Innumeracy in the Wild

Innumeracy in the Wild

Innumeracy in the Wild

Misunderstanding and Misusing Numbers

Ellen Peters

University of Oregon

OXFORD
UNIVERSITY PRESS

Oxford University Press is a department of the University of Oxford.
It furthers the University's objective of excellence in research, scholarship,
and education by publishing worldwide. Oxford is a registered trade mark of
Oxford University Press in the UK and in certain other countries.

Published in the United States of America by Oxford University Press
546 Fifth Avenue, New York, NY 10036, United States of America.

© Oxford University Press 2020

First published in paperback in 2026

CIP data is on file at the Library of Congress.

ISBN 9780190861094 (hardback)
ISBN 9780197847428 (Paperback)

Paperback printed by Marquis Book Printing, Canada

The manufacturer's authorized representative in the EU for product safety is
Oxford University Press España S.A. of Parque Empresarial San Fernando de Henares,
Avenida de Castilla, 2 – 28830 Madrid (www.oup.es/en or product.safety@oup.com).
OUP España S.A. also acts as importer into Spain of products made by the manufacturer.

Contents

VI. TWO ADDITIONAL WAYS OF KNOWING NUMBERS

VII. NUMBERS ARE JUST NUMBERS: THE IMPOTENCE OF DATA VERSUS THE POWER OF INFORMATION

VIII. BECOMING MORE NUMERATE

Preface

This book answers three main questions: Does numeric ability matter to the quality of judgments and decisions we make? If it does, how, when, and why is it important? How can we use this knowledge to improve decision making? A now sizeable body of psychological and applied findings highlights the critical importance of numeric ability (often called *numeracy*; i.e., the ability to process and use numbers effectively) to the quality of the decisions we make and, ultimately, the life outcomes we experience.

The topic is particularly important today because innumeracy is widespread. For example, a minority of high school seniors in 2015 (~25%) were considered math proficient.[1] As one high school graduate said in a recent survey "I am horrible at math. It doesn't come easy for me and never has. I have always got nervous, anxious, and almost panicked when I see numbers."[2] Innumeracy and its negative consequences are not limited to individuals who have less education. A college graduate confessed "I was trying to count up how much money I had left for a bill. I was very sure that I had enough to last me longer [than] a few days. I ended up being very wrong and was late on a bill because of it."[3] Thus, innumeracy follows people out of the classroom and into their everyday lives.

Policy makers have further exacerbated existing numeracy issues by giving consumers and patients more numeric information. These policy shifts are intended to empower individuals to take charge of their own welfare. The evidence is clear, however, that not everybody is prepared to use this information effectively and that those who are less numerate tend to make worse decisions unless they are supported adequately. As a result, the topic has important practical implications (e.g., for health and financial outcomes), and the research suggests that different communication approaches or training are needed for different individuals or groups.

The topic is also of critical import to research on decision making that has long focused on the *heuristics* of the human mind, the mental shortcuts we take that generally support judgments but can produce irrational thinking (biases). These heuristics were originally proposed by psychologists Daniel Kahneman and Amos Tversky and are often written about as if they are universal phenomena. More numerate people, however, are less susceptible to a wide range of heuristics and biases including framing effects, ratio biases, and the use of less relevant sources of affect. Individual differences in numeracy are important because they highlight that heuristic use is not universal and that decision-making processes differ markedly across individuals and in systematic ways. Studying the role of numeracy in decision making reveals important factors in how people understand, process, and use numeric and non-numeric information in judgments and decisions, and it shows how individuals differ in these factors. Highly numerate individuals understand and use numbers and numeric operations more, but, in the end, decision quality is often not based on doing complicated math or running the numbers fully. Instead, the highly numerate are more likely to do simple number operations and to derive more precise affective meaning from numbers. They subsequently use this affect to form risk perceptions and make choices. For less numerate individuals, numbers are more difficult. Instead of using affective meaning from numbers, they use mental shortcuts and rely on the compelling power of anecdotes, emotional reactions to situations, and top-of-the-mind information.

Innumeracy in the Wild has three goals:

- To explore the complex psychological mechanisms that underlie numeracy's effects in judgment and decision making
- To illustrate the importance of numeracy to life outcomes
- To highlight how this evidence (its concepts, methods, and findings) can be exploited to enable those who are less good with numbers to use them more effectively and make better choices

Section I (Chapter 1) introduces three different ways that people can be numerate or innumerate. Sections II and III (Chapters 2–8) then cover the complex psychological mechanisms that underlie how, why, and for whom numbers influence decisions. Section IV (Chapters 9 and 10) reveals the importance of numeracy to real world outcomes in health, finances, and employment and describes emerging questions in objective numeracy research. Section V (Chapters 11–12) reviews how numeric abilities emerge in childhood and what factors support and impede its development. Section VI (Chapters 13–14) reveals more about the two other ways of knowing numbers introduced briefly in Chapter 1: an evolutionarily based ability to perceive numeric magnitude and subjective numeracy (including numeric self-efficacy or confidence in our number abilities). Section VII (Chapters 15–17) introduces short-term fixes to how numeric information is presented that help people make better use of numbers. This literature has focused primarily on helping people better understand and use numeric sources of uncertainty such as the chances of a negative outcome. Section VIII (Chapters 18–19) reveals longer term educational and psychological interventions to grow number ability in individuals and reflects on theoretical and practical issues in helping people make better decisions. Throughout the book, we will explore research findings and develop a theoretical understanding of why, how, and when numeracy matters while linking this theory to everyday topics that matter.

By the end of this book, I hope to have convinced you that numeracy issues deserve attention whether you are a researcher, a communicator (and who among us is not?), someone who is highly numerate, or someone who wants to be. More numerate people are better able to take charge of the numeric aspects of their lives, and current data point toward them being healthier, wealthier, and with more stable employment. At the same time, all is not lost if you are innumerate or think that you are. You can change your numeric abilities. Interventions exist to build adult numeric capacity, both in the short run and long term, so that decision makers can bring knowledge to bear on decisions, think probabilistically, use heuristic processing less, consider alternative scenarios, and reason better numerically. By the end of the book, you also will understand three types of numerical competency as well as methods to improve them so that you and others don't neglect numbers as much and don't get distracted by other information.

In this book, I review literature relevant to numeracy and decision making from psychology, animal cognition, economics, medicine, public policy, and education. Most of the research is correlational, and we need to know more about what causal inferences can be made. In particular, a key next step in this literature is more research that experimentally manipulates numeric competence, both to establish causality and to improve outcomes. Finally, the review of the emergence of number abilities in childhood was brief by necessity as were the developmental and animal literatures on number understandings. In all cases, entire books can and have been written on the subjects if you are interested in reading more about particular areas.

References

1. Carr, P. G. (2016, April 27). *NAEP twelfth-grade mathematics and reading results.* Washington, DC: National Center for Education Statistics. Retrieved from https://nces.ed.gov/WhatsNew/commissioner/remarks2016/04_27_2016.asp
2. Peters, E. (2018a). MTurk Cohort 2, ID AJJKCFQTPX1I3.
3. Peters, E. (2018b). MTurk Cohort 2, ID AH31QLJ57XC8W.

Acknowledgments

Although I have wanted to write a book since childhood, actually writing it was both more fun and more difficult than I could have imagined. None of it would have been possible without my husband, Martin Tusler. Tino, you mean the world to me. I could not have done this without you and not only because I would have starved.

To Michelle, you have always been and will always be the light of my life and the reason it is all worth doing. I'm so happy I got to write this book while living nearby you and Eric in Colorado. I have loved, loved talking with you about research and hearing your perspective as a teacher. It has made my book and my research better.

A very special thanks to Hal Arkes who was the program officer on my very first grant and offered his tremendous editorial expertise to this book. Thank you for introducing me to academia and for being both colleague and friend.

Thanks to Kathleen Hall Jamieson as well. Your keen insights and tips for good book writing were exasperating because you were right, and I struggled to turn my academic book into something more readable. They were also incredibly helpful for exactly the same reasons.

Many thanks to the Ohio State University and Jan Box-Steffensmeier for sabbatical time. Having a year to read, reflect, and write was incredibly precious and greatly appreciated. Thanks as well to the University of Colorado Boulder and especially the social psychology program and Irene Blair for welcoming my visit. I also much appreciated the hospitality of Kathleen Hall Jamieson and the Annenberg Public Policy Center at the University of Pennsylvania where I rounded out my sabbatical year.

To everyone in the Cognitive and Affective Influences in Decision making (CAIDe) lab, I am grateful to work with you. Thanks, in particular, to Brittany Shoots-Reinhard, Tyler MacDonald, and Hayley Svensson for assistance on this book and to Brittany Shoots-Reinhard and Pär Bjälkebring who showed up every day and made everything happen.

Thanks to the funding agencies, and especially the National Science Foundation and National Institutes of Health, whose financial support has allowed me to pursue many of the questions and topics introduced in this book.

Finally, many thanks to my advisors, mentors, colleagues, students, and postdocs who played in this sandbox of ideas with me, including Paul Slovic, Judy Hibbard, Liana Fraenkel, Angie Fagerlin, Valerie Reyna, Dan Kahan, Eric Johnson, Myron Rothbart, Janet Kleber, Bill Klein, David Baker, Mary Kate Tompkins, Dan Schley, and Dana Chesney.

SECTION I

INTRODUCTION

1

The Types and Extent of Innumeracy

It's been said there are three kinds of people in the world, those who can count and those who can't count. In this book, instead of counting three kinds of people, we will dissect three ways that people can be good or bad with numbers and why each one matters. Thus, this book is intended primarily for academic researchers interested in numeracy and decision making. I think it will also be useful to researchers in related fields. And I hope it will prove valuable to those who are highly numerate and perplexed by the less numerate people around them, as well as to the less numerate who want to do better. We'll look first at brief examples of each of the three numeric competencies and the kinds of everyday situations they support.

First, people can score high or low on tests of their understanding and use of mathematical concepts (called *objective numeracy*). In a 2013 *New York Times* op-ed, Angelina Jolie[1] wrote about her experiences with genetic testing and prophylactic mastectomy. Jolie's doctors had informed her that she had an 87% risk of breast cancer due to her genetics. She took that information and reasoned like a highly numerate person. She thought long and hard about her numeric risks and ultimately chose to have a preventive double mastectomy to reduce her risk. Subsequently, Jolie's story and her fears for herself and her children were covered widely by *People Magazine* and other outlets. The less objectively numerate, however, are less sensitive to abstract numeric information. Instead, they use information like Jolie's story that is concrete and easier to evaluate. In fact, after Jolie's story went public, the proportion of early-stage breast cancer patients who chose preventive mastectomies rose from about 2% to 17%, with the fastest growth in average-risk women for whom surgery conferred no survival benefit.[2,3] Chapters 2–8 of this book will expand on how individuals lower and higher in objective numeracy understand and use information differently in judgments and decisions.

Second, people can be good or bad with numbers based on their confidence with numbers. Some people believe they are good at understanding and using mathematical concepts (they are high in what we will call *subjective numeracy*); others think they are terrible with numbers (they are low in subjective numeracy). In fact, people often say "I am not a math person." When I asked participants in one study to write about a time they had a hard time

Innumeracy in the Wild. Ellen Peters, Oxford University Press (2020). © Oxford University Press 2020.
DOI: 10.1093/oso/9780190861094.003.0001

with numbers, one person wrote "I am horrible at math. It doesn't come easy for me and never has. I have always got nervous, anxious, and almost panicked when I see numbers."[4] Another person said "I have never gotten along well with numbers, so don't use them too much."[5] To foreshadow Chapter 14, those who are less subjectively numerate do not try as hard with numbers, and their lack of persistence is related to lower comprehension and use of numbers in decisions.

Finally, our third way of being good or bad with numbers is an evolutionarily old sense of how big is a quantity. Using this intuitive number sense, we can discriminate quickly the numeric difference between two numbers (like mortgage rates), and we can make fast numeric estimates (e.g., of the number of coins in a jar). People differ in this intuitive number sense. Those who discriminate more precisely perceive numbers to be further apart and more different than people who are worse at numeric discriminations. This intuitive ability, as we will see in Chapter 13, is found in other species, and it appears to underlie the development of objective numeracy in children. Among human adults, it can compensate for low objective numeracy abilities. We rely on it instead of objective numeracy in some judgments and decisions.

These three ways of being good or bad with numbers are important because numbers permeate our daily lives. They instruct, inform, and give meaning to information about topics ranging from our science and health to politics, finances, and even sports and hobbies. Understanding and using them underlies our extraordinary ability to control the world around us as we choose in the short-term and forecast far out into the future. They are central to decisions that we make whenever we ask how much, how many, how big, how likely, how often, how long, or what time. Overall, our grasp of number is one of humankind's most distinctive and important traits.

These numeric competencies, for example, support personal finance activities like saving and budgeting. They also underlie some aspects of disease management, such as for diabetes and kidney disease. Without good numeric competencies, these everyday activities can be major obstacles for people because of the complex quantitative information involved.[6] A diabetic patient once wrote "Life with type 1 is manageable, but . . . if I were dropped in the desert, I'd die pretty quickly. In fact, if I want to walk to the shops, or even eat a piece of fruit, I have to plan, think about what happened since my last injection and what is likely to happen before my next one; I have to carry emergency supplies; I have to do blood tests. I can't even have a drink without having to do maths."[7] This patient clearly believed that thinking mathematically matters.

Numbers matter in much more common ways, too, like how to find a restaurant five blocks west and two blocks south, double a brownie recipe, and estimate the gasoline you need to drive from point A to point B. Even shopping environments present challenges that more numerate individuals likely cannot imagine being problematic. Examples include using sales signs, calculating or estimating unit prices to ascertain value, keeping a running total to avoid running short of funds at the grocery story, and applying for credit.[8] These examples point toward the potentially critical importance of these numeric competencies to the experienced quality of judgments, decisions, and life outcomes.

Definition and Extent of the Three Numeric Competencies

Before we get to the topic of judgment and decision making in the next sections, let's look first at definitions of the three numeric competencies and what we know about the existing extent of innumeracy based on nationally representative US samples. To foreshadow the rest of this chapter, you'll see that a wide and disappointing range of objective numeracy exists, that people claim to be more subjectively numerate than objective numeracy data reveal, and that we know less about how much adults differ in intuitive number sense.

Objective Numeracy

Objective numeracy has been defined variously as the ability to understand and use basic probability and mathematical concepts[9] and as "the degree to which individuals can obtain, process, and understand the basic [quantitative] health information and services they need to make appropriate health decisions" (p. vi).[10] Medical researchers further described the concept of health numeracy as representing "a constellation of skills necessary to function effectively in the health care environment and act appropriately on health care information" (p. 1).[11] The Organisation for Economic Cooperation and Development (OECD)[12] defined it as "the ability to access, use, interpret and communicate mathematical information and ideas in order to engage in and manage the mathematical demands of a range of situations in adult life" (p. 59).

As suggested earlier, many people have limited skills for dealing with life's numeric information. The OECD[12] estimated that 29% of American adults (about 73 million in 2018) are at or below Level 1 of numeracy; only 9% are at the highest Levels 4 and 5 of numeracy (about 23 million adults). See Table 1.1. Those with lowest numeracy are limited to doing simple operations; they can count, sort, and perform basic arithmetic operations with whole numbers or money. As a result, they likely cannot select the health plan with the lowest cost based on annual premiums and deductibles for a family or calculate the difference in the percent of patients who survive one treatment versus another.[13] The next 33% of the population can do more complicated math, for example, with percentages, fractions, simple measurement, and estimation; they can also use simple tables and graphs.[12] Only those at the highest numeracy levels (Level 4 or 5) have the quantitative skills necessary to understand and use all of the numeric information integral to management of a complex disease like diabetes.[13]

Demographic differences also are associated with objective numeracy scores. For example, more educated people tend to be more numerate. Even highly educated individuals, though, can be innumerate[14]—think about PhDs in non-numeric fields. Greater numeracy is associated further with being male, younger, having a higher income, and having health insurance prior to the Affordable Care Act.[13]

Table 1.1 Proportion (Number) of US Adults at Each Numeracy Level

Numeracy level	% (number[a]) US adults	Key abilities associated with level[b]
Below Level 1	9% (22,790,483)	Simple processes: counting, sorting, using whole numbers or money. Little or no text or distractors.
Level 1	20% (50,645,519)	Basic one-step or simple processes (counting, sorting, simple arithmetic, simple percents such as 50%). Little text and minimal distractors.
Level 2	33% (83,565,106)	More complicated math with two+ steps, percents and fractions, simple measurement, estimation; simple tables and graphs.
Level 3	26% (65,839,174)	Less explicit and unfamiliar numeric tasks that require several steps, problem solving, interpretation and basic analysis of data and statistics in texts, tables, and graphs.
Level 4/5	9% (22,790,483)	Complex, abstract, unfamiliar contexts. Multiple steps, analysis, statistics and chance, change, formulas.

[a]Based on 2018 estimated adult population from US Census Bureau.[15]
[b]From Desjardins et al.[12]

Note: Individuals at lower levels do not have the abilities associated with a higher level of numeracy. Approximately 3% of OECD sample is missing data because those individuals were unable to speak or read in the languages used for the assessment.

Estimates in other countries follow a similar pattern, but of 23 countries surveyed, the United States scored 21st. Whereas about 35% of Americans scored at or above Level 3, more than 60% of Japanese participants did so and other countries followed closely (Finland, Sweden, Netherlands, Norway, Denmark, Slovak Republic, and Belgium). Among 16- to 24-year-olds, the United States scored last. Lest we worry too much, some researchers are skeptical, however, whether these between-country comparisons are meaningful due to data uncertainty.[16]

Despite numeracy issues, many people want quantitative information (such as risk information in genetic counseling for cancer[17]) and believe (incorrectly sometimes) that they understand and use it appropriately. Here are some notable examples in health and personal finances.

- In an online survey of parents, 79% of them were familiar with growth charts, and most thought they understood them well.[18] However, when provided with multiple-choice questions, only 64% could identify a child's weight when shown a plotted point on a growth chart, and only 23% could correctly interpret as normal a chart that showed a child in the 10th percentile for both height and weight. Like other innumeracy-related examples, these misunderstandings may be important because parents may use their (inaccurate) understanding to guide health decisions for their children.
- Patients often have to figure out when to take a missed medication dose, but as many as 40% of Americans cannot do so;[19] 33% of hospital patients could not even determine how many pills of a prescription to take.[20] These issues are issues of numeracy. They are important because an estimated 70% of Americans take at least one prescription drug daily; more than 50% take two or more drugs.[21]
- Based on the National Adult Literacy Survey, almost half of the general population has difficulty with relatively simple numeric tasks such as calculating (using a calculator) the difference between a regular price and a sales price or estimating the cost per ounce of a grocery item.[22]
- Economist Annamaria Lusardi found that individuals had substantial trouble with simple interest rate calculations.[23] She asked the question "You owe $3,000 on your credit card. You pay a minimum payment of $30 each month. At an Annual Percentage Rate of 12% (or 1% per month), how many years would it take to eliminate your credit card debt if you made no additional new charges? Less than 5 years; Between 5 and 10 years; Between 10 and 15 years; Never, you will continue to be in debt; and Do not know." Only 35% correctly answered that they could never

pay off the debt; an additional surprising 22% simply said they did not know. These responses are alarming given that Americans' outstanding credit debt (mostly comprised of credit card loans) totaled $1.03 trillion in 2018.[24]

We know more about the objective numeracy skills of the general population of US adults than we do about experts. Nonetheless, we do know that well-educated experts can be objectively innumerate. For example, a recent Twitter post pointed out that the BBC inappropriately translated the statistic "One of four women who had an abortion in 2016 were using the most reliable methods of contraception" into the headline "Contraception failing one in four women."[25] Of course, contraceptives are much more effective (e.g., 98% effective when used properly). What they should have said was that "One of four aborted pregnancies was due to failed contraception." But, as Barbie infamously coined, "Math class is tough."[26] Research indicates, however, that journalists are often surprised by the importance of quantitative data to their work,[27] and, as in the BBC example, they can misinterpret it.[28]

Physicians, in particular, tend to be more objectively numerate than the average nonphysician. For example, when medical students and female veterans were given the same three-question numeracy measure, 77% of the medical students[29] answered all three questions correctly compared to only 16% of the veterans.[30]

However, studies with physicians and healthcare professionals point toward numeracy skills that are lower than desired given this era of evidence-based medicine.[31,32] For example, one study queried 29 HIV hotline counselors from US state and national hotlines who counseled low-risk women. None of the counselors provided an accurate likelihood of a patient being infected given that she tested positive (the conditional risk).[33] In another study by psychologist Gerd Gigerenzer, half of counselors in public AIDS counseling centers reported that HIV infection was certain in a low-risk man who tested HIV-positive.[34] In actuality, low-risk men who test positive for HIV can have as little as a 50% chance of infection. This numeric incomprehension extends to cancer treatment. Medical students and surgical residents were told about a patient considering adjuvant chemotherapy for bladder cancer. They then were asked how much chemotherapy reduced risk based on presented survival data. Although many participants had a good understanding of the risk reduction, less numerate trainees were seven times more likely than more numerate trainees to misunderstand.[32]

Subjective Numeracy and Intuitive Number Sense

We know less about the distributions of subjective numeracy and especially intuitive number sense in the United States and elsewhere. Subjective numeracy concerns a person's confidence in her ability to understand numeric information and use mathematical concepts (aka, numeric self-efficacy) and (sometimes) her preferences for numbers over words. In this book, we will also treat math anxiety as an aspect of subjective numeracy. Numeric confidence, in particular, appears to support persistence in numeric tasks and has effects, independent of objective numeracy, on decision processes and outcomes (see Chapter 14).

People tend to rate themselves as higher in subjective numeracy than might be expected from the extent of objective innumeracy seen in studies. For example, 63% of a US nationally representative sample responded that understanding medical statistics was "easy" or "very easy,"[35] despite the poor objective numeracy figures in Table 1.1. More concretely, large proportions of US adults do not understand medical statistics. As examples, we estimated that 55% of the US population cannot calculate the proportion of patients of a given age who will suffer at least one of three adverse events.[13] Eighty-eight percent likely can't calculate the 5-year fracture risk for a female patient from a medication when provided a table of annual risks broken out by gender.

In a recent study, my graduate student, Mary Kate Tompkins, attempted to look at numeric overconfidence more directly.[36] She told 96 participants "You just completed 8 math problems. How many of these math problems (from 0 to 8) do you think you answered correctly?" She then quantified the proportion of participants who were underconfident (17% answered more problems correctly than they thought they did), calibrated (21% knew exactly how many they answered correctly), and overconfident (63% answered fewer problems correctly than they thought they did). Those higher in objective numeracy were more likely to be underconfident or calibrated (22% and 37%, respectively) and less likely to be overconfident (41%). Those lower in objective numeracy were considerably less likely to be underconfident or calibrated (12% and 6%, respectively). Instead, they were largely overconfident (82%).

We know the least about the adult distribution of intuitive number sense, the third numeric competency, because no nationally representative samples exist. We do know that our understanding of numbers begins early in infancy through the approximate number system (ANS) and develops throughout childhood. In Chapter 11, we will take a closer look at what this number sense is, how it is measured, and how it changes from infancy to adulthood. We will then explore what we know about its effects in adult decision making.

Moving Forward

Does it really make a difference if someone is less numerate with respect to each of these numeric competencies? Perhaps these competencies do not really matter (but, as you'll see, they do), or perhaps most people are numerate enough given that we do not really use what we learned in algebra, arithmetic, and statistics courses? (But we do, and, as you'll learn, the highly numerate have better habits with numbers that allow them to make better decisions.) Or, given society's vast experiences with numbers and the less numerate, perhaps communicators already explain or present important numbers in ways that the less numerate can understand them? Later, however, you will read about the evidence on common mistakes made by communicators and you will learn evidence-based methods to improve numeric communication.

In this chapter, I introduced the problem of widespread innumeracy particularly with respect to objective numeracy. In the Appendix for this chapter, I describe available measures of objective numeracy and subjective numeracy for the interested reader. Intuitive number sense is so different that we'll hold off until the Appendix for Chapter 13 to learn more about its measurement. The discussion of measures is relatively technical, and you can certainly skip it until a time when you're curious about how to measure objective or subjective numeracy or how to identify someone (including yourself!) as high or low in numeracy. As a teaser, if you answer the following objective numeracy question correctly, it means you are high in objective numeracy: you fall in the top half of objective numeracy among well-educated American adults. Here's the question:[37] "Out of 1,000 people in a small town, 500 are members of a choir. Out of these 500 members in the choir, 100 are men. Out of the 500 inhabitants who are not in the choir, 300 are men. What is the probability that a randomly drawn man is a member of the choir? Please indicate the probability in percent." You can find the correct answer in the footnote of Table A.1 in the Appendix.

In the chapters that follow, we will consider decision makers as thinkers and information processors, and we will look, in particular, at how thinking and information processing differ depending on how numerically competent one is. You will learn in Chapters 2–8 how more and less objectively numerate people understand and use the same information differently in judgments and choices. Understanding the logic, rules, and habits that underlie decisions of the highly numerate may assist the less numerate and those who think they are less numerate. Then, Chapter 9 reveals relations of objective numeracy to life outcomes. In Chapter 10, I describe issues and opportunities in objective numeracy research. Chapters 11 and 12 then review evidence about how the numeric competencies develop to give readers a flavor of where things go right and wrong in childhood. Chapter 13 moves on to highlight the relation of intuitive number sense to decision making. Chapter 14 then points out how subjective numeracy matters to decision making and outcomes independent of objective numeracy and, in some cases, in interaction with objective numeracy.

A recurrent theme of this book has been and will continue to be that numeracy matters in ways both big and small. I do not mean to suggest that it is all that matters. I also do not want you to think that numeracy is unchangeable. Everyone has the ability to become more numerate and reason more effectively with numbers in everyday life. Numeracy is (mostly) not inherent, and, by the end of this book, you should have accumulated more knowledge about what you and others can do to make more numerate decisions. In Chapters 15–18, in particular, you will learn ways that numeracy-related solutions can be brought to bear. In these chapters, I argue that supporting and growing the numeracy skills of adults is possible and invaluable for quality of life.

Finally, throughout the book, I will focus on numeracy's psychological mechanisms. I will choose examples across domains, such as from health, finances, and consumer choices, that best exemplify each psychological process. As a result, you will see a mixture of examples across domains as we move forward. This choice could be viewed as a "bug," a flaw of the book. However, I believe strongly that this bug is really a helpful feature. It allows me to illustrate numeracy as a general phenomenon linked systematically to specific tendencies to process information that have similar effects across domains. I hope that you agree.

References

1. Jolie, A. (2013, May 14). My medical choice. *New York Times* pp. A25. Retrieved from https://www.nytimes.com/2013/05/14/opinion/my-medical-choice.html
2. Kummerow, K. L., Du, L., Penson, D. F., Shyr, Y., & Hooks, M. A. (2015). Nationwide trends in mastectomy for early-stage breast cancer. *JAMA Surgery, 150*(1), 9–16.
3. Pesce, C., Liederbach, E., Wang, C., Lapin, B., Winchester, D. J., & Yao, K. (2014). Contralateral prophylactic mastectomy provides no survival benefit in young women with estrogen receptor-negative breast cancer. *Annals of Surgical Oncology, 21*(10), 3231–3239.
4. Peters, E. (2018a). MTurk Cohort 2, ID AJJKCFQTPX1I3.
5. Peters, E. (2018b). MTurk Cohort 2, ID A1MMC6X3ZNJ9OT.
6. Narva, A. S., Norton, J. M., & Boulware, L. E. (2016). Educating patients about CKD: The path to self-management and patient-centered care. *Clinical Journal of the American Society of Nephrology, 11*(4), 694–703.
7. Snow, R. (2017). Bereavement without a death. *BMJ, 357*, j2012.

8. Viswanathan, M., Rosa, J. A., & Harris, J. E. (2005). Decision making and coping of functionally illiterate consumers and some implications for marketing management. *Journal of Marketing, 69*(1), 15–31.

9. Peters, E., Västfjäll, D., Slovic, P., Mertz, C. K., Mazzocco, K., & Dickert, S. (2006). Numeracy and decision making. *Psychological Science, 17*(5), 407–413.

10. Ratzan, S. C., & Parker, R. M. (2000). Introduction. In C. R. Selden, M. Zorn, S. C. Ratzan, & R. M. Parker (Eds.), *National Library of Medicine current bibliographies in medicine* (pp. v–vi). Bethesda, MD: National Institutes of Health, US Department of Health and Human Services.

11. Berkman, N. D., Sheridan, S. L., Donahue, K. E., Halpern, D. J., Viera, A., Crotty, K., . . . Viswanathan, M. (2011). *Health literacy interventions and outcomes: An updated systematic review.* Evidence Report/Technology Assessment No. 199. Rockville, MD: Agency for Healthcare Research and Quality.

12. Desjardins, R., Thorn, W., Schleicher, A., Quintini, G., Pellizzari, M., Kis, V., & Chung, J. E. (2013). *OECD skills outlook 2013: First results from the survey of adult skills.* Paris, France: OECD.

13. Peters, E., Meilleur, L., & Tompkins, M. K. (2014). Numeracy and the Affordable Care Act: Opportunities and challenges. Appendix A. IOM (Institute of Medicine). In *Health Literacy and Numeracy: Workshop Summary* (pp. 91–132). Washington, DC: The National Academies Press.

14. Lipkus, I. M., Samsa, G., & Rimer, B. K. (2001). General performance on a numeracy scale among highly educated samples. *Medical Decision Making, 21,* 37–44.

15. US Census Bureau. (2018). *US Census Bureau quick facts.* Retrieved from https://www.census.gov/quickfacts/fact/table/US/PST045218#PST045218

16. Spiegelhalter, D. (2013). Are you 45% more likely to die in a UK hospital rather than a US hospital?. *BMJ, 347,* f5775.

17. Anderson, B. L., Obrecht, N. A., Chapman, G. B., Driscoll, D. A., & Schulkin, J. (2011). Physicians' communication of Down syndrome screening test results: The influence of physician numeracy. *Genetics in Medicine, 13*(8), 744–749.

18. Ben-Joseph, E. P., Dowshen, S. A., & Izenberg, N. (2009). Do parents understand growth charts? A national, internet-based survey. *Pediatrics, 124*(4), 1100–1109.

19. Kutner, M., Greenberg, E., Jin, Y., Boyle, B., Hsu, Y., & Dunleavy, E. (2007, April). Literacy in everyday life: Results from the 2003 National Assessment of Adult Literacy (NAAL). National Center for Education Statistics. Institute of Education Sciences. Retrieved from https://nces.ed.gov/Pubs2007/2007480_1.pdf

20. Williams, M. V., Parker, R. M., Baker, D. W., Parikh, N. S., Pitkin, K., Coates, W. C., & Nurss, J. R. (1995). Inadequate functional health literacy among patients at two public hospitals. *JAMA, 274*(21), 1677–1682.

21. Zhong, W., Maradit-Kremers, H., Sauver, J. L. S., Yawn, B. P., Ebbert, J. O., Roger, V. L., . . . & Rocca, W. A. (2013, July). Age and sex patterns of drug prescribing in a defined American population. *Mayo Clinic Proceedings, 88*(7), 697–707.

22. Kirsch, I. S., Jungeblut, A., Jenkins, L., & Kolstad, A. (2002). *Adult literacy in America: A first look at the findings of the National Adult Literacy Survey, Vol. 201* (3rd ed.). Washington, DC: National Center for Education, US Department of Education.

23. Lusardi, A., & Tufano, P. (2009). *Debt literacy, financial experiences, and overindebtedness* (No. w14808). Cambridge, MA: National Bureau of Economic Research.

24. US Federal Reserve. (2018, July 9). *Consumer Credit – G.19.* Retrieved from https://www.federalreserve.gov/releases/g19/current/

25. Goldacre, B. (2017, July 7). Dear, lovely BBC. Numbers don't work like this. [Twitter Post] Retrieved from https://twitter.com/bengoldacre/status/883228257784647680

26. Croman, J. (2017, March 18). Teen Talk Barbie controversy 1992. Retrieved from https://www.youtube.com/watch?v=jSL2-rbE9AM.
27. Maier, S. R. (2003). Numeracy in the newsroom: A case study of mathematical competence and confidence. *Journalism & Mass Communication Quarterly, 80*(4), 921–936.
28. Silver, N. (2017, September 21). The media has a probability problem. Retrieved from https://fivethirtyeight.com/features/the-media-has-a-probability-problem/
29. Sheridan, S. L., & Pignone, M. (2002). Numeracy and the medical student's ability to interpret data. *Effective Clinical Practice: ECP, 5*(1), 35–40.
30. Schwartz, L. M., Woloshin, S., Black, W. C., & Welch, H. G. (1997). The role of numeracy in understanding the benefit of screening mammography. *Annals of Internal Medicine, 127*(11), 966–972.
31. Friederichs, H., Scholling, M., Marschall, B., & Weissenstein, A. (2014). Assessment of risk literacy among German medical students: A cross-sectional study evaluating numeracy skills. *Human and Ecological Risk Assessment, 20*(4), 1139–1147.
32. Johnson, T. V., Abbasi, A., Schoenberg, E. D., Kellum, R., Speake, L. D., Spiker, C., . . . Master, V. A. (2014). Numeracy among trainees: Are we preparing physicians for evidence-based medicine? *Journal of Surgical Education, 71*(2), 211–215.
33. Ellis, K. M., & Brase, G. L. (2015). Communicating HIV results to low-risk individuals: Still hazy after all these years. *Current HIV Research, 13*(5), 381–390.
34. Gigerenzer, G., Hoffrage, U., & Ebert, A. (1998). AIDS counselling for low-risk clients. *AIDS Care, 10*(2), 197–211.
35. Nelson, W. L., Moser, R. P., & Han, P. K. J. (2012). Exploring objective and subjective numeracy at a population level: Findings from the 2007 Health Information National Trends Survey (HINTS). *Journal of Health Communication: International Perspectives, 18*(2), 192–205. doi:10.1080/10810730.2012.688450
36. Tompkins, M. K. (2018). The role of subjective numeracy in financial outcomes and interventions of numeric-ability beliefs (doctoral dissertation, The Ohio State University).
37. Cokely, E. T., Galesic, M., Schulz, E., Ghazal, S., & Garcia-Retamero, R. (2012). Measuring risk literacy: The Berlin Numeracy Test. *Judgment and Decision Making, 7*(1), 21–47.

SECTION II

THE OBJECTIVELY INNUMERATE

2
Innumeracy, Incomprehension, and Inconsistency

Numbers can trip people up even when they are very smart in other ways. For example, treatment options for lung cancer can be described in terms of survival (e.g., 90% and 100% of patients given surgery or radiation treatment, respectively, survive treatment) or mortality (10% and 0%, respectively, died during treatment). Although the numbers are logically the same in both frames, surgeons were more likely to choose radiation therapy when options were described with survival statistics.[1] Information framing should not matter but does to experts and non-experts alike because the frame (mortality vs. survival) has an effect independent of the numeric evidence.

In Chapters 2–4, I discuss how the less objectively numerate produce poorer decisions by making four related points about them:

1. They misunderstand and are more inconsistent in responses to numeric data;
2. They respond more to concrete, easy-to-evaluate information, such as good stories, than to numbers;
3. They rely more on feelings (that are not feelings about numeric data); and
4. How information is framed has a different influence on them than on the highly numerate.

It is as important to understand how and why people make poor decisions as it is to understand how they can make better ones (Chapters 5–7 focus on what the highly numerate do better). By the end of both sections, you will understand how compelling information trips people up and how you can process information in judgments and decisions so that you and others don't neglect numbers.

Innumeracy in the Wild. Ellen Peters, Oxford University Press (2020). © Oxford University Press 2020.
DOI: 10.1093/oso/9780190861094.003.0001

Two Types of Information and Information Processing

Two fundamentally different and often conflicting types of information and information processing underlie judgments and decisions and appear to create problematic effects for those lower in objective numeracy. The first type of information is the set of experienced beliefs and emotions that people generally find true (survival is good; mortality is bad). The second type is data-based information, which consists of central numbers in decisions that tell us how likely, how much, how big, how often, how long, or what time. Decision makers process both kinds of information, and some researchers believe that the best decisions emerge from their combination.[2] Decision makers often find experiential information more intuitive, however, and easier to process and use. Our emotions in the moment, for example, alter how we feel about a hazard and how we perceive its risks and benefits.[3] Decision makers also can think carefully through their decisions. For example, one particularly analytic method for making decisions concerns calculating the expected values of options and then choosing the option that maximizes expected value. See Box 2.1 for how to calculate an expected value.

Box 2.1 Calculating an Expected Value

The expected value of an option, such as a gamble, is the probability-weighted average of all possible values. To calculate it, you take the probability of the first outcome multiplied by the value of that outcome plus the probability of the second outcome multiplied by its outcome value, and so on, until you run out of outcomes. For example, a gamble that has a 50% chance of winning $4 and a 50% chance of winning $20 has an expected value of .5 multiplied by 4 (= $2) plus .5 multiplied by 20 (= $10), or $12. The expected value is the average amount you would expect to win each time you played a gamble if you played it an infinite number of times. The expected value of a more complicated option, say a policy option, is calculated in similar manner. Unlike with simple gambles, however, the policy maker must ascertain the possible outcomes for each option. Next, she would estimate the likelihood and worth (or value) of each outcome. The calculation itself is then as easy as it is for gambles. However, the estimation process may be difficult.

Data-based information, however, can conflict with experienced beliefs and emotions. To resolve the conflict, we can either update our beliefs and emotions or we can neglect data, misinterpret it, and rely on intuitive thinking in decisions. These latter phenomena are the focus of Chapters 2–4. As you might imagine, the less numerate do less well with data-based information (especially calculations such as expected values), and they rely more on intuitive thinking. In addition, as we'll discover in the remainder of this chapter, the less objectively numerate do not understand numeric information as well and they are less able to use it consistently.

Numeric Incomprehension

Many people believe, just like Joe Friday on *Dragnet*, that "all we want are the facts, ma'am." After all, if everybody gets the same information, then the important stuff will rise to the top for all to use. This approach sounds reasonable, but people often misunderstand provided information, which can lead to worse decisions. For example, parents often do not understand what children's combined height and weight measurements mean for whether their weight is considered normal.[4] As a result, they may make worse decisions about diet, medical providers, and treatments. In another example, women were asked to estimate the risk of death from breast cancer with and without mammography. Most participants overestimated mammography's benefits, but more numerate women were more likely to be accurate.[5] These different understandings then may influence decisions about whether the amount of risk reduction offered by a treatment or preventive action is worth its costs. Similar results with diabetics may be critical to the outcomes they experience. Physician Russell Rothman, for example, found that only 37% of patients could calculate the number of carbohydrates consumed from a 20-ounce bottle of soda that contained 2.5 servings; higher comprehension of food labels was significantly correlated with greater numeracy and may result ultimately in better glucose control by the more numerate.[6] The positive relation between numeracy and comprehension of numeric data remains after controlling for other measures of intelligence, need for cognition, education, and other demographic variables.[7] Although most of the research linking numeracy and comprehension has been conducted in health domains,[7-11] it seems likely that effects would be similar in other contexts.[12] Indeed, objective numeracy and financial literacy have long been linked.[13,14]

Less Numerate Are Less Accurate and Overestimate Risk More

We can see the effects of lower comprehension in risk perceptions. For example, a series of studies in breast cancer indicated that less numerate women overestimate their personal risk of breast cancer compared to the highly numerate after controlling for demographics (e.g., race, years of education, family history of breast cancer, and number of breast biopsies[15-18]); one study did not replicate the link, however.[19] Researcher Torstein Låg and his colleagues similarly found that, compared to the more numerate, less numerate men and women ($N = 202$) provided greater risk overestimates than the more numerate for 10-year disease risks (breast cancer, prostate cancer, colon cancer, HIV/AIDS, and cardiovascular disease) in a random sample of Norwegians.[7] Their results were particularly useful in terms of the role of objective numeracy because the researchers controlled for demographics (gender, age, marital status, and education), subjective numeracy, and various intelligence measures. They are also important because risk perceptions are critical to health-behavior theories[20] and they relate to actions like uptake of flu shots, mammograms, and aspirin.[21-23] Note that the less numerate's risk perceptions also must reflect something other than inaccuracy given that they systematically perceive greater risk than the highly numerate in these examples. In particular, feelings about outcomes such as cancer are likely involved (see Chapter 4). Numeracy does not appear related, however, to comparative risk perceptions (how one's risk compares to similar others).[18,24]

The Less Numerate and Benefit Perceptions

The relation of numeracy with benefit perceptions appears more complicated. For example, among advanced cancer patients without other treatment options, lower objective numeracy was associated with less accurate and greater benefit expectations for experimental cancer treatments.[25] Among women considering preventive cancer treatment, however, less numerate women again were less accurate but they perceived less benefit from it.[26] In this latter paper, we studied 105 early-stage breast cancer patients facing a treatment decision to prevent possible cancer recurrence. We provided personalized 10-year survival estimates for four possible treatments and explored numeracy's association with patients' individualized 10-year cancer-free survival perceptions. The average patient underestimated treatment benefit, and, at higher survival odds, the less numerate were significantly less accurate, underestimating treatment benefits increasingly more than the highly numerate.

Two possible explanations exist for these contrasting benefit-perception results, one based more on emotions and the other on cognitive mechanisms. First, and consistent with prior research, emotional reactions may have driven benefit perceptions[27] but with different emotions experienced by the two patient groups. Advanced cancer patients in the former paper may have been more motivated to hope, with this positive emotion increasing benefit perceptions. Early-stage breast-cancer patients, in the latter paper, may have experienced more fear, which reduced benefit perceptions.[27] As we'll see later in Chapter 4, emotional reactions to outcomes, such as cancer, have stronger effects on the less objectively numerate than on the more numerate. Cancer-recurrence fears may have driven down benefit estimations in our study, similar to earlier findings by Johnson and Tversky. An alternative cognitive explanation exists based on the best-known descriptive theory in decision making, *Prospect Theory*.[28] Specifically, having advanced cancer history may predispose patients to think about their disease in terms of losses. When faced with losses, people tend to prefer taking more risk rather than accepting certain losses. Such risk taking could be consistent with these advanced-cancer patients perceiving greater benefit from a highly risky treatment. Our breast cancer patients, who were considering cancer prevention, may have construed the choice as maintaining health, a gain. When faced with gains, people tend to prefer avoiding risks.[29] Consistent with Prospect Theory's risk aversion, these patients may have underestimated (rather than overestimated) treatment benefit. Understanding how numeracy interacts with cognitive, emotional, and motivational demands of the situation is an important direction for future research.

Numeric Inconsistency

Less objectively numerate individuals also are less consistent in their use of numbers. For example, sometimes researchers or policy makers want to understand the value of different health states (such as living with cancer or osteoporosis). As pointed out in Box 2.1, estimating values (also called *utility*) can be difficult. Nonetheless, various numeric measures have been devised. The classic method is the *standard gamble task*. In it, participants are told to choose between living in a particular health state for the next 10 years or a gamble of a painless treatment that has a chance of death but otherwise guarantees perfect health. For example, Ralph might be indifferent between living with cancer and a painless treatment that offers a 20% chance of death and an 80% chance of perfect health. If so, a policy maker would say that his value for cancer was .80. Other methods of measuring value also exist and should produce similar results. However, physicians Steve Woloshin, Lisa Schwartz, and their colleagues found that use of these measures revealed a marked problem among the less numerate who produced quite different values depending on which value estimation technique was used. The highly numerate valued health states more consistently across different methods.[30]

Researchers have found similar inconsistencies among the less numerate between retrospective and diary measures of sexual intercourse[31] and in inaccurate dietary reporting.[32] The less objectively numerate also reported unstable breast cancer risk perceptions when asked to report them on a frequentistic scale (How many women out of 100 will get cancer?) versus a percentage scale (what percent of women from 0% to 100% will get cancer?). Similarly, asking about risks over a lifetime produced quite different results than asking about the 1-year risk (and calculating the implied lifetime risk).[33] Such inconsistent results could be due to a lack of numeric comprehension, a lack of ability among the less numerate to aggregate numeric information over time or sex partners, or a lack of ability to recall numbers.[34]

Some researchers suggest using more complex measures that allow for finer distinctions among highly numerate individuals and using simpler tasks for the less objectively numerate so that they can produce more consistent responses.[35] However, even relatively simple tasks, such as estimating a probability on a 0–100% scale, pose numeracy issues. Less numerate individuals, for example, are more likely to judge the probability of living or dying in the next 10 years as 50%, but this 50% response often meant "I don't know" as opposed to being the statistical response intended by researchers.[36]

Nonetheless, the less numerate are sometimes as consistent as the highly numerate in numeric responses.[37] For example, the less numerate were as reliable as the highly numerate when asked unexpectedly to re-evaluate how much they would pay to avoid a medication side effect.[38] We need to understand more about how numeracy relates to numeric inconsistencies when faced with various response scales.

Of course, sometimes decision makers have adequate ability to understand and consistently use numbers in a decision. Nonetheless, they choose not to do so because they mindfully or mindlessly trade off effort and accuracy in decision making.[39] They simplify their task when the level of effort to make an accurate decision becomes undesirable. They also will simplify when the desire for accuracy decreases (e.g., the decision is deemed less important). Because, by definition, understanding and processing numeric information is more difficult for the less objectively numerate, they will be more likely than the highly numerate to simplify in decisions involving numbers. The highly numerate, who have stronger preferences for numbers over words than the less numerate,[40] are likely to desire greater accuracy with numbers and to be willing to put in more effort. The tendency of the less numerate to simplify their decisions is the focus of the next chapter.

References

1. McNeil, B. J., Pauker, S. G., Sox, H. C., Jr., & Tversky, A. (1982). On the elicitation of preferences for alternative therapies. *New England Journal of Medicine, 306,* 1259–1262.
2. Damasio, A. R. (1994). *Descartes' error: Emotion, reason, and the human brain.* New York: Avon.
3. Slovic, P., Finucane, M., Peters, E., & MacGregor, D. G. (2002). Rational actors or rational fools: Implications of the affect heuristic for behavioral economics. *The Journal of Socio-Economics, 31*(4), 329–342.
4. Ben-Joseph, E. P., Dowshen, S. A., & Izenberg, N. (2009). Do parents understand growth charts? A national, internet-based survey. *Pediatrics, 124*(4), 1100–1109.
5. Schwartz, L. M., Woloshin, S., Black, W. C., & Welch, H. G. (1997). The role of numeracy in understanding the benefit of screening mammography. *Annals of Internal Medicine, 127*(11), 966–972.
6. Rothman, R. L., Housam, R., Weiss, H., Davis, D., Gregory, R., Gebretsadik, T., . . . Elasy, T. A. (2006). Patient understanding of food labels: The role of literacy and numeracy. *American Journal of Preventive Medicine, 31*(5), 391–398.
7. Låg, T., Bauger, L., Lindberg, M., & Friborg, O. (2014). The role of numeracy and intelligence in health-risk estimation and medical data interpretation. *Journal of Behavioral Decision Making, 27*(2), 95–108.
8. Gossett, D. R., Nayak, S., Bhatt, S., & Bailey, S. C. (2013). What do healthy women know about the consequences of delayed childbearing? *Journal of Health Communication, 18*(suppl 1), 118–128.
9. Riechel, C., Alegiani, AC., Kopke, S., Kasper, J., Rosenkranz, M., Thomalla, G., . . . Heesen, C. (2016). Subjective and objective knowledge and decisional role preferences in cerebrovascular patients compared to controls. *Patient Preference and Adherence, 10,* 1453–1460.
10. Rolison, J. J., Morsanyi, K., & O'Connor, P. A. (2016). Can I count on getting better? Association between math anxiety and poorer understanding of medical risk reductions. *Medical Decision Making, 36*(7), 876–886.
11. Zikmund-Fisher, B. J., Exe, N. L., & Witteman, H. O. (2014). Numeracy and literacy independently predict patients' ability to identify out-of-range test results. *Journal of Medical Internet Research, 16*(8), e187.
12. Lipkus, I. M., Samsa, G., & Rimer, B. K. (2001). General performance on a numeracy scale among highly educated samples. *Medical Decision Making, 21*(1), 37–44.
13. Fernandes, D., Lynch Jr, J. G., & Netemeyer, R. G. (2014). Financial literacy, financial education, and downstream financial behaviors. *Management Science, 60*(8), 1861–1883.
14. Lusardi, A., & Tufano, P. (2015). Debt literacy, financial experiences, and overindebtedness. *Journal of Pension Economics & Finance, 14*(4), 332–368.

15. Black, W. C., Nease, R. F. Jr., & Tosteson, A. N. (1995). Perceptions of breast cancer risk and screening effectiveness in women younger than 50 years of age. *Journal of the National Cancer Institute, 87*(10), 720–731.

16. Davids, S. L., Schapira, M. M., McAuliffe, T. L., & Nattinger, A. B. (2004). Predictors of pessimistic breast cancer risk perceptions in a primary care population. *Journal of General Internal Medicine, 19*(4), 310–315.

17. Gurmankin, A. D., Baron, J., & Armstrong, K. (2004). Intended message versus message received in hypothetical physician risk communications: Exploring the gap. *Risk Analysis, 24*(5), 1337–1347.

18. Woloshin, S., Schwartz, L. M., Black, W. C., & Welch, H. G. (1999). Women's perceptions of breast cancer risk: How you ask matters. *Medical Decision Making, 19,* 221–229.

19. Dillard, A. J., McCaul, K. D., Kelso, P. D., & Klein, W. M. (2006). Resisting good news: Reactions to breast cancer risk communication. *Health Communication, 19*(2), 115–123.

20. Weinstein, N. D. (1993). Testing four competing theories of health-protective behavior. *Health Psychology, 12*(4), 324–333.

21. Brewer, N. T., Salz, T., & Lillie, S. E. (2007). Systematic review: The long-term effects of false-positive mammograms. *Annals of Internal Medicine, 146*(7), 502–510.

22. Carman, K. G., & Kooreman, P. (2014). Probability perceptions and preventive health care. *Journal of Risk and Uncertainty, 49*(1), 43–71.

23. Sheeran, P., Harris, P. R., & Epton, T. (2014). Does heightening risk appraisals change people's intentions and behavior? A meta-analysis of experimental studies. *Psychological Bulletin, 140*(2), 511–543.

24. Haggstrom, D. A., & Schapira, M. M. (2006). Black-white differences in risk perceptions of breast cancer survival and screening mammography benefit. *Journal of General Internal Medicine, 21*(4), 371–377.

25. Weinfurt, K. P., Castel, L. D., Li, Y., Sulmasy, D. P., Balshem, A. M., Benson, A. B., . . . Meropol, N. J. (2003). The correlation between patient characteristics and expectations of benefit from phase I clinical trials. *Cancer, 98*(1), 166–175.

26. Lipkus, I. M., Peters, E., Kimmick, G., Liotcheva, V., & Marcom, P. (2010). Breast cancer patients' treatment expectations after exposure to the decision aid program adjuvant online: The influence of numeracy. *Medical Decision Making, 30*(4), 464–473.

27. Johnson, E. J., & Tversky, A. (1983). Affect, generalization, and the perception of risk. *Journal of Personality and Social Psychology, 45*(1), 20–31.

28. Kahneman, D., & Tversky, A. (1979). Prospect theory: An analysis of decision under risk. *Econometrica, 47*(2), 263–291.

29. Rothman, A. J., & Salovey, P. (1997). Shaping perceptions to motivate healthy behavior: The role of message framing. *Psychological Bulletin, 121*(1), 3–19. (1998?)

30. Woloshin, S., Schwartz, L. M., Moncur, M., Gabriel, S., & Tosteson, A. N. A. (2001). Assessing values for health: numeracy matters. *Medical Decision Making, 21*(5), 382–390.

31. McAuliffe, T. L., DiFranceisco, W., & Reed, B. R. (2010). Low numeracy predicts reduced accuracy of retrospective reports of frequency of sexual behavior. *AIDS and Behavior, 14*(6), 1320–1329.

32. Bowen, M. E., Cavanaugh, K. L., Wolff, K., Davis, D., Gregory, B., & Rothman, R. L. (2013). Numeracy and dietary intake in patients with type 2 diabetes. *The Diabetes Educator, 39*(2), 240–247.

33. Schapira, M. M., Davids, S. L., McAuliffe, T. L., & Nattinger, A. B. (2004). Agreement between scales in the measurement of breast cancer risk perceptions. *Risk Analysis, 24*(3), 665–673.

34. Zillmann, D., Callison, C., & Gibson, R. (2009). Quantitative media literacy: individual differences in dealing with numbers in the news. *Media Psychology, 12*(4), 394–416.

35. Dave, C., Eckel, C. C., Johnson, C. A., & Rojas, C. (2010). Eliciting risk preferences: When is simple better?. *Journal of Risk and Uncertainty, 41*(3), 219–243.
36. Bruine de Bruin, W., & Carman, K. G. (2012). Measuring risk perceptions: What does the excessive use of 50% mean?. *Medical Decision Making, 32*(2), 232–236.
37. Dieckmann, N. F., Slovic, P., & Peters, E. M. (2009). The use of narrative evidence and explicit likelihood by decisionmakers varying in numeracy. *Risk Analysis, 29*(10), 1473–1488.
38. Pachur, T., & Galesic, M. (2013). Strategy selection in risky choice: The impact of numeracy, affect, and cross-cultural differences. *Journal of Behavioral Decision Making, 26*(3), 260–271.
39. Payne, J. W., Bettman, J. R., & Johnson, E. J. (1993). *The adaptive decision maker.* New York: Cambridge University Press.
40. Fagerlin, A., Zikmund-Fisher, B. J., Ubel, P. A., Jankovic, A., Derry, H. A., & Smith, D. M. (2007). Measuring numeracy without a math test: Development of the Subjective Numeracy Scale. *Medical Decision Making, 27*(5), 672–680.

3

Reliance on Heuristics and Concrete, Easy-to-Evaluate Attributes

As we have seen, people with lower objective numeracy comprehend numbers less well and respond more inconsistently to them. The less numerate also prefer non-numeric over numeric evidence more than the highly numerate.[1] For example, they prefer hearing weather forecasts relatively more in words ("rain is likely") rather than in percentages (a 75% chance of rain). These three characteristics (incomprehension, inconsistency, and preferences for non-numeric information) point toward less numerate decision makers being more likely to rely on intuitive, non-numeric, and easy-to-process beliefs and emotions rather than relying on data-based information.

In decision making, some of the most well-known examples of reliance on intuitions versus data come from the mental shortcuts or heuristics described by Nobel Prize Winner Daniel Kahneman in his best-selling book, *Thinking, Fast and Slow*.[2] Heuristics are simple ways to make judgments and choices. When using them, people generally focus on a single easily accessible piece of information in a complex decision and ignore other information. Using a heuristic approach is efficient and generally produces satisfactory judgments, but it can cause errors.[3] For example, in research on what is called the *representativeness heuristic*, Kahneman and his colleague, psychologist Amos Tversky, asked participants to respond to a story about Jack.[4] Jack sounded like (he was a reasonable representation of) an engineer with hobbies that included home carpentry, sailing, and mathematical puzzles. He was further described as being part of a group of 100 people comprised of either 30 engineers and 70 lawyers or 70 engineers and 30 lawyers. Participants relied more than they should on Jack's story and mostly ignored the 30% (or 70%) likelihood of someone in the group being an engineer. For decision makers on limited cognitive budgets (and all of us are), using intuitive heuristics instead of data-based information is tempting.

But the use of heuristics, while common, is not ubiquitous. In fact, a consistent minority of research participants do not use each heuristic. In the earlier lung cancer example, physician Barbara McNeil and her colleagues[5]

Innumeracy in the Wild. Ellen Peters, Oxford University Press (2020). © Oxford University Press 2020.
DOI: 10.1093/oso/9780190861094.003.0001

had described two treatment options in either a positive survival frame or a negative mortality frame. *Information framing*, on average, mattered to patients, physicians, and graduate students alike. In particular, surgery was preferred over radiation therapy by 75% of the participants in the survival frame compared to only 58% in the mortality frame. Note, however, that not all participants chose surgery in the survival frame and radiation in the mortality frame. Individual differences existed that could not be explained with the notion of a framing effect.

As someone who likes math, it surprised me that anyone would show this effect. Don't you simply transform one number into the other? If 90% survived treatment, of course 10% perished. In Chapters 3 and 4, however, we will find that the less objectively numerate succumb more to the power of easily accessible and imaginable information, like stories, emotional reactions, and information frames. Easy-to-process information is compelling, and it takes effort and ability to overcome its power to use summarized statistics and other information that reveal the superior option.

To foreshadow the rest of this section, the published studies generally demonstrate that, compared to the highly numerate, the less objectively numerate rely more on simpler, one-attribute decision making. The rest of Chapter 3 is organized around two heuristics: *availability* and *representativeness*. Chapter 4 examines the affect heuristic and framing effects. In each chapter, you will read first about what the heuristic is and why it's important. Then, you will learn about objective numeracy differences. By the end of both chapters, you will know the kinds of information that are seemingly irresistible to the less numerate. After that, we will turn to the information-processing inclinations of the highly numerate that allow them to make better decisions. By building this awareness of what less and more objectively numerate individuals do, you may be able to recognize and reduce heuristic use and develop the habits of the highly numerate.

Good Stories Are Compelling

Representativeness and Neglect of Statistics

Imagine you met someone new and are trying to judge the likelihood that she is a basketball player or that he will be friendly. How would you decide? You might, for example, make these respective judgments based on her height and the number of times you see him smile. In other words, you might use the *representativeness heuristic*.[6] People who use this heuristic judge the likelihood of a scenario (Is he friendly?) based on thinking about its similarity with a stereotype or other organizing framework (Friendly people smile a lot. Does he?). The more similar or representative the scenario is of the stereotype, the higher is the perceived likelihood of belonging (e.g., to the group "friendly people").

Let's take another example that involves larger versus smaller sample sizes. People often do not understand that larger samples produce more reliable results. Psychologists Daniel Kahneman and Amos Tversky tested this idea in their classic "hospital problem."[7] In responses to it, the majority of participants did not realize that a smaller hospital would have a greater likelihood (than a larger hospital) to have more days on which more than 60% of the babies born were boys. They believed instead that infant births in both hospitals would be similar because both hospitals appear equally similar to a stereotypical hospital. See Box 3.1 for how to solve the hospital problem. The same thing is true of research results. Studies that have larger sample sizes (more vs. fewer study participants) also yield more reliable, less variable results.

Using the representativeness heuristic is often helpful (as heuristic use generally is). However, providing easy-to-imagine details (e.g., about an individual) can make a stereotype more salient and increase the similarity of a person to a group. Increased similarity, in turn, can increase judged likelihood of the person being in a group. Detailed stories, however, can be unreliable and may lead to ignoring relevant statistical information. In general, the less objectively numerate are swayed more than the highly numerate by the compelling power of stories. Let's look at examples of base-rate neglect and conjunction errors that emerge due to use of the representativeness heuristic. We'll then read about the availability heuristic and its effects.

Base-Rate Neglect

The average American woman's lifetime risk of developing breast cancer is 12.5%. This number is the *base rate* for breast cancer, its overall likelihood to occur in the given population (American women, in this case). If Irene is at average risk for breast cancer and a doctor tells Irene that she tested positive on a mammogram, then her likelihood of breast cancer is higher than that base rate, but it is not 100%. In fact, psychologist Gerd Gigerenzer found that even doctors are surprised at how little the original base rate should be modified with the new test result.[9] In Irene's case, if the test was 90% accurate and she is like the average American woman, the chance that she has breast cancer given the positive mammogram is only 56%. She has about even odds to have cancer or not. See Box 3.2 for how to solve this problem. However, people tend to neglect base rates and not appreciate their importance, especially when

Box 3.1 Solving the Hospital Problem

This problem concerns the *law of large numbers*, the statistical rule that we need large sample sizes (of coin flips or hospitals) for results to converge to the expected average (e.g., based on randomness of coin flips and babies' genders in hospitals). Let's try an example before we get to the hospital problem itself. Imagine flipping a coin 5 times and it lands on heads 4 times (80% of the time). Now imagine flipping the coin 10,000 times and getting 8,000 heads (also 80% of the time). Which event is more likely? People often have an intuition that coin flips will eventually average out to 50% heads, but it takes a lot of flips (a large number). If you flip a fair coin only 5 times, it sometimes never lands on heads. Other times, it will land on heads once, twice, or even all 5 times. But with 10,000 coin flips, it will always land on heads about 50% of time. This law of large numbers is simple statistics. The larger the sample size, the closer and more consistently we get to the expected 50% heads. More extreme events (flipping a coin and getting lots of or very few heads) are more likely in small samples. The same thing is true for hospitals. Fewer babies are born in smaller than larger hospitals. It's as if they "flip the baby gender coin" fewer times each day. As a result, smaller hospitals are more likely than larger hospitals to have more than 60% male babies (they're also more likely to have fewer male babies, like 40%, on any given day). Although people often have a pretty good understanding that sample sizes of 5 and 5,000,000 will likely produce different results, they do not have good intuitions about the difference between 30 and 1,000.[2] This intuitive lack trips up responses on the hospital problem. Compared to the less numerate, however, highly numerate participants appeared to have better intuitions about sample sizes, and they were more likely to solve the hospital problem correctly.[8]

they also have specific information about an individual or an event. Base rates are not the only important information to use, but they provide a place to start when thinking about likelihood.

Base rates are important to consider in a lot of problems including the "Jack the engineer" problem described earlier. In it, researchers described a group of 100 people, 30 of them were engineers and 70 were lawyers. The base rate for engineers in the group was therefore 30%. When no other information is provided and people are asked how likely it is that an individual chosen at random from the group is an engineer, they tend to use the base rate and

Box 3.2 Positive Mammograms and Bayes' Theorem

We can solve this problem together with a bit of math, taking it one simple step at a time. First, you need four pieces of information to know a woman's risk once she has a positive mammogram: that she tested positive (we won't use this piece of information until the very end), her base rate for breast cancer, the hit rate of the test, and the test's false alarm rate. Irene is at average risk for breast cancer so we know that she has a 1 out of 8 (12.5%) chance of cancer across her lifetime; this number is her base rate for cancer. Then, we need the hit rate and false alarm rate for mammography because no test is completely accurate. Here, I use a 90% hit rate (also called sensitivity) and a 10% false alarm rate. The hit rate means that 90% of women who have breast cancer will be told that their mammogram identified cancer (10% will be told that it didn't, even though they actually have cancer). Based on the false alarm rate, among the women who do not have cancer, 10% will be told inaccurately that they do have cancer. Now, we can calculate the likelihood that Irene has cancer given that she tested positive in five easy steps:

1. The first thing to do is to imagine 1,000 women like Irene, some of whom have cancer and some don't. This number goes in the bottom right cell of the table.
2. Irene's base rate for breast cancer is 12.5%. Of our 1,000 women, 125 of them have cancer, and the rest, 875, do not; these numbers go in the far right column of the table below.
3. Now, let's figure out how many of the women who have cancer will be accurately identified as having it. We're going to work in the second "has cancer" row and use the hit rate of 90% because this number tells us how many women with cancer will be accurately diagnosed. In row 2, we multiply .90 times 125 to determine that about 113 women will be accurately identified as having cancer. The remaining 12 women still have cancer but have a negative mammogram.
4. Now, we turn to the women who do not have cancer (the third row). We know that the false alarm rate is 10%. This number is the proportion of women without cancer who nonetheless will be told they have it. In row 3, we multiply .10 by the 875 women who don't have cancer to determine that about 88 women will have a positive mammogram even though they do not have cancer.
5. For our final step, we use our last piece of information, that Irene tested positive. Now, we only look at those women who had a positive mammogram (the second column). How many are there? Well, there are 201 women total who had a positive mammogram, but some of them have cancer (113 in the second row) and some do not (88 in the third row). Of those women who had a positive mammogram in this column, what percent of them actually have cancer? This is the answer we need for Irene. To calculate it, you divide the 113 women

in this column who have cancer by the total 201 women who tested positive. Based on these results, Irene has only a 56% chance of having breast cancer given her average cancer risk and the test's accuracy.

	Positive mammogram	Negative mammogram	Totals
Has cancer	113	12	125 (per base rate)
No cancer	88	787	875
Total	201	799	1,000 women total

If Irene had come from a low-risk population of women who very rarely had breast cancer (say, a cancer base rate of 5%), her chances of having cancer given a positive mammogram would be only 32%. If she came from a high-risk population that had a genetic mutation, then her base rate for cancer would be much higher. Let's say her base rate is 72%. Using the same test characteristics and this new base rate, her odds of having breast cancer if she had a positive mammogram are now an extraordinarily higher 96%.

answer about 30%.[6] However, the person can be described in a manner that makes them seem more like an engineer:

Jack is a 45-year-old man. He is married and has four children. He is generally conservative, careful, and ambitious. He shows no interest in political and social issues and spends most of his free time on his many hobbies which include home carpentry, sailing, and mathematical puzzles. The probability that Jack is one of the 30 engineers in the sample of 100 is ___%" (p. 241).[4]

In this case, people estimated the likelihood of Jack being an engineer as quite high. They largely ignored the base rate because the story about Jack was salient, easy to evaluate, and powerful.[4] Jack "seemed like" a stereotypical engineer even when the base rate indicated that he was most likely a lawyer. However, the base rate was not completely ignored, suggesting that some people ignored the base rate more than others. In fact, base rate neglect and use of this heuristic occurs more often among less numerate individuals.[10-12] See Box 3.3 for overcoming the representativeness heuristic.

These numeracy differences in base-rate neglect emerge because the less numerate do not think about using base rates. It turns out that they are capable of using them, however. In particular, providing prompts that made either base rates or stereotype information more salient (researchers essentially

---

Box 3.3 Explaining Base Rate Neglect

When reading a story that describes Jack in great detail and makes him sound like a stereotypical engineer, people tend to start with a high likelihood that he's an engineer. After all, he sounds like an engineer. That concrete description is very compelling and especially for less numerate people who do not think about the fact that only 30% of the people in the group are engineers. Based on Box 3.2, however, we know that this 30% base rate is really important. (Remember from Box 3.2 that Irene's odds of having breast cancer given a positive mammogram test were 56% if she had average cancer risk and 97% if she was at high risk.)

Jack's base rate, the group's 30% engineers, is critical. You should start with that number as your initial estimate (assuming it's trustworthy) and then think about whether his concrete description is meaningful. Did it come from a reliable source? Does it only describe engineers, or might a lawyer also be described in this way? If you decide that the story is somewhat informative and reliable, you would adjust your initial 30% estimate upward. If it's not, then you would stick with your original 30% estimate. Later in the chapter, you will learn that other stories, anecdotes, and narratives are also compelling but should be used only to adjust away from a trustworthy base rate.

---

repeated the same information) caused the less numerate to use base rate information more.[11] Thus, the less numerate were able to use base rates in a manner similar to the highly numerate but did not do so spontaneously. These salience manipulations made little difference to base rate use among the highly numerate, as if they judged their balance of information use as appropriate already (despite underusing base rates). More research is needed to uncover whether stronger salience manipulations would overcome mindless thinking and increase base-rate use.[13]

Other studies that did not include numeracy have identified manipulations that increase base-rate use, and these manipulations would be good places to start additional research. For example, base-rate use increases when base-rate information was placed after the compelling description instead of before,[14,15] when participants were asked to think "like a scientist analyzing data" versus to make "clinical judgments,"[16] and when participants were told that the task was a statistical problem versus a psychology problem from a human communicator.[17] Base-rate neglect similarly decreased when repeated measures were used, specifically when participants were asked in serial fashion to judge likelihood given a base rate of 10% and then 30%. These findings are often interpreted as due to the norms of conversation (e.g., If you provided more information, you must think I need it, so therefore I will use it).[17] However, from a numeracy perspective, I expect that many of the manipulations simply encourage greater numeric processing (e.g., think like a scientist) and will increase base-rate use among the less numerate. Less clear to me are their likely effects on the highly numerate who neglect base rates despite their numeric skills. These results suggest a lack of appreciation of base rates' importance (an education issue) or a lack of attention to base rates (attention can be manipulated).[18] More research on the effects of various manipulations in combination with numeracy should reveal more about the causes of base-rate neglect and the information processes of more and less numerate individuals.

Conjunction Errors

In another example of the compelling power of stories, psychologists Amos Tversky and Daniel Kahneman described "Linda" as if she was a stereotypical feminist: She "is 31 years old, single, outspoken, and very bright. She majored in philosophy. As a student, she was deeply concerned with issues of discrimination and social justice, and also participated in antinuclear demonstrations."[6] Following the description, participants were asked to judge whether Linda was more likely to be a bank teller or a bank teller and active in the feminist movement. Contrary to the rules of probability, most people (~80%) believed that Linda was more likely to be both a bank teller and feminist. However, this conjunction (Linda being both a bank teller and a feminist) is contained within the other option (Linda is a feminist), making it impossible for it to be more likely (although it could be as likely). Tversky and Kahneman[6] attributed this error to the representativeness heuristic because people appeared to judge likelihood based on how representative or similar Linda was of a stereotypical feminist rather than judging it based on the rules of probability. See Box 3.4 to solve the Linda problem.

As expected based on their misunderstandings of numeric concepts, lower objective numeracy has been associated with more conjunction errors. Specifically, the less numerate are more likely to say that the conjunction (Linda is a feminist bank teller) is true rather than that the single event (Linda is a bank teller) is true, even after controlling for non-numeric intelligence measures.[19-24] However, conjunction problems are difficult even for the highly numerate, and errors among the highly numerate are common too.

Two possible explanations exist for these errors by the highly numerate. First, it may be that some of the highly numerate understand the necessary probabilistic concept about conjunctions but do not think to use it. Evidence in support of this explanation is that errors among the highly numerate

Box 3.4 Overcoming Conjunction Fallacies

People often judge the likelihood that Linda is a feminist bank teller as more than her likelihood of being a bank teller. Similarly, they will judge the likelihood of going to the dentist to get a cavity filled as greater than their likelihood of going to the dentist for any reason. In both cases, one answer is concrete and appears more likely. It is closer to a well-known story (either the story about Linda or the familiar reason for going to the dentist). The stories are compelling, but they can also mislead. In the Venn diagram below, I illustrate how you should think about the Linda problem. There are bank tellers (a relatively small number) and there are feminists (a relatively large number). At the intersection of the two circles are the people who are feminist bank tellers. Linda's story is either irrelevant, or it could be thought relevant to how much the circles overlap. Are there more or fewer bank tellers who are also feminist? In any event, the likelihood of being a feminist bank teller can never be greater than the likelihood of the larger category of bank tellers.

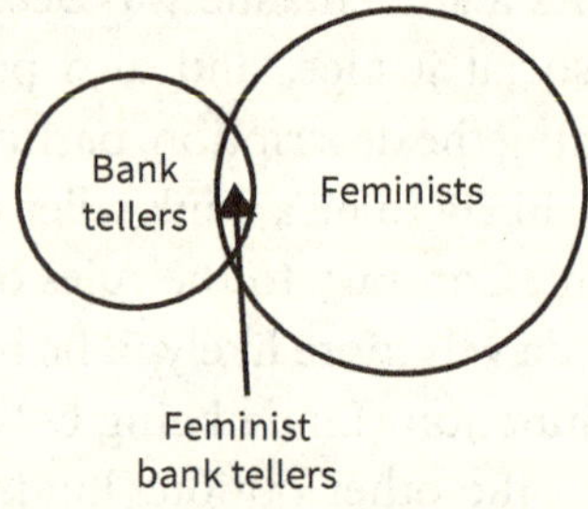

decrease with increased numeric thinking. For example, across studies, greater numeracy is more likely to be related to fewer conjunction errors when participants responded first to many repeated probability questions or to other probabilistic decision tasks and then to the conjunction task.[19,21,22] I believe these repeated questions and tasks increase numeric reasoning so that the highly numerate think to access and use their probabilistic knowledge more. This speculation is consistent with prior research indicating that priming participants to think more numerically improves reasoning on probabilistic decision tasks[25,26] and particularly among more objectively numerate participants.[27,28] The second explanation is based on the highly numerate (and the less numerate) using confirmatory processes that support intuitive impressions (e.g., based on Linda's description). The highly numerate, however, are more open to switching, if directed, to nonconfirmatory reasons. Psychologist Laura Scherer and her colleagues found that asking participants to generate arguments decreased conjunction errors among the highly numerate (compared to not generating arguments), but only if participants generated reasons for why the correct option was the right answer.[20]

The first explanation (priming numeric reasoning among those who know the necessary probabilistic concept) seems more plausible to me. Across studies and conditions, more and less numerate participants, on average, tended to commit the conjunction error. As a result, I think that conjunction errors can be largely explained by individuals across the numeracy spectrum not understanding the probabilistic concept involved (especially the less numerate) or not recognizing its appropriate use in the situation (the highly numerate). In fact, we often reason from conjunctions of events (I'm coughing and sneezing. Do I have a cold?), and this familiar reasoning may interfere with accessing the reasoning needed to avoid the compelling power of Linda's story and the conjunction fallacy.[24] This rationale also may explain why the highly numerate were less confident about their correct than incorrect responses.[20] Thus, highly numerate participants are more likely to know the correct logic, but they do not always recognize when to use it (see also psychology graduate student results[29]). Less numerate people likely did not know the correct logic and so directing them to consider the situation more deeply makes little difference. In Chapter 8, we will look at other examples where highly numerate individuals are no better than the less numerate at solving particularly difficult probabilistic problems (e.g., cumulative risk[30]) or they are helped more than the less numerate by having the experimenter focus them more on probabilities.[27,28]

Overall, those lower in objective numeracy are more likely than the highly numerate to judge the likelihoods of events based on assessments of similarity rather than the rules of probability. These effects are independent of measures of non-numeric intelligence. This use of the representativeness heuristic results in the less numerate being more likely to neglect base rates and commit conjunction fallacies. For the person who wants to use base rates more, however, research suggests that you remind yourself to think like a scientist or statistician. Avoiding conjunction fallacies may be more difficult. You first need to understand this probabilistic rule (see Box 3.4) and then be suspicious of compelling stories and think about reasons why the less compelling option is the correct one.

Availability and the Power of Narratives

Our next heuristic, the availability heuristic, concerns judging the likelihood of an event based on how easy it is to think about examples of its occurrence.[3]

In particular, when you can more easily imagine an event happening, it seems more likely. Ease of thought can be increased by telling compelling stories such as personal testimonials and narratives. These stories have powerful effects, while more abstract and pallid statistical information (e.g., the base rates described earlier) often fails to move people to action.[31,32] For example, easier-to-imagine stories can sway jury decisions. In one study, participants read a court case involving drunk driving.[33] The defendant had run a stop sign while driving from a Christmas party and collided with a garbage truck. The defendant's blood alcohol had not been tested at the time, and he was now being tried on the basis of circumstantial evidence. When the evidence was presented in a vivid manner ("On his way out the door, Sanders staggered against a serving table, knocking a bowl of guacamole dip to the floor and splattering guacamole on the white shag carpet"), the defendant was judged as more likely to be guilty than when it was presented in a pallid manner ("On his way out the door, Sanders staggered against a serving table, knocking a bowl to the floor").

The power of individual examples also plays out in the news. Take, for example, the snowball thrown on the senate floor by US Senator Jim Inhofe. He ignored available statistical information and instead singled out recent cold days to argue global warming as a hoax.[34] If people are biased toward using experienced intuitions linked to vivid stories when logic and intuition conflict,[35,36] then stories will be problematic sometimes. They will be used to denigrate politically inconvenient truths and fan fear of unlikely threats.

Although Tversky and Kahneman[6] suggested that heuristic use is natural and common, people higher in objective numeracy again are less likely to use the availability heuristic compared to the less numerate. For example, highly numerate jurors in a hypothetical court case were influenced more by numeric error rates. At the same time, the vividness of an error made by the laboratory technician affected the less numerate more.[37] The power of narratives is also stronger among the less numerate. We asked highly educated participants to react to three terrorism forecasts, presented one at a time. In each, an intelligence forecaster provided both an assessment of its likelihood (1%, 5%, 10%) and narrative evidence (a story) concerning a possible terrorist attack (e.g., a foreign newspaper printed a militant group's warning of an attack).[38] After each forecast, participants rated the narrative's credibility and coherence and rated how likely they perceived the possible attack. As predicted, less objectively numerate individuals were insensitive to the numeric likelihood assessments. Instead, their risk perceptions were associated with perceptions of the narratives; the more credible and coherent the narrative evidence appeared, the more likely they rated the attack. The highly numerate were relatively less sensitive to perceptions of the narratives and rated the likelihood of an attack as higher when its provided likelihood was higher. Similar results of the less numerate being more sensitive to narrative information (than the highly numerate) and less sensitive to numeric information have been found in medical scenarios (vaccines;[39,40] tropical dysentery[41]). Look back at Box 3.3 for tips on how to overcome the power of compelling stories.

This view of narratives as easier to use and more compelling than statistics is not the whole story, however. Health policy researchers Jessica Greene and Judy Hibbard[42] recently conducted a study in which they used a lengthy and informative narrative in cartoon form about Helen, a diabetic patient who had to switch doctors. Unlike prior studies, the narrative information did not compete with numeric information (in fact, it provided additional numeric information). Instead, the narrative appeared to direct thinking toward difficult issues for diabetic patients. More numerate participants (based on self-reports of numeric ability) were more likely to choose the highest quality physician in the narrative condition (65%) compared with two other non-narrative conditions (51% and 50%). The narrative presence had no effect on the less numerate. These results suggest that decision makers sometimes use narratives as more than a simple substitute for numeric information. Instead, narratives can direct people to elaborate on important numeric and non-numeric information.[43] More studies at the intersection of numeracy and communication/journalism research may reveal limits on availability-heuristic effects and highlight improved methods for helping more and less numerate individuals make better choices.

References

1. Fagerlin, A., Zikmund-Fisher, B. J., Ubel, P. A., Jankovic, A., Derry, H. A., & Smith, D. M. (2007). Measuring numeracy without a math test: Development of the Subjective Numeracy Scale. *Medical Decision Making, 27*(5), 672–680.
2. Kahneman, D. (2011). *Thinking, fast and slow.* New York: Farrar, Straus and Giroux.
3. Tversky, A., & Kahneman, D. (1974). Judgment under uncertainty: Heuristics and biases. *Science, 185*(4157), 1124–1131.
4. Kahneman, D., & Tversky, A. (1973). On the psychology of prediction. *Psychological Review, 80*(4), 237–251.
5. McNeil, B. J., Pauker, S. G., Sox, H. C., Jr., & Tversky, A. (1982). On the elicitation of preferences for alternative therapies. *New England Journal of Medicine, 306,* 1259–1262.
6. Tversky, A., & Kahneman, D. (1983). Extensional versus intuitive reasoning: The conjunction fallacy in probability judgment. *Psychological Review, 90*(4), 293–315.
7. Kahneman, D., & Tversky, A. (1972). Subjective probability: A judgment of representativeness. *Cognitive Psychology, 3*(3), 430–454.

8. Chesney, D. L., & Obrecht, N. A. (2012). Statistical judgments are influenced by the implied likelihood that samples represent the same population. *Memory & Cognition*, 40(3), 420–433.

9. Gigerenzer, G., Gaissmaier, W., Kurz-Milcke, E., Schwartz, L. M., & Woloshin, S. (2007). Helping doctors and patients make sense of health statistics. *Psychological Science in the Public Interest*, 8(2), 53–96.

10. Obrecht, N. A., & Chesney, D. L. (2013). Sample representativeness affects whether judgments are influenced by base rate or sample size. *Acta Psychologica*, 142(3), 370–382.

11. Obrecht, N. A., & Chesney, D. L. (2016). Prompting deliberation increases base-rate use. *Judgment and Decision Making*, 11(1), 1–6.

12. Weil, A. M., Wolfe, C. R., Reyna, V. F., Widmer, C. L., Cedillos-Whynott, E. M., & Brust-Renck, P. G. (2015). Proficiency of FPPI and objective numeracy in assessing breast cancer risk estimation. *Learning and Individual Differences*, 43, 149–155.

13. Arkes, H. R. (2016). A levels of processing interpretation of dual-system theories of judgment and decision making. *Theory & Psychology*, 26(4), 459–475.

14. Krosnick, J. A., Li, F., & Lehman, D. R. (1990). Conversational conventions, order of information acquisition, and the effect of base rates and individuating information on social judgments. *Journal of Personality and Social Psychology*, 59(6), 1140–1152.

15. Obrecht, N. A., Chapman, G. B., & Gelman, R. (2009). An encounter frequency account of how experience affects likelihood estimation. *Memory & Cognition*, 37(5), 632–643.

16. Zukier, H., & Pepitone, A. (1984). Social roles and strategies in prediction: Some determinants of the use of base-rate information. *Journal of Personality and Social Psychology*, 47(2), 349–360.

17. Schwarz, N., Strack, F., Hilton, D., & Naderer, G. (1991). Base rates, representativeness, and the logic of conversation: The contextual relevance of "irrelevant" information. *Social Cognition*, 9(1), 67–84.

18. Armel, K. C., Beaumel, A., & Rangel, A. (2008). Biasing simple choices by manipulating relative visual attention. *Judgment and Decision Making*, 3(5), 396–403.

19. Liberali, J. M., Reyna, V. F., Furlan, S., Stein, L. M., & Pardo, S. T. (2012). Individual differences in numeracy and cognitive reflection, with implications for biases and fallacies in probability judgment. *Journal of Behavioral Decision Making*, 25(4), 361–381.

20. Scherer, L. D., Yates, J. F., Baker, S. G., & Valentine, K. D. (2017). The influence of effortful thought and cognitive proficiencies on the conjunction fallacy: Implications for dual-process theories of reasoning and judgment. *Personality and Social Psychology Bulletin*, 43(6), 874–887.

21. Sinayev, A., & Peters, E. (2015). Cognitive reflection vs. calculation in decision making. *Frontiers in Psychology*, 6, 532.

22. Toplak, M. E., West, R. F., & Stanovich, K. E. (2011). The Cognitive Reflection Test as a predictor of performance on heuristics-and-biases tasks. *Memory & Cognition*, 39(7), 1275.

23. Winman, A., Juslin, P., Lindskog, M., Nilsson, H., & Kerimi, N. (2014). The role of ANS acuity and numeracy for the calibration and the coherence of subjective probability judgments. *Frontiers in Psychology*, 5, 851.

24. Wedell, D. H. (2011). Probabilistic reasoning in prediction and diagnosis: Effects of problem type, response mode, and individual differences. *Journal of Behavioral Decision Making*, 24(2), 157–179.

25. Hoover, J. D., & Healy, A. F. (2017). Algebraic reasoning and bat-and-ball problem variants: Solving isomorphic algebra first facilitates problem solving later. *Psychonomic Bulletin & Review*, 1–7.

26. Hsee, C. K., & Rottenstreich, Y. (2004). Music, pandas, and muggers: On the affective psychology of value. *Journal of Experimental Psychology: General*, 133(1), 23–30.

27. Bless, H., Betsch, T., & Franzen, A. (1998). Framing the framing effect: The impact of context cues on solutions to the "Asian disease" problem. *European Journal of Social Psychology*, *28*, 287–291.

28. Riege, A. H., & Teigen, K. H. (2013). Additivity neglect in probability estimates: Effects of numeracy and response format. *Organizational Behavior and Human Decision Processes*, *121*(1), 41–52.

29. Kahneman, D., & Tversky, A. (1982). The psychology of preferences. *Scientific American*, *246*(1), 160–173.

30. Peters, E., Kunreuther, H., Sagara, N., Slovic, P., & Schley, D. R. (2012). Protective measures, personal experience, and the affective psychology of time. *Risk Analysis*, *32*(12), 2084–2097.

31. Borgida, E., & Nisbett, R. E. (1977). The differential impact of abstract vs. concrete information on decisions. *Journal of Applied Social Psychology*, *7*(3), 258–271.

32. Epstein, S. (1994). Integration of the cognitive and the psychodynamic unconscious. *American Psychologist*, *49*, 709–724.

33. Reyes, R. M., Thompson, W. C., & Bower, G. H. (1980). Judgmental biases resulting from differing availabilities of arguments. *Journal of Personality and Social Psychology*, *39*(1), 2–12.

34. Sheppard, K. (2015, February 26). Jim Inhofe brings a snowball to the senate floor to prove climate change is a "hoax." Retrieved from https://www.huffingtonpost.com/2015/02/26/jim-inhofe-climate-snow_n_6763868.html

35. Daws, R. E., & Hampshire, A. (2017). The negative relationship between reasoning and religiosity is underpinned by a bias for intuitive responses specifically when intuition and logic are in conflict. *Frontiers in Psychology*, *8*, 2191.

36. Metz, S. E., Weisberg, D. S., & Weisberg, M. (2018). Non-scientific criteria for belief sustain counter-scientific beliefs. *Cognitive Science*, *42*(5), 1477–1503.

37. Scurich, N. (2015). The differential effect of numeracy and anecdotes on the perceived fallibility of forensic science. *Psychiatry, Psychology and Law*, *22*(4), 616–623.

38. Dieckmann, N. F., Slovic, P., & Peters, E. M. (2009). The use of narrative evidence and explicit likelihood by decisionmakers varying in numeracy. *Risk Analysis*, *29*(10), 1473–1488.

39. Betsch, C., Haase, N., Renkewitz, F., & Schmid, P. (2015). The narrative bias revisited: What drives the biasing influence of narrative information on risk perceptions? *Judgment and Decision Making*, *10*(3), 241–264.

40. Bruine de Bruin, W., Wallin, A., Parker, A. M., Strough, J., & Hanmer, J. (2017). Effects of anti-versus pro-vaccine narratives on responses by recipients varying in numeracy: A cross-sectional survey-based experiment. *Medical Decision Making*, *37*(8), 860–870.

41. Gibson, R., Callison, C., & Zillmann, D. (2011). Quantitative literacy and affective reactivity in processing statistical information and case histories in the news. *Media Psychology*, *14*(1), 96–120.

42. Greene, J., Hibbard, J. H., & Sacks, R. M. (2017). Testing a personal narrative for persuading people to value and use comparative physician quality of care information: An experimental study. *Medical Care Research and Review*. Online publication September 9, 2017. doi: 10.1077558717730156

43. Kreuter, M. W., Green, M. C., Cappella, J. N., Slater, M. D., Wise, M. E., Storey, D., . . . Hinyard, L. J. (2007). Narrative communication in cancer prevention and control: A framework to guide research and application. *Annals of Behavioral Medicine*, *33*(3), 221–235.

4

Feelings and Frames

Reliance on Feelings: The Affect Heuristic

Kahneman and Tversky introduced the representativeness and availability heuristics as cognitive in nature, consistent with psychology's focus at the time.[1] Emotional reactions were largely ignored, with a few exceptions.[2–5] Led by psychologist Paul Slovic, we noticed this lack of attention to the role of emotions and developed the affect heuristic.[5] According to it, decision makers rely in part on emotional reactions to stimuli (their affect) to inform judgments and make choices. We postulated that affect acts as a simple cue and that reliance on it has allowed people to survive throughout evolutionary history. In particular, affect helps people quickly identify what is safe to approach and what is best avoided. Perhaps a tribute to its importance, a punk band called "The Affect Heuristic" sings "I want to feel."[6]

Affect can be characterized in terms of valence (good versus bad feelings), arousal (calm versus energized feelings), or discrete emotions (e.g., angry, happy, sad feelings). Research on the affect heuristic tends to focus on valence and defines affect as a "specific quality of 'goodness' or 'badness' (1) experienced as a feeling state (with or without consciousness) and (2) demarcating a positive or negative quality of a stimulus" (p. 397).[5] Other researchers focus on the power of discrete emotions such as fear or anger (e.g., in risk perceptions[7]). The two foci are related, of course, with one popular approach, the *circumplex model*, characterizing emotional states[8] as emerging from two neurophysiological systems related to valence and arousal.[9] Different patterns of activation within the two systems of this circumplex model then create discrete emotional states.

The affect heuristic (not the punk rock band) arose out of early studies of reactions to hazards, activities, and technologies. In these studies, risk and benefit perceptions were positively correlated in the world but negatively correlated in people's minds and judgments.[10] For example, people tended to judge alcoholic beverages, handguns, and smoking as low in benefit and high in risk whereas they judged other hazards and technologies as high in benefit and low in risk (e.g., antibiotics, vaccinations). Later research revealed that this inverse relation between perceived risk and perceived benefit of an

Innumeracy in the Wild. Ellen Peters, Oxford University Press (2020). © Oxford University Press 2020.
DOI: 10.1093/oso/9780190861094.003.0001

activity (e.g., using pesticides) was linked to the strength of positive or negative affect associated with that activity.[11]

Affect-heuristic results implied that people base their judgments of an activity or a technology not only on what they think about it, but also on how they feel about it. In particular, instead of considering complex information, they use affect in heuristic fashion. If their feelings about an activity or technology were positive, they tended to perceive its risks as low and benefits as high. If their feelings toward it were negative, they tended to judge the opposite—high risk and low benefit. With this model, feelings about a hazard come prior to, and direct, judgments of risk and benefit. In fact, under time pressure, the negative correlation between risk and benefit perceptions grew stronger, as if affective reactions to hazards arise early in the mind and direct risk and benefit perceptions until corrected by later deliberation.[12] See Box 4.1.

Before we continue, I want you to be able to distinguish between three varieties of affect important to studies of objective numeracy and the affect heuristic. In particular, affect can be integral or incidental to a judgment or choice. *Integral affect* means that the feelings are part of how you represent the object being considered. They are built into how you think about and react to the object. These integral feelings can be due to prior learning about the object (broccoli smelled bad and tasted bad every time I've had it and therefore I have negative feelings about it) or to comparisons you make in the moment (an annual income of $65,000 feels much more positive in comparison to $50,000 than to $75,000). Integral affect is like a built-in bookcase that is integral to a living room. It can be changed, but it is part of your current representation of

Box 4.1 The Affect Heuristic and Risk and Benefit Perceptions

The objective risks and benefits of most hazards and activities are logically unrelated. For example, nuclear power has benefits. It can be produced in almost unlimited amounts and without dependence on imports from other countries. Those benefits are unrelated to its risks of radioactive hazards and waste. You could have the same benefits in the absence of the risks and perhaps someday science will produce this energy technology. Nonetheless, the human mind relies on feelings to simplify risk and benefit judgments so that they seem like opposites. We say that they use an *affect heuristic*. For example, you might feel bad about pesticides and use those negative feelings to judge them as riskier and with fewer benefits. Thinking longer about a hazard's risks and benefits helps to overcome use of this heuristic.

an object like chocolate cake or people who bully. The research just described regarding risk and benefit perceptions being guided by affect specifically concern integral affect to hazards.[12]

Two types of integral affect exist that are important for this book. First are integral feelings about outcomes (defined broadly here to include hazards, technologies, activities, or the possible end results of a choice such as a side effect from a prescription drug). The second type of integral affect concerns feelings about quantitative information in a judgment or choice (e.g., good or bad feelings about a probability).

A third type of affect, *incidental affect*, is defined as feelings such as mood states that are independent of a stimulus but can be misattributed to it. These feelings are unrelated to the decision itself except that they may co-occur in time (e.g., a negative mood from a long workday can co-occur with judging the chances that your teenager will come home past curfew).

All three types (integral affect to outcomes, integral affect to numbers, and incidental affect) have been used to predict and explain a wide variety of judgments and decisions ranging from choices among bets and willingness to pay for insurance to risk perceptions of medical interventions and valuation of human lives.[5,13,14]

However, more and less objectively numerate individuals rely differently on the three varieties of affect. In particular, and as we'll see in Chapter 6, the more numerate derive more integral (built-in) affect from numeric information which then appears to facilitate their greater use of numeric information in judgments and choices.[15-17] Without affective meaning, studies indicate that numeric information is used less. The less objectively numerate, on the other hand, rely more on built-in integral affect to non-numeric outcomes (e.g., cancer fears). The less numerate also use incidental affect (e.g., moods or feelings in the moment) more in their judgments. The next section will illustrate how the less numerate rely more on incidental affect and integral affect to non-numeric outcomes in judgment and choice in ways that mislead them. Understanding these concepts will help you better apprehend how the highly numerate lean less on these non-numeric sources of affect by thinking more with numbers and having a better integral feel for them.

Integral Affect to Outcomes and Incidental Affect Are Used by the Less Objectively Numerate

Integral (Built-In) Affect to Outcomes and Greater Risk Perceptions

Greater reliance on the affect heuristic and, in particular, integral affect to outcomes may explain the systematically greater risk perceptions held by the less objectively numerate as compared to the more numerate.[18-24] From Chapter 2, we might think that less numerate individuals are less accurate and respond more inconsistently and randomly in their risk perceptions compared to the highly numerate.[22,25,26] Instead, however, they appear to infer risk based on their integral affect to possible outcomes. For example, in response to the 2008 economic crisis, the less numerate reported greater negative emotional responses and they perceived more risk to personal savings, investments, retirement, and jobs as compared to the more numerate.[24] In this study, we surveyed public responses starting on September 29, 2007, the day the Dow experienced its then-largest single-day drop of 779 points. We asked a nationwide panel to respond to seven surveys, with the last survey concluding in October 2009. At least 600 respondents participated in each survey, and 413 completed all seven surveys. Not only did the less numerate report greater negative emotions to the crisis and more perceived risk, but stronger emotional reactions significantly predicted greater risk perceptions after controlling for perceptions of one's future prospects, confidence in the government and business, current mood state, and demographics (gender, income, age, education, political attitude). These results imply that, compared to the highly numerate, the less numerate relied more on integral (built-in) affect to outcomes (negative feelings to the financial crisis in this case) in forming perceptions of risk. The more numerate instead may have relied more on what they knew about objective information concerning likelihoods and outcomes. In other words, the less numerate rely more than the highly numerate on the affect heuristic when affect concerns integral affect to outcomes.

The less objectively numerate, however, do not always perceive greater risk than the highly numerate. Anomalies may be explained by hypothetical studies that elicited little negative integral affect. For example, in one study, individuals ($N = 463$) responded to questions about their chances of ever developing a fatal cancer on a scale from 0 (absolutely no chance) to 100 (absolutely certain).[27] Those who perceived a higher probability (>50%) of ever developing cancer in the future were more numerate than those who perceived a lower probability (50% or less). Similarly, in another study, participants ($N = 401$ women) were asked about hypothetical women's risks of breast cancer.[28] Greater objective numeracy led to more accurate risk perceptions (consistent with most prior findings), but the less numerate did not perceive greater risk than the highly numerate (in fact, the opposite occurred for the high cancer-risk scenario). Participants in both studies, however, may have experienced relatively little affect to presented hypothetical scenarios as they came from a frequently interviewed internet panel[27] or from a combination of college undergraduates and individuals from the community and internet sites (e.g., Facebook).[28] If true, then little affect existed to guide risk perceptions of the less numerate. In studies where the less numerate perceived greater risk from cancer, the samples tended to be patients recruited from medical centers[19,20] who may have responded more emotionally to cancer scenarios.

Other inconsistencies in the literature may be caused by more and less numerate individuals processing the same information differently. For example, decision makers often neglect probability in affect-rich situations (where integral affect to the outcomes is strong versus weak).[29] If the less objectively numerate rely more on the affect heuristic, we would expect them to neglect probabilities as they used integral affect more while the highly numerate used probabilities. Contrary to predictions, both more and less numerate individuals neglect probabilities in these cases, perhaps suggestive of affect-heuristic use across the numeracy spectrum. However, psychologists Thorsten Pachur and Mirta Galesic[30] discovered that probability neglect of the highly numerate was due to them following a more reasoned-based strategy, whereas the less numerate chose based on their feelings, consistent with the affect heuristic. Future research should focus on disentangling cognitive versus affective processes in decision making from other effects that may influence how more and less objectively numerate individuals perceive risks.

Incidental Affect and the Less Numerate

Less objectively numerate individuals also use the affect heuristic based on incidental affect more than the highly numerate. For example, participants in one of our studies were asked to evaluate the attractiveness of a hospital based on three numeric quality-of-care indicators (e.g., 93% of pneumonia patients survived treatment at Hospital A). Evaluations from less numerate individuals were related to their self-reported mood states (as if they used these feelings to infer "I feel bad; therefore, the hospital must be bad"). Ratings of those higher in numeracy relied more on provided numeric quality-of-care indicators.[31] The highly numerate appeared able to parse out (or separate) the possible influence of incidental affect irrelevant to the judgment task.

Recently, researchers demonstrated the hypothesized causal influence of incidental affect on judgments of the less numerate.[14] In a well-designed experiment, a source of incidental negative affect (i.e., fear-inducing pictures versus neutral pictures) appeared briefly immediately before participants indicated how much they were willing to pay (WTP) to insure against a probability of losing a costly voucher (probabilities were varied within subject; 1%, 5%, 10%, 25%, 50%, 75%, 90%, 95%, 99%). The researchers then modeled whether WTP values reflected the probabilities. Consistent with the affect heuristic, less numerate individuals neglected probability more after seeing negative versus neutral images. No such effect was seen among the highly numerate.

Inconsistent with the affect heuristic, however, WTP to insure against a possible negative event was not higher among the less numerate when negative versus neutral pictures were shown.

Overall, extant results are most consistent with less objectively numerate individuals relying more on two varieties of affect—incident affect and integral affect to outcomes—in judgment and choice. Like research on the other heuristics reviewed, when data-based information conflicts with easy-to-process affective reactions, less numerate individuals are more susceptible to using incidental affect and integral (built-in) affect to outcomes in their judgments. In Chapter 6, we will see that those higher in objective numeracy derive strong and precise integral affect from numeric information and use it instead.

It's All in How It's Presented: Numeric Framing Effects

Is the glass half-full or half-empty? Is old age so bad when you consider the alternative? We can interpret in a positive light some of the most negative things in life (and vice versa). Having to clean your house (ugh!) can be recast as having a nice place to live. Getting endless questions about homework means that your kids' brains are growing. These reinterpretations may seem meaningless, but framing information positively versus negatively can influence related judgments and decisions. The differences are important because they change, for example, how attractive sales prices and medical treatment options appear. Parents may even make different resuscitation decisions for premature infants depending on whether their prognosis is presented in terms of survival or death statistics.[32] In the decision literature, numeric framing generally includes attribute framing and risky-choice framing,[33] both described later. Also included in this section is the relation of objective numeracy to a different way of framing numeric information, the use of frequency versus percentage information. To foreshadow these findings, attribute-framing and frequency-percentage framing effects are especially prevalent among less objectively numerate individuals. In risky-choice framing, more and less numerate individuals show similar framing effects but different psychological processes.

Attribute Framing

The simplest form of framing, *attribute framing*, focuses on evaluations of an object based on a single attribute. In a well-known example, perceptions of the quality of cooked ground beef depended on whether the beef was labeled as "75% lean" (a positive frame) or "25% fat" (a negative frame).[34] Participants tasted cooked ground beef described as "75% lean" or "25% fat." They rated the former as better tasting and less greasy, as if they responded to the given frame without thinking about its equivalent alternative frame despite being able to rely on the concreteness of taste. In their review, psychologist Irwin Levin and his colleagues[33] argued that the effect was due to associative processing. In their model, positive labeling of an attribute led to information encoding that evoked favorable associations in memory, whereas negative labeling of the same attribute caused an encoding that evoked unfavorable associations. Relatedly, the provided frame may act as a source of integral (built-in) affect that informs subsequent judgments in affect-heuristic fashion.[5,35] In a meta-analysis, attribute-framing studies revealed robust effects, with an average effect size that was small to medium.[36] Effect sizes differed across studies, which leaves room for further explanation with individual differences.

Because attribute frames generally involve a single attribute and percentage that the experimenter transforms between the positive and negative frame, objective numeracy seemed likely to have an effect in our early numeracy research. In fact, when we asked participants to evaluate the quality of work done by a series of students, described, for example, as answering 87% of the questions on a test correctly (positive frame) or 13% incorrectly (negative frame), less objectively numerate individuals were more susceptible to the framing effect. They evaluated the quality of student work more positively when exam scores were presented in a positive versus negative light, whereas the highly numerate showed little effect of frame.[17,37–41] We speculated that the highly numerate transform the given frame into the alternative frame (87% correct equals 13% incorrect) so that they have both frames available. We thought that the less numerate were left with only the provided frame, which is why they demonstrated strong attribute-framing effects.[17] Consistent with attribute-framing effects emerging when number transformations are not done, bonobos and chimpanzees (who do not know formal math) also demonstrate human-like attribute-framing effects.[42]

Behavioral scientist Ayel Gamliel and colleagues[43] further found that the effect was specific to objective numeracy (and not Chapter 14's subjective numeracy), consistent with the importance of number transformations as an underlying mechanism. In a later study, they hypothesized that greater framing effects among the less numerate would be caused by decreased attention and sensitivity to provided numbers across a series of scenarios.[44] Their hypothesis was not supported. Instead, the less objectively numerate were as sensitive as the highly numerate to provided percentage information. For example, across the numeracy spectrum, all participants rated a course more positively (and by about the same amount) when told "There is a 90% chance that the lecturer will upload the presentations to the course's web-site" than when told "There is a 60% chance . . . " At the same time, the less numerate nonetheless demonstrated greater framing effects than the highly numerate.

I believe these seemingly conflicting results emerged because of the nature of repeated judgments in the following way. First and consistent with our 2006 results,[17] the less numerate evaluated the first course described based on its frame. Thus, they rated a course described positively (90% succeed) as more attractive than one framed negatively (10% fail). The highly numerate likely transformed between the formats (10% failure means that 90% succeed) and found the frames about equally attractive. With additional stimuli that differed from the first stimulus only in terms of given percentages, more and less numerate participants likely processed later percentages in relation to the initial one. In other words, less numerate participants may have rated "90% succeed" as quite positive (and more positive than the highly numerate), and then both groups adjusted their ratings downward by about the same amount for the next courses in which 75% and 60% succeeded. If true, this process would allow attribute-framing effects to exist only for the less objectively numerate and numeric sensitivity to emerge regardless of numeracy.

Although numeracy-related attribute-framing effects appear robust, they have not always replicated. For example, some researchers have demonstrated nonsignificant effects in a direction consistent with prior results.[45,46] Other nonreplications may be due to increasing numeric reasoning through the use of repeated measures. Psychologist Fabio Del Missier and colleagues[47] failed to replicate the effect, but participants responded to seven attribute-framing and seven risky-choice framing problems. They suggested their null effect may have been due to a surprisingly small framing effect in their study relative to prior ones. However, the smaller-than-usual framing effect may have been due to their repeated measures priming numeric reasoning among their participants. If less objectively numerate individuals are capable of these relatively simple transformations (but do not think to perform them), then increasing numeric reasoning should decrease the overall framing effect and any numeracy differences, potentially explaining their data. See Chapter 10 for further discussion of the role of repeated measures in priming numeric reasoning and decreasing numeracy differences.

Overall, objective numeracy differences in attribute-framing effects are most consistent with highly numerate individuals being "more likely to transform given information frames into normative equivalents" (p. 32).[48] They therefore have a more complex array of information available for consideration than do the less numerate. The most likely candidate for reducing attribute-framing effects is to encourage these transformations[49] (see Chapter 5).

Risky Choice Framing

A different framing effect, *risky-choice framing*, was introduced by psychologists Amos Tversky and Daniel Kahneman[50] with the famous Asian Disease problem. In it, the outcomes of risky and safe options in a choice scenario are described either in positive terms (the number of people who will be saved) or negative terms (the number of people who will die). Decision makers tend to exhibit a preference reversal between frames. Specifically, most participants given the positively framed version of the task (a sure saving of 200 lives versus a one-third chance of saving all 600 lives and a two-thirds chance of saving no lives) chose the option with the certain outcome. However, in the negative frame (a sure loss of 400 lives versus a one-third chance of losing no lives and a two-thirds chance of losing all 600 lives), they selected the risky option. Tversky and Kahneman explained the effect as being due to perceptions of diminishing returns from additional lives (600 lives is definitely more than 200 lives, but it doesn't feel like three times more; it feels like less). As a result, in the positive frame, the perception of 600 lives saved is not three times larger than the 200 lives saved for sure, and there is only a one-third chance of saving the 600 lives. Thus, participants perceive the value of saving 200 for sure as larger and choose this certain option. In the negative frame, a similar process results in participants perceiving a two-thirds chance of losing 600 lives as smaller than losing 400 lives for sure.

Risky-choice framing effects have been robust, with small- to medium-sized effects in meta-analyses.[36,51] Effect sizes vary across studies, suggestive of individual differences. Having greater numeracy skills could encourage numeric transformation from one frame to the other, a reframing of the problem that leaves the highly numerate with both frames available and perhaps smaller framing effects.

However, objective numeracy does not alter the size of the risky-choice framing effect,[37,47] although the more and less numerate do process information differently. With psychologist Irwin Levin, we asked participants to respond to choices among options that were framed as either positive or negative. They also rated how attractive they found the separate sure and risky options.[37] We found that risky-choice framing effects did not vary by objective numeracy. Numeracy was associated, though, with the usual attribute-framing effects in ratings of the sure options. In other words, the less numerate showed larger attribute-framing effects, and the highly numerate rated the two frames about the same. In ratings of the risky options, however, the less numerate showed only a tendency toward their usual attribute-framing effect. The highly numerate instead rated risky options in the negative frame as more positive than those in the positive, inconsistent with the usual attribute-framing effect but consistent with risk-seeking tendencies in the loss domain predicted by Kahneman and Tversky.[50] This tendency may be the basis for their ultimately showing similar risky-choice framing effects as the less numerate.

Finally, we examined information processing underlying these risky choices by predicting risky choices with the individual option ratings, the provided frame, and their interactions with objective numeracy. Choices of the less numerate indicated a large effect of the provided frame above and beyond any influence of their option ratings, whereas choices of the highly numerate were almost completely accounted for by their ratings of the separate options.[37] These results are consistent with an increased tendency of the highly numerate to integrate complex numeric information into their preferences and a tendency for the less numerate to respond more superficially to the verbal cues identifying the positive and negative frames. Thus, only information processing among the less numerate was consistent with original theorizing about risky-choice framing effects.[50]

Participants, or at least highly numerate participants, nonetheless may have adequate ability to avoid risky-choice framing effects but require prompting to use that ability, similar to other recent decision studies.[52,53] Specifically, the overall size of risky-choice framing effects attenuates when participants elaborate more[54-59] and when the scenario is presented as a statistical problem. For example, when a subtle header in the upper right corner of the page said "statistical research," no framing effect emerged, whereas the framing effect appeared as usual when the header stated "medical research."[60] These studies did not include numeracy as a variable, but it is reasonable that they primed numeric reasoning at least among the highly numerate. We need more research on when manipulations such as accountability, numeric priming, and instructions might produce more numeric reasoning for everybody (thus, potentially attenuating numeracy differences) versus when they might produce more numeric reasoning only in the highly numerate (exacerbating numeracy differences).

Frequencies Have Greater Impact Than Percentages on the Less Numerate

The less numerate are more susceptible to other kinds of numeric framing effects as well. Numeric risks, for example, can be presented in percentage or frequency formats (e.g., 9% versus 9 out of 100 people, respectively, will suffer a side effect). Frequency formats elicit greater affective imagery[2] and result in greater risk perceptions, consistent with the affect heuristic. Numeracy research, however, indicates that this effect is limited to less numerate individuals. Across a variety of pro-social, medical, and terrorism-related domains, the less objectively numerate perceived greater risk when exposed to normatively equivalent information presented as frequencies versus percentages.[25,17,46,61] The highly numerate were relatively insensitive to the format differences. For example, we asked participants from an internet panel to "imagine that they suffered from headaches severe enough to cause them to miss work."[46] The medication would reduce the frequency and severity of their headaches, but it came with some risk of a side effect; this risk was presented in either a percentage or frequency format (e.g., "10% of patients [10 out of every 100 patients] get a bad blistering rash"). Less objectively numerate patients perceived significantly greater risk from the frequency than percentage format. The highly numerate showed no such effect. Similar to attribute-framing effects, we have attributed this numeracy difference to the highly numerate being more likely to transform the given frame into its logical equivalent (10% out of 100 = 10 out of 100). Thus, unlike the less numerate, they had the advantage of having both frames available and showed little effect of the presented frame.[17,46]

This ability to transform numbers between logically equivalent formats could be an advantage for the highly numerate. It allows them access to more complete information rather than being left with only the concrete information provided. However, this supposed advantage could lead them to perceiving more risk in both formats because they would always have available the affective imagery from having frequency information. The less numerate, by this logic, should perceive more risk only if specifically given the frequency format. Data from two studies supported this possibility, with the highly numerate perceiving risk in both frame conditions at a similar level to the less numerate who were provided the frequency frame.[17,46] Risk perceptions of the less numerate were lower when given percentage information. The frequency frame appears to be "sticky" for the highly numerate.

However, the less objectively numerate appear to not always use the numeric frame as a source of affect. They sometimes substitute easier-to-process affective information instead.[25,61] For example, in Study 1 of a paper on terrorism risks, we examined perceived risks based on a likelihood assessment and a brief statement about potential lives lost and property damage if the attack occurred.[25] Half the participants also received a narrative description of the evidence concerning the attack. When narrative evidence was included, responses to frequency versus percentage formats did not differ between the more or less numerate although the less numerate perceived greater risk overall. The presence of the compelling narrative appeared to reduce numeric sensitivity (its format in this case) for the less numerate. This finding points toward a hypothesis consistent with the affect heuristic, namely, that increasing affect (e.g., with a narrative) will increase risk perceptions, reduce sensitivity to numeric levels, and reduce sensitivity to different numeric frames (they are part of the number after all). These effects should happen particularly among the less numerate who use integral affect to outcomes, such as those described in narratives, as a simple cue rather than using other relevant information in the problem. The frequency/percent effect did not replicate in one paper for reasons that are unclear.[62] It may be that other study conditions (e.g., narrative presence, prior experiences in life, order effects in the experimental setting, encouragement to elaborate) also determine the extent to which the less numerate attend enough to numbers for their format to matter.

A side note: Some researchers have confused the effect of frequency versus percentage formats on risk perceptions discussed earlier with that of natural frequency versus single-event probabilities on comprehension of numeric risk information in Bayes-type problems.[63] For example, despite contrary assertions, the research concerning how objective numeracy interacts with the effects of frequency versus percentage formats on risk perceptions makes no claims about numeric comprehension.[64] In fact, comprehension is not assessed. Instead, the research concerns more general risk perceptions, often measured on verbal scales ranging from no/low risk to high risk,[25] rather than on numeric 0–100% scales.

The Cumulative Risk of Incomprehension and Heuristic Use

The less numerate understand numeric information less well and make less logical judgments and choices based on the literature reviewed in Chapters 2–4, but the question remains whether these differences matter. For example, heuristic use causes errors, such as base-rate neglect, but it also produces judgments that are generally satisfactory for the individual. As psychologist David Funder pointed out "Detection of an error implies the existence of a mistake only when the process that produces the error also produces incorrect judgments in real life" (p. 76).[65] To me, it also seems likely that not understanding information once or misjudging it once should not matter much in most circumstances.

However, I think that these small errors may accumulate over time, with possible negative consequences for the less numerate and the quality of the life outcomes they experience. I offer as an analogy smoking a single cigarette. No one cigarette will have measurable consequence to health, but, over time, smoking causes immense mortality through its links with diseases of almost every major organ in the body.[66] Similarly, the general point can be made that poor judgment and bad decisions related to innumeracy may accrue slowly over a person's lifetime and result in lower well-being. Consistent with this reasoning, psychologist Wändi Bruine de Bruin and her colleagues found that individuals who relied more on heuristics also experienced more negative decision outcomes ("threw out food or groceries you had bought because they went bad," "had a check bounce," "been in a jail cell overnight," "declared bankruptcy").[67] Indeed, in Chapter 9, you will read about worse life outcomes experienced by the less objectively numerate. Although a single use of a heuristic generally causes no noticeable harm (and it can be beneficial in the moment), I believe their negative consequences accrue somewhat invisibly over time and result in worse outcomes over long periods.

What We Know and Don't Know

You will recognize two general points made in Chapters 2–4. First, the less objectively numerate are more likely than the highly numerate to allow compelling non-numeric information to drive their judgments. This information is easy to evaluate, and thus powerful, for individuals who find numeric information difficult. It includes story-like descriptions of a person or situation, narratives, integral (built-in) affect about outcomes, incidental affect such as mood states, and the frame in which information is presented. As a result, the less numerate are more susceptible to using heuristics, mental shortcuts that simplify the judgment process but leave the decision maker open to errors. Recent research points toward differences between more and less numerate individuals in the use of some classic heuristics (availability, representativeness, and affect heuristic). Less evidence exists concerning whether numeracy relates to other simple heuristics.[68,69] This heuristic use offers many benefits including speed, efficiency, and judgments that are generally good enough. The accumulation of small errors over time, however, may add up to produce extensive damage in the health, employment, and financial lives of the less numerate. More research is needed, however, linking numeracy to outcomes through these mediating decision processes.

However (and here is the second general point), the situation is by no means hopeless for the less numerate. It is possible to solve all of the heuristic problems described in Chapters 2–4 with particular rules and principles (see the boxes). In addition, people can improve their numeracy skills (see Chapter 18), information providers (communicators) can provide numeric information in easier-to-use formats, and patients and consumers can request these formats (see Chapters 15–17). Finally, as we will see in Chapters 5–8, the highly numerate have certain habits and inclinations with respect to processing numeric information. The less numerate may be able to learn these same habits.

In Chapter 5, we will focus on the highly numerate's tendency to process information in more complex ways, including performing number operations, integrating more sources of information, and reacting less to heuristic-related concrete attributes in judgment and choice. Usually, but not always, these processes result in the highly numerate forming more logical judgments and making better choices and the less numerate appearing less logical. Although not well studied, teaching the less numerate these relatively simple processes and inclinations so that they embrace them in their judgments and decisions over time offers promise for improving their decisions.

References

1. Kahneman, D., & Frederick, S. (2002). Representativeness revisited: Attribute substitution in intuitive judgment. In T. Gilovich, D. W. Griffin, & D. Kahneman (Eds.), *Heuristics and biases: The psychology of intuitive judgment* (pp. 49–81). New York: Cambridge University Press.
2. Albarracín, D., & Kumkale, G. T. (2003). Affect as information in persuasion: A model of affect identification and discounting. *Journal of Personality and Social Psychology, 84*(3), 453.
3. Loewenstein, G. F., Weber, E. U., Hsee, C. K., & Welch, E. S. (2001). Risk as feelings. *Psychological Bulletin, 127,* 267–286.
4. Schwarz, N., & Clore, G. L. (1983). Mood, misattribution, and judgments of well-being: Informative and directive functions of affective states. *Journal of Personality and Social Psychology, 45*(3), 513–523.
5. Slovic, P., Finucane, M., Peters, E., & MacGregor, D. G. (2002). Rational actors or rational fools: Implications of the affect heuristic for behavioral economics. *The Journal of Socio-Economics, 31*(4), 329–342.
6. The Affect Heuristic. (2018). Retrieved from https://theaffecttheuristic.bandcamp.com/music
7. Lerner, J. S., & Keltner, D. (2001). Fear, anger, and risk. *Journal of Personality and Social Psychology, 81*(1), 146–159.

8. Posner, J., Russell, J. A., & Peterson, B. S. (2005). The circumplex model of affect: An integrative approach to affective neuroscience, cognitive development, and psychopathology. *Development and Psychopathology, 17*(3), 715–734.

9. Russell J. A. (1980). A circumplex model of affect. *Journal of Personality and Social Psychology, 39*(6), 1161–1178.

10. Fischhoff, B., Slovic, P., Lichtenstein, S., Reid, S., & Coombs, B. (1978). How safe is safe enough? A psychometric study of attitudes towards technological risks and benefits. *Policy Sciences, 9*, 127–152.

11. Alhakami, A. S., & Slovic, P. (1994). A psychological study of the inverse relationship between perceived risk and perceived benefit. *Risk Analysis, 14*(6), 1085–1096.

12. Finucane, M. L., Alhakami, A., Slovic, P., & Johnson, S. M. (2000). The affect heuristic in judgments of risks and benefits. *Journal of Behavioral Decision Making, 13*, 1–17.

13. Kahneman, D., Schkade, D., & Sunstein, C. R. (1998). Shared outrage and erratic awards: The psychology of punitive damages. *Journal of Risk and Uncertainty, 16*, 49–86.

14. Traczyk, J., & Fulawka, K. (2016). Numeracy moderates the influence of task-irrelevant affect on probability weighting. *Cognition, 151*, 37–41.

15. Slovic, P., Finucane, M. L., Peters, E., & MacGregor, D. G. (2004). Risk as analysis and risk as feelings: Some thoughts about affect, reason, risk, and rationality. *Risk Analysis, 24*(2), 311–322.

16. Bateman, I., Dent, S., Peters, E., Slovic, P., & Starmer, C. (2007). The affect heuristic and the attractiveness of simple gambles. *Journal of Behavioral Decision Making, 20*(4), 365–380.

17. Peters, E., Västfjäll, D., Slovic, P., Mertz, C. K., Mazzocco, K., & Dickert, S. (2006). Numeracy and decision making. *Psychological Science, 17*(5), 407–413.

18. Låg, T., Bauger, L., Lindberg, M., & Friborg, O. (2014). The role of numeracy and intelligence in health-risk estimation and medical data interpretation. *Journal of Behavioral Decision Making, 27*(2), 95–108.

19. Black, W. C., Nease, R. F. Jr., & Tosteson, A. N. (1995). Perceptions of breast cancer risk and screening effectiveness in women younger than 50 years of age. *Journal of the National Cancer Institute, 87*(10), 720–731.

20. Davids, S. L., Schapira, M. M., McAuliffe, T. L., & Nattinger, A. B. (2004). Predictors of pessimistic breast cancer risk perceptions in a primary care population. *Journal of General Internal Medicine, 19*(4), 310–315.

21. Gurmankin, A. D., Baron, J., & Armstrong, K. (2004). Intended message versus message received in hypothetical physician risk communications: Exploring the gap. *Risk Analysis, 24*(5), 1337–1347.

22. Woloshin, S., Schwartz, L. M., Black, W. C., & Welch, H. G. (1999). Women's perceptions of breast cancer risk: How you ask matters. *Medical Decision Making, 19*, 221–229.

23. Peters, E., Kunreuther, H., Sagara, N., Slovic, P., & Schley, D. R. (2012). Protective measures, personal experience, and the affective psychology of time. *Risk Analysis, 32*(12), 2084–2097.

24. Burns, W. J., Peters, E., & Slovic, P. (2012). Risk perception and the economic crisis: A longitudinal study of the trajectory of perceived risk. *Risk Analysis, 32*(4), 659–677.

25. Dieckmann, N. F., Slovic, P., & Peters, E. M. (2009). The use of narrative evidence and explicit likelihood by decisionmakers varying in numeracy. *Risk Analysis, 29*(10), 1473–1488.

26. Betsch, C., Haase, N., Renkewitz, F., & Schmid, P. (2015). The narrative bias revisited: What drives the biasing influence of narrative information on risk perceptions?. *Judgment and Decision Making, 10*(3), 241–264.

27. Milligan, M. A., Bohara, A. K., Pagan, J. A. (2010). Assessing willingness to pay for cancer prevention. *International Journal of Health Care Finance & Economics, 10*(4), 301–314.

28. Weil, A. M., Wolfe, C. R., Reyna, V. F., Widmer, C. L., Cedillos-Whynott, E. M., & Brust-Renck, P. G. (2015). Proficiency of FPPI and objective numeracy in assessing breast cancer risk estimation. *Learning and Individual Differences, 43,* 149–155.

29. Rottenstreich, Y., & Hsee, C. K. (2001). Money, kisses, and electric shocks: On the affective psychology of risk. *Psychological Science, 12*(3), 185–190.

30. Pachur, T., & Galesic, M. (2013). Strategy selection in risky choice: The impact of numeracy, affect, and cross-cultural differences. *Journal of Behavioral Decision Making, 26*(3), 260–271.

31. Peters, E., Dieckmann, N. F., Västfjäll, D., Mertz, C. K., Slovic, P., & Hibbard, J. H. (2009). Bringing meaning to numbers: The impact of evaluative categories on decisions. *Journal of Experimental Psychology: Applied, 15*(3), 213–227.

32. Haward, M. F., Murphy, R. O., & Lorenz, J. M. (2008). Message framing and perinatal decisions. *Pediatrics 122,* 109–118.

33. Levin, I. P., Schneider, S. L., & Gaeth, G. J. (1998). All frames are not created equal: A typology and critical analysis of framing effects. *Organizational Behavior and Human Decision Processes, 76*(2), 149–188.

34. Levin, I. P., & Gaeth, G. J. (1988). Framing of attribute information before and after consuming the product. *Journal of Consumer Research, 15*(3), 374–378.

35. Peters, E. (2006). The functions of affect in the construction of preferences. In S. Lichtenstein & P. Slovic (Eds.), *The construction of preference* (pp. 454–463). New York: Cambridge University Press.

36. Piñon, A., & Gambara, H. (2005). A meta-analytic review of framing effect: Risky, attribute and goal framing. *Psicothema, 17*(2), 325–331.

37. Peters, E., & Levin, I. P. (2008). Dissecting the risky-choice framing effect: Numeracy as an individual-difference factor in weighting risky and riskless options. *Judgment and Decision Making Journal, 3*(6), 435–448.

38. Choi, H., Wong, J. B., Mendiratta, A., Heiman, G. A., & Hamberger, M. J. (2011). Numeracy and framing bias in epilepsy. *Epilepsy & Behavior, 20*(1), 29–33.

39. Garcia-Retamero, R., & Galesic, M. (2010). How to reduce the effect of framing on messages about health. *Journal of General Internal Medicine, 25*(12), 1323–1329.

40. Okamoto, M., Kyutoku, Y., Sawada, M., Clowney, L., Watanabe, E., Dan, I., & Kawamoto, K. (2012). Health numeracy in Japan: Measures of basic numeracy account for framing bias in a highly numerate population. *BMC Medical Informatics and Decision Making, 12*(1), 104.

41. Garcia-Retamero, R., & Cokely, E. T. (2014). The influence of skills, message frame, and visual aids on prevention of sexually transmitted diseases. *Journal of Behavioral Decision Making, 27*(2), 179–189.

42. Krupenye, C., Rosati, A. G., & Hare, B. (2015). Bonobos and chimpanzees exhibit human-like framing effects. *Biology Letters, 11*(2), 20140527.

43. Gamliel, E., Kreiner, H., & Garcia-Retamero, R. (2016). The moderating role of objective and subjective numeracy in attribute framing. *International Journal of Psychology, 51*(2), 109–116.

44. Gamliel, E., & Kreiner, H. (2017). Outcome proportions, numeracy, and attribute-framing bias. *Australian Journal of Psychology, 69*(4), 283–292.

45. Levin, I. P., Bossard, E. A., Gaeth, G. J., & Yan, H. Y. (2014). The combined role of task, child's age and individual differences in understanding decision processes. *Judgment and Decision Making, 9*(3), 274–286.

46. Peters, E., Hart, P. S., & Fraenkel, L. (2011). Informing patients: The influence of numeracy, framing, and format of side effect information on risk perceptions. *Medical Decision Making, 31*(3), 432–436.

47. Del Missier, F., Mäntylä, T., & Bruine de Bruin, W. (2012). Decision-making competence, executive functioning, and general cognitive abilities. *Journal of Behavioral Decision Making, 25*(4), 331–351.

48. Peters, E. (2012). Beyond comprehension: The role of numeracy in judgments and decisions. *Current Directions in Psychological Science, 21*(1), 31–35.

49. Cheng, F. F., Wu, C. S., & Lin, H. H. (2014). Reducing the influence of framing on internet consumers' decisions: The role of elaboration. *Computers in Human Behavior 37*, 56–63.

50. Tversky, A., & Kahneman, D. (1981). The framing of decisions and the psychology of choice. *Science, 211*, 453–458.

51. Kühberger, A. (1998). The influence of framing on risky decisions: A meta-analysis. *Organizational Behavior and Human Decision Processes, 75*(1), 23–55.

52. Scherer, L. D., Yates, J. F., Baker, S. G., & Valentine, K. D. (2017). The influence of effortful thought and cognitive proficiencies on the conjunction fallacy: Implications for dual-process theories of reasoning and judgment. *Personality and Social Psychology Bulletin, 43*(6), 874–887.

53. Riege, A. H., & Teigen, K. H. (2013). Additivity neglect in probability estimates: Effects of numeracy and response format. *Organizational Behavior and Human Decision Processes, 121*(1), 41–52.

54. Simon, A. F., Fagley, N. S., & Halleran, J. G. (2004). Decision framing: Moderating effects of individual differences and cognitive processing. *Journal of Behavioral Decision Making, 17*(2), 77–93.

55. LeBoeuf, R. A., & Shafir, E. (2003). Deep thoughts and shallow frames: On the susceptibility to framing effects. *Journal of Behavioral Decision Making, 16*(2), 77–92.

56. Miller, P. M., & Fagley, N. S. (1991). The effects of framing, problem variations, and providing rationale on choice. *Personality and Social Psychology Bulletin, 17*(5), 517–522.

57. Smith, S. M., & Levin, I. (1997). Need for cognition and choice framing effects. *Journal of Behavior Decision Making, 9*(4), 283–290.

58. Takemura, K. (1993). The effect of decision frame and decision justification on risky choice. *Japanese Psychological Research, 35*(1), 36–40.

59. Takemura, K. (1994). Influence of elaboration on the framing of decision. *The Journal of Psychology, 128*(1), 33–39.

60. Bless, H., Betsch, T., & Franzen, A. (1998). Framing the framing effect: The impact of context cues on solutions to the "Asian disease" problem. *European Journal of Social Psychology, 28*, 287–291.

61. Dickert, S., Kleber, J., Peters, E., & Slovic, P. (2011). Numeracy as a precursor to pro-social behavior: The impact of numeracy and presentation format on the cognitive mechanisms underlying donation decisions. *Judgment and Decision Making, 6*(7), 638–650.

62. Hill, W. T., & Brase, G. L. (2012). When and for whom do frequencies facilitate performance? On the role of numerical literacy. *Quarterly Journal of Experimental Psychology, 65*(12), 2343–2368.

63. Johnson, E. D., & Tubau, E. (2015). Comprehension and computation in Bayesian problem solving. *Frontiers in Psychology, 6*, 938.

64. Brase, G. L., & Hill, W. T. (2017). Adding up to good Bayesian reasoning: Problem format manipulations and individual skill differences. *Journal of Experimental Psychology: General, 146*(4), 577–591.

65. Funder, D. C. (1987). Errors and mistakes: Evaluating the accuracy of social judgment. *Psychological Bulletin, 101*(1), 75–90.

66. US DHHS. (2014). *The health consequences of smoking—50 years of progress. A report of the Surgeon General.* Atlanta, GA: US Department of Health and Human Services.

67. Bruine de Bruin, W., Parker, A. M., & Fischhoff, B. (2007). Individual differences in adult decision-making competence. *Journal of Personality and Social Psychology, 92*(5), 938–956.
68. Tversky, A., & Kahneman, D. (1974). Judgment under uncertainty: Heuristics and biases. *Science, 185*(4157), 1124–1131.
69. Gigerenzer, G., Todd, P. M., & ABC Research Group, T. (1999). *Simple heuristics that make us smart.* Oxford: Oxford University Press.

THE HABITS OF THE HIGHLY NUMERATE

5

Thinking Harder with Numbers

Chapters 5–8 focus on the highly numerate. By this section's end, you will understand better how more objectively numerate people deal more successfully than the less numerate with the numbers that permeate modern life and how you and others can, too. For example, you might recall that the less objectively numerate are susceptible to how people describe information to them. They rate the quality of work done by a student as higher when her exam grade is 87% correct (a positive frame) than when it is described as 13% incorrect (a negative frame of the same grade).[1] The highly numerate receive the same framed information but, as you will see in this chapter, they think harder with numbers. In this case, they are more likely than the less numerate to transform the number they were given (13% incorrect) into the other frame (that's 87% correct!). As a result, they seem to have both frames available and are less vulnerable to someone else's choice of frame.

In Chapters 5–8, I discuss how the more objectively numerate make better decisions most of the time based on three related inclinations to process numeric information. The highly numerate:

- Attend more to and think harder about numbers (Chapter 5);
- Develop more precise feelings about numbers in decisions (Chapter 6); and
- Are more sensitive to and consistent with numbers (Chapter 7);
- However, their numerical reasoning can be insufficient (Chapter 8).

Chapters 5–8 continue to take the view that, although objective numeracy is measured with a math test, its effects extend far beyond number comprehension to inclinations and habits for dealing with numeric and non-numeric information in judgment and choice. I believe this dispositional nature of numeracy is critical and is likely caused by the highly numerate having chronically greater cognitive access to numeric knowledge structures[2] that increases their likelihood of processing numbers in decisions. By the end of this chapter, you will recognize these habits of the highly numerate, when they are useful, and (hopefully) how you can make them of service to you and others.

Innumeracy in the Wild. Ellen Peters, Oxford University Press (2020). © Oxford University Press 2020.
DOI: 10.1093/oso/9780190861094.003.0001

Attention to and Search for Numbers

Numbers are provided in decisions because they are thought helpful, but that simple fact does not guarantee that everybody concentrates on them. Less numerate patients, for example, trust doctor-provided numeric information less than the highly numerate do.[3] The highly numerate also prefer numbers more than the less numerate[4] and have more positive emotions about math,[5] suggesting that the more and less numerate may interact differently with numbers in decision making.

Consistent with these reactions, the highly numerate attend to and search for numeric information more than the less numerate. Numeracy research has recently begun to use what are called *process-tracing methods* to assess attention to numeric and non-numeric information.[6] The most common method is *eye tracking*. With it, researchers record and study movements of the eye as study participants look at one piece of information (such as a number) and then another (such as a word or graph).

Limited research exists in this area so far, but more objectively numerate individuals appear to look at abstract numeric information earlier than the less numerate when competing non-numeric information is available. For example, participants ($N = 159$) read hypothetical test results indicating that an individual had a 17% chance of having colon cancer.[7] This risk was presented as a percentage and in a graph (you will learn more about the benefits of using graphs in Chapter 16). When participants indicated their feelings and risk perceptions about this 17% risk based on their gut feelings, the more and less objectively numerate relied intuitively on different information-processing strategies. Specifically, more numerate participants were more likely to look at the percentage information first, whereas the less numerate looked initially at the graph. A second group did the same task after being instructed to think carefully. No numeracy differences emerged in this second group. The combined results suggest that the less numerate can process numeric risks in a similar manner to the highly numerate (if asked to think carefully), but they do not do so intuitively.

The highly numerate also look relatively longer at important numbers more than the less numerate.[8,9] For example, when asked about the risks of a hypothetical radon level in their home ($N = 68$), those higher in numeracy spent relatively more time looking at numeric risks (50 in 100 extra cancer deaths); less time on an illustrated, familiar, smoking-risk comparison; and similar time on a difficult-to-evaluate radon level (i.e., 220 bq/cubic meter).[10]

Psychologist Janet Kleber further found that more objectively numerate individuals looked relatively longer at product quantities on consumer goods packages and especially at familiar quantities (i.e., grams rather than ounces for Austrian participants).[11] They were also willing to pay more for larger than smaller quantities (e.g., 200 g vs. 100 g of chocolate). The less numerate looked longer at non-numeric information on product packages, such as brand names, and valued larger and smaller quantities about the same. Longer looking at quantity information explained the highly numerate's greater sensitivity to quantity in price judgments. More numerate people may benefit by noticing more often when manufacturers reduce package sizes while leaving price the same (e.g., ice cream containers are now 1.5 quarts, 25% smaller than what was the standard half-gallon size).[12]

Studies conducted thus far with process-tracing methods are sparse. Additional research (with larger samples) ultimately should help us understand how people process numeric and non-numeric information in decision making[6] and how methods to alter attention may assist (see Chapter 17 for more on such methods).

Thinking More with Numbers

Early on, we reasoned that the highly numerate deliberate more about numbers in decision making, including retrieving and using appropriate numerical principles, but we had little direct evidence at the time. The literature has developed substantially since then and, by this chapter's end, you will appreciate the deliberative processing inclinations of the highly numerate, who complete more number operations during decisions, deliberate longer, and are more aware of what they know and don't know with respect to numeric information.

Number Operations Including Transformations

Although we are rarely advised to use math in decisions, the highly numerate appear to apply their skills nonetheless to doing numeric operations in judgments and decisions. For example, we asked participants ($N = 100$) to rate the work quality of undergraduates described in positive frames (e.g., Emily got 74% correct) or negative frames (e.g., Emily got 26% incorrect).[1] As hypothesized, the less numerate rated work quality substantially higher in the positive than negative frame, but the highly numerate were relatively insusceptible to frame. Similarly, we saw in Chapter 4 that the less objectively numerate perceived greater risk when the likelihood of a negative event was described in frequentistic formats (e.g., 10 of 100 mental patients are estimated to commit violence) than when they are described in probabilistic terms ("10% of 100").[1] We speculated that these numeracy differences were due to the highly numerate being more likely to calculate a number transformation (74% correct equals 26% incorrect and 10 out of 100 equals 10%). As a result, they would have both information frames available and would be less susceptible than the less numerate to how information was provided.[1] Consistent with our early speculation, more objectively numerate participants reported doing more simple numeric operations, such as transforming probabilities, than the less numerate when making choices between a fixed amount of money and a gamble.[13]

With former graduate student Aleksandr Sinayev, we designed an experiment to examine these possible numeracy-related transformations.[14] We reasoned that, if the highly numerate transformed numbers from one format to the other (e.g., from the provided 75% sugar-free to 25% sugar), then they should falsely remember having seen information they calculated (i.e., 25% sugar).[15] If the less objectively numerate do not do these number operations as expected, then they should not have the same false memories. Undergraduate participants ($N = 79$) responded to both frames of 12 framing scenarios. Half responded to all positive frames first, and the other half responded to all negative frames first. After each response, they were asked whether they had just seen 10 pieces of information, one of which was the hypothesized transformation. For example, participants read "Health Bars . . . [are] 75% sugar-free" and were asked to rate their healthiness on a scale from −3 (very unhealthy) to +3 (very healthy). Immediately after responding, they responded whether each of 10 items had been shown verbatim in the previous scenario. In fact, they had been shown five of the items (Health Bars, 75%) but had not been shown the remaining five items (Dairy Bars, 39%), one of which was the "foil of interest" (25% in this example).

As hypothesized, the less objectively numerate showed larger framing effects, even after controlling for non-numeric intelligence measures. Critically, compared to the less objectively numerate, highly numerate individuals incorrectly said that they had seen the foil of interest more often (respective errors of 12% and 24%, p <.01 after controlling for intelligence proxies). People who made more foil-of-interest errors exhibited smaller framing effects. Finally, the number of these errors partially explained the highly numerate's tendency to show smaller framing effects. In essence, highly numerate decision makers "considered the opposite" by performing relatively simple number transformations, and doing so appeared to reduce their susceptibility to framing biases. To avoid being manipulated by how others frame information, see Box 5.1.

Box 5.1 Avoiding Attribute-Framing Effects

Less numerate individuals are more susceptible to attribute-framing effects in which options described in positive terms are evaluated more highly than those described in negative terms. For example, they rate medications more positively when described in terms of the proportion of patients who remain side effect-free than when described with the proportion who suffer the side effect. The effect can be explained by the less numerate encoding the option in terms of integral (built-in) affect to the non-numeric positive or negative frame while neglecting the numeric information. The highly numerate instead focus first or more on the combined numeric and frame information, and they transform the provided frame into its logically equivalent alternative frame (25% chance of my best friend taking the course equals a 75% chance he will not take the course). As a result, the highly numerate have more information available, including integral affect to both frames, so that they are not swayed unreasonably by a single frame. You can lessen framing effects by listening carefully to the initial information (e.g., 17% sugar) and calculating the opposite equivalent frame. For example, the proportion of sugar and non-sugar ingredients in this candy bar must add up to 100%, and 100% minus 17% = 83%. Therefore, the candy bar is 83% sugar-free and 17% sugar.

The highly numerate transform numbers into proportions, too. For example, we told participants about a number of children that would be helped by their donation (always five children) and the total number in need of help (e.g., 10 or 1,000 starving children; Study 2).[16] Highly numerate individuals were willing to donate more for projects that offered assistance to the same number but greater proportion of children in need (note that the proportion was not provided but had to be calculated or estimated). Conversely, less numerate individuals were insensitive to this proportion. They used a numerically simpler strategy and, across studies, donated more based on either the number of children helped or the total number in need. Thus, the less numerate used a single attribute in their donation decisions whereas the more numerate used a more complex array of information and responded to the proportion of children helped. Similar numeracy-related findings emerged in another study when choosing between two options.[17] In this case, however, the highly numerate chose to save a greater proportion of lives only if it did not mean saving fewer lives. Thus, the highly numerate were not captive to their numeric abilities. Instead, they used their ability flexibly to draw meaning from information (e.g., by calculating proportions) and to identify logically appropriate strategies (i.e., save more lives).

The highly numerate use more complex number operations, too. Compared to less numerate consumers, the more numerate used more complete arithmetic operations and made better choices when two shops offered different deals on the same product (cell phones or microwave ovens).[18] When asked to describe how they chose the best deal, more numerate consumers used more complete arithmetic operations than the less numerate. Tracking eye movements in a second study revealed that those higher in objective numeracy also looked at the pricing information in more detail than the less numerate and in a way that was consistent with them calculating final prices.

With my postdoctoral fellow, Par Bjälkebring, we also found that the highly numerate calculated expected values in risky decisions more than the less numerate.[5] (See Box 2.1 if you need a reminder about expected values.) In our study, participants were asked about four hypothetical risky choices (choices between a sure amount and a gamble). For each one, they first rated their preferences between winning the gamble (e.g., 50% chance of winning $4 and a 50% chance of winning $20) and specific amounts of money for sure. For example, participants responded to the preceding gamble versus $7, $8, $9, $10, and $11. They then indicated an indifference value ("How much money would you need to win for sure in order to be indifferent (have no preference) between it and the gamble just described?"). More objectively numerate individuals were more likely than the less numerate to give exact expected-value responses on all four gambles, controlling for non-numeric intelligence as well as two other numeric competencies (subjective numeracy and intuitive number sense).[5,19] The highly numerate do not always appear to calculate expected values more than the less numerate, however.[13] Methodological differences between studies may explain differences (e.g., more expected value responding may emerge when participants respond to fewer gambles and/or explicitly set a price for the gamble [our two studies] rather than verbally report how they made choices [Cokely & Kelley's study]).

Deliberate Longer

The number-processing habits and inclinations of the highly numerate extend beyond doing calculations to deliberating longer in decisions involving numbers. Similar to individuals who score higher on other cognitive ability measures, they may process information more deeply early, encoding it in a meaningful way in memory so that they can recall it and make better subsequent decisions.[20–22] In fact, the highly numerate spent more time than the less numerate on base-rate tasks[23] and conjunction problems[24] (see Chapter 3 for a reminder of these tasks). This increased time in task partially explained the effects of numeracy on superior decisions.[9,25] At the same time, research has demonstrated that more objectively numerate individuals adapt to their circumstances[26] so that it seems likely that they will deliberate less when it is to their advantage.[13] In fact, those higher in objective numeracy put more effort than the less numerate into making high-payoff decisions but not into low-payoff decisions where objective numeracy did not provide as much benefit.[27] Additional research is needed to identify moderators of numeracy-related deliberation time and its impacts on decision quality.

Recognizing What You Know and Don't Know (Knowledge Calibration)

Recognizing the extent of one's knowledge (or lack thereof) is a metacognitive ability critical to effective decision making. However, individuals are often overconfident and report knowing more than they actually know (e.g., they estimate that they answered 90% of questions correctly but only answered 55% correct).[28,29] Perfect calibration occurs when people estimate the same number of correct responses to general knowledge questions as they actually did answer correctly (e.g., someone who estimated and scored 70% correct). Being more calibrated may help people shift from focusing primarily on evidence that supports their a priori beliefs to focusing on disconfirming evidence because they are more aware of what they don't know. As a result, they may make better decisions.[30]

Consistent with them tending to make better decisions, the highly numerate tend to be more calibrated about what they know than the less numerate, controlling for non-numeric intelligence.[25,31] Their greater calibration may be due to the more numerate spending more time deliberating in decisions.[25] Calibration studies, however, have focused primarily on general knowledge questions, but overconfidence exists in many domains (e.g., driving), where numeracy relations are unknown.

So far, we have discussed greater calibration leading to better decisions. However, overconfidence may propel people's pursuit of lofty goals. For example, men overestimated their math performance more than women did.[32] This gender-related overconfidence then predicted men's greater intentions to pursue math courses and careers, suggesting that gender gaps in STEM fields could be due to men's overconfidence rather than women's underconfidence. Given that overconfidence has been used to explain persistent high rates of stock market trading, entrepreneurial activities, and corporate mergers and acquisitions despite frequent failures,[33–35] the meaning of this gender difference is unclear. One popular decision textbook, however, concluded that "No problem in judgment and decision making is more prevalent and more potentially catastrophic than overconfidence" (p. 217).[36]

Future Research on Thinking Harder

We now know that more objectively numerate people think harder with numbers in a variety of ways including doing more number operations in decisions, thinking longer, and understanding better what they know and don't know. Many researchers have controlled for non-numeric intelligence measures, and numeracy effects have remained significant.[5,14,19,25,31] Consistent with this line of thought, highly numerate individuals reported being more likely to choose the best option in decisions rather than choosing options that were good enough: they are maximizers rather than satisficers.[37] Future research should examine:

- Are "thinking harder" effects confined to tasks using numeric stimuli and/or numeric response scales?
- Are the superior decisions of the highly numerate due to them preparing better to make decisions through deeper encoding of information that makes it and its meaning more accessible for later processing? Such early selection processes could help the decision maker prepare for the task at hand and flexibly change strategies as needed. Alternatively, are their superior decisions explained by them being better able to correct initial faulty intuitions? Some dual-process theorists identify later correction processes as critical to good decisions.[38]
- The highly numerate may selectively attend earlier and more to numeric than non-numeric information. If true, what are the benefits and costs of such selective attention?
- Might these attention effects point toward a numeracy-related impact of irrelevant numbers? Given that the highly numerate think harder about numbers, do they also inhibit less relevant numbers in decisions better than the less numerate, or can they be "tricked" by numbers?

References

1. Peters, E., Västfjäll, D., Slovic, P., Mertz, C. K., Mazzocco, K., & Dickert, S. (2006). Numeracy and decision making. *Psychological Science, 17*(5), 407–413.
2. Srull, T. K., & Wyer, R. S. (1979). The role of category accessibility in the interpretation of information about persons: Some determinants and implications. *Journal of Personality and Social Psychology, 37*(10), 1660–1672.
3. Gurmankin, A. D., Baron, J., & Armstrong, K. (2004). The effect of numerical statements of risk on trust and comfort with hypothetical physician risk communication. *Medical Decision Making, 24*(3), 265–271.
4. Fagerlin, A., Zikmund-Fisher, B. J., Ubel, P. A., Jankovic, A., Derry, H. A., & Smith, D. M. (2007). Measuring numeracy without a math test: Development of the Subjective Numeracy Scale. *Medical Decision Making, 27*(5), 672–680.
5. Peters, E., & Bjälkebring, P. (2015). Multiple numeric competencies: When a number is not just a number. *Journal of Personality and Social Psychology, 108*(5), 802–822.
6. Schulte-Mecklenbeck, M., Johnson, J. G., Böckenholt, U., Goldstein, D. G., Russo, J. E., Sullivan, N. J., & Willemsen, M. C. (2017). Process-tracing methods in decision making: On growing up in the 70s. *Current Directions in Psychological Science, 26*(5), 442–450.
7. Keller, C., Kreuzmair, C., Leins-Hess, R., & Siegrist, M. (2014). Numeric and graphic risk information processing of high and low numerates in the intuitive and deliberative decision modes: An eye-tracker study. *Judgment and Decision Making, 9*(5), 420–432.
8. Fleig, H., Meiser, T., Ettlin, F., & Rummel, J. (2017). Statistical numeracy as a moderator of (pseudo)contingency effects on decision behavior. *Acta Psychologica, 174*, 68–79.
9. Jasper, J. D., Bhattacharya, C., & Corser, R. (2017). Numeracy predicts more effortful and elaborative search strategies in a complex risky choice context: A process-tracing approach. *Journal of Behavioral Decision Making, 30*(2), 224–235.
10. Keller, C. (2011). Using a familiar risk comparison within a risk ladder to improve risk understanding by low numerates: A study of visual attention. *Risk Analysis, 31*(7), 1043–1054.
11. Kleber, J., Florack, A., & Peters, E. (in preparation). The influence of numeracy on the perception and elaboration of quantity information on product packages.
12. Çakır, M., & Balagtas, J. V. (2014). Consumer response to package downsizing: Evidence from the Chicago ice cream market. *Journal of Retailing, 90*(1), 1–12.
13. Cokely, E. T., & Kelley, C. M. (2009). Cognitive abilities and superior decision making under risk: A protocol analysis and process model evaluation. *Judgment and Decision Making, 4*(1), 20–33.
14. Sinayev, A., & Peters, E. (2012). Numeric conversions explain why numeracy ameliorates the framing effect. Talked presented at the annual conference for the Society of Judgment and Decision Making, November 18, 2012, Minneapolis, MN.
15. Jacoby, L. L., & Whitehouse, K. (1989). An illusion of memory: False recognition influenced by unconscious perception. *Journal of Experimental Psychology: General, 118*(2), 126–135.
16. Kleber, J., Dickert, S., Peters, E., & Florack, A. (2013). Same numbers, different meanings: How numeracy influences the importance of numbers for pro-social behavior. *Journal of Experimental Social Psychology, 49*(4), 699–705.
17. Mata, A. (2016). Proportion dominance in valuing lives: The role of deliberative thinking. *Judgment and Decision Making, 11*(5), 441–448.
18. Graffeo, M., Polonio, L., & Bonini, N. (2015). Individual differences in competent consumer choice: The role of cognitive reflection and numeracy skills. *Frontiers in Psychology, 6*, 844.

19. Peters, E., Fennema, M. G., & Tiede, K. E. (2019). The loss-bet paradox: Actuaries, accountants, and other numerate people rate numerically inferior gambles as superior. *Journal of Behavioral Decision Making, 32*, 15–29. https://doi.org/10.1002/bdm.2085.

20. Baron, J. (1978). Intelligence and general strategies. In G. Underwood (Ed.), *Strategies of information processing* (pp. 403–450). London: Academic Press.

21. Cokely, E. T., Kelley, C. M., & Gilchrist, A. L. (2006). Sources of individual differences in working memory: Contributions of strategy to capacity. *Psychonomic Bulletin & Review, 13*(6), 991–997.

22. Sternberg, R. J. (1977). Component processes in analogical reasoning. *Psychological Review, 84*(4), 353–378.

23. Pennycook, G., Cheyne, J. A., Barr, N., Koehler, D. J., & Fugelsang, J. A. (2014). Cognitive style and religiosity: The role of conflict detection. *Memory & Cognition, 42*(1), 1–10.

24. Scherer, L. D., Yates, J. F., Baker, S. G., & Valentine, K. D. (2017). The influence of effortful thought and cognitive proficiencies on the conjunction fallacy: Implications for dual-process theories of reasoning and judgment. *Personality and Social Psychology Bulletin, 43*(6), 874–887.

25. Ghazal, S., Cokely, E. T., & Garcia-Retamero, R. (2014). Predicting biases in very highly educated samples: Numeracy and metacognition. *Judgment and Decision Making, 9*(1), 15–34.

26. Peters, E., Dieckmann, N., Dixon, A., Hibbard, J. H., & Mertz, C. K. (2007). Less is more in presenting quality information to consumers. *Medical Care Research and Review, 64*(2), 169–190.

27. Traczyk, J., Sobkow, A., Fulawka, K., Kus, J., Petrova, D., & Garcia- Retamero, R. (2018). Numerate decision makers don't use more effortful strategies unless it pays: A process tracing investigation of skilled and adaptive strategy selection in risky decision making. *Judgment and Decision Making, 13*(4), 372–381.

28. Griffin, D., & Brenner, L. (2004). Perspectives on probability judgment calibration. In D. J. Koehler & N. Harvey (Eds.), *Blackwell handbook of judgment and decision making* (pp. 177–199). Malden, MA: Blackwell Publishing.

29. Moore, D. A., & Healy, P. J. (2008). The trouble with overconfidence. *Psychological Review, 115*(2), 502–517.

30. Arkes, H. R. (1991). Costs and benefits of judgment errors: Implications for debiasing. *Psychological Bulletin, 110*(3), 486–498.

31. Winman, A., Juslin, P., Lindskog, M., Nilsson, H., & Kerimi, N. (2014). The role of ANS acuity and numeracy for the calibration and the coherence of subjective probability judgments. *Frontiers in Psychology, 5*, 851.

32. Bench, S. W., Lench, H. C., Liew, J., Miner, K., & Flores, S. A. (2015). Gender gaps in overestimation of math performance. *Sex Roles, 72*(11–12), 536–546.

33. Camerer, C., & Lovallo, D. (1999). Overconfidence and excess entry: An experimental approach. *American Economic Review, 89*(1), 306–318.

34. Malmendier, U., & Tate, G. (2005). CEO overconfidence and corporate investment. *The Journal of Finance, 60*(6), 2661–2700.

35. Odean, T. (1998). Volume, volatility, price, and profit when all traders are above average. *The Journal of Finance, 53*(6), 1887–1934.

36. Plous, S. (1993). *The psychology of judgment and decision making.* New York: McGraw-Hill.

37. Misuraca, R., Teuscher, U., & Carmeci, F. A. (2016). Who are maximizers? Future oriented and highly numerate individuals. *International Journal of Psychology, 51*(4), 307–311.

38. Stanovich, K. E., & West, R. F. (2008). On the relative independence of thinking biases and cognitive ability. *Journal of Personality and Social Psychology, 94*(4), 672–695.

6

The Highly Numerate Understand the Feel of Numbers

Decisions are hard sometimes because we don't have a feel for what a number means. What is a billion dollars? What about 1,198,500,000 people? What is 37%? I recently saw that one cigarette contains 12–106 micrograms of formaldehyde. Everyone knows smoking is bad for you and formaldehyde certainly sounds bad, but how bad should I feel about that amount of formaldehyde? What about its cumulative effects across many cigarettes? The gist of this chapter is that the highly numerate are better at understanding the the affective good/bad meaning of these and other numbers in decisions.

Communicators provide numeric information because they think those numbers provide information that we can think about, understand, and use in decisions. But numbers also have extensive, subtle effects on our feelings. It turns out that numbers, even familiar ones like numbers of lives or dollars, make little difference to decisions until we can feel them. Instead of a Spock-like comprehension of data, numbers come alive with feelings, and using them in decisions appears to rely on this process.[1] When it comes to decision making, what the number makes us think about is important, but so is how it makes us feel.

This chapter takes up Chapter 4's distinction between three different types of affect (also called *emotion* or *feeling*) that we rely on as we judge and decide. In this chapter, I focus on (a) *integral affect* derived from numeric information. You might recall that integral affect is affect that is built into how you represent an object, in this case a number. The highly numerate derive clearer and more precise integral affect from numbers (e.g., good and bad feelings about a 9% chance). Chapter 4 focused instead on the less numerate and the other two types of affect: (b) *integral (built-in) affect toward outcomes* (e.g., negative feelings about a medication-induced migraine) and (c) *incidental affect* (positive or negative feelings, such as mood states that are incidental to a decision but influence it nonetheless; think about dealing with your wayward teen after having your parking spot stolen).

Innumeracy in the Wild. Ellen Peters, Oxford University Press (2020). © Oxford University Press 2020.
DOI: 10.1093/oso/9780190861094.003.0001

The topic of affect is critical to the study of numeracy and decision making because everyday judgments and choices often require considering competing numbers and emotionally compelling information (e.g., a medication's .0001% chance of scary side effects; statistical evidence about a crime vs. stereotypes; cost vs. luxury). How one resolves these conflicts can have important consequences, and objective numeracy appears to help determine their resolution. Less objectively numerate individuals are influenced more by the latter two types of emotional information (integral built-in affect toward outcomes—but not numbers—and incidental affect) whereas the highly numerate derive more integral affect from numeric information and use this affect in decisions instead of other mental shortcuts they might substitute otherwise. Thus, the highly numerate do use affect in decisions but it is a systematically *different* source of affect than that used by the less numerate.

Number Comparisons and Number-Related Integral Affect

Specifically, people higher in objective numeracy are more likely than the less numerate to compare numbers and "draw from this deliberation a more precise [secondary] affective reaction that would guide their decisions" (p. 410).[2] Imagine, for example, that you are at Costco looking at television sets. A brand new 55-inch Ultra HD TV sells for $1,649.99. The picture looks fantastic, but how do you feel about the price? Then, you notice the slightly smaller 49-inch TV next to it that also has a great picture but is only $389.99. Now, the original price tag feels dismal by comparison. This comparison-produced "faint whisper of emotion" (p. 312)[1] appears to underlie how we respond to many decisions, including opportunities for risk and reward.[3,4] Whereas economists generally separate thinking from feeling, psychological studies point toward thinking (e.g., about numbers) as producing subtle feelings that then motivate and guide choice. Although these numeric comparisons and ensuing integral number-related affect can lead us astray, as you'll see later in this chapter, more often they help us judge and choose better.

Let's look at a concrete experimental example that we call the "bets effect." In it, participants rate the attractiveness of playing a bet on a 21-point scale (0 = not at all attractive to 20 = extremely attractive). They are shown only one of two bets. The No-Loss bet (7/36 chances to win $9; otherwise, win $0) has a higher expected value than the Loss bet (7/36 chances to win $9; otherwise lose 5¢). Thus, logically, people, and especially highly numerate people, should rate the No-Loss bet as more attractive. Instead, participants consistently rate the objectively worse Loss bet as more attractive, and they report positive feelings about the $9 in the loss's presence but neutral feelings in its absence.[3] In other words, the same $9 present in both bets comes alive with feeling when the comparison of the $9 to the 5¢ loss is available, and these feelings drive the bet's attractiveness. We extended this result by demonstrating that highly numerate people were the ones who reported more positive affect to the $9 and rated the objectively worse loss bet as subjectively more attractive.[2] This nonintuitive result was so surprising that our senior author insisted we replicate it four times before attempting to publish it. Since then, we have demonstrated the bets effect multiple times including with highly numerate professionals (accountants and actuaries who should have stable feelings about $9, but don't).[5] In the same paper, we asked nonexperts "What did you think about while you were deciding how attractive the bet would be to play?" As expected, highly numerate participants reported comparing the $9 to the 5¢ loss more often than the less numerate (26% and 13%, respectively).

The highly numerate also draw greater affective meaning from probabilities, and this affect appears to underlie their sensitivity to different probability levels. In one study, for example, highly numerate participants reported greater negative emotion to a 90% chance of losing a valued belonging than a 50% chance of losing it.[6] Furthermore, they were willing to pay more to insure against higher than lower probabilities of loss. Reactions of the less numerate were relatively insensitive to different probability levels. In another study showing similar probability neglect among the less numerate, their choices relied instead on incidental feelings to irrelevant pictures presented prior to each choice.[7] Choices of the highly numerate were sensitive to probability and unrelated to incidental affect.

Many choices appear to benefit from the highly numerate's ability to draw affective meaning from abstract numbers. Choices involving probabilities, for example, can become biased if the decision maker considers the probability's numerator separate from its denominator. To explain further, a chance like 63 out of 1,000 contains a numerator, the 63, and a denominator, the 1,000. Having 63 people at risk for a disease means very different things if they are from a group of 70 (a 90% chance) than a group of 1,000 (a 6.3% chance). However, the less objectively numerate neglect denominators sometimes whereas the highly numerate more appropriately use both numerator and denominator, drawing greater affective meaning from their combination. We can see this phenomenon in *denominator-neglect problems* (aka, ratio bias, numerosity bias).[2] In one example, participants were given a chance to win a hypothetical prize by drawing a colored jellybean from a bowl. They often elected to draw from the large bowl with a greater absolute number but smaller proportion of colored beans (9 in 100, 9%) rather than from the small bowl containing fewer colored beans but a higher winning probability (1 in 10, 10%), even though the probabilities were explicitly stated beneath each bowl (see Figure 6.1).[8] Some researchers claimed the effect is due to compelling affective images from the nine winning beans in the large bowl dominating thoughts about the small bowl's superior, explicitly presented 10% chance. Psychologists Valerie Reyna and Charles Brainerd[9] argued instead that confusion concerning the relations of the numerator to the denominator in each bowl resulted in denominator neglect, a "minor mental book-keeping confusion rather than a fundamental flaw" (p. 95). However, availability of the explicit probabilities should have eliminated this confusion.

In 2006, we hypothesized instead that this denominator neglect was due to numeracy differences in deriving precise affective meaning from the explicit probabilities. In particular, we reasoned that the less numerate would attend less to and draw less precise affective meaning from the comparison of 9% and 10% and, thus, make worse choices.[2] Consistent with this hypothesis, we found that 33% of less numerate adults chose the larger, inferior bowl compared to only 5% of the more objectively numerate. The choice effect remained significant, controlling for a measure of general intelligence (SAT scores). In addition, compared to the less numerate, the highly numerate reported greater affective precision about Bowl A's 9% chance ("How clear a feeling do you have

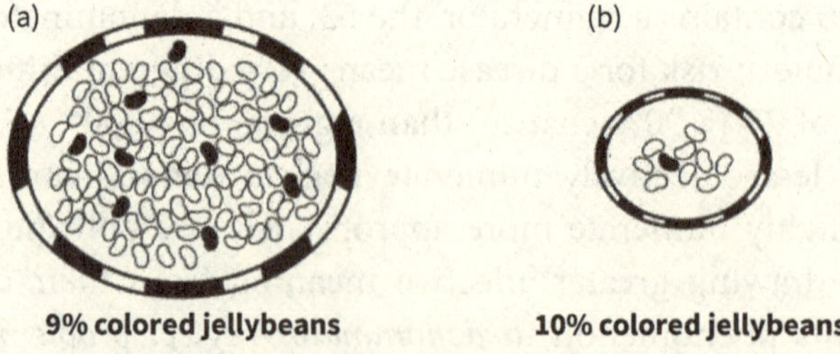

Figure 6.1 The highly numerate are more likely to choose the superior Bowl B and show less denominator neglect.

about [its] goodness or badness?"). Their affect to the inferior 9% odds ("How good or bad does [it] make you feel?") was directionally more negative. Thus, the highly numerate drew more precise affective meaning from the numbers, and this process (similar to the "bets effect") appeared to underlie their greater use of probabilities. Across studies, the highly numerate consistently show less denominator neglect, controlling for general intelligence.[9–13]

Denominator-neglect findings are important in many studies including medical ones. The highly numerate, for example, may be less likely to imagine the numerator (the story you read about the patient who suffered an awful medication side effect, or the terrible images that pop to mind when you might have cancer). They may focus instead on the overall statistics (the numerator and denominator) because the statistics come alive with affective meaning for them in ways that they do not for the less objectively numerate.

I think that these numeracy-linked comparison and affective processes are often at play and can be used to improve judgments at least among those higher in objective numeracy. More numerate women, for example, distinguished better between fetal risk levels when comparative risk numbers from an unrelated risk were provided.[14] The less numerate did not distinguish between risk levels whether or not this comparative information was provided. As we'll discuss in Chapters 15–17, other strategic choices of how to present risk information can assist the less numerate.

The results of the bets-effect, denominator-neglect, and other studies demonstrate the affective significance of numbers to preference and choice. They show that the meaning, utility, and weighting of even very familiar numbers such as $9 or an 80% chance of losing a bet is not fixed but depends greatly on integral feelings that the decision maker derives from numeric information. Rather than being a heuristic cue that is substituted for more relevant information, integral (built-in) affect to numbers is one way that we translate data into meaningful information, and it is inherent to how we employ quantitative reasoning in decision making. Numbers may be counted, sorted, and manipulated by our thinking minds, but, in the end, numbers influence and inform choices through our feeling minds. Our thoughts and feelings about numbers together contribute to good decision making.

You Think (and Feel) Too Much! The Overuse of Numbers

Although generally thought helpful to judgments and decisions, our ability to derive integral affect from and use numbers can lead us astray. Psychologist

Angie Fagerlin and her colleagues,[15] for example, asked women how relieved or anxious they were to find out that women have a 13% average lifetime risk of breast cancer. Their responses depended on whether or not they had estimated this risk number earlier. Among women who first estimated the average woman's lifetime chance of breast cancer, they not only overestimated it (mean estimate of 46%), but this now-salient number was used as a comparison to the provided 13%. The estimators felt relieved and perceived less risk. Women who simply received the 13% estimate (and made no earlier estimate) were more anxious about the risk. The researchers concluded that "Patient education sometimes generates results opposite from those intended. For example, after undergoing risk counseling to help them make decisions about breast cancer prevention, some women (aged 40+) became less motivated to undergo mammography, perhaps because they perceived the risk (13% on average) to be too low to be concerned about" (p. 294).[15]

Greater numeracy may hurt judgments involving unfamiliar numeric metrics too, simply because the highly numerate are more likely to make inferences based on salient numeric information. For example, when asked to evaluate how ecological was a car with carbon emissions described as "0.135 kg of CO_2/km" or "135 g of CO_2/km," the highly numerate perceived the former car as significantly more ecological than the latter logically identical car.[16] The less numerate were insensitive to these differences. These findings may be explained by previously described numeracy differences in inclinations to compare numbers combined with psychologist Christopher Hsee's innovative work on evaluability.[17,18]

Evaluability is illustrated by an experiment in which Hsee asked people to assume they were music majors looking for a used music dictionary.[17] In a joint-evaluation condition, participants were shown two dictionaries, A and B, and asked how much they would be willing to pay for each. Dictionary A had 10,000 entries and was like new, whereas Dictionary B had 20,000 entries and it was like new except that its cover was torn. Willingness-to-pay under joint evaluation was far higher for Dictionary B, presumably because it had twice as many entries. However, when one group of participants evaluated only A and another group evaluated only B (Hsee called these two conditions separate evaluation), the mean willingness to pay was much higher for Dictionary A. Hsee argued that, without a direct comparison in separate evaluation, the number of entries is hard to evaluate. The evaluator knows that more entries are better but does not have a precise notion of how good or bad a specific number is: 10,000 and 20,000 are both large. However, the torn cover is evaluable because it translates easily into a precise good/bad response and thus carries more weight in separate evaluation. Most people find a defective dictionary unattractive and a like-new one attractive. Under joint evaluation, the buyer can see that B is far superior on the more important attribute, number of entries. Thus, the number of entries becomes evaluable (we have a more precise affective impression of it) through the comparison process. His separate-evaluation participants knew the number of entries in the dictionary they were shown, but, without experience with such dictionaries and without a comparison, the number of entries elicited an imprecise affective impression and thus little influenced their judgments.

Although only a few studies exist, I suspect the highly numerate are more prone than the less numerate to the benefits and costs of evaluability because of their greater inclinations to compare numbers. For example, in the preceding carbon emissions study, both formats of CO_2/km were relatively unfamiliar and meaningless to participants who saw only a single number.[16] Thus, they responded in separate evaluation. However, the highly numerate (but not the less numerate) appeared to think harder about the information and make it easier to evaluate by considering its comparative numeric magnitude (participants knew that bigger numbers were worse and, in the context of all numbers, 0.135 is smallish whereas 135 is biggish). The highly numerate arguably overthought and responded to a nonexistent numeric difference because of number-processing inclinations that the less numerate do not share. Similarly, an average breast cancer risk becomes easier to evaluate when a woman considers her earlier estimate and compares the two risk numbers.[15] The bets task results can also be explained by evaluability.[2,5,19] Highly numerate individuals (but not the less numerate) appear to evaluate the Loss and No-Loss bets, respectively, in conditions similar to joint evaluation (two monetary amounts are available to compare, $9 and 5¢) and separate evaluation (no win or loss amounts are available for comparison). The highly numerate then rated the objectively worse Loss bet as subjectively more attractive than the No-Loss bet because they compared the $9 and 5¢ loss and felt quite positive about the $9. When the $9 was not evaluable in the absence of the loss, the highly numerate's feelings about the $9 were relatively neutral, and they rated this objectively superior bet as less attractive. Less numerate individuals were not as inclined to compare numbers[5] and were less subject to the evaluability principle.

If more objectively numerate individuals compare numbers more than the less numerate, then we should expect the more numerate to show other evaluability effects, too.[20–21] For example, the highly numerate may overuse irrelevant numbers (e.g., points used to reward healthy behavior that provide no additional information over other available information[21]) more than the less numerate. In this case, however, the number overuse may benefit them!

Numeracy provides cognitive machinery, both simple and sophisticated, that guides us and sometimes misleads us. Understanding these processes better could help researchers recognize potential problems, tailor interventions, and improve outcomes. The evaluability concept implies that measurable and comparable quantities, such as monetary costs, will direct decisions, particularly among the highly numerate. At the same time, more difficult to measure, potentially more important attributes could fade into the background.[22] For example, Trump White House budget office staff proposed eliminating funding for the Special Olympics specifically "because its benefits could not be measured."[23] A focus on measurable economic costs (as opposed to social costs and benefits) could lead to a degradation of resources we greatly value, including education, the environment, healthcare, family and friendships, and happiness. If this difference is greater for the more numerate than the less numerate, the more numerate may suffer individual consequences more. If the more numerate are policy makers, we all may suffer more.

References

1. Slovic, P., Finucane, M. L., Peters, E., & MacGregor, D. G. (2004). Risk as analysis and risk as feelings: Some thoughts about affect, reason, risk, and rationality. *Risk Analysis*, *24*(2), 311–322.
2. Peters, E., Västfjäll, D., Slovic, P., Mertz, C. K., Mazzocco, K., & Dickert, S. (2006). Numeracy and decision making. *Psychological Science*, *17*(5), 407–413.
3. Bateman, I., Dent, S., Peters, E., Slovic, P., & Starmer, C. (2007). The affect heuristic and the attractiveness of simple gambles. *Journal of Behavioral Decision Making*, *20*(4), 365–380.
4. Slovic, P., Finucane, M., Peters, E., & MacGregor, D. G. (2002). Rational actors or rational fools: Implications of the affect heuristic for behavioral economics. *The Journal of Socio-Economics*, *31*(4), 329–342.
5. Peters, E., Fennema, M. G., & Tiede, K. E. (2019). The loss-bet paradox: Actuaries, accountants, and other numerate people rate numerically inferior gambles as superior. *Journal of Behavioral Decision Making*, *32*, 15–29. https://doi.org/10.1002/bdm.2085.
6. Petrova, D. G., van der Pligt, J., & Garcia-Retamero, R. (2014). Feeling the numbers: On the interplay between risk, affect, and numeracy. *Journal of Behavioral Decision Making*, *27*(3), 191–199.
7. Traczyk, J., & Fulawka, K. (2016). Numeracy moderates the influence of task-irrelevant affect on probability weighting. *Cognition*, *151*, 37–41.
8. Denes-Raj, V., & Epstein, S. (1994). Conflict between intuitive and rational processing: When people behave against their better judgment. *Journal of Personality and Social Psychology*, *66*(5), 819–829.
9. Reyna, V. F., & Brainerd, C. J. (2008). Numeracy, ratio bias, and denominator neglect in judgments of risk and probability. *Learning and Individual Differences*, *18*(1), 89–107.

10. Ghazal, S., Cokely, E. T., & Garcia-Retamero, R. (2014). Predicting biases in very highly educated samples: Numeracy and metacognition. *Judgment and Decision Making*, *9*(1), 15–34.

11. Låg, T., Bauger, L., Lindberg, M., & Friborg, O. (2014). The role of numeracy and intelligence in health-risk estimation and medical data interpretation. *Journal of Behavioral Decision Making*, *27*(2), 95–108.

12. Liberali, J. M., Reyna, V. F., Furlan, S., Stein, L. M., & Pardo, S. T. (2012). Individual differences in numeracy and cognitive reflection, with implications for biases and fallacies in probability judgment. *Journal of Behavioral Decision Making*, *25*(4), 361–381.

13. Stone, E. R., Parker, A. M., & Townsend, L. D. (2018). Distinguishing the ratio bias from unsystematic error: Situation and Individual-difference effects. *Journal of Behavioral Decision Making*. Retrieved from https://doi.org/10.1002/bdm.2068

14. Pighin, S., Savadori, L., Barilli, E., Rumiati, R., Bonalumi, S., Ferrari, M., & Cremonesi, L. (2013). Using comparison scenarios to improve prenatal risk communication. *Medical Decision Making*, *33*(1), 48–58.

15. Fagerlin, A., Zikmund-Fisher, B. J., & Ubel, P. A. (2005). How making a risk estimate can change the feel of that risk: Shifting attitudes toward breast cancer risk in a general public survey. *Patient Education and Counseling*, *57*(3), 294–299.

16. Cadario, R., Parguel, B., & Benoit-Moreau, F. (2016). Is bigger always better? The unit effect in carbon emissions information. *International Journal of Research in Marketing*, *33*(1), 204–207.

17. Hsee, C. K. (1996). The evaluability hypothesis: An explanation for preference reversals between joint and separate evaluations of alternatives. *Organizational Behavior and Human Decision Processes*, *67*, 242–257.

18. Hsee, C. K., Loewenstein, G. F., Blount, S., & Bazerman, M. H. (1999). Preference reversals between joint and separate evaluations of options: A review and theoretical analysis. *Psychological Bulletin*, *125*(5), 576–590.

19. Peters, E., & Bjälkebring, P. (2015). Multiple numeric competencies: When a number is not just a number. *Journal of Personality and Social Psychology*, *108*(5), 802–822.

20. Hsee, C. K., & Zhang, J. (2004). Distinction bias: Misprediction and mischoice due to joint evaluation. *Journal of Personality and Social Psychology*, *86*(5), 680–695.

21. Hsee, C. K., Yu, F., Zhang, J., & Zhang, Y. (2003). Medium maximization. *Journal of Consumer Research*, *30*(1), 1–14.

22. Mintzberg, H. (2017, July 14). What could possibly be wrong with "efficiency"? Plenty. [Blog post]. Retrieved from http://www.mintzberg.org/blog/what-could-possibly-be-wrong-with-efficiency-plenty

23. Green, E. L., & Haberman, M. (2019, March 29). After Trump casts blame for a Special Olympics cut, Betsy DeVos flashes pique. *The New York Times*. Retrieved from https://www.nytimes.com/

7

Numeric Sensitivity and Consistent Use of Numbers

Logically, decision makers should be sensitive to numeric differences concerning important outcomes. All else equal, you should choose the medical treatment with lower likelihood of side effects and eschew the bank with higher fees. In Chapter 7, however, you will see that the highly numerate are more numerically sensitive as well as consistent compared to the less numerate. The mechanisms reviewed thus far are likely candidates for these differences in number sensitivity. In particular, the less numerate are drawn to compelling, easy-to-evaluate, non-numeric information whereas the highly numerate attend earlier and longer to numeric information; think harder about numbers, including comparing and transforming them; and have a better feel for them. Little research, however, has explicitly linked these psychological processes to numeracy-related sensitivity to numbers. As you read Chapter 7, what affective and/or deliberative mechanisms do you think underlie each effect?

Sensitivity to Numeric Levels

Imagine two cancer patients, one faced with a 92% chance of surviving cancer-free for 10 years and the other with a 64% likelihood. Would you feel better about your chances if you were one patient versus the other? Which patient might consider more aggressive treatment if it was an option? Answers to these questions may depend on one's numeracy. Whereas less numerate decision makers appear to use non–number-related emotional information in judgments and decisions, the highly numerate instead are more sensitive to decision-related numbers such as likelihoods[1,2] and expected values.[3–8]

- We examined numeracy's association with treatment efficacy perceptions among 105 women with early-stage breast cancers who were faced with a treatment decision to prevent possible cancer recurrence.[9] We gave them personalized 10-year survival estimates for four treatments. Perceptions of more numerate patients were significantly more sensitive to these

Innumeracy in the Wild. Ellen Peters, Oxford University Press (2020). © Oxford University Press 2020.
DOI: 10.1093/oso/9780190861094.003.0001

statistics than were those of the less numerate. In particular, given higher (e.g., 92%) versus lower (e.g., 64%) survival odds, the highly numerate were somewhat pessimistic, perceiving their personal survival odds, respectively, at about 80% and 40%. Less numerate patients, however, were not only pessimistic, but they were largely insensitive to the medical statistics personalized for them. They perceived their average personal survival chances as between 40% and 45%, regardless of provided statistics. Similar numeracy-related results emerged even when patients responded on a non-numeric subjective-benefit scale.

- Similarly, we found that highly numerate participants rated the attractiveness of hypothetical hospitals based on provided numeric quality-of-care indicators (e.g., proportions of patients satisfied with their care).[10] We could tell because the highly numerate rated hospitals as more attractive when told that the hospital had higher numeric quality as opposed to lower numeric quality. The less numerate instead provided evaluations related to their current feelings (self-reported good or bad mood).

- When provided numeric and non-numeric information about vaccines, the highly numerate (measured through subjective numeracy) were more sensitive than the less numerate to differences in hypothetical risks, perceiving greater differences in risk between an 85% and a 5% chance of adverse events.[11]

- Highly numerate individuals were sensitive to probabilistic risk disclosures in hypothetical informed consent, whereas the less numerate were relatively insensitive to even extreme risk differences.[12]

- More than the less numerate, highly numerate people tend to be more patient, choosing larger later rewards over immediate smaller rewards even when choices are incentivized (and participants receive more cash when they make better choices).[13–15]

- They also tend to choose riskier options, with larger probabilistic rewards that have higher expected values over smaller, certain rewards.[13,15] In fact, one experiment revealed that cognitive load reduced objective numeracy and increased both patient and risk-seeking choices, suggesting a causal effect of numeracy.[16]

- Decision-related numbers, in fact, are used more by the highly numerate across a variety of contexts ranging from vaccines,[11] food nutrition labels,[17] and energy consumption of various activities (e.g., turning off lights, driving less).[18–20]

The preceding effects were mostly attributed to objective numeracy without consideration of the possible roles of other, less studied numeric competencies.

In Chapters 13 and 14, we will explore whether some effects attributed to objective numeracy may be due to the approximate number system and the ability to discriminate magnitudes or to subjective numeracy.[21,22] For example, we know now that the highly numerate are more sensitive to expected values. However, the highly numerate seldom actually calculate expected values.[3,21,23] Instead, they seem to do a series of simpler number operations, extract more precise affective meaning from the data,[24,25] use proportional differences or ratios more,[26] or discriminate numeric magnitudes better.[27] However, we found that participants who set prices for gambles that were closer to the gambles' expected values were not only higher in objective numeracy, but they were also better at discriminating magnitudes.[21]

Overall, numeracy appears to influence abilities to interpret and use numeric information in hypothetical and consequential situations. As the preceding summaries suggest, the highly numerate differentiate more than the less numerate between numeric risks, benefits, expected values, and other numbers. Although not always studied, the less numerate may have used their feelings about possible harms (their integral, built-in affect to outcomes) to inform their judgments while neglecting the likelihood of harm.[12] Their insensitivity calls into question whether the less numerate can be informed adequately about numeric information.

But Numeracy Differences in Sensitivity Don't Always Emerge

This last depressing possibility (that we may not be able to adequately inform the less numerate about numeric information) is offset by a more hopeful picture painted by the lack of similar numeracy differences in other studies.

- First, some situations appear to motivate numeric processing (e.g., certain diseases such as breast cancer among women[28]).
- Instructions to think carefully can cause the less numerate to take on this habit of the highly numerate so that numeracy differences attenuate.[23,29]
- Responding to repeated questions (or seeing the same number repeated[30]) can highlight numeric strategies over other strategies that the less numerate might use otherwise. For example, less numerate participants showed greater attribute-framing effects than the highly numerate, rating a 90% chance of success as more positive than a 10% chance of failure.[31] However, when responding to multiple scenarios in which only the proportion changed (e.g., from 90% success to 75%, proportion sensitivity

did not depend on numeracy. Instead, across numeracy levels, individuals rated a 90% chance of success as more positive than a 75% or 60% chance. Having only the proportions change appeared to highlight the importance of their use.

- Finally, information presentation matters.
  - Providing a familiar risk comparison (a visual comparison of radon risk levels to cigarette smoking risk levels based on an equivalent number of packs smoked per day) also allowed the less numerate to distinguish between risk levels.[32,33] The more numerate were more consistently risk sensitive with and without the familiar comparison.
  - The less numerate can also use numbers in a manner more similar to the highly numerate when we provide the affective meaning of the numbers or lower the cognitive effort needed to process numeric information.[10,34]

In sum, although numeracy differences in sensitivity often occur, the less numerate can discriminate between numeric levels when circumstances permit. The preceding results point toward them being capable of numeric strategies but of not thinking to use them during decisions or choosing not to use them. Providing them access to the habits of the highly numerate or the products of their processing (e.g., affective meaning[10]) can attenuate these numeracy differences (see Chapters 15–17).

Consistency in Judgment and Choice

The highly numerate have another advantage: they are more consistent than the less numerate in their use of numeric information, and they respond more sensibly to numbers. Their greater consistency emerges, for example, when experimenters use different measurement methods (e.g., methods to value health states, count the number of sexual encounters, and assess the likelihood of negative events).[13,35–37] In risk-inconsistency studies, participants are asked to provide the percent chance of an event happening or not happening over a given time frame (e.g., getting into a car accident) on a line ranging from 0% (no chance) to 100% (certain).[38] They are also asked to consider subsets and supersets (e.g., going to the dentist to get a cavity filled and going to the dentist for any reason) and to consider all of these events over 1-year and 5-year time frames. Participant risk-inconsistency scores are calculated based on the number of inconsistent responses they generated in three categories: time (estimating a 5-year risk to be less than its 1-year risk), frame (estimated risks for complementary events exceed 100%, e.g., the likelihood of driving accident free and getting into an accident), and subsets (estimated likelihood for a subset event being judged as higher than that for a superset). In separate studies out of different labs, more numerate individuals were more consistent.[13,37] These consistency differences seem to be due to the more numerate thinking more with numbers and having a better sense of what they know and do not know (recall Chapter 5's discussion on these points).

More numerate individuals also choose more consistently than the less numerate when options are explicitly described (e.g., Option A offers a 47% chance to win $56 and a 53% chance to win $28; Option B offers 29% of $121 and 71% of $17) versus when the same options are experienced through sampling (e.g., Option B could be presented as a decks of 100 cards, 29 of which offered $121 if turned over, and 71 cards earned $17).[39] For example, highly numerate individuals tend to sample more from options, such as decks of cards, and explore the same option repeatedly instead of alternating between options.[40,41] They also explored options with higher outcome variability more than those with lower variability, thus making it more likely to maximize learning. These systematic choices to explore likely explained their greater choice consistency when options were described versus when they were experienced. In fact, when participants experienced options, but had to sample each option a fixed number of times (and therefore received the same information), more and less numerate participants made similarly consistent choices.[40] Thus, the highly numerate make effective choices to learn more and respond appropriately across different related situations.

The superior decisions of the highly numerate are almost certainly due in part to their greater numeric sensitivity and consistency. They also appear to produce their own additional information through number transformations, other calculations, comparing numbers to assist in evaluation, producing a more precise affective feeling for numbers, and/or choosing to learn more.[3,21,24,40] They then are able to integrate more and more complex information into their preferences compared to the less numerate who are more likely to respond more superficially to non-numeric sources of information such as a narrative or a positive/negative frame.[42,43]

The highly numerate have a numeric hammer, and they are inclined to use it. They not only know number operations better than the less numerate, but they likely access that numeric knowledge more quickly and easily.[44] Most of the time, these processes result in the highly numerate making better decisions.

References

1. Pachur, T., Schulte-Mecklenbeck, M., Murphy, R. O., & Hertwig, R. (2018). Prospect theory reflects selective allocation of attention. *Journal of Experimental Psychology: General, 147*(2), 147–169.
2. Traczyk, J., & Fulawka, K. (2016). Numeracy moderates the influence of task-irrelevant affect on probability weighting. *Cognition, 151*, 37–41.
3. Cokely, E. T., & Kelley, C. M. (2009). Cognitive abilities and superior decision making under risk: A protocol analysis and process model evaluation. *Judgment and Decision Making, 4*(1), 20–33.
4. Bateman, H., Eckert, C., Geweke, J., Louviere, J., Satchell, S., & Thorp, S. (2016). Risk presentation and portfolio choice. *Review of Finance, 20*(1), 201–229.
5. Chen, Y. W., Wang, J. X., Kirk, R. M., Pethtel, O. L., & Kiefner, A. E. (2014). Age differences in adaptive decision making: The role of numeracy. *Educational Gerontology, 40*(11), 825–833.
6. Jasper, J. D., Bhattacharya, C., Levin, I. P., Jones, L., & Bossard, E. (2013). Numeracy as a predictor of adaptive risky decision making. *Journal of Behavioral Decision Making, 26*(2), 164–173.
7. Levin, I. P., Bossard, E. A., Gaeth, G. J., & Yan, H. (2014). The combined role of task, child's age and individual differences in understanding decision processes. *Judgment and Decision Making, 9*(3), 274–286.
8. Pertl, M. T., Zamarian, L., & Delazer, M. (2017). Reasoning and mathematical skills contribute to normatively superior decision making under risk: Evidence from the game of dice task. *Cognitive Processing, 18*(3), 249–260.
9. Lipkus, I. M., Peters, E., Kimmick, G., Liotcheva, V., & Marcom, P. (2010). Breast cancer patients' treatment expectations after exposure to the decision aid program adjuvant online: The influence of numeracy. *Medical Decision Making, 30*(4), 464–473.
10. Peters, E., Dieckmann, N. F., Västfjäll, D., Mertz, C. K., Slovic, P., & Hibbard, J. H. (2009). Bringing meaning to numbers: The impact of evaluative categories on decisions. *Journal of Experimental Psychology: Applied, 15*(3), 213–227.
11. Betsch, C., Renkewitz, F., & Haase, N. (2013). Effect of narrative reports about vaccine adverse events and bias-awareness disclaimers on vaccine decisions: A simulation of an online patient social network. *Medical Decision Making, 33*(1), 14–25.
12. Couper, M. P., & Singer, E. (2009). The role of numeracy in informed consent for surveys. *Journal of Empirical Research on Human Research Ethics, 4*(4), 17–26.
13. Sinayev, A., & Peters, E. (2015). Cognitive reflection vs. calculation in decision making. *Frontiers in Psychology, 6*, 532–547.
14. Burks, S. V., Carpenter, J. P., Goette, L., & Rustichini, A. (2009). Cognitive skills affect economic preferences, strategic behavior, and job attachment. *Proceedings of the National Academy of Sciences, 106*(19), 7745–7750.
15. Frederick, S. (2005). Cognitive reflection and decision making. *Journal of Economic Perspectives, 19*(4), 25–42.
16. Deck, C., & Jahedi, S. (2015). The effect of cognitive load on economic decision making: A survey and new experiments. *European Economic Review, 78*, 97–119.
17. Visschers, V. H., & Siegrist, M. (2010). When reduced fat increases preference. How fat reduction in nutrition tables and numeracy skills affect food choices. *Appetite, 55*(3), 730–733.
18. Attari, S. Z., DeKay, M. L., Davidson, C. I., & Bruine de Bruin, W. (2010). Public perceptions of energy consumption and savings. *Proceedings of the National Academy of Sciences of the United States of America, 107*(37), 16054–16059.

19. Attari, S. Z. (2014). Perceptions of water use. *Proceedings of the National Academy of Sciences of the United States of America, 111*(14), 5129–5134.

20. Schley, D. R., & DeKay, M. L. (2015). Cognitive accessibility in judgments of household energy consumption. *Journal of Environmental Psychology, 43*, 30–41.

21. Peters, E., & Bjälkebring, P. (2015). Multiple numeric competencies: When a number is not just a number. *Journal of Personality and Social Psychology, 108*(5), 802–822.

22. Schley, D. R., & Peters, E. (2014). Assessing economic value symbolic-number mappings predict risky and riskless valuations. *Psychological Science, 25*(3), 753–761.

23. Peters, E., Fennema, M. G., & Tiede, K. E. (2019). The loss-bet paradox: Actuaries, accountants, and other numerate people rate numerically inferior gambles as superior. *Journal of Behavioral Decision Making, 32*, 15–29. https://doi.org/10.1002/bdm.2085.

24. Peters, E., Västfjäll, D., Slovic, P., Mertz, C. K., Mazzocco, K., & Dickert, S. (2006). Numeracy and decision making. *Psychological Science, 17*(5), 407–413.

25. Reyna, V. F. (2004). How people make decisions that involve risk: A dual-processes approach. *Current Directions in Psychological Science, 13*(2), 60–66.

26. Matthews, P. G., Lewis, M. R., & Hubbard, E. M. (2016). Individual differences in nonsymbolic ratio processing predict symbolic math performance. *Psychological Science, 27*(2), 191–202.

27. Dehaene, S. (1992). Varieties of numerical abilities. *Cognition, 44*(1–2), 1–42.

28. Fagerlin, A., Zikmund-Fisher, B. J., Ubel, P. A., Jankovic, A., Derry, H. A., & Smith, D. M. (2007). Measuring numeracy without a math test: Development of the Subjective Numeracy Scale. *Medical Decision Making, 27*(5), 672–680.

29. Keller, C., Kreuzmair, C., Leins-Hess, R., & Siegrist, M. (2014). Numeric and graphic risk information processing of high and low numerates in the intuitive and deliberative decision modes: An eye-tracker study. *Judgment and Decision Making, 9*(5), 420–432.

30. Obrecht, N. A., & Chesney, D. L. (2016). Prompting deliberation increases base-rate use. *Judgment and Decision Making, 11*(1), 1–6.

31. Gamliel, E., & Kreiner, H. (2017). Outcome proportions, numeracy, and attribute-framing bias. *Australian Journal of Psychology, 69*(4), 283–292.

32. Pighin, S., Savadori, L., Barilli, E., Rumiati, R., Bonalumi, S., Ferrari, M., & Cremonesi, L. (2013). Using comparison scenarios to improve prenatal risk communication. *Medical Decision Making, 33*(1), 48–58.

33. Keller, C., Siegrist, M., &Visschers, V. (2009). Effect of risk ladder format on risk perception in high- and low-numerate individuals. *Risk Analysis, 29*(9), 1255–1264.

34. Peters, E., Meilleur, L., & Tompkins, M. K. (2014). Numeracy and the Affordable Care Act: Opportunities and challenges. Appendix A. IOM (Institute of Medicine). In *Health Literacy and Numeracy: Workshop Summary* (pp. 91–132). Washington, DC: The National Academies Press.

35. Woloshin, S., Schwartz, L. M., Moncur, M., Gabriel, S., & Tosteson, A. N. A. (2001). Assessing values for health: Numeracy matters. *Medical Decision Making, 21*(5), 382–390.

36. McAuliffe, T. L., DiFranceisco, W., & Reed, B. R. (2010). Low numeracy predicts reduced accuracy of retrospective reports of frequency of sexual behavior. *AIDS and Behavior, 14*(6), 1320–1329.

37. Del Missier, F., Mäntylä, T., & De Bruin, W. B. (2012). Decision-making competence, executive functioning, and general cognitive abilities. *Journal of Behavioral Decision Making, 25*(4), 331–351.

38. Bruine de Bruin, W., Parker, A. M., & Fischhoff, B. (2007). Individual differences in adult decision-making competence. *Journal of Personality and Social Psychology, 92*(5), 938–956.

39. Hertwig, R., Barron, G., Weber, E. U., & Erev, I. (2004). Decisions from experience and the effect of rare events in risky choice. *Psychological Science, 15*(8), 534–539.

40. Ashby, N. J. (2017). Numeracy predicts preference consistency: Deliberative search heuristics increase choice consistency for choices from description and experience. *Judgment and Decision Making, 12*(2), 128–139.
41. Lejarraga, T. (2010). When experience is better than description: Time delays and complexity. *Journal of Behavioral Decision Making, 23*(1), 100–116.
42. Dieckmann, N. F., Slovic, P., & Peters, E. M. (2009). The use of narrative evidence and explicit likelihood by decisionmakers varying in numeracy. *Risk Analysis, 29*(10), 1473–1488.
43. Peters, E., & Levin, I. P. (2008). Dissecting the risky-choice framing effect: Numeracy as an individual-difference factor in weighting risky and riskless options. *Judgment and Decision Making, 3*(6), 435–448.
44. Srull, T. K., & Wyer, R. S. (1979). The role of category accessibility in the interpretation of information about persons: Some determinants and implications. *Journal of Personality and Social Psychology, 37*(10), 1660–1672.

8

Numerically Imperfect Reasoning Among the Highly Numerate

In this chapter, we examine two ways that even the highly numerate come up numerically short-handed. First, sometimes their numeric knowledge is imperfect or they don't think to use it. Second, all of us, including the highly numerate, can be motivated by goals other than numeric accuracy.

Imperfect Knowledge and Reasoning

Although the highly numerate certainly understand and use numeric information better than the less objectively numerate, they are nonetheless imperfect number crunchers. For example, patients are sometimes asked to assess the value of different health states using highly numeric measures.[1] In one classic method, participants choose between gambles involving imagined health states (e.g., "Would you prefer to live with your current health for the next 10 years or try a painless treatment that has a 90% chance of perfect health for 10 years but a 10% chance of immediate death?"). By varying the gamble's probabilities, researchers can identify an indifference point at which the participant indicates no preference between the two options. The authors expected to find that participants' most feared disease (e.g., cancer) would be valued the least. In fact, most (76%) of the highly numerate did so (vs. 36% of the less numerate), but 24% of the highly numerate failed the task.[1]

The highly numerate also remain surprisingly prone to some of Chapter 3's heuristics and especially those heuristics that contain compelling stories. Integrating statistics with stories in these judgments is either particularly difficult or does not seem necessary. In base-rate neglect problems (see Box 3.3), for example, participants regardless of numeracy use easy-to-imagine details about a person such as "Jack the engineer" more than provided statistics (the base rate of engineers in the group).[2] The highly numerate tend to recognize the importance of the base rate more than the less numerate but underuse them. The errors committed in conjunction problems further highlight the compelling power of easy-to-imagine stories. In a relatively simple type of conjunction error, we examined errors between superset items that should be rated as more likely than or equally likely as subset items. For example, participants should rate the likelihood of going to the dentist for any reason higher than or equal to its subset, going to the dentist to get a cavity filled. However, the subset is somewhat easier to imagine even though no specific "story" is told, and study participants sometimes rate it incorrectly as more likely. In our study, less numerate participants averaged 8.7% errors whereas the highly numerate averaged 4.3%.[3] Other conjunction problems describe a more concrete story and produce more errors. In the Linda problem, for example, a stereotypical description of a feminist bank teller is provided and participants are asked whether she is more likely to be a bank teller (the superset) or a feminist bank teller (the subset) (see Box 3.4). Without further instruction, even highly numerate participants responded incorrectly 75–88% of the time.[4] When instructed to argue why the logically correct option is the smart option to choose, fewer of the most numerate chose incorrectly. Nonetheless, 63% of them chose incorrectly compared to 100% of the least numerate. Stories are powerful even among the most numerate, and math ability and numeric processing inclinations are not always enough.

The highly numerate also have imperfect knowledge or reasoning capacity for what we call *conditional probability* (Bayes reasoning) problems (see Box 3.2). In prototypical medical diagnosis problems, we rely on symptoms and test results to make inferences about some underlying condition or disease. For example, I may want to know the likelihood of a disease given some symptom (e.g., what is the probability that I have tendinitis given that my wrist hurts every time I type?). Other times, we know some test result (such as whether a screening test indicates I have cancer) and want to know the likelihood of disease (because tests are imperfect). In a recent study, only 7% and 14%, respectively, of the less and more educated were able to answer correctly a Bayesian problem similar to that in Box 3.2.[5] In Bayes problems, information presentation and further instructions (e.g., Box 3.2) can increase correct responses although they tend to help more numerate individuals who already have some understanding of the basic concepts.[6–9]

Nonlinear thinking, such as cumulative odds, is also quite difficult for everyone.[10] For example, only 1.2% of college student respondents answered this problem correctly: "Imagine that, when the Columbus Clippers and the Eugene Emeralds minor league baseball teams have played each other, the Columbus Clippers won only 10% of the time. If the teams have a four-game series, by your calculations, what are the chances that the Clippers will win at least once?" (see Box 8.1 for how to calculate the correct answer, 34%).

Box 8.1 Calculating Cumulative Odds

People are often tripped up by cumulative calculations due to the nonlinear thinking required. In one paper, we asked participants to imagine that when two "minor league baseball teams have played each other, the Columbus Clippers won only 10% of the time. If the teams have a four-game series, by your calculations, what are the chances that the Clippers will win at least once?" Only 1% of participants provided the correct response to this problem.[10] There are multiple ways to calculate these odds correctly. First, you could calculate the chances they would win exactly one game, two games, three and four games, and add these four odds together, but this is complicated. The easier method is to think about the other team winning all four games and calculate those odds. If you then subtract that calculation from 100%, it would give you the odds of anything else happening—in this case, the Clippers winning one or more games. The likelihood of the other team winning all four games is .90 times .90 times .90 times .90 = $.90^4$ = .66 or 66%. Then, 100% minus 66% = 34% chance that the Clippers would win at least one game out of the four-game series.

Objective numeracy was unrelated to correct responses and to any of the simple strategies used by participants (e.g., if the likelihood of winning one game was 10%, then participants perceived that the chance of winning at least one of those games was also 10%).

Errors in calculating cumulative odds can be problematic for common decisions. For example, psychologists Patricia Linville, Gregory Fischer, and Baruch Fischhoff[11] asked participants to estimate the risk of HIV transmission based on a single sexual encounter and then to estimate how much the risk would change with 10 and 100 exposures. Participants overestimated the one-time risk to be 5% and then estimated the 10- and 100-exposure risks as 10% and 20%, respectively. However, if the risk of one exposure was 5%, the risk of 10 exposures would be 40% (100% − $(100\% - 5\%)^{10}$ = 100% − $95\%^{10}$ = 1 − $.95^{10}$ = .4 = 40%; see Box 8.1). By a similar calculation, the risk of 100 exposures would be 99%. Thus, people can overestimate a one-time chance but vastly underestimate the risk of repeated exposures. This problem deserves more attention because people are often given annual risks (e.g., flooding in a certain area, pregnancy given birth control) but do not understand what they mean for longer time periods.[12]

The highly numerate look like the less numerate on other kinds of numeric thinking, too.

- Purchase decisions that involve ratios (e.g., calories per serving; price per ounce).[13]
- Percentage price differences based on different targets. For example, a $1,500 moped was perceived as relatively more expensive than a $1,000 moped when described as 50% higher in price than when the less expensive moped was described as 33% less.[14]
- Treatment effectiveness in groups with different baseline risks. A treatment helped 25 people in each of two groups avoid heart disease. The same 25% reduction, however, appeared larger when evaluated in the context of the low-risk group (without and with the medication, respectively, 30% and 5% develop heart disease) than the high-risk group (90% and 65%, respectively, develop heart disease).[15]

In sum, greater numeracy helps people understand and respond more logically to many numeric complexities in their lives. Nonetheless, in the range of numeracy skills generally studied, patchy reasoning persists. The highly numerate neglect base rates and commit conjunction fallacies at surprising rates. Bayes reasoning and nonlinear calculations pose enduring difficulties. As is frequently the case, one of the joys and horrors of being human is that we have more to learn!

Everyone Is a Motivated Reasoner, Including the Highly Numerate

In most of the studies discussed thus far, the highly numerate made better, more numerically accurate decisions than the less numerate. However, numeric accuracy is not always a decision maker's primary goal. The less numerate, for example, may have a goal of avoiding difficult number processing (or act as if they do). For example, they are more likely to substitute the answer to an easier question (how do I feel about this risk?) for the answer to the hard question asked (what is the integration of the probability and possible outcomes for this hazard?).[16] Consistent with the idea of having alternative goals, the less numerate reacted defensively to cancer-screening results, agreeing more, for example, with statements such as "I like to ignore the fact that I could get cancer."[17] In this case, the presumed primacy of the highly numerate's accuracy goals meant that they did not show the same defensive reactions.

However, as it turns out, the highly numerate also can "use their numeric hammer" to create perceptions more in line with their prior beliefs, too.

They may even be better at creating consistent perceptions because being a motivated reasoner is thought to take cognitive effort[18] and the highly numerate have more capacity for numeric effort. In fact, more numerate individuals exposed themselves longer than the less numerate to political news that agreed rather than disagreed with their prior attitudes.[19] Consistent with numeracy research,[20] the highly numerate sought out more information than the less numerate. However, their information seeking was focused on information that confirmed what they already believed.

Thus, with politically divisive risk issues, two competing numeracy predictions exist. If the decision maker's goal is accuracy, then more numerate people should behave more like scientists, with risk perceptions converging on the facts regardless of political ideology. The less numerate instead might rely on their political attitudes, feelings, or compelling stories as a mental shortcut to determine their risk attitudes. However, we sometimes have goals other than accuracy. For example, we have strong and pervasive goals to feel like we belong.[21] such as to our own political conservative or liberal "tribe," and we have goals to maintain consistent beliefs.[18] People then are motivated to seek out, process, and use information in a motivated manner to attain their goals, whatever they may be.

If being a motivated reasoner also requires cognitive effort, the highly numerate have more ability to seek out and perceive information in ways that allow them to double down on their political beliefs. As a result, the highly numerate could show greater political polarization than the less numerate.

With risk expert Dan Kahan, we explored these alternative hypotheses in risk perceptions of climate change and nuclear power. Overall and as expected, more liberal individuals perceived greater risk than conservatives. This polarization, however, was significantly stronger among those higher, rather than lower, in objective numeracy and scientific literacy, supporting the highly numerate perceiving risks based on goals other than accuracy.[22] Similarly stronger political divisiveness in risk perceptions have been found among individuals with more (compared to less) education.[23]

We interpreted our findings to mean that those with greater ability were better able to attain their alternative goal of protecting their political identity and beliefs, *and* they had greater ability to do so. Thus, our participants espoused beliefs, in essence, to protect membership in their chosen "tribe." Alternative explanations exist. For example, they may have protected more confidently held beliefs[23] or more fluent beliefs learned through family and friends.[24] Whichever explanation is true, highly numerate individuals, even when they have the ability to be numerically accurate, will sometimes choose to actively or passively seek out and process information in ways that bless rather than question what they would like to see.

This predicted information-processing effect emerged in recent studies that asked participants to answer a math question in a politically neutral skin cream problem or a politically divisive gun control problem.[25,26] In each problem, a 2 × 2 table provided them with counts of who experienced better and worse outcomes (see Figure 8.1). In the skin cream problem, for example, patients used or didn't use the cream, and it either increased or decreased a rash. In the numerically identical gun control problem, cities that banned (or didn't ban) concealed handguns in public had crime rates that either increased or decreased. Respondents randomly assigned to one of these four conditions simply indicated whether they thought the treatment (cream or gun ban) was helpful or harmful. The problems were set up so that doing simple comparisons with the most salient cell (the upper left corner of Figure 8.1's 2 × 2 table) would cause people to arrive at an incorrect response, but analyzing all four cells appropriately would reveal the correct response.

We did not expect political ideology to influence responses on the neutral skin cream problem. However, as expected, highly numerate individuals were more likely than the less numerate to respond correctly. After all, it is a math problem. The problem is difficult, and less than 50% of the highly numerate answered correctly.

In the gun control problem, however, the highly numerate might have had goals other than accuracy. Remember that the most salient cell was misleading with respect to the numerically correct response. In addition, we expected

	Decrease in crime	Increase in crime
Cities that <u>did</u> ban carrying concealed handguns in public	223	75
Cities that <u>did not</u> ban carrying concealed handguns in public	107	21

What result does the study support?

o Cities that enacted a ban on carrying concealed handguns were more likely to have a <u>decrease in crime</u> than cities without bans.

o Cities that enacted a ban on carrying concealed handguns were more likely to have an <u>increase in crime</u> than cities without bans.

Figure 8.1 A 2 × 2 covariation bias table used in experiments.[25,26]

liberal participants to believe a priori (and have a goal to continue to believe so as to remain part of their "tribe") that banning concealed handguns would decrease crime while conservatives would believe the opposite. If true, then the highly numerate may focus on different numeric information (simple comparisons to the most salient value vs. the numerical operation that correctly combines all four cells) depending on what the correct response is. In fact, gun control results were revealed as more politically motivated. Arriving at the correct answer depended both on greater numeracy and political ideology. In particular, more numerate individuals, whether more liberal or more conservative, arrived at the correct response more often in those conditions where the correct response was consistent with their political ideology. More numerate liberals were more likely to respond correctly when gun bans led to decreased crime, whereas more numerate conservatives were more likely to respond correctly when gun bans led to increased crime. However, when simple comparisons to the most salient value revealed answers that were ideologically consistent, the highly numerate were significantly more likely to choose the incorrect response than when those comparisons revealed an ideologically inconsistent answer. In fact, the highly numerate were 45 percentage points more likely to get the right answer if the data backed up their views than if they didn't. Less numerate people were far less polarized.

Psychologist Leaf van Boven[27] found similar politically divisive motivated-math effects. Their participants judged numeric information as more important to government policies when it supported their ideologically preferred policy option than when it did not. For example, supporters of a Muslim immigration ban, when considering different probabilities, rated the likelihood of terrorist immigrants being Muslim (a relatively high probability) as more important than the chances of Muslim immigrants being terrorists (a very low probability). Opponents of the ban provided the opposite importance ratings. As anticipated, these effects were significantly and meaningfully larger among those higher than lower in objective numeracy.

Thus, greater numeracy can be associated with better or worse reasoning if we define accuracy as the correct goal. More accurate in my opinion, though, is that the highly numerate use their numeric ability strategically to meet their personal needs, and salient needs are not necessarily numerical accuracy.[28] As news anchor Megyn Kelly once queried political consultant Karl Rove, "Is this just math that you do as a Republican to make yourself feel better?"[29] In the preceding gun control problem, highly numerate individuals, whether Republican and Democrat, demonstrated similar motivated-math effects.[25,26] Although ancient Greek to modern-day philosophers have assumed that making good decisions involves effortful deliberation that overrides both cognitive and emotion-driven errors,[30] sometimes greater thought can be used to service our other motivated goals. In these cases, what looks like greater bias may emerge from the highly numerate.

Critically, we need to know more about when and why people prioritize accuracy goals and how to encourage such goals when they do not, especially when doing so has long-term societal and individual benefits but short-term individual costs. The strength of the association between the issue and political ideology appears important to this question. For example, when a policy had low party polarization and a specific political party had made a numeric political appeal, the highly numerate were simply more accurate.[31] The less numerate largely neglected the numeric information, relying instead on the political-party cue, similar to prior research linking decisions of the less numerate to easy-to-evaluate information and heuristic processing (see Chapter 3).

Also unclear is the locus of the motivated math. Although I have interpreted these effects as due to numeracy rather than education, science literacy, or general intelligence, researchers thus far have measured only their construct of interest (e.g., numeracy[25]) or included multiple measures but analyzed them separately.[23] In addition, some researchers have found that partisan responding to knowledge questions disappears or at least is greatly attenuated with payment for accuracy.[32-34] They claim that their findings question results of motivated reasoning in risk perceptions. However, the results can also be explained by paid participants having multiple goals. When paid for accuracy, that goal likely becomes more salient, and, as a result, partisan differences in correct responding reduce. In these studies, however, partisan differences in perceptions of information credibility increase with pay, suggesting that motivated partisan processing did not disappear altogether.[33] Other accounts can also explain these paid-participant data (e.g., wanting more money and correctly guessing what the experimenter wants,[35] perhaps combined with using uncertainty about correct responses to get more pay[36]).

What We Know and Do Not Know

Let's pause now and consider what we know and don't know about objective numeracy and its effects in judgments and decisions. We know, for example, that decision makers balance accuracy with effort.[37] However, for some people (the highly numerate), numbers are relatively easy, whereas for others (the less numerate) they are fraught with negative emotion and are considerably more difficult compared to other more salient and less diagnostic information. We also don't just "choose." We process information, and our numeric abilities appear to guide this information processing.

At this point in the book, you will recognize the surprising number of ways that information processing in decisions differs by objective numeracy. In particular, the less objectively numerate use information that is easier to evaluate, including emotional reactions (except to numbers) and compelling stories (see Chapters 2–4). In Chapters 5–7, you learned that the highly numerate have numerical habits and inclinations that guide them to better decisions (usually). The less objectively numerate may be able to acquire some of these habits of the highly numerate. In particular, the highly numerate do not always crunch the numbers thoroughly, but they do tend to think longer in numeric decisions, perform more number operations (some simple, some complex), and use these operations to "calculate" a feeling for the numbers. As psychologist Daniel Willingham[38] has suggested "Thinking well requires knowing facts" (p. 21). Knowing numeric facts provides a firm foundation for the highly numerate to think more about numbers and make better decisions.

Of course, it likely does not matter much when someone misunderstands one numeric fact. Similarly, in most circumstances, a less-than-ideal judgment or choice is not usually very costly, and it may be quicker and less effortful for the decision maker. This argument implies that the abilities and habits of the highly numerate may not matter. Furthermore, it suggests that the less objectively numerate may face hiccups occasionally, but their lack of ability ultimately should have little impact on them.

However, as you saw in Chapter 4, I believe that the risks of innumeracy accumulate over time. It's not that the less objectively numerate misunderstand once; they misunderstand across situations and time. It's likely that they also often rely on easy-to-evaluate non-numeric information to form judgments and make choices instead of relying on the numeric information that forms the backbone of many good decisions. If the risks of incomprehension and poor decision making accumulate as I believe, then the less numerate should experience poorer life outcomes. The next chapter examines exactly that idea.

References

1. Woloshin, S., Schwartz, L. M., Moncur, M., Gabriel, S., & Tosteson, A. N. A. (2001). Assessing values for health: Numeracy matters. *Medical Decision Making, 21*(5), 382–390.
2. Obrecht, N. A., & Chesney, D. L. (2016). Prompting deliberation increases base-rate use. *Judgment and Decision Making, 11*(1), 1–6.
3. Sinayev, A., & Peters, E. (2015). Cognitive reflection vs. calculation in decision making. *Frontiers in Psychology, 6*, 532–547.

4. Scherer, L. D., Yates, J. F., Baker, S. G., & Valentine, K. D. (2017). The influence of effortful thought and cognitive proficiencies on the conjunction fallacy: Implications for dual-process theories of reasoning and judgment. *Personality and Social Psychology Bulletin*, *43*(6), 874–887.

5. Peters, E., Fennema, M. G., & Tiede, K. E. (2019). The loss-bet paradox: Actuaries, accountants, and other numerate people rate numerically inferior gambles as superior. *Journal of Behavioral Decision Making*, *32*, 15–29. https://doi.org/10.1002/bdm.2085.

6. McNair, S., & Feeney, A. (2015). Whose statistical reasoning is facilitated by a causal structure intervention?. *Psychonomic Bulletin & Review*, *22*(1), 258–264.

7. Hoffrage, U., Gigerenzer, G., Krauss, S., & Martignon, L. (2002). Representation facilitates reasoning: What natural frequencies are and what they are not. *Cognition*, *84*(3), 343–352.

8. Chapman, G. B., & Liu, J. (2009). Numeracy, frequency, and Bayesian reasoning. *Judgment and Decision Making*, *4*(1), 34–40.

9. Wolfe, C. R., & Reyna, V. F. (2010). Semantic coherence and fallacies in estimating joint probabilities. *Journal of Behavioral Decision Making*, *23*(2), 203–223.

10. Peters, E., Kunreuther, H., Sagara, N., Slovic, P., & Schley, D. R. (2012). Protective measures, personal experience, and the affective psychology of time. *Risk Analysis*, *32*(12), 2084–2097.

11. Linville, P. W., Fischer, G. W., & Fischhoff, B. (1993). AIDS risk perceptions and decision biases. In J. B. Pryor & G. D. Reeder (Eds.), *The social psychology of HIV infection* (pp. 5–38). Hillsdale, NJ: Lawrence Erlbaum.

12. Rolison, J. J., Hanoch, Y., & Miron-Shatz, T. (2012). What do men understand about lifetime risk following genetic testing? The effect of context and numeracy. *Health Psychology*, *31*(4), 530–533.

13. Tsiros, M., & Chen, H. A. (2017). Convexity neglect in consumer decision making. *Journal of Marketing Behavior*, *2*(4), 253–290.

14. Kruger, J., & Vargas, P. (2008). Consumer confusion of percent differences. *Journal of Consumer Psychology*, *18*(1), 49–61.

15. Vogt, F., Mason, D., & Marteau, T. M. (2012). Crediting treatments for good outcomes that would have happened anyway: The impact of baseline risk on treatment perceptions. *Medical Decision Making*, *32*(2), 301–310.

16. Kahneman, D., & Frederick, S. (2002). Representativeness revisited: Attribute substitution in intuitive judgment. In T. Gilovich, D. W. Griffin, & D. Kahneman (Eds.), *Heuristics and biases: The psychology of intuitive judgment* (pp. 49–81). New York: Cambridge University Press.

17. Smith, S. G., Kobayashi, L. C., Wolf, M. S., Raine, R., Wardle, J., & von Wagner, C. (2016). The associations between objective numeracy and colorectal cancer screening knowledge, attitudes and defensive processing in a deprived community sample. *Journal of Health Psychology*, *21*(8), 1665–1675.

18. Taber, C. S., & Lodge, M. (2006). Motivated skepticism in the evaluation of political beliefs. *American Journal of Political Science*, *50*(3), 755–769.

19. Knobloch-Westerwick, S., Mothes, C., & Polavin, N. (2017). Confirmation bias, ingroup bias, and negativity bias in selective exposure to political information. *Communication Research*. Retrieved from https://doi.org/10.1177/0093650217719596

20. Ashby, N. J. (2017). Numeracy predicts preference consistency: Deliberative search heuristics increase choice consistency for choices from description and experience. *Judgment and Decision Making*, *12*(2), 128–139.

21. Baumeister, R. F., & Leary, M. R. (1995). The need to belong: Desire for interpersonal attachments as a fundamental human motivation. *Psychological Bulletin*, *117*(3), 497.

22. Kahan, D. M., Peters, E., Wittlin, M., Slovic, P., Ouellette, L. L., Braman, D., & Mandel, G. (2012). The polarizing impact of science literacy and numeracy on perceived climate change risks. *Nature Climate Change, 2*(10), 732–735.

23. Drummond, C., & Fischhoff, B. (2017). Individuals with greater science literacy and education have more polarized beliefs on controversial science topics. *Proceedings of the National Academy of Sciences, 114*(36), 9587–9592.

24. Fazio, L. K., Brashier, N. M., Payne, B. K., & Marsh, E. J. (2015). Knowledge does not protect against illusory truth. *Journal of Experimental Psychology: General, 144*(5), 993–1002.

25. Kahan, D. M., Peters, E., Dawson, E. C., & Slovic, P. (2017). Motivated numeracy and enlightened self-government. *Behavioural Public Policy, 1*(1), 54–86.

26. Kahan, D. M., & Peters, E. (2017, August 26) Rumors of the "nonreplication" of the 'motivated numeracy effect' are greatly exaggerated. *Yale Law & Economics Research Paper No. 584.* Retrieved from https://ssrn.com/abstract=3026941

27. Van Boven, L., Ramos, J., Montal-Rosenberg, R., Kogut, T., Sherman, D. K., & Slovic, P. (2019). It depends: Partisan evaluation of conditional probability importance. *Cognition, 188*, 51–63. https://doi.org/10.1016/j.cognition.2019.01.020

28. Mata, A., Sherman, S. J., Ferreira, M. B., & Mendonça, C. (2015). Strategic numeracy: Self-serving reasoning about health statistics. *Basic and Applied Social Psychology, 37*(3), 165–173.

29. Oremus, W. (2012, November 7). The five stages of Fox News grief. Retrieved from http://www.slate.com/blogs/the_slatest/2012/11/07/karl_rove_on_fox_news_the_five_stages_of_conservative_grief.html

30. de Vries, M., Fagerlin, A., Witteman, H. O., & Scherer, L. D. (2013). Combining deliberation and intuition in patient decision support. *Patient Education and Counseling, 91*(2), 154–160.

31. Mérola, V., & Hitt, M. P. (2015). Numeracy and the persuasive effect of policy information and party cues. *Public Opinion Quarterly, 80*(2), 554–562.

32. Bullock, J. G., Gerber, A. S., Hill, S. J., & Huber, G. A. (2015). Partisan bias in factual beliefs about politics. *Quarterly Journal of Political Science, 10*, 519–578.

33. Khanna, K., & Sood, G. (2018). Motivated responding in studies of factual learning. *Political Behavior, 40*(1), 79–101.

34. Prior, M., Sood, G., & Khanna, K. (2015). You cannot be serious: The impact of accuracy incentives on partisan bias in reports of economic perceptions. *Quarterly Journal of Political Science, 10*, 489–518.

35. Kahan, D. (2016, March 2). Incentives and politically motivated reasoning: We can learn something but only if we don't fall into the "external validity trap." Retrieved from http://www.culturalcognition.net/blog/2016/3/2/incentives-and-politically-motivated-reasoning-we-can-learn.html

36. Dieckmann, N. F., Gregory, R., Peters, E., & Hartman, R. (2017). Seeing what you want to see: How imprecise uncertainty ranges enhance motivated reasoning. *Risk Analysis, 37*(3), 471–486.

37. Payne, J. W., Bettman, J. R., & Johnson, E. J. (1993). *The adaptive decision maker.* New York: Cambridge University Press.

38. Willingham, D. T. (2009). *Why don't students like school.* San Francisco, CA: Jossey-Bass.

OBJECTIVE NUMERACY, LIFE OUTCOMES, AND RESEARCH ISSUES AND OPPORTUNITIES

9

Numeracy's Secret Connection with Life Outcomes

Why should we care if people don't always understand or use numbers well? After all, their physician, financial advisor, friend, or family member can straighten them out. Our lives are intertwined with other helpful people, and many decisions are made for us. Physicians, for example, usually treat our diseases with standard methods, and everybody contributes to Social Security for their retirement. However, leeway exists for better behaviors and for errors, both big and small. Because some of these behaviors and errors involve numerical data, being numerate may confer opportunities while being innumerate exacts costs. In particular, persistent lower comprehension and poorer decisions by the less numerate may accumulate over time and, ultimately, act as a risk factor that reduces the quality of their life outcomes relative to the highly numerate.

In this chapter, I review available evidence for numeracy's relations with outcomes in health, employment, and personal finances. Most studies have focused on health, so we begin there. One note: health researchers often use subjective numeracy measures as proxies for objective numeracy as if they were identical. The measures, of course, are related; but, as you will see in Chapter 14, subjective numeracy relates differently to decision-making processes and outcomes than does objective numeracy. Nonetheless, the current state of the literature often does not discriminate their effects on health behaviors and outcomes. Thus, I treat them as interchangeable in this chapter.

Health Behaviors and Outcomes

So why should math grades from long ago matter to how healthy I am today? The grades, of course, do not matter, but staying or getting healthy involves frequent use of basic math skills such as arithmetic and probabilistic understanding. You have to schedule appointments, get to them on time, use medications appropriately (including their timing and dosage), estimate how

Innumeracy in the Wild. Ellen Peters, Oxford University Press (2020). © Oxford University Press 2020.
DOI: 10.1093/oso/9780190861094.003.0001

often you've experienced headaches or other symptoms, count or estimate calories consumed or burned through exercise, and understand and react to the probabilistic nature of diseases and treatments. Making good use of health insurance, too, requires understanding its heavily numeric premiums, deductibles, and copayments.

Numeracy skills, in fact, have become increasingly relevant as the amount of quantitative data available to patients has increased with greater access to the internet and electronic records and growing expectations for patients and physicians to share in medical decision making.[1,2] Information access and shared decision making are related to patients taking more control of their health and medical decisions.[3,4] Better outcomes should emerge, but only, of course, if patients can understand and use available information.

Consistent with the idea of a numeracy-empowered patient, psychologist Rocio Garcia-Retamero and her colleagues[5] related patient numeracy scores to clinical outcomes in their medical records. They found that patients lower in objective numeracy took 20% more prescription medications than the highly numerate and were 40% more likely to have at least one chronic disease. Their patients' subjective numeracy scores were unrelated to these objective clinical outcomes (greater subjective numeracy was associated with more positive perceptions of physical and mental health). Their objective numeracy results held after controlling for education, other demographics, risky habits, body mass index (BMI), trust in physicians, and satisfaction with role in decision making, some of which we could reasonably assume were related to and even causal of numeracy (e.g., education). Similarly in other studies, less numerate hospital patients had a greater number of comorbidities[6] and less numerate high school students reported worse health (e.g., how many times have you been sick in bed over the past year; doctor visits in past 6 months) controlling for socioeconomic status.[7]

In the remainder of this section, you will see that numeracy further relates to behaviors and outcomes in specific diseases. (Here, we consider cancer and diabetes but see the Appendix for other diseases). You will see that numeracy's health effects appear due, at least in part, to issues of health-related incomprehension and poorer decisions among the less numerate. Numeracy, however, also relates to systemic issues, like having health insurance, which may explain some numeracy-related health differences. Finally, we will briefly look at what little is known about the possible impacts of physician numeracy on patients.

Cancer

In addressing cancer, as in other decisions, highly numerate patients are more sensitive to treatment statistics whereas the less numerate appear to respond more heuristically to fears about cancer or medication side effects.[8,9] For example, more numerate patients preferred hypothetical cancer treatments that maximized numeric survival rates more than the less numerate did.[10] Consistent with this preference, highly numerate women reported being more willing than the less numerate to take a chemopreventive drug if they were found to be at high breast cancer risk.[11]

Cancer screening behaviors relate inconsistently with numeracy, perhaps because cancer-screening costs (e.g., false positives) can outweigh its benefits.[12] For example, physicians Philip Ciampa and Russell Rothman found that older adults (age 50 years and older with no history of cancer) who were higher in objective numeracy or subjective numeracy were more likely to get colorectal cancer screening compared to those lower in either numeracy.[13] Similarly, more numerate patients provided numeric information were more likely to intend to be screened for colorectal cancer,[14,15] but numeracy did not predict actual uptake.[14] Other researchers also have not found relations between numeracy and screening for colorectal, breast, or cervical cancers.[16,17]

Only one known study has examined associations of numeracy with smoking, a major cause of cancer. In this study of current and former smokers, for every 1-point increase in numeracy, the odds of quitting increased by about 24%.[18] Such results could be due to less numerate smokers knowing less about smoking's health risks so that they have less motivation to quit.[19] Improvements to warning labels on cigarette packages and other evidence-based communication efforts, however, makes deeper risk knowledge more accessible.[20,21]

Diabetes

Numeracy relates relatively consistently to managing diabetes, a highly numeric disease for which patients must estimate portion sizes, calculate carbohydrate intake, extract data from food labels, interpret blood sugar readings and other clinical data, and adjust and administer medications. Less numerate patients make considerable mistakes, and even the highly numerate are not immune to important comprehension errors. For example, in one study, only 77% of individuals higher in numeracy and health literacy could correctly identify that a blood glucose result was abnormally high or low.[22] Even worse, only 38% of those lower in numeracy and literacy could do so although many diabetics must understand and act on such results multiple times per day to manage their disease effectively. We estimated that only about 9% of US adults could do all the numeric tasks posed by diabetes.[23]

Most importantly, greater numeracy has been linked with better diabetic health among adults, including achieving lower hemoglobin A1c (HbA1c), which measures blood glucose control.[24,25] Furthermore, diabetic children with more numerate parents had lower HbA1c levels than diabetic children with less numerate parents.[26] One study failed to find this numeracy–HbA1c-level association, but its results may have been limited by a numeracy measure that did not distinguish well between more and less numerate patients.[27]

Consistent with them having better control of their diabetes, greater numeracy also has been associated with lower BMI, better portion-size estimation skills, and superior comprehension of growth charts and nutrition labels.[28-31] In addition, some researchers have suggested that numeracy's positive role in diabetic health may be due to higher numeracy being associated with greater confidence in performing diabetes self-care.[27,32]

Numeracy and Other Disease-Management Issues

Numeracy relates to a variety of other disease-management issues that the interested reader can find in the Appendix. For example, heart disease is the leading cause of death for both men and women. Getting hospital care quickly can be critical to decreasing its risks of death and disability. More numerate patients, however, were about four times more likely than the less numerate to seek medical attention within the critical first hour after coronary symptom onset (e.g., chest pain or tightness, perhaps because they better understood the probabilistic connection between the symptom and disease).[33] Thus, across diseases, worse health outcomes among the less numerate may be due at least in part to their lower numeric comprehension and worse decisions.

Systemic Differences

Some numeracy-related health differences, however, could be due to systemic issues that disadvantage the less numerate. For example, the less numerate were less likely to have health insurance (e.g., supplemental Medicare coverage[34]; Medicare Part D's prescription drug coverage;[35,36] and long-term care insurance[37]), which can pay for medications and other necessary healthcare.

Furthermore, less numerate patients were less likely to have access to the internet (and therefore were less able to access information that plays a role in patients taking more active care of their health).[38]

Overall, compared to more numerate patients, the less numerate suffer from more diseases, take more prescription medications, may make worse choices about cancer treatments (and certainly make less informed choices), and have less control over active disease like diabetes. They also are less likely to have the advantages that accrue from access to health information and health insurance.

Physician Innumeracy

You might recall from Chapter 1 that physicians also differ in objective numeracy: Some are better with numbers, others are worse. These differences might not be of interest if they didn't have measurable patient impact. However, researchers have noted at least two physician-numeracy impacts. First, surgeons with lower objective numeracy were less likely to involve patients in decisions about their health compared to more numerate surgeons.[39] In addition, physicians who perceived their numeric ability to be higher (they were more subjectively numerate) were more likely to report communicating or intending to communicate numeric health information than those who were less subjectively numerate.[40,41] These differences are potentially problematic because more shared decision making and provision of numbers such as the likelihoods of medication side effects may benefit individuals higher and lower in numeracy.[2,42]

A matching of patient and physician numeracy may produce the best outcomes for patients. Just as less numerate physicians prefer not to share decision making with their patients, less subjectively numerate patients also tend to desire less shared decision making compared to those who perceive themselves as better with numbers.[43–45]

However, physician numeracy is generally higher than patient numeracy, and patient perceptions of their shared health decision making appear to reflect this average difference. For example, less numerate US patients reported that they would prefer to be more passive about medical decisions than they currently are, as if more numerate physicians are sharing too much decision making with them.[46] In this same study, highly numerate patients were generally satisfied with their level of involvement in their healthcare. Similarly, the less subjectively numerate (compared to those who were more subjectively numerate) reported more negative interactions with their health providers[47,48] including reporting that their provider was less likely to ensure that they understood information.[13]

Overall, more and less numerate physicians exist, but physicians are generally more numerate than their patients. Both differences have potential patient impact, but we need more studies. Studies are needed, in particular, to understand how physician do and should identify patient numeracy and how they do and should adjust their subsequent communications with patients.

Numeracy in the Workplace

In some ways, numeracy relates more obviously to aspects of the job market than it does to health. In a speech at the National Academies of Science, former President Barack Obama commented that, "Reaffirming and strengthening America's role as the world's engine of scientific discovery and technological innovation is essential to meeting the challenges of this century. That's why I am committed to making the improvement of STEM education over the next decade a national priority."[49] Education in science, technology, engineering, and mathematics (STEM) is considered critical to better jobs, workforce development and innovation, an improved economy, and global leadership. Science and engineering jobs, in particular, are thought to benefit from greater numeracy (mathematics, the M in STEM). Think about the movie, *Hidden Figures*, for example, and the critical roles played by black female mathematicians who worked as human computers at the National Aeronautics and Space Administration (NASA) during the US–Russia race to space.

However, numeracy skills are required for many jobs. According to the Organisation for Economic Cooperation and Development (OECD),[50] the use of numeracy skills was reported, not only in engineering and science, but also across a wide range of occupations (plant and machine operators, service and sales workers, clerical support, technicians, and managers) and industries (construction, agriculture, manufacturing, real estate, financial). Work skills that require numeracy include calculating prices, costs, and budgets; the use of fractions, decimals, and percentages; using calculators; preparing graphs and tables; using algebra or formulas; and using advanced math or statistics (calculus, trigonometry, regressions). Relative to other OECD countries, US and Canadian participants reported using numeracy skills most frequently. Men also reported using numeracy skills at work more often than women, and indefinite workers reported using more numeracy skills than temporary workers.[50] Of interest, one study demonstrated that overestimating math ability, rather than the extent of math ability, was related to gender differences in interest in pursuing math careers.[51] Men overestimated more than women, and their overestimates accounted for their greater intent to pursue math fields.

Overall, numeracy likely affects employment in a number of ways, but little research exists. Studies have linked greater numeracy (independent of education and literacy) to higher income levels and to being employed.[52,53] For example, getting an incorrect response on a probability question was associated with a 6.1% point increase in the probability of being unemployed for 12 months or longer, controlling for age, gender, years of education, and household wealth.[54] On the job, more numerate loan officers were more accurate than less numerate officers in assessing their borrowers' credit risk.[55] Thus, numeracy skills appear important to the workplace, but research is limited in terms of the extent of its importance, reasons why it matters when it does (e.g., unemployment), and whether other skills may compensate.

Financial Behaviors and Outcomes

Objective numeracy is perhaps most obviously related to doing better financially due to the inherently quantitative nature of personal finances. As you read this section, think about whether your numeracy might help or interfere with your finances and how you could do better.

Savings and Wealth

Indeed, numeracy strongly predicts a set of financial behaviors, as well as overall wealth, over and above general intelligence.

- Individuals with greater numeracy are more likely to invest in stocks and plan for retirement.[56–61]
- The less numerate were more likely to have saved no money for retirement, controlling for demographics and non-numeric intelligence.[62]
- More numerate individuals ultimately are wealthier, perhaps due to numeracy's relations with better financial behaviors, lower unemployment, and better health.[59] In one English sample aged older than 50 years, highly numerate people had accrued more wealth after controlling for education and cognitive abilities such as literacy, memory, and executive function.[57] These numeracy effects were not small: "Amongst 50- to

59-year-old men, those with the highest numerical ability are nearly 2.5 times more likely to be found in the highest wealth quintile than in the lowest, while those with the worst numerical ability are over 6 times more likely to be found in the lowest wealth quintile than in the highest" (p. 154).[57]

Other Financial Behaviors

Poorer financial decisions by the less numerate likely underlie these overall savings and wealth differences.

- For example, less numerate older adults in England were less likely than the more numerate to shop around for an annuity to get the best long-term deal.[63]
- In the United States, less numerate adults were more likely to report having a predatory loan, being denied credit for a loan, making a late payment on a loan in the past year, and not having paid credit cards in full, after controlling for other variables such as non-numeric intelligence and education.[62]
- The less numerate were also more likely to default on mortgage loans after controlling for demographics and other intelligence measures[64] and to overdraw their bank account.[54]
- Although lower numeracy was related to greater difficulty in understanding credit card debt,[65] some studies found no relation of numeracy to overindebtedness.[66,67] However, these analyses controlled for variables that likely shared significance variance with numeracy (e.g., debt literacy test scores, nonproductive use of loan, total assets), which may explain why numeracy itself did not emerge as a significant predictor.

Adult Aging and Financial Exploitation

Finally, older adults tend to be less numerate than younger adults.[68] As a result, they may be at higher risk for being financially exploited because they may be tricked by numbers more easily than younger adults. In fact, lower numeracy among older adults was associated with more reports of theft and scams, financial victimization, and other signs of possible financial exploitation.[69] Older adult innumeracy is an important problem.[68]

I suspect that many numeracy-related findings in personal finances are due to a combination of factors, including the less numerate making more numeric errors and failing to appreciate past trends in the growth of riskier investments and the benefits of cumulative growth as compared to the highly numerate. These findings do not appear due to general intelligence as most of these personal finances studies controlled for various non-numeric intelligence measures. However, researchers have not examined subjective numeracy effects in this literature, and subjective numeracy effects may be important in combination with objective numeracy. You will see some initial results in Chapter 14.

There Is Nothing Funny About Innumeracy

People find it embarrassing to be illiterate (less able to read) and will go to great lengths to hide it. But they often do not mind being innumerate and even find it joke-worthy. In a speech at the National Science Foundation, Michelle Obama, former First Lady of the United States, said "I know for me, I'm a lawyer because I was bad at [science and math]. (Laughter.) All lawyers in the room, you know it's true. We can't add and subtract, so we argue. (Laughter)."[70] The problem is that if you avoid math in your life, you may end up less healthy and less wealthy.

Innumeracy is no laughing matter. Although people will say "I'm not a math person" as casually as "I hate broccoli," math ability appears to play a critical role in people's lives. Hopefully, by now, you have begun to appreciate the importance of being numerate and the potential of becoming more numerate.

Let's Pause Before Moving Forward

So far, we have learned that innumeracy in the wild means that people don't understand critical numeric information in their daily lives and they make poorer judgments and decisions as a result. This incomprehension and poorer decision making then appear to act as risk factors that ultimately exact substantial costs on their health, employment, and wealth. Thus, in a sense, our math skills crawl out of the classroom and intrude on our daily lives. I hope that, as you read this book, you learn skills for yourself and your family that help you avoid numeric mistakes and take advantage of numeric opportunities around you.

This analysis, of course, assumes that numeracy causes these outcomes, but the data presented thus far have been correlational. A more correct interpretation of the data presented is that greater numeracy "relates to" better-quality decision making and better outcomes in health, the workplace, and finances. The obvious question is why? Does greater numeracy cause people to make better decisions that lead them to be healthier, labor more successfully, and achieve greater wealth? Or does being healthier and having greater wealth allow people to become more numerate, the reverse path of what we have discussed? Alternatively, maybe numeracy does not matter, but smarter people, who also happen to be more numerate, make better-quality decisions and enjoy better life outcomes. In Chapter 10, we discuss these and other issues.

References

1. Schroy, P. C., Emmons, K. M., Peters, E., Glick, J. T., Robinson, P. A., Lydotes, M. A., . . . Heeren, T. C. (2012). Aid-assisted decision making and colorectal cancer screening: A randomized controlled trial. *American Journal of Preventive Medicine, 43*(6), 573–583.
2. Elwyn, G., Frosch, D., Thomson, R., Joseph-Williams, N., Lloyd, A., Kinnersley, P., . . . Edwards, A. (2012). Shared decision making: A model for clinical practice. *Journal of General Internal Medicine, 27*(10), 1361–1367.
3. Epstein, R. M., & Street, R. L. (2011). The values and value of patient-centered care. *The Annals of Family Medicine, 9*(2), 100–103.
4. Tang, P. C., Ash, J. S., Bates, D. W., Overhage, J. M., & Sands, D. Z. (2006). Personal health records: Definitions, benefits, and strategies for overcoming barriers to adoption. *Journal of the American Medical Informatics Association, 13*(2), 121–126.
5. Garcia-Retamero, R., Andrade, A., Sharit, J., & Ruiz, J. G. (2015). Is patients' numeracy related to physical and mental health? *Medical Decision Making, 35*(4), 501–511.
6. Tisminetzky, M., Gurwitz, J., McManus, D. D., Saczynski, J. S., Erskine, N., Waring, M. E., . . . Goldberg, R. (2016). Multiple chronic conditions and psychosocial limitations in patients hospitalized with an acute coronary syndrome. *American Journal of Medicine, 129*(6), 608–614.
7. Lubinski, D., & Humphreys, L. G. (1992). Some bodily and medical correlates of mathematical giftedness and commensurate levels of socioeconomic status. *Intelligence, 16*(1), 99–115.
8. Lipkus, I. M., Peters, E., Kimmick, G., Liotcheva, V., & Marcom, P. (2010). Breast cancer patients' treatment expectations after exposure to the decision aid program adjuvant online: The influence of numeracy. *Medical Decision Making, 30*(4), 464–473.
9. Lopez-Perez, B., Barnes, A., Frosch, D. L., & Hanoch, Y. (2017). Predicting prostate cancer treatment choices: The role of numeracy, time discounting, and risk attitudes. *Journal of Health Psychology, 22*(6), 788–797.
10. Wong, Y. N., Egleston, B. L., Sachdeva, K., Eghan, N., Pirollo, M., Stump, T. K., . . . Meropol, N. J. (2013). Cancer patients' trade-offs among efficacy, toxicity, and out-of-pocket cost in the curative and noncurative setting. *Medical Care, 51*(9), 838–845.

11. Kaplan, C. P., Kim, S. E., Wong, S. T., Sawaya, G. F., Walsh, J. M. E., & Perez-Stable, E. J. (2012). Willingness to use tamoxifen to prevent breast cancer among diverse women. *Breast Cancer Research and Treatment, 133*(1), 357–366.

12. Welch, H. G., Schwartz, L., & Woloshin, S. (2011). *Overdiagnosed: Making people sick in the pursuit of health.* Boston: Beacon Press.

13. Ciampa, P. J., Osborn, C. Y., Peterson, N. B., & Rothman, R. L. (2010). Patient numeracy, perceptions of provider communication, and colorectal cancer screening utilization. *Journal of Health Communication, 15*(suppl 3), 157–168.

14. Schwartz, P. H., Perkins, S. M., Schmidt, K. K., Muriello, P. F., Althouse, S., & Rawl, S. M. (2017). Providing quantitative information and a nudge to undergo stool testing in a colorectal cancer screening decision aid: A randomized clinical trial. *Medical Decision Making, 37*(6), 688–702.

15. Smith, S. G., Kobayashi, L. C., Wolf, M. S., Raine, R., Wardle, J., & von Wagner, C. (2016). The associations between objective numeracy and colorectal cancer screening knowledge, attitudes and defensive processing in a deprived community sample. *Journal of Health Psychology, 21*(8), 1665–1675.

16. Aggarwal, A., Speckman, J. L., Paasche-Orlow, M. K., Roloff, K. S., & Battaglia, T. A. (2007). The role of numeracy on cancer screening among urban women. *American Journal of Health Behavior, 31*(1), S57–S68.

17. Schapira, M. M., Neuner, J., Fletcher, K. E., Gilligan, M. A., Hayes, E., & Laud, P. (2011). The relationship of health numeracy to cancer screening. *Journal of Cancer Education, 26*(1), 103–110.

18. Martin, L. T., Haas, A., Schonlau, M., Derose, K. P., Rosenfeld, L., Rudd, R., & Buka, S. L. (2012). Which literacy skills are associated with smoking?. *Journal of Epidemiology and Community Health, 66*(2), 189–192.

19. Lillard, D. R. (2017). Educational heterogeneity in the association between smoking cessation and health information. In K. Bolin, B. Lindgren, M. Grossman, D. Gyrd-Hansen, T. Iversen, R. Kaestner, & J. Sindelar (Eds.), *Human capital and health behavior.* Bingley, UK: Emerald Group Publishing.

20. Evans, A. T., Peters, E., Strasser, A. A., Emery, L. F., Sheerin, K. M., & Romer, D. (2015). Graphic warning labels elicit affective and thoughtful responses from smokers: Results of a randomized clinical trial. *PloS One, 10*(12), e0142879.

21. Peters, E., Shoots-Reinhard, B., Evans, A. T., Shoben, A., Klein, E., Tompkins, M. K., . . . Tusler, M. (2018). Pictorial warning labels and memory for cigarette health-risk information over time. *Annals of Behavioral Medicine, 53*(4), 358–371.

22. Zikmund-Fisher, B. J., Exe, N. L., & Witteman, H. O. (2014). Numeracy and literacy independently predict patients' ability to identify out-of-range test results. *Journal of Medical Internet Research, 16*(8), e187.

23. Peters, E., Meilleur, L., & Tompkins, M. K. (2014). Numeracy and the Affordable Care Act: Opportunities and challenges. Appendix A. IOM (Institute of Medicine). In *Health Literacy and Numeracy: Workshop Summary* (pp. 91–132). Washington, DC: The National Academies Press.

24. Cavanaugh, K., Huizinga, M. M., Wallston, K. A., Gebretsadik, T., Shintani, A., Davis, D., . . . Rothman, R. L. (2008). Association of numeracy and diabetes control. *Annals of Internal Medicine, 148*(10), 737–746.

25. Marden, S., Thomas, P. W., Sheppard, Z. A., Knott, J., Lueddeke, J., & Kerr, D. (2012). Poor numeracy skills are associated with glycaemic control in type 1 diabetes. *Diabetic Medicine, 29*(5), 662–669.

26. Hassan, K., & Heptulla, R. A. (2010). Glycemic control in pediatric type 1 diabetes: Role of caregiver literacy. *Pediatrics, 125*(5), E1104–E1108.

27. White, R. O., Osborn, C. Y., Gebretsadik, T., Kripalani, S., & Rothman, R. L. (2011). Development and validation of a Spanish diabetes-specific numeracy measure: Dnt-15 Latino. *Diabetes Technology & Therapeutics, 13*(9), 893–898.

28. Huizinga, M. M., Carlisle, A. J., Cavanaugh, K. L., Davis, D. L., Gregory, R. P., Schlundt, D. G., & Rothman, R. L (2009). Literacy, numeracy, and portion-size estimation skills. *American Journal of Preventive Medicine, 36*(4), 324–328.

29. Dallacker, M., Hertwig, R., Peters, E., & Mata, J. (2016). Lower parental numeracy is associated with children being under- and overweight. *Social Science & Medicine, 161*(), 126–133.

30. Rothman, R. L., Housam, R., Weiss, H., Davis, D., Gregory, R., Gebretsadik, T., . . . Elasy, T. A. (2006). Patient understanding of food labels: The role of literacy and numeracy. *American Journal of Preventive Medicine, 31*(5), 391–398.

31. Huizinga, M. M., Elasy, T. A., Wallston, K. A., Cavanaugh, K., Davis, D., Gregory, R. P., . . . Rothman, R. L. (2008). Development and validation of the Diabetes Numeracy Test (DNT). *BMC Health Services Research, 8* (96). https://bmchealthservres.biomedcentral.com/articles/10.1186/1472-6963-8-96

32. Osborn, C. Y., Cavanaugh, K., Wallston, K. A., & Rothman, R. L. (2010). Self-efficacy links health literacy and numeracy to glycemic control. *Journal of Health Communication, 15*(s2), 146–158.

33. Petrova, D., Garcia-Retamero, R., Catena, A., Cokely, E., Heredia Carrasco, A., Arrebola Moreno, A., & Ramirez Hernandez, J. A. (2017). Numeracy predicts risk of pre-hospital decision delay: A retrospective study of acute coronary syndrome survival. *Annals of Behavioral Medicine, 51*(2), 292–306.

34. Chan, S., & Elbel, B. (2012). Low cognitive ability and poor skill with numbers may prevent many from enrolling in Medicare supplemental coverage. *Health Affairs, 31*(8), 1847–1854.

35. Kuye, I. O., Frank, R. G., & McWilliams, J. M. (2013). Cognition and take-up of subsidized drug benefits by Medicare beneficiaries. *JAMA Internal Medicine, 173*(12), 1100–1107.

36. Szrek, H., & Bundorf, M. K (2011). Age and the purchase of prescription drug insurance by older adults. *Psychology and Aging, 26*(2), 308–320.

37. McGarry, B. E., Temkin-Greener, H., Chapman, B. P., & Grabowski, D. C., & Li, Y. (2016). The impact of consumer numeracy on the purchase of long-term care insurance. *Health Services Research, 51*(4), 1612–1631.

38. Jensen, J. D., King, A. J., Davis, L. A., & Guntzviller, L. M. (2010). Utilization of internet technology by low-income adults: The role of health literacy, health numeracy, and computer assistance. *Journal of Aging and Health, 22*(6), 804–826.

39. Garcia-Retamero, R., Wicki, B., Cokely, E. T., & Hanson, B. (2014). Factors predicting surgeons' preferred and actual roles in interactions with their patients. *Health Psychology, 33*(8), 920–928.

40. Anderson, B. L., Obrecht, N. A., Chapman, G. B., Driscoll, D. A., & Schulkin, J. (2011). Physicians' communication of Down syndrome screening test results: The influence of physician numeracy. *Genetics in Medicine, 13*(8), 744–749.

41. Han, P. K. J., Dieckmann, N. F., Holt, C., Gutheil, C., & Peters, E. (2016). Factors affecting physicians' intentions to communicate personalized prognostic information to cancer patients at the end of life: An experimental vignette study. *Medical Decision Making, 36*(6), 703–713.

42. Peters, E., Hart, P. S., Tusler, M., & Fraenkel, L. (2014). Numbers matter to informed patient choices: A randomized design across age and numeracy levels. *Medical Decision Making, 34*(4), 430–442.

43. Goggins, K. M., Wallston, K. A., Nwosu, S., Schildcrout, J. S., Castel, L., & Kripalani, S. (2014). Health literacy, numeracy, and other characteristics associated with hospitalized

patients' preferences for involvement in decision making. *Journal of Health Communication*, *19*(suppl 2), 29–43.

44. Hanoch, Y., Miron-Shatz, T., Rolison, J. J., Omer, Z., & Ozanne, E. (2015). Shared decision making in patients at risk of cancer: The role of domain and numeracy. *Health Expectations*, *18*(6), 2799–2810.

45. Kenealy, T., Goodyear-Smith, F., Wells, S., Arroll, B., Jackson, R., & Horsburgh, M. (2011). Patient preference for autonomy: Does it change as risk rises?. *Family Practice*, *28*(5), 541–544.

46. Galesic, M., & Garcia-Retamero, R. (2011). Do low-numeracy people avoid shared decision making? *Health Psychology*, *30*(3), 336–341.

47. Manganello, J. A., & Clayman, M. L. (2011). The association of understanding of medical statistics with health information seeking and health provider interaction in a national sample of young adults. *Journal of Health Communication*, *16*(suppl 3), 163–176.

48. Smith, S. G., Wolf, M. S., & Wagner, C. V. (2010). Socioeconomic status, statistical confidence, and patient–provider communication: An analysis of the Health Information National Trends Survey (HINTS 2007). *Journal of Health Communication*, *15*(suppl 3), 169–185.

49. Rayfield, J. (2009, November 23) Obama: "Scientific discovery and technological innovation' are 'essential to meeting the challenges of this century." Retrieved from https://talkingpointsmemo.com/news/obama-scientific-discovery-and-technological-innovation-are-essential-to-meeting-the-challenges-of-this-century

50. Desjardins, R., Thorn, W., Schleicher, A., Quintini, G., Pellizzari, M., Kis, V., & Chung, J. E. (2013). *OECD Skills Outlook 2013: First results from the survey of adult skills*. Paris: OECD.

51. Bench, S. W., Lench, H. C., Liew, J., Miner, K., & Flores, S. A. (2015). Gender gaps in overestimation of math performance. *Sex Roles*, *72*(11–12), 536–546.

52. Charette, M. F., & Meng, R. (1998). The determinants of literacy and numeracy, and the effect of literacy and numeracy on labour market outcomes. *Canadian Journal of Economics-Revue Canadienne D Economique*, *31*(3), 495–517.

53. Kelly, E., McGuinness, S., & O'Connell, P. J. (2012). Transitions to long-term unemployment risk among young people: Evidence from Ireland. *Journal of Youth Studies*, *15*(6), 780–801.

54. Dohmen, T., Falk, A., Huffman, D., Marklein, F., & Sunde, U. (2009). Biased probability judgment: Evidence of incidence and relationship to economic outcomes from a representative sample. *Journal of Economic Behavior & Organization*, *72*(3), 903–915.

55. Brown, M., Kirschenmann, K., & Spycher, T. (2020). *Numeracy and on-the-job performance: Evidence from loan officers*. *Economic Inquiry*, *58*(2), 998–1022, https://doi.org/10.1111/ecin.12873.

56. Christelis, D., Jappelli, T., & Padula, M. (2010). Cognitive abilities and portfolio choice. *European Economic Review*, *54*(1), 18–38.

57. Banks, J., & Oldfield, Z. (2007). Understanding pensions: Cognitive function, numerical ability and retirement saving. *Fiscal Studies*, *28*(2), 143–170.

58. Almenberg, J., & Dreber, A. (2015). Gender, stock market participation and financial literacy. *Economics Letters*, *137*, 140–142.

59. Banks, J., O'Dea, C., & Oldfield, Z. (2011). Cognitive function, numeracy and retirement saving trajectories. *The Economic Journal*, *120*(548), F381–F410.

60. Estrada-Mejia, C., de Vries, M., & Zeelenberg, M. (2016). Numeracy and wealth. *Journal of Economic Psychology*, *54*, 53–63.

61. Smith, J. P., McArdle, J. J., & Willis, R. (2010). Financial decision making and cognition in a family context. *The Economic Journal*, *120*(548), F363–F380.

62. Sinayev, A., & Peters, E. (2015). Cognitive reflection vs. calculation in decision making. *Frontiers in Psychology*, *6*, 532.

63. Banks, J., Crawford, R., & Tetlow, G. (2015). Annuity choices and income drawdown: Evidence from the decumulation phase of defined contribution pensions in England. *Journal of Pension Economics & Finance, 14*(4), 412–438.

64. Gerardi, K., Goette, L., & Meier, S. (2013). Numerical ability predicts mortgage default. *Proceedings of the National Academy of Sciences of the United States of America, 110*(28), 11267–11271.

65. Soll, J. B., Keeney, R. L., & Larrick, R. P. (2013). Consumer misunderstanding of credit card use, payments, and debt: Causes and solutions. *Journal of Public Policy & Marketing, 32*(1), 66–81.

66. French, D., & McKillop, D. (2016). Financial literacy and over-indebtedness in low-income households. *International Review of Financial Analysis, 48*, 1–11.

67. Schicks, J. (2014). Over-indebtedness in microfinance an empirical analysis of related factors on the borrower level. *World Development, 54*, 301–324.

68. Peters, E., Hess, T. M., Västfjäll, D., & Auman, C. (2007). Adult age differences in dual information processes: Implications for the role of affective and deliberative processes in older adults' decision making. *Perspectives on Psychological Science, 2*(1), 1–23.

69. Wood, S. A., Liu, P. J., Hanoch, Y., & Estevez-Cores, S. (2016). Importance of numeracy as a risk factor for elder financial exploitation in a community sample. *Journals of Gerontology Series B-Psychological Sciences and Social Sciences, 71*(6), 978–986.

70. Peters, G., & Wooley, J. T. (2011, September 26). Michelle Obama: Remarks by the First Lady at the National Science Foundation Family-Friendly Policy Rollout. The American Presidency Project. Retrieved from http://www.presidency.ucsb.edu/ws/?pid=120669

10

Issues and Opportunities in Objective Numeracy Research

We know by now that the more objectively numerate are better decision makers than the less numerate. They also have better life outcomes, especially in health and personal finances. That is not everything we need to know, however, about numeracy's impact on people's lives. For example, we learned in Chapter 8 that numeric accuracy is not the only goal that decision makers have (e.g., in evaluating the effects of gun control bans, a goal to belong or to maintain consistent beliefs may be more important), and we need to know more about when and why people prioritize accuracy goals over other goals.

In this chapter, I discuss three additional cross-cutting questions in objective numeracy research. The first two issues concern the correlational nature of most objective numeracy research and two alternative explanations for the effects of numeracy on decisions and life outcomes. The third issue concerns researchers' experimental design decisions and what results might teach us about how to improve numeric reasoning.

- Can intelligence explain what we have called *numeracy effects* such that smarter people understand more, make better decisions, and enjoy better outcomes?
- Might better health and more wealth produce greater numeracy instead?
- Experimenters sometimes make choices about what tasks to include in their studies for reasons of efficiency, power, or generalizability. Might these choices, however, differentially affect those higher than lower in objective numeracy? Can the differences teach us something about how to improve numeric reasoning?

It's Not General Intelligence; It's Numeric Intelligence

In presentations, I'm often asked whether numeracy's effects are simply due to some people being smarter than others. Several reasons point towards

Innumeracy in the Wild. Ellen Peters, Oxford University Press (2020). © Oxford University Press 2020.
DOI: 10.1093/oso/9780190861094.003.0001

numeric intelligence being special however. To begin, objective numeracy is a part of general intelligence, but it is also separable from other aspects of intelligence. For example, inferior-parietal lesions can destroy numerical knowledge without impairing non-numerical knowledge.[1] Retired bookkeepers and accountants showed similar numerical memory to young adults even though they demonstrated the expected age-related declines in non-numerical memory.[2] The lack of age-related decline in numeric memory seemed due to how much these bookkeepers and accountants valued numbers. In another study demonstrating the independence of different types of skills, 99% of non-expert participants had adequate literacy skills, but only 17% had better than ninth-grade numeracy skills.[3] These reported differences in adequate literacy versus adequate numeracy are common in patient populations.[4,5]

Numeracy's effects on decision tasks also tend to be independent of general intelligence. Results from studies in Chapters 2–8 demonstrate that objective numeracy retains independent predictive power in a wide variety of decision tasks including risk comprehension, framing effects, conjunction fallacies, risk comprehension, risky choices, and intertemporal preferences.[6–12] In fact, psychologists Keith Stanovich and Richard West have demonstrated that general intelligence (measured with self-reported SAT scores among college students) related weakly to performance in a wide variety of judgment and decision-making tasks,[13] including some tasks from this book that relate specifically to numeracy (e.g., conjunction fallacy, base-rate neglect, use of affect in judgments). In addition, tests in relatively homogenous populations (in terms of intelligence) such as college students nonetheless reveal numeracy effects.[8] Thus, it is not that people who are smarter—for example, with words and abstract reasoning—make better decisions. Instead, numeracy-related decision findings appear inextricably linked to numeric intelligence rather than to some other intelligence.

Similarly, health and financial behaviors and outcomes have been related to objective numeracy after controlling for non-numeric intelligence measures.[7,14,15] In many of these studies, researchers found numeracy effects independent of health literacy,[16] measures of memory and executive function,[17] and/or demographics.[18] One note: controlling for variables known to be associated with and even causal of numeracy (e.g., income, education)[19–21] will take away from some of the legitimate power of numeracy in predictions. Nonetheless, controlling for them can be beneficial because, for example, education and numeracy are not synonymous. However, a better approach is to control for non-numeric intelligences, such as working memory or abstract reasoning, that also develop with greater education. Although some studies support the possibility of greater general intelligence producing better health outcomes,[22] these researchers have not attempted to discriminate between different types of intelligence, such as numeric versus non-numeric intelligence, leaving their separate effects unknown. Finally, financial studies have examined objective numeracy effects after controlling for other forms of intelligence more consistently than health studies.

The Reverse Causal Path Is Sometimes Possible

Second, is it possible that greater health and wealth sometimes produce greater numeracy? Most numeracy research implicitly assumes that greater numeracy likely causes superior life outcomes. Correlational data, however, leave open the possibility of the reverse causal path, and some data are consistent with that possibility.

For example, researchers have demonstrated this potential reverse causal path with poorer health and with poverty. Middle schoolers who had been born preterm were less numerate than those who had been born full-term. This middle-school numeracy difference then explained the effect of having been a preterm baby on having less wealth in adulthood.[23] Similarly, being impoverished (in wealth or time) represents an overwhelming cognitive load that reduces non-numeric cognitive abilities.[24] It may reduce numeric intelligence as well, although researchers have not included numeracy tests.

Additionally, researchers have suggested that having a chronic disease, such as cognitive impairment, Parkinson's, epilepsy, and kidney disease may suppress numeric abilities[25-27] although not all diseases are associated with lower numeracy (e.g., multiple sclerosis[28]). Because their data are correlational, being less numerate could have contributed to development of these diseases (although this explanation seems unlikely), or a third variable (e.g., a genetic abnormality) could have caused both lower numeracy and the disease.

Being admitted to a hospital also reduces how well patients and consumers think.[29] Consider having to make key health decisions under time pressure, stress, acute sickness, or sleep deprivation. Reductions to thinking well likely will reduce thinking well with numbers, too. Thus, situations common to important health and financial decisions may result in reduced numeric ability at the moment of judgment or choice.

This reverse causal explanation, however, cannot explain all numeracy results. As we have discussed, robust numeracy effects exist in risk comprehension, decision making, and life outcomes after controlling for non-numeric intelligence measures such as health literacy, reading ability, memory, and reasoning. It is reasonable to assume that these other intelligence measures also should decline with poorer health if numeracy does. The reversal causal explanation also tends to be unreasonable when numeracy predicts protective behaviors such as exercise.[14,30] Nonetheless, reversal causal paths seem plausible in some circumstances (e.g., being born pre-term,[23] living in poverty[24]).

Ultimately, we need experiments in which researchers attempt to experimentally increase numeracy rather than measure it. I review early evidence in Chapter 18 for numeracy-training studies with children and adults, respectively, which demonstrate some of the hypothesized causal effects on decision processes and outcomes.

Experimenter Choices, Repeated Measures, and Other Order Effects

As experimenters, we sometimes make choices about what tasks to include in our studies to be more efficient, have more power to detect hypothesized effects, or show generalizability across different decision tasks. Less well considered, however, is whether these choices may have different impacts on those higher versus lower in objective numeracy. For example, in Chapter 7, we learned that the highly numerate tend to be more sensitive to differences in numeric levels than the less numerate. However, when responding to repeated almost identical tasks, in which only numeric information changes, less numerate people appear to recognize task similarity and look more like the highly numerate by becoming more responsive to differences in numeric levels in framing problems[31] and conjunction scenarios.[32]

Researchers instead might ask participants to respond to multiple different tasks. Such an approach can be efficient (we can test multiple hypotheses with the same people rather than having to test each hypothesis in a separate sample), and it might allow us to claim generalizability of numeracy effects across tasks. However, because the study of numeracy and decision making is relatively new, I believe we need to think carefully about possible interaction effects. Prior tasks, including what we think of as unrelated tasks, may change information processing and therefore performance on subsequent tasks, and those effects may differ by numeracy. For example:

- Increasing thinking can decrease the influence of integral (built-in) affect to outcomes (e.g., your feelings about nuclear power) on subsequent responses.[33–35] However, some people may think more about numeric information (and less about integral affect to outcomes) in response to such instructions whereas others, such as the less numerate, may think even more about the integral affect to outcomes instead if they have a strong desire to avoid numbers.

- Altering someone's incidental affect (how positive or negative they feel at the moment) changes risk perceptions,[36,37] but these experimental influences are stronger for the less numerate than the highly numerate when numeric information is also provided.[38] Experimenters need to think carefully about whether responding to an earlier task might alter incidental affect, which then would have subsequent different effects on the more and less numerate in later tasks. For example, having participants respond to an emotionally compelling narrative about a hazard may make them feel bad. Less numerate participants then may use this negative mood as information to inform risk perceptions in the next supposedly unrelated task, whereas the more numerate use provided task-relevant numeric information.
- Priming number processing (e.g., by answering some math problems) causes participants to use numeric information more in subsequent judgments.[39,40] Thus, for example, researchers may find that having participants respond first versus last to objective numeracy questions may result, respectively, in more and less use of numeric information. However, more numerate individuals will likely show greater effects than the less numerate.[41,42]
- Relatedly, if tasks all involve difficult statistical reasoning (e.g., conjunction and base-rate neglect tasks[32]), completing the first task may prime additional numeric reasoning such that errors reduce more among high-ability participants[39,43,44] than low-ability participants who do not have the necessary knowledge even when primed. In other words, responding to multiple numeric tasks may point highly numerate people toward "thinking more like a statistician" on subsequent tasks.

Although we know that responding to multiple numeric tasks can alter how decision makers respond to tasks later in the sequence, experimenters nonetheless interpret repeated-measures results as if they were based on single decisions. Neuroimaging studies are exemplars. They often rely on participants making hundreds of decisions, for example, about numeric magnitudes or about probabilistic gains and losses. Other examples exist, too. Sometimes, participants will make multiple choices among health insurance plans based on different formats of a website in an experiment. In reality, they would have gathered information from a single website and made one choice.

Can we use information from these experiments to generalize to one-shot decisions, given that information processing changes and may change differently for the more and less objectively numerate?

Other types of order effects may exist too. For example, decision makers normally choose immediately after information exposure, but, in experiments, they may answer a series of comprehension and other questions that require them to process numeric information repeatedly and then choose. How similar are the natural and experimental choices and the underlying psychological mechanisms for those higher and lower in objective numeracy? I think that information processing in these various scenarios may be too different to draw conclusions from one to the other, but future research will reveal whether I'm correct.

Thus, choices made by the experimenter can decrease numeracy differences in performance on simple decision tasks (e.g., framing studies[31]) and increase them in more difficult tasks (e.g., conjunction errors[7,45,46]). We also know that the highly numerate strategically use their numeric hammer, putting in more and less effort depending on its benefit to the decision maker. As a result, we should expect that the more and less numerate make different adjustments, including using different heuristics, when they provide multiple versus single responses.[47,48] These findings, in turn, point toward creative interventions to improve decision-making processes (e.g., when should we ask a consumer pointed questions that encourage more numeric processing and practice?). Research will uncover how numeracy-based information processing unfolds over time and will improve our theoretical understanding of numeracy and decision making.

Moving Backward to Move Forward

Next, we journey backward (in a sense) to discover how numeric abilities emerge and what barriers sometimes impede learning progress. You might recognize yourself or your child. Chapter 11 concerns the approximate number system (ANS). Its discussion is somewhat technical, and you should feel free to skip it. However, the ANS will surface again in Chapter 13, and I encourage you to return to this more technical section if you would like to understand it better. Chapter 12 concerns the genetic underpinnings of the numerical competencies we have discussed as well as the effects of formal education, including barriers to math learning in school.

References

1. Dehaene, S. (1997). *The number sense: How the mind creates mathematics*. New York: Oxford University Press.
2. Castel, A. D. (2007). Aging and memory for numerical information: The role of specificity and expertise in associative memory. *The Journals of Gerontology Series B: Psychological Sciences and Social Sciences, 62*(3), P194–P196.
3. Kumar, D., Sanders, L., Perrin, E. M., Lokker, N., Patterson, B., Gunn, V., . . . Rothman, R. L. (2010). Parental understanding of infant health information: Health literacy, numeracy, and the parental health literacy activities test (PHLAT). *Academic Pediatrics, 10*(5), 309–316.
4. Griffey, R. T., Melson, A. T., Lin, M. J., Carpenter, C. R., Goodman, M. S., & Kaphingst, K. A. (2014). Does numeracy correlate with measures of health literacy in the emergency department?. *Academic Emergency Medicine, 21*(2), 147–153.
5. Huizinga, M. M., Carlisle, A. J., Cavanaugh, K. L., Davis, D. L., Gregory, R. P., Schlundt, D. G., & Rothman, R. L (2009). Literacy, numeracy, and portion-size estimation skills. *American Journal of Preventive Medicine, 36*(4), 324–328.
6. Låg, T., Bauger, L., Lindberg, M., & Friborg, O. (2014). The role of numeracy and intelligence in health-risk estimation and medical data interpretation. *Journal of Behavioral Decision Making, 27*(2), 95–108.
7. Sinayev, A., & Peters, E. (2015). Cognitive reflection vs. calculation in decision making. *Frontiers in Psychology, 6*, 532.
8. Peters, E., Västfjäll, D., Slovic, P., Mertz, C. K., Mazzocco, K., & Dickert, S. (2006). Numeracy and decision making. *Psychological Science, 17*(5), 407–413.
9. Benjamin, D. J., Brown, S. A., & Shapiro, J. M. (2013). Who is 'behavioral'? Cognitive ability and anomalous preferences. *Journal of the European Economic Association, 11*(6), 1231–1255.
10. Cokely, E. T., Galesic, M., Schulz, E., Ghazal, S., & Garcia-Retamero, R. (2012). Measuring risk literacy: The Berlin Numeracy Test. *Judgment and Decision Making, 7*(1), 25–47.
11. Frederick, S. (2005). Cognitive reflection and decision making. *Journal of Economic Perspectives, 19*(4), 25–42.
12. Weller, J. A., Dieckmann, N. F., Tusler, M., Mertz, C. K., Burns, W. J., & Peters, E. (2013). Development and testing of an abbreviated numeracy scale: A Rasch analysis approach. *Journal of Behavioral Decision Making, 26*(2), 198–212.
13. Stanovich, K. E., & West, R. F. (2008). On the relative independence of thinking biases and cognitive ability. *Journal of Personality and Social Psychology, 94*(4), 672–695.
14. Dieckmann, N. F., Peters, E., Leon, J., Benavides, M., Baker, D. P., & Norris, A. (2015). The role of objective numeracy and fluid intelligence in sex-related protective behaviors. *Current HIV Research, 13*(5), 337–346.
15. Smith, J. P., McArdle, J. J., & Willis, R. (2010). Financial decision making and cognition in a family context. *Economic Journal, 120*(548), F363–F380.
16. Apter, A. J., Cheng, J., Small, D., Bennett, I. M., Albert, C., Fein, D. G., . . . Van Horne, S. (2006). Asthma numeracy skill and health literacy. *Journal of Asthma, 43*(9), 705–710.
17. Banks, J., & Oldfield, Z. (2007). Understanding pensions: Cognitive function, numerical ability and retirement saving. *Fiscal Studies, 28*(2), 143–170.
18. Dohmen, T., Falk, A., Huffman, D., Marklein, F., & Sunde, U. (2009). Biased probability judgment: Evidence of incidence and relationship to economic outcomes from a representative sample. *Journal of Economic Behavior & Organization, 72*(3), 903–915.

19. Baker, D. P., Eslinger, P. J., Benavides, M., Peters, E., Dieckmann, N. F., & Leon, J. (2015). The cognitive impact of the education revolution: A possible cause of the Flynn Effect on population IQ. *Intelligence, 49*, 144–158.

20. French, D., & McKillop, D. (2016). Financial literacy and over-indebtedness in low-income households. *International Review of Financial Analysis, 48*, 1–11.

21. Schicks, J. (2014). Over-indebtedness in microfinance an empirical analysis of related factors on the borrower level. *World Development, 54*, 301–324.

22. Calvin, C. M., Batty, G. D., Der, G., Brett, C. E., Taylor, A., Pattie, A., . . . Deary, I. J. (2017). Childhood intelligence in relation to major causes of death in 68 year follow-up: Prospective population study. *BMJ, 357*, j2708.

23. Basten, M., Jaekel, J., Johnson, S., Gilmore, C., & Wolke, D. (2015). Preterm birth and adult wealth: Mathematics skills count. *Psychological Science, 26*(10), 1608–1619.

24. Mani, A., Mullainathan, S., Shafir, E., & Zhao, J. (2013). Poverty impedes cognitive function. *Science, 341*(6149), 976–980.

25. Delazer, M., Kemmler, G., & Benke, T. (2013). Health numeracy and cognitive decline in advanced age. *Aging Neuropsychology and Cognition, 20*(6), 639–659.

26. Choi, H., Wong, J. B., Mendiratta, A., Heiman, G. A., & Hamberger, M. J. (2011). Numeracy and framing bias in epilepsy. *Epilepsy & Behavior, 20*(1), 29–33.

27. Abdel-Kader, K., Dew, M. A., Bhatnagar, M., Argyropoulos, C., Karpov, I., Switzer, G., & Unruh, M. L. (2010). Numeracy skills in CKD: Correlates and outcomes. *Clinical Journal of The American Society of Nephrology, 5*(9), 1566–1573.

28. Gaissmaier, W., Giese, H., Galesic, M., Garcia-Retamero, R., Kasper, J., Kleiter, I., . . . Heesen, C. (2017). Numeracy of multiple sclerosis patients: A comparison of patients from the PERCEPT study to a German probabilistic sample. *Patient Education and Counseling, 101*(1), 74–78.

29. Ginde, A. A., Clark, S., Goldstein, J. N., & Camargo, C. A. (2008). Demographic disparities in numeracy among emergency department patients: Evidence from two multicenter studies. *Patient Education and Counseling, 72*(2), 350–356.

30. Maher, C., Lewis, L., Katzmarzyk, P. T., Dumuid, D., Cassidy, L., & Olds, T. (2016). The associations between physical activity, sedentary behaviour and academic performance. *Journal of Science and Medicine in Sport, 19*(12), 1004–1009.

31. Gamliel, E., & Kreiner, H. (2017). Outcome proportions, numeracy, and attribute-framing bias. *Australian Journal of Psychology, 69*(4), 283–292.

32. Klaczynski, P. A. (2014). Heuristics and biases: Interactions among numeracy, ability, and reflectiveness predict normative responding. *Frontiers in Psychology, 5*, 665–677.

33. Finucane, M. L., Alhakami, A., Slovic, P., & Johnson, S. M. (2000). The affect heuristic in judgments of risks and benefits. *Journal of Behavioral Decision Making, 13*, 1–17.

34. Keysar, B., Hayakawa, S. L., & An, S. G. (2012). The foreign-language effect: Thinking in a foreign tongue reduces decision biases. *Psychological Science, 23*(6), 661–668.

35. Small, D. A., Loewenstein, G., & Slovic, P. (2007). Sympathy and callousness: The impact of deliberative thought on donations to identifiable and statistical victims. *Organizational Behavior and Human Decision Processes, 102*(2), 143–153.

36. Johnson, E. J., & Tversky, A. (1983). Affect, generalization, and the perception of risk. *Journal of Personality and Social Psychology, 45*(1), 20–31.

37. Lerner, J. S., & Keltner, D. (2001). Fear, anger, and risk. *Journal of Personality and Social Psychology, 81*(1), 146–159.

38. Traczyk, J., & Fulawka, K. (2016). Numeracy moderates the influence of task-irrelevant affect on probability weighting. *Cognition, 151*, 37–41.

39. Hoover, J. D., & Healy, A. F. (2017). Algebraic reasoning and bat-and-ball problem variants: Solving isomorphic algebra first facilitates problem solving later. *Psychonomic Bulletin & Review, 24*(6), 1922–1928.

40. Hsee, C. K., & Rottenstreich, Y. (2004). Music, pandas, and muggers: On the affective psychology of value. *Journal of Experimental Psychology: General, 133*(1), 23–30.

41. Bless, H., Betsch, T., & Franzen, A. (1998). Framing the framing effect: The impact of context cues on solutions to the 'Asian disease' problem. *European Journal of Social Psychology, 28*, 287–291.

42. Riege, A. H., & Teigen, K. H. (2013). Additivity neglect in probability estimates: Effects of numeracy and response format. *Organizational Behavior and Human Decision Processes, 121*(1), 41–52.

43. LeBoeuf, R. A., & Shafir, E. (2003). Deep thoughts and shallow frames: On the susceptibility to framing effects. *Journal of Behavioral Decision Making, 16*(2), 77–92.

44. Stanovich, K. E., & West, R. F. (1998). Individual differences in rational thought. *Journal of Experimental Psychology: General, 127*(2), 161.

45. Scherer, L. D., Yates, J. F., Baker, S. G., & Valentine, K. D. (2017). The influence of effortful thought and cognitive proficiencies on the conjunction fallacy: Implications for dual-process theories of reasoning and judgment. *Personality and Social Psychology Bulletin, 43*(6), 874–887.

46. Toplak, M. E., West, R. F., & Stanovich, K. E. (2011). The Cognitive Reflection Test as a predictor of performance on heuristics-and-biases tasks. *Memory & Cognition, 39*(7), 1275.

47. Peters, E., & Levin, I. P. (2008). Dissecting the risky-choice framing effect: Numeracy as an individual-difference factor in weighting risky and riskless options. *Judgment and Decision Making, 3*(6), 435–448.

48. Pachur, T., & Galesic, M. (2013). Strategy selection in risky choice: The impact of numeracy, affect, and cross-cultural differences. *Journal of Behavioral Decision Making, 26*(3), 260–271.

SECTION V

THE EMERGENCE OF NUMBER UNDERSTANDING

11

The Approximate Number System (ANS) and Discriminating Magnitudes

In past chapters, we learned that people with greater objective numeracy make better decisions and enjoy better life outcomes. These discoveries now set the stage for the importance of our next topic—understanding how numerical abilities emerge. I expect Chapters 11 and 12 will help you make sense of your own abilities and those of others, and they will point out opportunities and barriers for the children in your lives.

As you'll discover in this chapter, we are born with an innate sense of number and an ability to perform simple arithmetic operations with sets of objects. Children, for example, can inevitably tell intuitively and at a glance which of two handfuls of M&Ms has more candy. They will grab the larger amount before they can count, much to the chagrin of parents everywhere.

This low-level understanding of numbers begins early in infancy through the *approximate number system* (ANS), which allows us an intuitive understanding of numerical magnitude (how big one quantity is relative to another). Research points to this quick intuitive grasp of "bigness" as a critical foundation for later mathematical learning. Here, we explore how the ANS develops in humans and its evolutionary roots in other species. This initial ANS section is somewhat technical and you could proceed past it to Chapter 12 on "Genetics and Formal Education." If you do skip it now, consider returning later, when we return to the ANS's role in decision making in Chapter 13. I'll remind you then.

What Is the ANS?

The ANS itself is a system for representing approximate quantities that are bigger than 3 or 4. The quantities it represents do not rely on language or symbols such as "6" and "four" but instead are what we call nonsymbolic; for example, sets of dots like ":::" or "::". A second system, sometimes called the *object tracking system*, precisely tracks small numbers of objects (1, 2, 3, and sometimes 4) through a process called *subitizing*.[1] In this chapter, I focus on

Innumeracy in the Wild. Ellen Peters, Oxford University Press (2020). © Oxford University Press 2020.
DOI: 10.1093/oso/9780190861094.003.0001

the ANS because it involves perceptions important to math abilities and, ultimately, to decision making.

ANS research has demonstrated that we perceive these numerical quantities in accordance with what is called *Weber's Law*. Weber's Law states that, to maintain a noticeable difference between two stimuli at larger magnitudes, the ratio of the original stimuli must be maintained. For example, if you can tell that an array of 10 dots is bigger than one of 9 dots, then you can probably tell that 100 dots is bigger than 90, but not that 100 dots is bigger than 99. This ratio dependence is true for numeric magnitudes as well as other physical magnitudes such as sound (quieter, louder), weight (more and less heavy), and light (lighter, darker).[1-7] We perceive numeric magnitudes spontaneously without counting, but we do so inexactly. Similar perceptions emerge whether quantities are shown nonsymbolically (sets of dots, "::::") or symbolically (symbols such as integers, whole numbers like "6" or "124," or spelled-out number words, like "six"). Researchers believe that perceiving the magnitude (bigness) of a symbolic quantity requires the mind to translate it into a nonsymbolic representation akin to a set of dots.

Evidence for inexact magnitude perceptions come from studies on what is known as the *distance effect* (see Figure 11.1). Psychologists Robert Moyer and Thomas Landauer[8] conducted the first distance effect studies with integers. In pioneering studies, they asked participants to make simple judgments about which of two numbers was larger (e.g., Is 2 greater than or less than 4?). The greater the distance between two numbers, the more quickly their order was judged and the fewer errors were made. In other words, it was harder to discriminate numbers adjacent to one another on the number line (5 and 6) than to discriminate far-apart values (5 vs. 9). Psychologist John Parkman[9] subsequently found a *size effect*. Specifically, people have more difficulty distinguishing larger numbers than smaller ones at the same numerical distance so that we can easily distinguish 5 from 15, but we find it harder to discriminate 105 from 115, even though both pairs are a distance of 10 apart. Symbolic distance and size effects are observed in the single- and double-digit ranges.[10-12] We have also demonstrated distance effects with proportions between 0 and 1 (presented as decimals, e.g., ".10", frequencies, e.g., "10 out of 100," and percentages, e.g., "10%").[13] Perceiving magnitudes through the ANS means that we perceive "four" and "six" as farther apart, as more different from each other, than "ten" and "twelve," even though both pairs are two numbers apart. Similar distance and size effects are shown with nonsymbolic sets of dots.

Researchers explain distance-effect results with a perceptual-comparator model, suggesting that "displayed numerals are converted to analogue magnitudes [akin to sets of dots], and the comparison is then made between

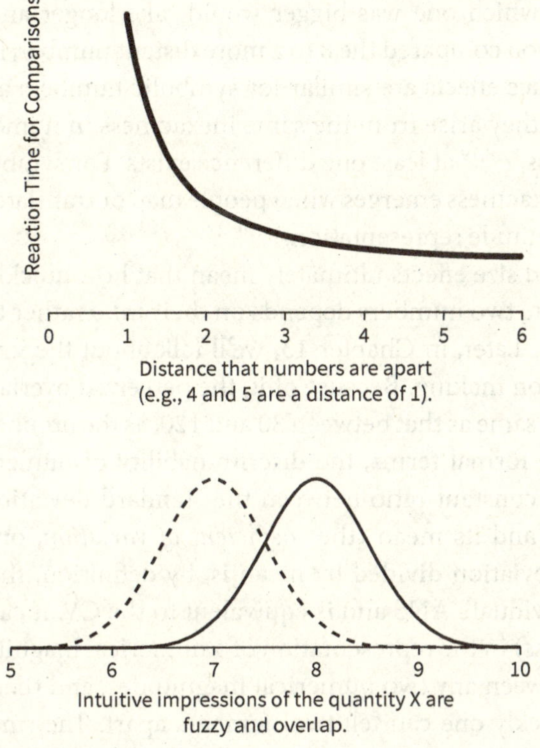

Figure 11.1 The distance effect.

these magnitudes in much the same way that comparisons are made between physical stimuli such as loudness or length of line" (p. 1520).[8] This model is the basis for most numerical-cognition models that attempt to explain our ability to discriminate magnitudes spontaneously (numerosity-code,[14] compressed number-line,[15] and accumulator models[16,17]).

In these perceptual comparisons, a perceived magnitude is represented inexactly by a *fuzzy distribution* of activations (see the bottom part of Figure 11.1). The fuzzy distribution means that mistakes can happen or correct answers might take longer. In particular, when two numbers are compared, their fuzzy distributions will overlap more with smaller distances between them, thus increasing reaction times (RTs) and errors in number-comparison tasks and explaining the distance effect. For example, imagine seeing the symbolic number "8" or the nonsymbolic set of dots ":::". In both cases, a magnitude of 8 would be most strongly activated (making it likely that you will quickly and correctly identify it), but, somewhat less likely, it could be a 7 or 9; 6 and 10 are possible, too, but even less likely. If you compared 8 to a nearby number, like 9, then their distributions would overlap considerably and deciding which one was bigger would take longer and produce more errors than if you compared the 8 to a more distant number, like 13. Although size and distance effects are similar for symbolic numbers and nonsymbolic dots (because they arise from the same inexactness in numerical magnitude representations,[8,18,19] at least one difference exists. For symbolic numbers, an additional inexactness emerges when people map or translate them onto nonsymbolic magnitude representations.[6,20–22]

Distance and size effects ultimately mean that how quickly and accurately we discriminate two numbers depends on their *ratio* rather than the distance between them. Later, in Chapter 13, we'll talk about the importance of this idea for decision making. Because of it, the perceived overlap between 8 and 12 is about the same as that between 80 and 120, as the numbers have the same ratio. In more formal terms, the discriminability of numerical magnitudes depends on a constant ratio between the standard deviation of the magnitude estimate and its mean (the *coefficient of variation*, or CV). This ratio of standard deviation divided by mean is, by definition, the *Weber fraction* (w) of an individual's ANS and is equivalent to the CV. It captures the variability (fuzziness) in the representation of a numerical magnitude, the amount of overlap between any two numerical magnitudes, and therefore how accurately and quickly one can tell two numbers apart. The smaller your w, the better you can discriminate between numerical magnitudes because their numerical magnitude perceptions overlap less. In the bottom of Figure 11.1, you would have more peaked, less spread-out distributions.

These behavioral results have been supported in neuroimaging studies of humans[23] and single-cell recordings in monkeys.[24,25] Strong evidence points to a biologically determined, domain-specific representation of numerical magnitude that is linked to the inferior parietal cortex and specifically the horizontal intraparietal sulcus in both adults and children.[26–29] All numerical formats, whether dots, integers, spelled-out, or spoken numerals, activate this area. Doing approximate arithmetic without time to calculate (e.g., quickly estimating whether 29 plus 19 equals 38) activates the same area. Thus, it is thought to be involved in abstract representation and manipulation of the quantity meaning of numbers.[23]

ANS Development

What is surprising to some people is that infants as young as 6 months can discriminate between numerical magnitudes even though they cannot name numbers or count.[30] Babies can't tell quantities apart as well as adults, but they can discriminate between pairs of dot sets with ratios of 2:1 (e.g., they can discriminate 16 vs. 8 dots, but not 12 vs. 8 dots). By the time they are 12 months old, their ANS development allows them to discriminate this latter 3:2 ratio.[31] We say that their ANS became "more acute."

Experimenters have been quite creative in testing infants, given that they cannot name numbers. For example, in testing 6-month-old infants' ability to discriminate quantities, researchers use what is called a *habituation paradigm*.[30] In it, the infants first see repeated presentations of a specific number of dots (e.g., "::::"). Then, they are shown either the same familiar number of dots or a novel set (e.g., "::::::::") that might surprise them if they perceived it as different from earlier quantities. In fact, at this 2:1 ratio, they looked longer at the novel set, suggesting that they could discriminate this ratio. However, they did not respond differently at smaller ratios, such as 3:2 (":::" vs. "::"). Infants can also do intuitive "math" that does not require counting or words. If you show a 6-month-old infant a doll and hide it behind a screen (so that the infant can see you hiding it), show the infant a second doll and, again, hide it behind the same screen, then the infant will expect two dolls when the screen is pulled. If a different number of dolls is present, say one or three dolls, the infant looks longer because she expects two dolls and is surprised.[32]

The ANS continues to develop into adulthood.[3] Using internet data from more than 10,000 participants aged 11–85 years, ANS acuity improved in children throughout their schooling and peaked at about 30 years old.[33] Discrimination of symbolic numbers also appears to change from more ratio-based representations in earlier childhood to more linear ones in later childhood[6,34] (although some researchers disagree[35,36]). For the interested reader, a summary of ANS-acuity measures useful for decision-making studies with adults can be found in the Appendix to Chapter 13.

Adults then can discriminate magnitudes at ratios of about 9:10 and 9:11, considerably better than 6-month-old infants' discrimination ratios of 2:1.[3,7,37–43] Approximate arithmetic skills also develop. For example, adults can add and subtract sets of dots without time to count them (e.g., 21 dots plus 13 dots) and nonetheless score 70–85% correct.[43] As adults age further, their ANS acuity does not appear to change, although older adults respond more slowly.[13,44,45] As you will see, we attain better number understanding through the use of language, but nonetheless have access to an evolutionarily older, language-free form of number understanding.

Numerical distance effects have been found across age groups and in many different languages, supporting the universality of magnitude representations.[13,46–49] Further support comes from studies demonstrating that adults without formal math education or even many words for numbers nonetheless possess similar numerical magnitude perceptions. For example, two indigenous Brazilian cultures have languages that contain only a few number words. The Pirahã are a small group of semi-nomadic people who live along a tributary of the Amazon River. They have only imprecise words for quantities. *Hói* indicates a "small size or amount" whereas *hoí* indicates a "somewhat larger size or amount," and all larger quantities are identified with the single term *baágiso* which means "many."[50] Not surprisingly, the Pirahã ability to count is quite limited. However, when experimenters showed them a quantity of thread spools and asked them to match that quantity with a set of balloons, Pirahã participants were quite accurate for sets of one to three objects. For larger quantities, their performance was poor and errors increased with larger numbers, consistent with Weber's Law and using estimation strategies of the ANS rather than counting the objects.

A second group, the Munduruku, has number words for more values (symbolic numbers 1–5). When asked to complete a distance-effect task (which of two sets of dots is larger), Munduruku participants performed about as well as French-speaking control participants although the French control group responded more quickly. The Munduruku also discriminated quantities marginally less well at ratios of 6:7 compared to French controls who discriminated ratios of 8:9.[41] The Munduruku, however, could estimate the addition of large numbers far beyond their language range, and, consistent with other research, their performance was even better when the ratio of larger to smaller number was bigger. The Munduruku also could exactly subtract sets of dots so long as all provided quantities fell within the range of their language (numbers 1–5). They could not perform exact subtraction, however, when the numbers of dots used for the initial number went beyond their language (even when the correct answer was within the range of numbers they could name) (e.g., for the subtraction of 8 minus 4, the number 8 is outside of their 1–5 language range). Exact arithmetic depends, in part, on having language for numbers.[41,51,52]

Humans Are Not Alone in This Intuitive Skill

Humans share the ability to "count" with other animals if you define counting as discriminating between quantities. Counting, in fact, is critical for survival and mating in the animal kingdom in creatures as diverse as honeybees,[53] salamanders and fish,[54] rats,[19,55] chickens,[56] monkeys,[57] lions,[58] and beluga whales.[59] Rats, for example, can correctly tell which button to press to get a food pellet when they hear eight sounds versus two sounds (a 4:1

discrimination ratio, worse than human infants).[19] The male túngara frog of Central America competes for female mates by having a competition with other males for making the most female-attracting pulsed calls. Females "count" and respond to these pulsed calls.[60] Some fish can discriminate almost as well as adult humans; three-spined sticklebacks can choose a larger shoal of sticklebacks from a smaller one at a ratio of 6:7[54] similar to the Munduruku peoples but somewhat less than those adult humans whose discrimination ratios are closer to 9:10.[41] Sticklebacks cannot count as humans do, but they have a keen sense of quantity that allows them to discriminate between quantities and choose the safety of larger numbers.

Like humans, animals also spontaneously use quantities based on ratios.[19] For example, untrained cotton-top tamarind monkeys oriented their heads toward a speaker more often when they said a novel number of syllables. "Novelty" was indexed by the ratio between two quantities independent of their absolute values.[61] Researchers have been quite interested in animal numerical cognition, and the number of publications on numerical abilities in vertebrates alone has increased markedly since 1900 (see Figure 11.2).[54]

Trained non-human primates can be quite sophisticated with numbers. For example, trained monkeys can order objects from 1 to 9 based on quantity.[62] Trained chimpanzees learned to point to the larger of two reward arrays (e.g., chocolate-covered peanuts) in order to receive the larger quantity (the smaller array was then given to their neighbor chimpanzee). However, they were unable to learn to point to the smaller reward array for their neighbor to receive (they would then get the larger reward array to which they did not point).[63] The researchers concluded that the chimpanzees performed poorly because they found the greater amount of candy too appealing. In a later study, the

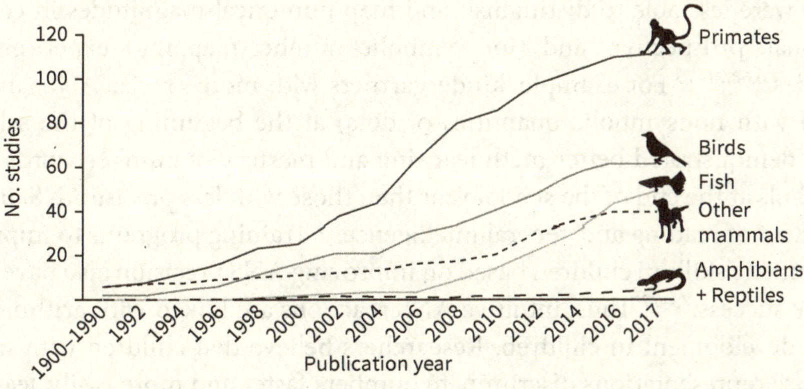

Figure 11.2 Number of publications on vertebrate numerical cognition 1900–2017.[54]

researchers tested adult chimpanzees trained to recognize symbolic numbers as representations for quantities. When symbolic numbers replaced the candy arrays, these chimpanzees now were able to do the more difficult task, pointing to the smaller number for their neighbor to receive (and they received the larger number).[64] Apparently, the more abstract, deliberative mode used to process symbolic numbers allowed these animals to use quantities without being distracted by the candy.

In sum, verbal and nonverbal animals appear to spontaneously activate nonverbal, language-independent quantity representations that allow all of us to "think unnamed numbers" without counting (p. 3).[65,66] However, as we will see next, human animals differ in this ability and, therefore, in how well they discriminate numerical magnitudes and estimate quantities, with implications for formal math ability.

Numeracy (Math) Abilities Emerge from ANS Acuity

The ratio-based discriminability of numerical magnitudes is at odds with modern society's base-10 system of symbolic mathematical operations.[43,67–70] Nonetheless, the ability to discriminate magnitudes appears to underlie early differences in math learning. Through education, children learn to associate or map learned symbolic numbers (e.g., "6" and "four") onto their appropriate underlying representations (::: and ••••). These processes then support learning of higher level mathematical concepts and operations. In particular, researchers have linked symbolic arithmetic operations in children, such as ordering, addition, subtraction, and multiplication, with their ANS acuity.[68] Children who were better able to distinguish numerical magnitudes and map symbolic numbers onto a visual number line were better at math than those who were less able to distinguish and map numerical magnitudes in correlational, prospective, and (for symbolic number-mapping) experimental studies.[6,68,71–73] For example, kindergartners with more precise ANS (measured with nonsymbolic quantities of dots) at the beginning of the school year demonstrated better math learning and mastery of number words and symbols at the end of the school year than those with less precise ANS, independent of reading and general intelligence.[74] Training programs to improve arithmetic skills in children based on improving ANS precision also have had some success.[75–77] Thus, intuitive ANS reactions are linked with arithmetic-skill development in children. Researchers believe that children with more precise representations discriminate numbers faster and more easily, leaving them with working-memory and other capacities available to develop more sophisticated math abilities. Alternatively, it is possible that differences in the quantity or quality of engagement in courses and training programs might increase both math ability and ANS acuity.

Adult math ability also relates to ANS-acuity differences.[6,13] In one large study, individual differences in ANS acuity (measured with a dot-discrimination task) had moderate correlations with SAT math scores (r = .22 and .31 in two studies) among college-bound adults, even after controlling for SAT verbal scores.[78] In my lab, numeracy and ANS acuity (assessed with a distance-effect task) were moderately correlated (r = .29) in a combined sample of undergraduate students and older adults.[13] A recent meta-analysis indicated that the true correlation between ANS acuity and symbolic mathematical ability may be smaller (r = .20).[67] However, inclusion of "catch" trials to identify nonattentive participants may allow for better identification of the effect. When we did not use "catch" trials, ANS acuity estimates had nonsignificant correlations with Math SAT scores.[79] Accounting for inattentive participants made a substantial difference, and better ANS acuity (smaller w's) then correlated with higher SAT Math scores (r = .36). Inattention, of course, is common,[80] and ANS researchers should assess inattention regularly.

Ideas and findings concerning this intuitive number sense suggests two things important to decision making that I would like you to remember for Chapter 13 (but I will also remind you). First, ANS acuity (a measure of intuitive number sense) correlates with objective math abilities so that some objective numeracy findings may be due to ANS acuity. Second, because ANS-acuity differences persist into adulthood and are associated with different perceptions of numbers based on their ratio differences, these acuity differences may exert their own systematic effects on our judgments and decisions. In Chapter 13, I review evidence concerning relations of ANS acuity to decision tasks independent of objective numeracy.

References

1. Feigenson, L., Dehaene, S., & Spelke, E. (2004). Core systems of number. *Trends in Cognitive Sciences, 8*(7), 307–314.
2. Dehaene, S., Izard, V., Spelke, E., & Pica, P. (2008). Log or linear? Distinct intuitions of the number scale in Western and Amazonian indigene cultures. *Science, 320*(5880), 1217–1220.
3. Halberda, J., & Feigenson, L. (2008). Developmental change in the acuity of the" number sense": The approximate number system in 3-, 4-, 5-, and 6-year-olds and adults. *Developmental Psychology, 44*(5), 1457–1465.
4. Nieder, A., Freedman, D. J., & Miller, E. K. (2002). Representation of the quantity of visual items in the primate prefrontal cortex. *Science, 297*(5587), 1708–1711.

5. Piazza, M., Pica, P., Izard, V., Spelke, E. S., & Dehaene, S. (2013). Education enhances the acuity of the nonverbal approximate number system. *Psychological Science, 24*(6), 1037–1043.

6. Siegler, R. S., & Opfer, J. E. (2003). The development of numerical estimation: Evidence for multiple representations of numerical quantity. *Psychological Science, 14*(3), 237–250.

7. Whalen, J., Gallistel, C. R., & Gelman, R. (1999). Nonverbal counting in humans: The psychophysics of number representation. *Psychological Science, 10*(2), 130–137.

8. Moyer, R. S., & Landauer, T. K. (1967). Time required for judgements of numerical inequality. *Nature, 215*(5109), 1519–1520.

9. Parkman, J. M. (1971). Temporal aspects of digit and letter inequality judgments. *Journal of Experimental Psychology, 91*(2), 191–205.

10. Dehaene, S., Dupoux, E., & Mehler, J. (1990). Is numerical comparison digital? Analogical and symbolic effects in two-digit number comparison. *Journal of Experimental Psychology: Human Perception and Performance, 16*(3), 626–641.

11. Gallistel, C. R., & Gelman, R. (1992). Preverbal and verbal counting and computation. *Cognition, 44*(1–2), 43–74.

12. Gallistel, C. R., & Gelman, R. (2005). *Mathematical cognition*. New York: Cambridge University Press.

13. Peters, E., Slovic, P., Västfjäll, D., & Mertz, C. K. (2008). Intuitive numbers guide decisions. *Judgment and Decision Making, 3*(8), 619–635.

14. Butterworth, B. (2010). Foundational numerical capacities and the origins of dyscalculia. *Trends in Cognitive Sciences, 14*(12), 534–541.

15. Dehaene, S. (1992). Varieties of numerical abilities. *Cognition, 44*(1–2), 1–42.

16. Link, S. (1990). Modeling imageless thought: The relative judgment theory of numerical comparisons. *Journal of Mathematical Psychology, 34*(1), 2–41.

17. Gallistel, C. R., & Gelman, R. (2000). Non-verbal numerical cognition: From reals to integers. *Trends in Cognitive Sciences, 4*(2), 59–65.

18. Kaufman, E. L., Lord, M. W., Reese, T. W., & Volkmann, J. (1949). The discrimination of visual number. *American Journal of Psychology, 62*(4), 498–525.

19. Meck, W. H., & Church, R. M. (1983). A mode control model of counting and timing processes. *Journal of Experimental Psychology: Animal Behavior Processes, 9*(3), 320–334.

20. Chesney, D. L., & Matthews, P. G. (2013). Knowledge on the line: Manipulating beliefs about the magnitudes of symbolic numbers affects the linearity of line estimation tasks. *Psychonomic Bulletin & Review, 20*(6), 1146–1153.

21. Izard, V., & Dehaene, S. (2008). Calibrating the mental number line. *Cognition, 106*(3), 1221–1247.

22. Rips, L. J. (2013). How many is a zillion? Sources of number distortion. *Journal of Experimental Psychology: Learning, Memory, and Cognition, 39*(4), 1257–1264.

23. Piazza, M., Izard, V., Pinel, P., Le Bihan, D., & Dehaene, S. (2004). Tuning curves for approximate numerosity in the human intraparietal sulcus. *Neuron, 44*(3), 547–555.

24. Nieder, A., & Miller, E. K. (2003). Coding of cognitive magnitude: Compressed scaling of numerical information in the primate prefrontal cortex. *Neuron, 37*(1), 149–157.

25. Nieder, A., & Miller, E. K. (2004). A parieto-frontal network for visual numerical information in the monkey. *Proceedings of the National Academy of Sciences, 101*(19), 7457–7662.

26. Cantlon, J. F., Brannon, E. M., Carter, E. J., & Pelphrey, K. A. (2006). Functional imaging of numerical processing in adults and 4-y-old children. *PLoS Biology, 4*(5), e125.

27. Dehaene, S., Piazza, M., Pinel, P., & Cohen, L. (2003). Three parietal circuits for number processing. *Cognitive Neuropsychology, 20*(3-6), 487–506.

28. Pinel, P., Dehaene, S., Riviere, D., & LeBihan, D. (2001). Modulation of parietal activation by semantic distance in a number comparison task. *Neuroimage, 14*(5), 1013–1026.

29. Pinel, P., Piazza, M., Le Bihan, D., & Dehaene, S. (2004). Distributed and overlapping cerebral representations of number, size, and luminance during comparative judgments. *Neuron, 41*(6), 983–993.

30. Xu, F., & Spelke, E. S. (2000). Large number discrimination in 6-month-old infants. *Cognition, 74*(1), B1–B11.

31. Cantrell, L., & Smith, L. B. (2013). Open questions and a proposal: A critical review of the evidence on infant numerical abilities. *Cognition, 128*(3), 331–352.

32. Wynn, K. (1992). Addition and subtraction by human infants. *Nature, 358*(6389), 749–750.

33. Halberda, J., Ly, R., Wilmer, J. B., Naiman, D. Q., & Germine, L. (2012). Number sense across the lifespan as revealed by a massive Internet-based sample. *Proceedings of the National Academy of Sciences, 109*(28), 11116–11120.

34. Opfer, J. E., & Siegler, R. S. (2007). Representational change and children's numerical estimation. *Cognitive Psychology, 55*(3), 169–195.

35. Barth, H. C., & Paladino, A. M. (2011). The development of numerical estimation: Evidence against a representational shift. *Developmental Science, 14*(1), 125–135.

36. Opfer, J. E., Siegler, R. S., & Young, C. J. (2011). The powers of noise-fitting: Reply to Barth and Paladino. *Developmental Science, 14*(5), 1194–1204.

37. Barth, H., Kanwisher, N., & Spelke, E. (2003). The construction of large number representations in adults. *Cognition, 86*(3), 201–221.

38. Cordes, S., Gelman, R., Gallistel, C. R., & Whalen, J. (2001). Variability signatures distinguish verbal from nonverbal counting for both large and small numbers. *Psychonomic Bulletin & Review, 8*(4), 698–707.

39. Inglis, M., & Gilmore, C. (2014). Indexing the approximate number system. *Acta Psychologica, 145*, 147–155.

40. Lindskog, M., Winman, A., Juslin, P., & Poom, L. (2013). Measuring acuity of the approximate number system reliably and validly: The evaluation of an adaptive test procedure. *Frontiers in Psychology, 4*, 510.

41. Pica, P., Lemer, C., Izard, V., & Dehaene, S. (2004). Exact and approximate arithmetic in an Amazonian indigene group. *Science, 306*(5695), 499–503.

42. Price, G. R., Palmer, D., Battista, C., & Ansari, D. (2012). Nonsymbolic numerical magnitude comparison: Reliability and validity of different task variants and outcome measures, and their relationship to arithmetic achievement in adults. *Acta Psychologica, 140*(1), 50–57.

43. Park, J., & Brannon, E. M. (2013). Training the approximate number system improves math proficiency. *Psychological Science, 24*(10), 2013–2019.

44. Geary, D. C., & Lin, J. (2010). Numerical cognition: Age-related differences in the speed of executing biologically primary and biologically secondary processes. *Experimental Aging Research, 24*(2), 101–137.

45. Ratcliff, R., Thapar, A., & McKoon, G. (2010). Individual differences, aging, and IQ in two-choice tasks. *Cognitive Psychology, 60*(3), 127–157.

46. Dehaene, S. (1996). The organization of brain activations in number comparison: Event-related potentials and the additive-factors method. *Journal of Cognitive Neuroscience, 8*(1), 47–68.

47. Dehaene, S. (1997). *The number sense: How the mind creates mathematics.* Oxford: Oxford University Press.

48. Ganayim, D., & Ibrahim, R. (2014). Number processing of Arabic and Hebrew bilinguals: Evidence supporting the distance effect. *Japanese Psychological Research, 56*(2), 153–167.

49. Koechlin, E., Naccache, L., Block, E., & Dehaene, S. (1999). Primed numbers: Exploring the modularity of numerical representations with masked and unmasked semantic

priming. *Journal of Experimental Psychology: Human Perception and Performance, 25*(6), 1882–1905.

50. Everett, C., & Madora, K. (2012). Quantity recognition among speakers of an anumeric language. *Cognitive Science, 36*(1), 130–141.

51. Everett, C. (2013a). Independent cross-cultural data reveal linguistic effects on basic numerical cognition. *Language and Cognition, 5*(1), 99–104.

52. Everett, C. (2013b). Without language, no distinctly human numerosity: A reply to Coolidge and Overmann. *Current Anthropology, 54*(1), 81–82.

53. Nieder, A. (2018). Honey bees zero in on the empty set. *Science, 360*(6393), 1069–1070.

54. Agrillo, C., & Bisazza, A. (2018). Understanding the origin of number sense: A review of fish studies. *Philosophical Transactions of the Royal Society B, 373*(1740), 20160511.

55. Platt, J. R., & Johnson, D. M. (1971). Localization of position within a homogeneous behavior chain: Effects of error contingencies. *Learning and Motivation, 2*(4), 386–414.

56. Rugani, R., Regolin, L., & Vallortigara, G. (2007). Rudimental numerical competence in 5-day-old domestic chicks (*Gallus gallus*): Identification of ordinal position. *Journal of Experimental Psychology: Animal Behavior Processes, 33*(1), 21–31.

57. Cantlon, J. F., & Brannon, E. M. (2006). Shared system for ordering small and large numbers in monkeys and humans. *Psychological Science, 17*(5), 401–406.

58. McComb, K., Packer, C., & Pusey, A. (1994), Roaring and numerical assessment in contests between groups of female lions, *Panthera leo. Animal Behaviour, 47*, 379–387.

59. Abramson, J. Z., Hernández-Lloreda, V., Call, J., & Colmenares, F. (2013). Relative quantity judgments in the beluga whale (*Delphinapterus leucas*) and the bottlenose dolphin (*Tursiops truncatus*). *Behavioural Processes, 96*, 11–19.

60. Rose, G. J. (2018). The numerical abilities of anurans and their neural correlates: Insights from neuroethological studies of acoustic communication. *Philosophical Transactions Royal Society, B, 373*(1740).

61. Hauser, M. D., Tsao, F., Garcia, P., & Spelke, E. S. (2003). Evolutionary foundations of number: Spontaneous representations of numerical magnitudes by cotton-top tamarins. *Proceedings of the Royal Society, London, B270*, 1441–1446.

62. Brannon, E. M., & Terrace, H. S. (1998). Ordering of the numerosities 1 to 9 by monkeys. *Science, 282*(5389), 746–749.

63. Boysen, S. T., & Berntson, G. G. (1995). Responses to quantity: Perceptual versus cognitive mechanisms in chimpanzees (*Pan troglodytes*). *Journal of Experimental Psychology: Animal Behavior Processes, 21*(1), 82–86.

64. Boysen, S. T., Mukobi, K. L., & Berntson, G. G. (1999). Overcoming response bias using symbolic representations of number by chimpanzees (*Pan troglodytes*). *Animal Learning & Behavior, 27*(2), 229–235.

65. Koehler, O. (1950). The ability of birds to count. *Bulletin of Animal Behaviour, 9*, 41–45.

66. Smeltzer, D. (2003). *Man and number*. Chelmsford, MA: Courier Corporation.

67. Chen, Q., & Li, J. (2014). Association between individual differences in non-symbolic number acuity and math performance: A meta-analysis. *Acta Psychologica, 148*, 163–172.

68. Halberda, J., Mazzocco, M. M., & Feigenson, L. (2008). Individual differences in non-verbal number acuity correlate with maths achievement. *Nature, 455*(7213), 665–668.

69. Libertus, M. E., Feigenson, L., & Halberda, J. (2011). Preschool acuity of the approximate number system correlates with school math ability. *Developmental Science, 14*(6), 1292–1300.

70. Schley, D. R., & Peters, E. (2014). Assessing economic value symbolic-number mappings predict risky and riskless valuations. *Psychological Science, 25*(3), 753–761.

71. Booth, J. L., & Siegler, R. S. (2008). Numerical magnitude representations influence arithmetic learning. *Child Development, 79*(4), 1016–1031.

72. De Smedt, B., Verschaffel, L., & Ghesquière, P. (2009). The predictive value of numerical magnitude comparison for individual differences in mathematics achievement. *Journal of Experimental Child Psychology, 103*(4), 469–479.

73. Fazio, L. K., Bailey, D. H., Thompson, C. A., & Siegler, R. S. (2014). Relations of different types of numerical magnitude representations to each other and to mathematics achievement. *Journal of Experimental Child Psychology, 123*, 53–72.

74. Gilmore, C. K., McCarthy, S. E., & Spelke, E. S. (2010). Non-symbolic arithmetic abilities and mathematics achievement in the first year of formal schooling. *Cognition, 115*(3), 394–406.

75. Siegler, R. S., & Ramani, G. B. (2009). Playing linear number board games—but not circular ones—improves low-income preschoolers' numerical understanding. *Journal of Educational Psychology, 101*(3), 545–560.

76. Wilson, A. J., Revkin, S. K., Cohen, D., Cohen, L., & Dehaene, S. (2006). An open trial assessment of "The Number Race," an adaptive computer game for remediation of dyscalculia. *Behavioral and Brain Functions, 2*(1), 20.

77. Wilson, A. J., Dehaene, S., Pinel, P., Revkin, S. K., Cohen, L., & Cohen. D. (2006). Principles underlying the design of "The Number Race," an adaptive computer game for remediation of dyscalculia. *Behavioral and Brain Functions, 2*(1), 19.

78. Libertus, M. E., Odic, D., & Halberda, J. (2012). Intuitive sense of number correlates with math scores on college-entrance examination. *Acta Psychologica, 141*(3), 373–379.

79. Chesney, D., Bjälkebring, P., & Peters. E. (2015). How to estimate how well people estimate: Evaluating measures of individual differences in the approximate number system. *Attention, Perception, & Psychophysics, 77* (8), 2781–2802.

80. Oppenheimer, D. M., Meyvis, T., & Davidenko, N. (2009). Instructional manipulation checks: Detecting satisficing to increase statistical power. *Journal of Experimental Social Psychology, 45*(4), 867–872.

12

Genetics and Formal Education

The emergence of math ability requires more than the intuitions of the approximate number system (ANS). Math competency develops primarily during the school years from kindergarten through high school or college. As implied by Chapter 11's findings of our innate ability to do approximate arithmetic, it is simply not the case that some people cannot do math (barring extreme examples of acalculia diagnoses[1]). However, barriers such as math anxiety can interfere with learning, and genetic differences play a role.

Genetic Underpinnings of Numerical Competencies

Although everyone can do math, how well an individual processes symbolic and nonsymbolic numeric information may depend partly on his or her genetics. Behavioral genetics examines what is called *heritability*, "the proportion of observed variation among individuals in a population that can be attributed to underlying genetic differences. It is a characteristic of a population rather than an individual (at the individual level the relative importance of genetic influences and environment can vary widely)" (p. 30).[2]

Studies indicate some genetic influence on both ANS acuity[3] and objective numeracy.[4–8] Psychologists, for example, assessed ANS acuity in 16-year-olds using a dot-discrimination task described in the Appendix of Chapter 13.[3] Their quantitative genetics analyses revealed modest heritability (32% of ANS-acuity variation). They concluded that the relatively low heritability may be due to ANS acuity being an evolutionarily preserved core-system trait with limited genetic variability across individuals.

Math ability (objective numeracy) at primary-school age has a higher heritability of about 60–75% that reduces to about 50–60% by age 12.[6,7] Part of this genetic influence is shared, however, with other cognitive abilities.[9–11] Nonetheless, at least 33% of the variance in math is unique and separate from reading and general cognitive ability.[4,7,9,12] The shared genetic influence appears due to "generalist genes"—domain-general genetic factors that exert influence on multiple abilities such as math, reading, and general intelligence.[13] Domain-specific genetic factors contribute to the independence of math skills from these other abilities.[5,10]

The proportion of variation in math skills explained by genes also may differ across populations in an interesting way.[14,15] In particular, genetic influences may be stronger for people with higher socioeconomic status. Their superior educational environments may allow them to attain something closer to their highest genetically endowed ability, thus maximizing genetic influences on math ability. For example, higher socioeconomic status may enable people to appropriately select environments that match their genetic predispositions, allowing for greater ability and positive feedback loops. These "[t]ransactional models propose that genetic differences between people matter for cognition because initial genetic differences lead to different environmental experiences" (p. 351).[15] Lower quality environments appear to mask genetic differences because they limit how much individuals can attain the best environments for themselves and thus realize their full genetic potential. These findings did not replicate in Europe, and researchers suggested it may be due to Europe's more equal distribution of educational opportunities as compared to the social inequities in education that occur in the United States; not all researchers agree.[15–16]

Given relations between greater objective numeracy and better life outcomes, improving the math education environment for your children seems critical.

Taking Stock of Where We Are

If your objective numeracy skills develop through the acuity of your ANS and your genetic background, then a certain immutability of number skills may exist, perhaps supporting the lament "I'm not a math person!" But we also know that you have been a math person since infancy. In addition, much about understanding and using numbers is not inherent. In the remainder of this chapter, we discuss the role of formal education, including barriers to math learning during childhood. You may recognize yourself or someone you know.

Before we proceed though, I want to remind you that formal education in childhood (or adulthood) is not the only way to grow your numeracy abilities. Chapters 2–7 pointed out ways to improve numeric decisions by cultivating the habits of the highly numerate. Chapters 13 and 14 will add to your numeracy repertoire by showing you ways that we compensate for and support the effects of our objective numeracy skills. You can also take other concrete steps, such as asking communicators, like physicians, to show you numeric information in more comprehensible formats (Chapters 15–17) and growing your numeracy using a variety of techniques (Chapter 18). Nonetheless, formal education is critical.

Formal Education

Formal Education and the Approximate Number System (ANS)

Having some formal education has been linked to greater ANS acuity. For example, adults schooled versus unschooled in objective numeracy better discriminated larger magnitudes (two-digit Arabic integers).[17] They discriminated smaller magnitudes (integers 1–9) equally well, as if formal schooling was less necessary for these small quantities.[18] Similar differences existed between more educated American and French participants and an Amazonian tribe called the Munduruku whose language includes formal words only for numbers 1–5. In particular, psychologist Stanislas Dehaene and his colleagues provided Munduruku and American participants with a line segment with 1 dot on the line's left side and 10 dots on its right endpoint.[19] The experimenter then indicated a quantity (e.g., dots, sequences of tones, spoken words) and participants were asked where that quantity belonged on the line segment. American participants were quite linear in their mapping: they put 3 and 8 dots near the spots for 3 and 8 on the 1–10 line. If 5½ dots existed, it would have been placed in the middle of the line. However, Munduruku adults mapped the quantities more logarithmically, like children do. In particular, 1 and 2 were spread out on the left side of the line, 3 and 4 were close to the middle of the line, and 5 to 9 were bunched up on the right side. When researchers discouraged counting and used a larger line segment that went up to 100, both American and Munduruku participants mapped numbers logarithmically. Thus, and consistent with prior research, humans appear to have logarithmic perceptions of numerical magnitudes and less acute ANS prior to formal education exposure. Developing a more acute ANS and learning to map numbers more linearly appears to require formal education and the attainment of verbal number words.

Less clear is whether the extent of schooling (more vs. less schooling among those who have some schooling) matters to ANS-acuity performance. Some researchers have concluded that it does not and that education-produced ANS differences are unlikely in North American and European adults where some schooling is mandatory for children.[17] However, business undergraduates in Sweden, who attained more formal math education as a degree requirement, improved their ANS acuity, suggesting the possibility of incremental formal education effects on ANS acuity.[20] ANS acuity did not improve in the same study among math majors (who already had more acute ANS in Year 1) or humanities majors (who generally did not take additional math courses).

Overall, greater formal education, probably mostly in childhood, appears to benefit ANS acuity and especially the linear mapping of quantities onto a number line. Experimental efforts to train ANS acuity in children and adults are reviewed in Chapter 18.

Formal Education and Objective Numeracy

Formal education, of course, also improves objective numeracy.[18,21,22] For example, in a study we conducted in the Peruvian Andes, each additional year of schooling led the average participant to score 0.67 points higher on an 18-question arithmetic test.[21] In a recent randomized controlled trial, interleaving consecutive problems, as opposed to having people practice the same skill or concept in a block of problems, had large effects on increased math learning among children.[23] The US Common Core State Standards Initiative curriculum provides math standards for children at each grade level (see the Appendix of this chapter for a brief review).

Some Numeracy Skills Are More Difficult to Learn

In the Common Core and other curricula, mathematical understanding is intended to progress smoothly from one topic to the next. Children, however, have more difficulty learning some mathematical concepts than others. For example, arithmetic with rational numbers such as fractions, decimals, probabilities, and proportions are especially difficult. In one study, middle schoolers were asked whether "12/13 + 7/8" is closest to 1, 2, 19, or 21. They scored at about chance levels, as if they guessed the answer.[24]

Processing these more sophisticated concepts is thought to be based nonetheless in Chapter 11's ANS. In particular, brain areas originally developed to represent whole numbers, like 5 and 14, have been co-opted for nonintuitive, symbolic processing of these other concepts, like 1/5 and 0.14.[24,25] However, confusion results when people separately represent the magnitudes of a fraction's denominator and numerator (the top and bottom numbers, respectively) but do not have a representation of the fraction itself. Other researchers recently proposed that a separate ratio-processing system exists to support processing fractions.[26]

Additional difficulties exist for the math learner, too.

- Whereas a whole number with more digits than another whole number is always larger, that relation is untrue for fractions and decimals (e.g., 1/2 > 23/237; .99 > .123).
- Performing arithmetic operations on whole numbers versus rational numbers that are not whole numbers (e.g., 7/8) poses more issues. For example, the steps needed to calculate with fractions change considerably depending on whether the operation is addition or multiplication.[24]

Still other researchers support the idea that people intuitively understand some forms of numbers better than other normatively equivalent forms. If true, then childhood education with them should proceed at a faster pace, and that improved understanding should continue into adulthood. In particular, a group of researchers claims that frequency representations are "privileged" over related probability formats.[27–30] Their claim is that simple frequencies are a more transparent, evolutionarily prepared form of presenting numerical information as compared to other forms, such as percentages. For example, only 4% of physicians in one study correctly estimated the probability of cancer when information about a cancer-screening test was presented in probabilities; 67% answered correctly when it was presented in natural frequencies.[30]

People do not always perform better with frequencies per se, however.[31–35] For example, when told by a hypothetical doctor "There is a 30% chance that the treatment will cure your cancer and a 4% chance that it will not cure it but will keep it from getting any worse" and asked "What is the chance that the treatment will benefit you by either curing your cancer or keeping it from getting worse?," participants scored higher when provided with the percentages shown versus their equivalent frequencies (36% and 19% correct, respectively).[32] Gigerenzer and colleagues have backed off the idea of simple frequencies as a basis for improved understanding over percentages.[36] Their claim that natural frequencies improve comprehension over single-event probabilities is well supported if one allows those natural frequencies to be in a frequency or percentage format. It seems likely to me, however, that its effect are due not to evolutionary preparedness, but rather to disentangling relations between subsets of items.[37] For example, when thinking about how likely it is that you have cancer given a positive screening-test result, it is easier to understand your chances when you can clearly see the number of people who tested positive, some of whom have cancer and some of whom do not (see Box 3.2). Overall, formal education with frequencies appears unlikely to improve math learning more than that with percentages.

Obstacles in Formal Education

Other obstacles exist, however, to mastering mathematical concepts during formal education including math anxiety and early experiences that limit mastery.

Missed Chances to Maximize Early Learning

Economist James Heckman argued that formal education offers the "biggest bang for the buck" early in childhood.[38] His rational was based on two observations. First, critical learning periods exist in development, and, second, early mastery of skills makes later learning easier and it leads children to value acquired skills more (which further promotes later learning opportunities). In other words, "skills beget skills" (p. 10156).[38] Mastering elementary mathematical concepts can create positive feedback loops for students that lead to greater math confidence that allows them to conquer increasingly difficult problems. Without this early mastery, however, and perhaps especially if students have fixed mindsets toward math,[39] children may experience negative feedback loops in which lower skills produce lower math confidence, which, in turn, reduces math learning and leaves the child further behind. Supporting children's math and math confidence (self-efficacy) is critical.

Math Anxiety

Math anxiety also emerges as a critical roadblock to math learning. Defined as a prospective feeling of tension, worry, or fear about performing math calculations, math anxiety occurs more often among women than men (although women may simply be more willing to admit to it).[40,41] It has been correlated with lower math scores and higher levels of general test anxiety and trait anxiety (with correlations in the range of .30 to .50).[40–42] It has also been associated with increasing physiological reactivity and reduced ability to keep math problems in mind when attempting to solve them.[43–45] These physiological reactions and accompanying self-efficacy (confidence) concerns then likely underlie the tendency of the math anxious to avoid math courses and content more than those who are not math anxious. This avoidance further leads them to learn less and perform less well.[40–42,46] Timed tests, doing another task at the same time, and more difficult tests exacerbate this negative relation between math anxiety and math performance.[40,47] At the individual level, math anxiety may have a particularly negative impact on those with higher working memory who rely more on this capacity in doing math problems than those lower in working memory.[44,45]

Multiple potential causes of math anxiety exist. First, math anxiety has some genetic basis, with about 40% of the variation in math anxiety at age 12 attributable to genetic factors.[48] Second, some researchers believe its roots are motivational, such that people who highly value good performance but who have low math confidence and poor performance expectations will be the most math anxious.[49,50]

Still other researchers have found that math anxiety is linked with a sort of social contagion. In particular, math-anxious female elementary school teachers may unintentionally undermine their girl pupils' math achievement but not their boys' achievement. Specifically, psychologist Sian Beilock and her colleagues[51] tested teacher math anxiety as well as their first- and second-graders' math achievement and beliefs in the gender stereotype of boys being better at math and worse at reading than girls at the beginning of the school year and its end. No relation existed between teacher math anxiety and student math achievement at the beginning of the school year. However, by the year's end, this relation appeared among girls but not boys ($r = -.28$ and $-.04$, respectively). In particular, female teacher anxiety was related to the most negative effect on math achievement among those girl pupils who believed the gender stereotype. Similarly, math anxious parents who provided frequent help with math homework had first- and second-grade children with worse math performance (but not reading performance) than parents who were not math anxious and/or did not provide frequent help.[52] However, the problem is not intractable, and increasing high-quality parent–child math interactions helps. For example, children who engaged with their math-anxious parents on math-relevant stories and associated problems on an iPad had higher math scores than those in a reading control group.[53]

Overall, math anxiety and a lack of math self-efficacy (confidence) appear to block math learning.[46] They also may cause early gender differences in math. In fact, studies have shown that gender differences in math self-efficacy begin as early as elementary school and are larger than gender differences in interest and achievement in math.[54] As a result, childhood interventions related to math confidence as well as math achievement appear critical and especially for girls.

Looking back, in Chapters 2–8, you learned how this math achievement (objective numeracy) may affect your decisions and outcomes as an adult.

Looking forward to Chapters 13–14, you will further learn that the ANS and math confidence have independent effects on some of these same outcomes.

References

1. Butterworth, B., Varma, S., & Laurillard, D. (2011). Dyscalculia: From brain to education. *Science, 332*(6033), 1049–1053.
2. Rusconi, E., & McLean, J. F. (2017). 2.1 Nature/nurture and the origin of individual differences in mathematics: Evidence from infant and behavioural genetics studies. In J. Adams, J., P. Barmby, P., & A. Mesoudi, A. (Eds.), *The Nature and Development of Mathematics: Cross Disciplinary Perspectives on Cognition, Learning and Culture*, 23–42.
3. Tosto, M. G., Petrill, S. A., Halberda, J., Trzaskowski, M., Tikhomirova, T. N., Bogdanova, O. Y., ... Plomin, R. (2014). Why do we differ in number sense? Evidence from a genetically sensitive investigation. *Intelligence, 43*, 35–46.
4. Grasby, K. L., Coventry, W. L., Byrne, B., Olson, R. K., & Medland, S. E. (2016). Genetic and environmental influences on literacy and numeracy performance in Australian school children in Grades 3, 5, 7, and 9. *Behavior Genetics, 46*(5), 627–648.
5. Hart, S. A., Petrill, S. A., Thompson, L. A., & Plomin, R. (2009). The ABCs of math: A genetic analysis of mathematics and its links with reading ability and general cognitive ability. *Journal of Educational Psychology, 101*(2), 388.
6. Haworth, C. M., Kovas, Y., Petrill, S. A., & Plomin, R. (2007). Developmental origins of low mathematics performance and normal variation in twins from 7 to 9 years. *Twin Research and Human Genetics, 10*(1), 106–117.
7. Kovas, Y., Haworth, C. M., Petrill, S. A., & Plomin, R. (2007). Mathematical ability of 10-year-old boys and girls: Genetic and environmental etiology of typical and low performance. *Journal of Learning Disabilities, 40*(6), 554–567.
8. Oliver, B., Harlaar, N., Hayiou Thomas, M. E., Kovas, Y., Walker, S. O., Petrill, S. A., ... Plomin, R. (2004). A twin study of teacher-reported mathematics performance and low performance in 7-year-olds. *Journal of Educational Psychology, 96*(3), 504.
9. Davis, O. S., Band, G., Pirinen, M., Haworth, C. M., Meaburn, E. L., Kovas, Y., ... Curtis, C. J. (2014). The correlation between reading and mathematics ability at age twelve has a substantial genetic component. *Nature Communications, 5*, 4204.
10. Petrill, S. A. (2016). Behavioural genetic studies of reading and mathematics skills. In Y. Kovas, S. Malykh, & D. Gaysina (Eds.), *Behavioural genetics for education* (pp. 60–76). London: Palgrave Macmillan.
11. Petrill, S. A., Kovas, Y., Hart, S. A., Thompson, L. A., & Plomin, R. (2009). The genetic and environmental etiology of high math performance in 10-year-old twins. *Behavior Genetics, 39*(4), 371–379.
12. Haworth, C., Dale, P. S., & Plomin, R. (2009). The etiology of science performance: Decreasing heritability and increasing importance of the shared environment from 9 to 12 years of age. *Child Development, 80*(3), 662–673.
13. Plomin, R., & Kovas, Y. (2005). Generalist genes and learning disabilities. *Psychological Bulletin, 131*(4), 592–617.
14. Rhemtulla, M., & Tucker-Drob, E. M. (2012). Gene-by-socioeconomic status interaction on school readiness. *Behavior Genetics, 42*(4), 549–558.
15. Tucker-Drob, E. M., Briley, D. A., & Harden, K. P. (2013). Genetic and environmental influences on cognition across development and context. *Current Directions in Psychological Science, 22*(5), 349–355.

16. Figlio, D. N., Freese, J., Karbownik, K., & Roth, J. (2017). Socioeconomic status and genetic influences on cognitive development. *Proceedings of the National Academy of Sciences, 2114*(51), 13441--1344601708491.

17. Nys, J., Ventura, P., Fernandes, T., Querido, L., & Leybaert, J. (2013). Does math education modify the approximate number system? A comparison of schooled and unschooled adults. *Trends in Neuroscience and Education, 2*(1), 13–22.

18. Zebian, S., & Ansari, D. (2012). Differences between literates and illiterates on symbolic but not nonsymbolic numerical magnitude processing. *Psychonomic Bulletin & Review, 19*(1), 93–100.

19. Dehaene, S., Izard, V., Spelke, E., & Pica, P. (2008). Log or linear? Distinct intuitions of the number scale in Western and Amazonian indigene cultures. *Science, 320*(5880), 1217–1220.

20. Lindskog, M., Winman, A., & Juslin, P. (2014). The association between higher education and approximate number system acuity. *Frontiers in Psychology, 5,* 462.

21. Baker, D. P., Eslinger, P. J., Benavides, M., Peters, E., Dieckmann, N. F., & Leon, J. (2015). The cognitive impact of the education revolution: A possible cause of the Flynn Effect on population IQ. *Intelligence, 49,* 144–158.

22. Peters, E., Baker, D. P., Dieckmann, N. F., Leon, J., & Collins, J. (2010). Explaining the effect of education on health: A field study in Ghana. *Psychological Science, 21*(10), 1369–1376.

23. Rohrer, D., Dedrick, R. F., Hartwig, M. K., & Cheung, C. N. (2019). A randomized controlled trial of interleaved mathematics practice. *Journal of Educational Psychology, 112*(1), 40--52.

24. Siegler, R. S., & Lortie-Forgues, H. (2017). Hard lessons: Why rational number arithmetic is so difficult for so many people. *Current Directions in Psychological Science, 26*(4), 346–351.

25. Carpenter, T. P., Corbitt, M. K., Kepner, H. S., Lindquist, M. M., & Reys, R. E. (1981). What are the chances of your students knowing probability? *Mathematics Teacher, 74*(5), 342–344.

26. Matthews, P. G., Lewis, M. R., & Hubbard, E. M. (2016). Individual differences in nonsymbolic ratio processing predict symbolic math performance. *Psychological Science, 27*(2), 191–202.

27. Brase, G. L., Martinie, S., & Castillo-Garsow, C. (2014). Intuitive conceptions of probability and the development of basic math skills. In E. J. Chernoff & B. Sriraman (Eds.), *Probabilistic thinking* (pp. 161–194). Dordrecht: Springer.

28. Gigerenzer, G. (1994). Why the distinction between single-event probabilities and frequencies is important for psychology (and vice versa). In G. Wright & P. Ayton (Eds.), *Subjective probability* (pp. 129–161). New York: Wiley.

29. Hoffrage, U., Gigerenzer, G., Krauss, S., & Martignon, L. (2002). Representation facilitates reasoning: What natural frequencies are and what they are not. *Cognition, 84*(3), 343–352.

30. Hoffrage, U., Lindsey, S., Hertwig, R., & Gigerenzer, G. (2000). Communicating statistical information. *Science, 290*(5500), 2261–2262.

31. Bodemer, N., Meder, B., & Gigerenzer, G. (2014). Communicating relative risk changes with baseline risk: Presentation format and numeracy matter. *Medical Decision Making, 34*(5), 615–626.

32. Cuite, C. L., Weinstein, N. D., Emmons, K., & Colditz, G. (2008). A test of numeric formats for communicating risk probabilities. *Medical Decision Making, 28*(3), 377–384.

33. Evans, J. S. B., Handley, S. J., Perham, N., Over, D. E., & Thompson, V. A. (2000). Frequency versus probability formats in statistical word problems. *Cognition, 77*(3), 197–213.

34. Waters, E. A., Weinstein, N. D., Colditz, G. A., & Emmons, K. (2006). Formats for improving risk communication in medical tradeoff decisions. *Journal of Health Communication, 11*(2), 167–182.

35. Woloshin, S., & Schwartz, L. M. (2011). Communicating data about the benefits and harms of treatment: A randomized trial. *Annals of Internal Medicine, 155*(2), 87–96.

36. Gigerenzer, G., & Galesic, M. (2012). Why do single event probabilities confuse patients? *BMJ: British Medical Journal (Online), 344:*, e245.

37. Reyna, V. F., & Brainerd, C. J. (2008). Numeracy, ratio bias, and denominator neglect in judgments of risk and probability. *Learning and Individual Differences, 18*(1), 89–107.

38. Knudsen, E. I., Heckman, J. J., Cameron, J. L., & Shonkoff, J. P. (2006). Economic, neurobiological, and behavioral perspectives on building America's future workforce. *Proceedings of the National Academy of Sciences, 103*(27), 10155–10162.

39. Dweck, C. S. (2006). *Mindset: The new psychology of success.* New York: Random House.

40. Ashcraft, M. H. (2002). Math anxiety: Personal, educational, and cognitive consequences. *Current Directions in Psychological Science, 11*(5), 181–185.

41. Betz, N. E. (1978). Prevalence, distribution, and correlates of math anxiety in college students. *Journal of Counseling Psychology, 25*(5), 441–448.

42. Gunderson, E. A., Ramirez, G., Levine, S. C., & Beilock, S. L. (2012). The role of parents and teachers in the development of gender-related math attitudes. *Sex Roles, 66*(3–4), 153–166.

43. Faust, M. W. (1992). *Analysis of physiological reactivity in mathematics anxiety.* Unpublished doctoral dissertation, Bowling Green State University, Bowling Green, Ohio.

44. Beilock, S. L. (2008). Math performance in stressful situations. *Current Directions in Psychological Science, 17*(5), 339–343.

45. Beilock, S. L., & Carr, T. H. (2005). When high-powered people fail: Working memory and "choking under pressure" in math. *Psychological science, 16*(2), 101–105.

46. Hackett, G., & Betz, N. E. (1981). A self-efficacy approach to the career development of women. *Journal of Vocational Behavior, 18*(3), 326–339.

47. Morsanyi, K., Busdraghi, C., & Primi, C. (2014). Mathematical anxiety is linked to reduced cognitive reflection: A potential road from discomfort in the mathematics classroom to susceptibility to biases. *Behavioral and Brain Functions, 10*(1), 31.

48. Wang, Z., Hart, S. A., Kovas, Y., Lukowski, S., Soden, B., Thompson, L. A., . . . Petrill, S. A. (2014). Who is afraid of math? Two sources of genetic variance for mathematical anxiety. *Journal of Child Psychology and Psychiatry, 55*(9), 1056–1064.

49. Kyttälä, M., & Björn, P. M. (2010). Prior mathematics achievement, cognitive appraisals and anxiety as predictors of Finnish students' later mathematics performance and career orientation. *Educational Psychology, 30*(4), 431–448.

50. Lauermann, F., Eccles, J. S., & Pekrun, R. (2017). Why do children worry about their academic achievement? An expectancy-value perspective on elementary students' worries about their mathematics and reading performance. *ZDM, 49*(3), 339–354.

51. Beilock, S. L., Gunderson, E. A., Ramirez, G., & Levine, S. C. (2010). Female teachers' math anxiety affects girls' math achievement. *Proceedings of the National Academy of Sciences, 107*(5), 1860–1863.

52. Maloney, E. A., Ramirez, G., Gunderson, E. A., Levine, S. C., & Beilock, S. L. (2015). Intergenerational effects of parents' math anxiety on children's math achievement and anxiety. *Psychological Science, 26*(9), 1480–1488.

53. Berkowitz, T., Schaeffer, M. W., Maloney, E. A., Peterson, L., Gregor, C., Levine, S. C., & Beilock, S. L. (2015). Math at home adds up to achievement in school. *Science, 350*(6257), 196–198.

54. Ganley, C. M., & Lubienski, S. T. (2016). Mathematics confidence, interest, and performance: Examining gender patterns and reciprocal relations. *Learning and Individual Differences, 47*, 182–193.

SECTION VI

TWO ADDITIONAL WAYS OF KNOWING NUMBERS

13
Discriminating Numbers Allows for Better Decisions

So far, we have mostly discussed objective numeracy and its importance to decision-making processes and life outcomes. By the end of Chapters 13 and 14, you will see that objective numeracy does not explain everything with respect to how we judge and decide when numbers are involved. Instead, systematic differences exist among adults in two additional ways of knowing and using numbers in judgments and decisions. In this chapter, we will look again at the approximate number system (ANS) and focus on its effects in decisions independent of objective numeracy. This chapter will add to your understanding of how numeric intuitions, rather than deliberations, likely influence how you respond to decision-related numbers. The ANS allows for an intuitive sense of numeric magnitude (how big one quantity is relative to another quantity) and the ability to estimate quantities and do approximate arithmetic without counting. Don't forget you can turn back to Chapter 11 to remind yourself about the ANS and its significance to human and non-human animals. Chapter 14 then will review subjective numeracy and how beliefs in your math abilities propel or thwart engagement with numbers as you judge and decide, independent of your actual skills. This numeric confidence (aka self-efficacy) contributes to our understanding of number use and nonuse in decisions by adding a motivational component. Findings with these two additional numeric competencies highlight important theoretical distinctions and pragmatic differences in decision making.

Let's start with the ANS and a description of someone that I think will help you intuit what our ANS skills contribute to decision making. Mark is a highly skilled carpenter who excels at estimating the angles, lengths, and areas that are critical to his craft. He can glance at a living room floor and know about how many square feet of oak he needs to rebuild it. At the same time, he claims he is "no good at math." It's surprising because his career requires him to be mathematically adept. Amazon, for example, sells multiple books solely dedicated to the use of math in carpentry. According to online career advice for carpenters, "Basic math skills are a must for any carpenter. Carpenters use arithmetic, algebra, geometry, calculus and statistics to measure materials,

Innumeracy in the Wild. Ellen Peters, Oxford University Press (2020). © Oxford University Press 2020.
DOI: 10.1093/oso/9780190861094.003.0001

add up volumes and complete other project-planning tasks."[1] The quote continues, however, by describing intuitive math abilities that are needed: "To finish a job on time and within budget, carpenters use estimating skills to calculate sizes, distances and quantities of material, and how much time and money they need to wrap up the project." These latter estimation skills may be the locus of Mark's success.

Being able to estimate well does not necessarily require great objective math abilities, and Chapter 11's discussion of ANS acuity (how precisely a person represents numeric magnitude) leaves open the possibility that Mark has good ANS acuity with underdeveloped objective numeracy skills. For Mark, a finely honed sense of number (really, of numeric magnitude) may compensate for his lack of math skills even if this same intuitive sense does not help him to precisely calculate his billings. In this chapter, we'll discuss the effects of our ability to discriminate numbers intuitively on judgments and decisions when you have to tell how far apart numbers are but perhaps do not need to know precisely what they are.

Number Sense in Human Decision Making

We know that this intuitive sense of numeric magnitude plays an important role in decisions made by non-human animals. It allows them to forage for food, choose mates, and avoid enemies when their numbers are too great (see Chapter 11). Humans, of course, have evolved beyond intuitions about quantities to know modern numeric abstractions. We can recognize, name, manipulate, and communicate with symbolic numbers in ways that have powered human progress for thousands of years.

However, we are animals, too, and this intuitive number sense remains pivotal to human decisions. Just as beluga whales and bottlenose dolphins can select the larger of two sets if their numeric difference is large enough (e.g., choosing eight fish over two fish),[2] human adults can quickly and intuitively, without calculation, know that 11 is more than 9 and a $45,000 salary is greater than $30,000. Also similar to non-human animals, human adults cannot discriminate well between small numeric differences such as sets of 19 and 20 objects. In fact, Pakistan and India have similar phrases "like 19 vs. 20," which mean that two things, job candidates or cars, are different but seem the same,[3] making choices between them difficult. Thus, human decision making relies in part on the same numeric magnitude-based mechanisms that evolved in other animals in response to their natural environments.

These intuitive decisions can be made without counting or doing precise arithmetic, and they depend on the ratio difference between two numeric values rather than their absolute difference. As we discovered in Chapter 11, and consistent with Weber's Law, the discriminability of two numeric magnitudes is a function of their ratio. Another way to state Weber's Law is that to maintain a noticeable difference between two stimuli (e.g., two weights or two numeric magnitudes) at larger magnitudes, the ratio difference between the original stimuli must be maintained. In other words, if you barely notice the difference between sets of 9 and 10 oranges, you will also just notice the difference between sets of 90 and 100 oranges, and you will not detect a smaller proportional difference, say between sets of 95 and 100 oranges. In decision making, a similar ratio-like dependence can be seen in the diminishing marginal values noted by mathematician Daniel Bernoulli[4] and that is reflected in *Prospect Theory*, the most widely accepted descriptive theory of how people perceive value.[5] In it, people perceive a dollar as more valuable when they have only $1 than when they have $100; the marginal value of $1 is lower when they have more. Value differences also are not linear; a $5 difference between $5 and $10 is valued about the same as the $10 difference between $10 and $20. Furthermore, getting $1,000 back on your tax return feels great when you expected $100, a joyful tenfold increase. However, that same $1,000 is not valued as much when you expected $990 (a trivial 1% difference). This similarity between ANS discriminability and perceived value suggests that how we value options in decision making may depend on this evolutionarily older faculty (see the section on value distortion later in this chapter).

You can see this ratio-based dependence in how people react to prices. In particular, consumers evaluate price differences based on their proportional difference from a reference. Psychologists Daniel Kahneman and Amos Tversky[6] came up with the following example: Imagine that you go to the store to purchase a very reasonably priced $20 calculator. Once you're at the store, however, you find out that you can get the same calculator across town for $10; would you drive there? Now imagine a similar situation where you could save the same $10 if you drove across town to purchase a $2,000 leather jacket for $1,990. Would you go to the effort? Many people would in the first case but not in the second. If you recognize yourself in these responses, how did you arrive at your understanding of the savings? You likely noticed that you would save $10 in both scenarios. Did you use your objective numeracy skills to calculate their respective 50% and .5% savings, or did you intuitively feel the proportional difference through the ANS? I suspect the latter.

In the examples so far, numerosities were seen all at once (e.g., four fish in a bucket, $10 savings). The ANS also can represent the likely magnitude of an option learned across variable experiences with it. For example, honeybees must choose where to fly for nectar each day. Animal cognition researcher Sharoni Shafir finds that they do so by tracking nectar magnitude across the times that they venture to a given location.[7] Such foraging for food is risky, and locations vary in terms of the average expected quantity of food available across experiences (more is better, of course) and also in its variability (a lot of nectar was available in a given location one day, but little was there the next time; less variability is better). Honeybees then "count" approximate nectar by taking into account nectar variability and expected value at each location. In the wild, honeybees (and fish and birds) choose foraging locations based on their coefficient of variability (the *coefficient of variation* [CV], the standard deviation of nectar magnitudes experienced in a given location divided by the average nectar found in that location).[7] The CV depicts relative risk (risk per unit of expected return), and smaller CVs are better, all else equal. Animals avoid risk (more variability) when they are not in danger of starvation (in Prospect Theory language, they are in the "domain of gains"), choosing guaranteed amounts of food rather than risk getting a smaller amount in the hopes of obtaining a much larger quantity. However, they become risk seeking when starvation is possible (the "domain of losses").[7]

Similar to non-human animals, people's risky choices also follow ANS representations.[5] For example, gambles vary in possible rewards (e.g., Gamble 1: 90% chance to win $0 and 10% chance to win $10 vs. Gamble 2: 10% chance of $0 and 90% chance of $10). A CV can be calculated for each gamble (similar to honeybees "calculating" the CV of a nectar location) by dividing the standard deviation of possible rewards by their expected value (see Box 2.1 if you need a reminder about how to calculate an expected value). With these two gambles, for example, their CVs are, respectively, 3 (the standard deviation of 10 and 9 zeros divided by the expected mean of 1) and .33 (the standard deviation of 9 ten's and 1 zero divided by the expected mean of 9). If people perceive higher CVs as less valuable (why take more risk per unit of expected return?), then humans should be (and are) more likely to choose options with lower CVs. When each gamble was paired against a sure thing offering its same expected value, only 32% chose Gamble 1 with the higher CV of 3 whereas 76% chose Gamble 2 with the CV of .33.[8] People noticed Gamble 2's relatively low risk for its expected value and chose it.

Just as animals learn about risks and benefits in their natural environment through exploration, humans also sometimes learn about options through experience (e.g., Would I like to live in this city given my experiences with its cultural and intellectual activities but also its noise and grime? Should I bring a raincoat given what I see outside?). In fact, psychologist Elke Weber and her colleagues[8] demonstrated that choices were more ANS-dependent when humans, like animals, learned about choices experientially, by sampling them and learning what happened with each choice over time. In their studies, participants drew cards from each of two decks, one of which always provided a certain reward whereas the other probabilistically rewarded nothing or some larger amount. ANS dependence mattered less when these same risky and certain options were described (e.g., respondents saw two pie charts depicting probabilities numerically and pictorially and outcomes numerically).

These researchers interpreted their findings in the context of dual-process theories, suggesting that experiential learning about options depends more on associative processing that humans share with other animals, whereas choosing by description depends less on these associative processes and more on rule-based processing. "To the extent that human decision making is mediated by associative rather than rule-based processing, one would expect similarity between choice patterns in human and animal data" (p. 431).[8] Thus, human decisions follow the intuitive dictates of the ANS less when decisions are described using abstract numeric symbols common to modern decisions (e.g., interest rates, medication risks and benefits, the likelihood of rain). Nonetheless, whether options are experienced or symbolically described, numeric proclivities dragged from our distant evolutionary past intrude on our perceptions of numeric information and valuations of certain and risky options.

An interesting question arises when abstract symbolic representations use different magnitudes to indicate the same value (12, 1 dozen). The ANS is thought nonetheless to discriminate magnitude (12 is greater than 1) and not value. If true, then a manipulation of numeric magnitude, independent of value, should systematically bias judgments.[9] Consistent with this idea, psychologists Frank Kanayet, John Opfer, and Wil Cunningham[10] disentangled people's neural responses to numeric magnitudes (1, 100) from those to monetary values (1¢, $1, 100¢, $100). Their results indicated that humans' older and newer systems for knowing numbers both mattered. In particular, brain activity in the intraparietal sulcus was correlated with changes in numeric magnitude (e.g., 100¢, $1) but not with changes in monetary value (e.g., 100¢, $100). Monetary value, however, was related to activity in evolutionarily newer orbitofrontal cortex (numeric magnitude was unrelated). Thus, their research revealed that different parts of the brain responded to monetary rewards based on ANS-perceived numeric magnitudes (intraparietal sulcus) than to the more abstract and symbolic monetary values critical to financial outcomes (orbitofrontal cortex).

Individual Differences in ANS Acuity Intrude on Decision Making

So far in this chapter, we have discussed how the ANS affects everyone similarly. These studies are important because they illustrate how the average human animal responds intuitively to numbers. The findings, however, overlook the individual differences in the ANS discussed in Chapter 11. There, we saw that individuals with more acute ANS (they discriminated magnitudes better than others) had stronger math abilities. One possible reason for this relation is that having a more acute ANS allows one to discriminate numbers more quickly and easily, leaving more time and cognitive capacity to learn additional math skills. This discrimination ability, however, could easily apply to decision making, too, so that people with a more acute ANS access numeric differences more quickly, leaving capacity and time to process information further in decisions. For the remainder of this chapter, we consider whether and how individuals with systematically different ANS acuity make different decisions.

Quantity Discrimination Processes in Judgment and Choice

The notion of intuitive quantity-discrimination processes means that our evolutionary past may sneak uninvited into decisions about topics that did not exist when these mechanisms first evolved in human and non-human animals. It also means that we can make predictions about what will happen based on what we know about the mathematical properties of how we perceive numeric-magnitude differences. Specifically, we know from Chapter 11 that numeric discriminability in human decision making can be approximated by a logarithmic function that represents the ANS's ratio-based perceptions of numeric magnitudes. Although power functions also conform to the behavioral data, a logarithmic function was a somewhat better fit to data from human numerical-estimation studies and monkey neural-response curves during a number-estimation task.[11,12] As a result, you can think about a logarithmic function as what translates objective magnitudes into perceived magnitudes. Individuals, however, will differ in the basis of that logarithmic function.

In a 2008 paper, we found it useful to think about ANS acuity differences in this way because logarithmic transformations of numbers have three systematic properties that can be used to predict and test possible effects of individual differences in ANS acuity on judgments and decisions.[13] In Box 13.1, I briefly explain these three properties and their underlying math, but you should feel free to skip the math.

To the ANS, a numeric magnitude is a numeric magnitude. Nothing exists in theorizing about the ANS to predict differences in how people respond to mortgage rates, the likelihoods of cancer under different medication regimens, dollar values, square feet of oak flooring, or numbers of oranges. All else equal, each of these types of magnitudes should be equally prone to ANS-based distortions (although, later, I will argue that probabilities may be

---

Box 13.1 Three Systematic Properties of Logarithmic Transformations

1. The difference between logarithmic transformations of two numbers means that their perceived difference will depend on their proportional difference rather than subtractive difference. If you're interested in the math (you can skip it), think about two numbers, 100 and 50. If we transform them logarithmically, then you can think about their perceived difference as $\log(100) - \log(50)$. A systematic property of logarithms is that this subtraction is equal to $\log(100$ divided by $50)$ or $\log(100/50)$. More generally, $\log(2x) - \log(x)$ equals $\log(2x/x)$ equals $\log(2)$ for any number pairs where one number is twice the other. In other words, based on logarithmic transformations, the subjective difference between 100 and 50 would be the same as that between 800 and 400 or 12 and 6.

2. If Person A has a smaller base for the logarithmic transformations than Person B (A has a more acute ANS), then A will always perceive a greater difference between two numbers compared to B. Mathematically, imagine that Person A's and Person B's representations, respectively, use a log base 3 transformation (we write this as "$\log_3$") and $\log_{10}$ transformation. In this case, with a proportional difference of two, B would perceive a difference of .30 ($\log_{10}(2x) - \log_{10}(x) = \log_{10}(2x/x) = \log_{10}(2) = .30$ for all x) whereas A would perceive a difference of .63 ($\log_3(2) = .63$). Thus, Person A would perceive a bigger subjective difference than B.

3. The larger the number and the larger the proportional difference between two numbers (the bigger the ratio), the greater will be the perceived difference between individuals with more versus less acute ANS. See Figure 13.1 for a graphical depiction. The perceived numbers on the y-axis are calculated as in point 2.

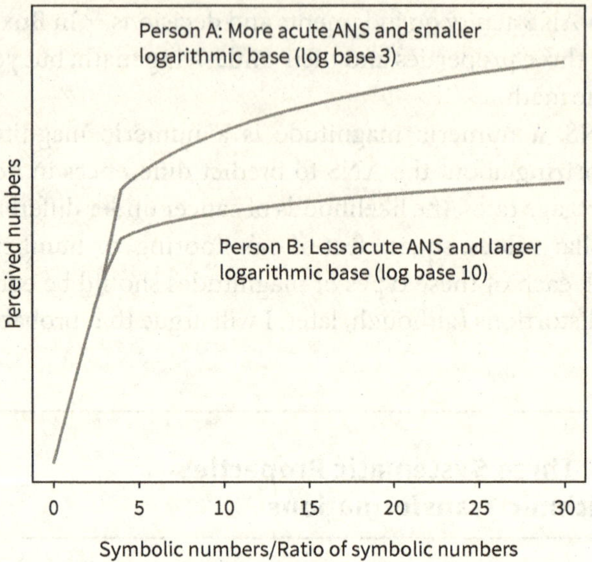

Figure 13.1 Hypothetical logarithmic mappings from symbolic numbers on the x-axis to subjective (or perceived) numbers on the y-axis. Each line represents a hypothetical individual with a different logarithmic base for transformation.

different because they are bound to a 0%–100% scale). Therefore, in decisions, individuals with more acute magnitude representations should discriminate between any two numbers better (more quickly and precisely) and perceive the numbers to be further apart than those with less precise representations, regardless of what type of quantity it is. Furthermore, perceptions of options should be based on proportional differences (ratios) between them rather than absolute differences.

Thus, subjective numerical-magnitude perceptions may intrude on judgments and choices in similar and systematic ways across different domains. This intuitive way of knowing numbers may help people, like Mark the carpenter, to compensate for not being able to calculate well. As you will learn later, it also has implications for numeric memory and distortion of values and probabilities that may be critical to a variety of judgments and choices.

Value Distortion

In some early research on value distortion,[13] we tested Box 13.1's three implications of logarithmic transformations on number discrimination and decisions: (1) ratios (relative differences) should matter more than absolute differences when it comes to the ANS's role in preferences, (2) a person with a more acute ANS (smaller base for the logarithmic transformation) should perceive a greater difference between two numbers compared to someone with a less acute ANS, and (3) the larger the proportional difference between two numbers (the bigger their ratio), the greater the perceived difference between two numbers for individuals with more versus less acute ANS. We also implicitly tested the notion that all types of magnitudes should be equally prone to ANS-based distortions by examining decisions based on monetary outcomes and numbers of lives.

Absolute Versus Relative Differences

In the first experiment,[13] participants were asked "to imagine that they were the chairperson on the board of 'Science for Life,' a charitable foundation in charge of distributing large sums of money to research institutions that develop treatments for serious diseases" and to select one proposal from three submitted proposals to receive $10 million. Institution X proposed to treat a disease and reduce deaths from 15,000/year to 5,000/year, Institution Y would reduce deaths from 160,000/year to 145,000/year, and Institution Z would reduce deaths from 290,000/year to 270,000/year. Note that a choice of Institution Z saves the greatest number of absolute lives (20,000) but the smallest proportion of lives (6.9%) whereas Institution X saves the fewest number of lives (5,000) but the greatest proportion (67%). We assessed ANS acuity with the distance-effect task described in the Appendix.

We hypothesized that people would choose based on proportions and especially those people with more acute ANS (who would perceive larger differences based on proportions) compared to those with less acute ANS. Consistent with the first two implications of logarithmic transformations mentioned earlier, individuals with more acute ANS made worse decisions, choosing Institution X that saved the fewest lives but greatest proportion of lives. In particular, 53% of those with the most acute ANS chose the illogical Institution X that saved the greatest proportion of lives (but fewest absolute lives) compared to 19% of those with the least acute ANS after controlling for objective numeracy and age. Although we expected greater objective numeracy to be associated independently with more choices of the normatively best Institution Z (which would save the greatest absolute number of lives), it was not a significant predictor. These results supported the first two implications of logarithmic representations of numeric magnitudes. First, choices were based on ratio rather than absolute differences, and, second, those with more acute ANS perceived greater value from the largest proportional mortality reduction than did those with less acute ANS.

Intertemporal Preferences (Hyperbolic Discounting)

In a second study in the same paper,[13] we used an intertemporal-preference task to examine the third implication of logarithmic representations (that perceived differences between individuals with more vs. less acute ANS would be bigger, with the larger ratio difference). In it, participants indicated two preferences on a scale ranging from −6 = much prefer (the smaller reward) now to +6 = much prefer (the larger reward) later. One choice ($100 now or $110 in a month) offered a smaller proportional difference between monetary rewards (10%) but a larger absolute difference ($10) than a second choice ($10 now or $15 in a week) that had a 50% proportional difference and only a $5 absolute difference. Logically, people should have a greater preference to delay the second choice because it has a better return rate. In addition, though, a logarithmic transformation from objective magnitudes to subjective magnitude perceptions predicts that, with increasingly acute ANS, individuals would prefer the $15 over $10 even more than they would prefer the $110 over $100 because the former has a larger ratio difference, 15:10 or 1.5 versus 110/100 or 1.1. As expected, preference differences for the larger later reward increased faster with greater ANS acuity for the $15 reward than they did for the $110 reward, supporting the third underlying implication of the ANS's logarithmic basis for preferences. Objective numeracy was not significantly related to either preference.

Findings thus far support the implications of logarithmic transformations on decisions. In addition, all types of magnitudes (monetary outcomes and numbers of lives so far) appear prone to ANS-based distortion. In fact, research highlights a common magnitude system for processing numeric magnitudes, time, and length.[14]

Risky Versus Certain Choices and Prospect Theory

These results point toward magnitude perceptions being a stable component of value across decision contexts. With my former graduate student Dan Schley, we tested this idea further.[15] We hypothesized that individuals who differ in ANS acuity would show predictable differences in how they value options (for those of you who know Prospect Theory, in the shape of their value functions). In particular, we should be able to see in judgments and choices the workings of logarithmic transformations of numeric quantities to perceived quantities.[13] First, individuals with more acute ANS should value options more than those with less acute ANS based on the magnitudes of their outcomes. Second, those with more acute ANS should do so even more at larger magnitudes (e.g., at $100 vs. $40; see the top line of Figure 13.1 for those with more acute ANS and the bottom line for those with less acute

ANS). Consequently, those with more acute ANS should value options more linearly.

In three studies, we assessed ANS acuity through a symbolic number mapping (SMap) measure reviewed in the Appendix[11] and tested both riskless (certain) and risky valuation.[15] The SMap measure was chosen due to its ease of use and because valuation tasks, like the SMap task, usually involve symbolic numbers common to decision making as opposed to nonsymbolic magnitudes (e.g., numbers of dots). In two riskless valuation studies,[15] we asked participants to indicate the farthest distance in miles they would be willing to drive to receive a specified amount of money (e.g., $5, $40, $100). In a third risky valuation study, participants made choices among pairs of gambles that changed adaptively based on their responses using dynamic experiments for estimating preferences (DEEP).[16] DEEP estimates how much people value the monetary outcomes (and how much they weigh probability level) in their choices.

Results from all three studies supported our hypothesis that valuation (whether risky or riskless) could be explained in part by individual differences in symbolic number mapping and the implications of logarithmic representations of numeric magnitudes.[15] Individuals with more precise SMap scores (greater ANS acuity) valued monetary outcomes more linearly compared to those with less precise scores. The third DEEP study also demonstrated that individuals with more precise SMap scores showed less loss aversion than those with less precise SMap scores (*loss aversion* occurs when, for example, a $40 loss hurts more than a $40 gain helps). In other words, losses loomed larger than gains, but less for people with more precise SMap scores. These results were independent of objective numeracy and are consistent with more linear magnitude representations among those with more acute ANS. Overall, ANS acuity appeared to guide valuation processes in both riskless valuations and risky choices.[15,17]

In another study, however, psychologist Andrea Patalano and her colleagues[18] concluded that the ANS was not involved in valuation processes. They used a purer ANS measure, a conventional dot-discrimination task. Whereas the SMap task relies on symbolic numbers, their ANS measure used nonsymbolic magnitudes. Three issues exist, however, with their study. First, the use of symbolic numbers in an ANS measure may be necessary to locate effects in decisions that themselves involve symbolic numbers.[15,19] The use of symbolic numbers, whether in decisions or magnitude discriminations, involves two types of noisy mental coding, both the noisy magnitudes themselves (see the bottom panel of Figure 11.1) and the noisy mapping of symbolic numbers onto their underlying magnitudes. Second, their study was underpowered for an individual-difference study if correlations of less than .40 were expected (final $N = 51$; for comparison, Schley and Peters[15] found correlations of SMap and objective numeracy with valuation ranging from .17 to .40 across three studies). Finally, they used a relatively unreliable version of an ANS measure.[20,21]

Overall, the ANS, or at least its measurement involving symbolic magnitudes, offers the possibility of stable individual differences across decision situations and product domains. Although economic value is intended to be a measure of the benefit provided by a good or service, perceptions of numeric magnitude (simply how big is a number, like 100) provide a perceptual undergird, explaining and/or confounding our notion of economic value.

Probability Distortion

Because probabilities themselves are numeric magnitudes, they may be subject to the same logarithmic transformations as monetary outcomes so that probability sensitivity also would relate to ANS acuity. The few existing studies do not support this hypothesis[15,18] although the lack of findings could be due to methodological issues (e.g., issues in fitting of Prospect Theory parameters,[15] lack of power[18]).

As a result, the relation of ANS acuity to probability is unclear. I think the relation is unlikely, though, due to the bounded nature of the probability scale (and because it is clear how to evaluate probabilities close to the end points of 0% and 100%).[22,23] Particularly when participants respond to a wide range of probabilities (e.g., from 1% to 99%), probability's bounded scale likely muddies the extent to which the ANS exerts influence on probability interpretation. Moreover, studies have uncovered a more consistent relation of objective numeracy to probability sensitivity (see Chapter 7). It is likely that objective numeracy, and not ANS acuity, will account for sensitivity to probabilistic information.

Memory for Decision-Related Information

Somewhat more examined is whether numeric memory relates to objective numeracy and/or ANS acuity. In Chapter 5, we reviewed evidence that individuals with greater objective numeracy attended more to numeric evidence and spent more time on numeric decisions than did those lower in objective numeracy. This greater processing of numeric information may help to explain findings that the highly numerate recall numbers better.[24–27] However, a separate link also exists between the ANS and numeric memory. Greater ANS acuity (measured with SMap, in particular) has been linked with children's superior memory for numbers, controlling for math knowledge.[28,29] We further demonstrated that adults with more versus less precise SMap scores had better numeric memory (but not non-numeric memory), after controlling for objective numeracy.[17] It is unclear at this point how much previous results linking objective numeracy and memory for numbers may be due to the highly numerate processing numbers more deeply versus their being better able to discriminate numeric magnitudes (based on objective numeracy's relation with ANS acuity). I suspect that both objective numeracy and ANS acuity will matter to numeric recall in decision tasks (that happen to assess memory, too) and that only ANS acuity will relate in memorization tasks.

Moving Forward with the ANS

Let's pause for a moment to review what we have just learned. The ANS allows us to represent and manipulate numeric quantities through representations of magnitude (of quantity or bigness) that are spontaneously activated in the presence of numeric information regardless of their format. A number of dots, an Arabic numeral, a spelled-out number all will activate these magnitude representations similarly. The representations are "inner marks" that allow verbal and nonverbal animals to "think unnamed numbers" (p. 3).[30,31] They also underlie our very distinctive human ability to grasp the abstract numbers that allow us to predict, manipulate, and even control the world around us.

Any influence of the ANS on decision making, unlike objective numeracy, appears to be primarily innate (see Chapter 11). It is generally thought to support better judgments and decisions, but researchers also can devise decision situations that take advantage of ANS-based proportional reasoning and essentially trick people into making worse decisions.[13] What is most important for you to understand about the ANS is that it provides an intuitive feel for how far apart are two numeric values, such as pairs of prices or interest rates, that may be importantly different for decisions you make. The ANS also may compensate for and/or complement your objective numeric abilities by allowing you to make quick numeric estimates that are good enough for the task at hand (like Mark the carpenter). Finally, although research is limited in this topic, you should have begun to understand situations where your ANS-based intuitions could mislead you (100¢ really is the same as $1, and 1 year is longer than 6 months!).

More broadly, results in the current chapter question what we mean by "preference" (a greater liking for one option over another) and "economic value" (the benefit provided by an option). What are preferences and economic value if their foundations rest on how we represent numeric magnitudes devoid of any decision context? What we call preference and value instead may emerge from two separate areas of the brain, one of which is sensitive to ANS acuity (numeric magnitudes and the intraparietal sulcus) and the other of which is due to something traditionally closer to what we call value (monetary values and the orbitofrontal cortex).[10] Links between ANS acuity and decisions, according to this view, are more likely mediated by intraparietal sulcus activations (linked to numeric magnitudes) than by those in orbitofrontal cortex (linked to monetary outcomes). This suggestion remains to be tested explicitly.

Understanding how lower level cognitive processes such as magnitude-discriminability effects influence higher level decision processes is intellectually interesting and has been useful in other domains such as reading and math.[32] It may be that decision makers consciously or unconsciously rely more on one numeric competence (ANS acuity vs. objective numeracy) in some decisions and a different numeric competence in other decisions. Prior research in decision making has certainly found that decision makers use different decision heuristics depending on the context.[33] Decision makers also may switch information-processing strategies within the same decision based on our various numeric competencies (using a number transformation based on objective numeracy in one moment and then an ANS-based intuitive feel for how far apart are two numbers). Understanding the link between ANS processes and decision making is likely to be useful in resolving theoretical arguments in decision making[8] and in identifying people and situations in which decisions would benefit from intervention.

References

1. Alyson, J. (2018, May 30). What skills are required to be a carpenter? http://work.chron.com/skills-required-carpenter-11775.html.
2. Abramson, J. Z., Hernández-Lloreda, V., Call, J., & Colmenares, F. (2013). Relative quantity judgments in the beluga whale (*Delphinapterus leucas*) and the bottlenose dolphin (*Tursiops truncatus*). *Behavioural Processes, 96*, 11–19.
3. Goldstein, D. (2018, May 1). Nineteen vs. twenty. Decision Science News. http://www.decisionsciencenews.com/2018/05/01/nineteen-vs-twenty/
4. Bernoulli, D. (1954). Exposition of a new theory on the measurement of risk. (Sommer, L. Trans.). *Econometrica, 22*(1), 22–36. (Original work published 1738.)

5. Kahneman, D., & Tversky, A. (1979). Prospect theory: An analysis of decision under risk. *Econometrica, 47*(2), 263–291.

6. Kahneman, D., & Tversky, A. (1984). Choices, values, and frames. *American Psychologist, 39*(4), 341–350.

7. Shafir, S. (2000). Risk-sensitive foraging: The effect of relative variability. *Oikos, 88*(3), 663–669.

8. Weber, E. U., Shafir, S., & Blais, A. R. (2004). Predicting risk sensitivity in humans and lower animals: Risk as variance or coefficient of variation. *Psychological Review, 111*(2), 430–445.

9. Shrivastava, S., Jain, G., Nayakankuppam, D., Gaeth, G. J., & Levin, I. P. (2017). Numerosity and allocation behavior: Insights using the dictator game. *Judgment and Decision Making, 12*(6), 527–536.

10. Kanayet, F. J., Opfer, J. E., & Cunningham, W. A. (2014). The value of numbers in economic rewards. *Psychological Science, 25*(8), 1534–1545.

11. Siegler, R. S., & Opfer, J. E. (2003). The development of numerical estimation: Evidence for multiple representations of numerical quantity. *Psychological Science, 14*(3), 237–250.

12. Nieder, A., & Miller, E. K. (2003). Coding of cognitive magnitude: Compressed scaling of numerical information in the primate prefrontal cortex. *Neuron, 37*(1), 149–157.

13. Peters, E., Slovic, P., Västfjäll, D., & Mertz, C. K. (2008). Intuitive numbers guide decisions. *Judgment and Decision Making, 3*(8), 619–635.

14. Crollen, V., Grade, S., Pesenti, M., & Dormal, V. (2013). A common metric magnitude system for the perception and production of numerosity, length, and duration. *Frontiers in Psychology, 4*, 449–458.

15. Schley, D. R., & Peters, E. (2014). Assessing economic value symbolic-number mappings predict risky and riskless valuations. *Psychological Science, 25*(3), 753–761.

16. Toubia, O., Johnson, E., Evgeniou, T., & Delquié, P. (2013). Dynamic experiments for estimating preferences: An adaptive method of eliciting time and risk parameters. *Management Science, 59*(3), 613–640.

17. Peters, E., & Bjälkebring, P. (2015). Multiple numeric competencies: When a number is not just a number. *Journal of Personality and Social Psychology, 108*(5), 802–822.

18. Patalano, A. L., Saltiel, J. R., Machlin, L., & Barth, H. (2015). The role of numeracy and approximate number system acuity in predicting value and probability distortion. *Psychonomic Bulletin & Review, 22*(6), 1820–1829.

19. Mueller, S. M., Schiebener, J., Delazer, M., & Brand, M. (2018). Risk approximation in decision making: Approximative numeric abilities predict advantageous decisions under objective risk. *Cognitive Processing, 19*(3), 297–315.

20. Chesney, D., Bjälkebring, P., & Peters. E. (2015). How to estimate how well people estimate: Evaluating measures of individual differences in the approximate number system. *Attention, Perception, & Psychophysics, 77*(8), 2781–2802.

21. Lindskog, M., Winman, A., Juslin, P., & Poom, L. (2013). Measuring acuity of the approximate number system reliably and validly: The evaluation of an adaptive test procedure. *Frontiers in Psychology, 4*, 510–527.

22. Bateman, I., Dent, S., Peters, E., Slovic, P., & Starmer, C. (2007). The affect heuristic and the attractiveness of simple gambles. *Journal of Behavioral Decision Making, 20*(4), 365–380.

23. Peters, E., Fennema, M. G., & Tiede, K. E. (2019). The loss-bet paradox: Actuaries, accountants, and other numerate people rate numerically inferior gambles as superior. *Journal of Behavioral Decision Making, 32*, 15–29. https://doi.org/10.1002/bdm.2085.

24. Besser, A. G., Sanderson, S. C., Roberts, J. S., Chen, C. A., Christensen, K. D., Lautenbach, D. M., . . . Green, R. C. (2015). Factors affecting recall of different types of personal genetic information about Alzheimer's disease risk: The REVEAL Study. *Public Health Genomics, 18*(2), 78–86.

25. Callison, C., Gibson, R., & Zillmann, D. (2009). How to report quantitative information in news stories. *Newspaper Research Journal, 30*(2), 43–55.

26. Galesic, M., & Garcia-Retamero, R. (2011). Communicating consequences of risky behaviors: Life expectancy versus risk of disease. *Patient Education and Counseling, 82*(1), 30–35.

27. Zillmann, D., Callison, C., & Gibson, R. (2009). Quantitative media literacy: Individual differences in dealing with numbers in the news. *Media Psychology, 12*(4), 394–416.

28. Thompson, C. A., & Siegler, R. S. (2010). Linear numerical-magnitude representations aid children's memory for numbers. *Psychological Science, 21*(9), 1274–1281.

29. Thompson, C. A., & Opfer, J. E. (2016). Learning linear spatial-numeric associations improves accuracy of memory for numbers. *Frontiers in Psychology, 7*, 24.

30. Koehler, O. (1950). The ability of birds to count. *Bulletin of Animal Behaviour, 9*, 41–45.

31. Smeltzer, D. (2006). *Man and number*. Mineola, NY: Dover Publications.

32. Holloway, I. D., & Ansari, D. (2009). Mapping numerical magnitudes onto symbols: The numerical distance effect and individual differences in children's mathematics achievement. *Journal of Experimental Child Psychology, 103*(1), 17–29.

33. Payne, J. W., Bettman, J. R., & Johnson, E. J. (1993). *The adaptive decision maker*. New York: Cambridge University Press.

14

Subjective Numeracy and Knowing What You Know

People are often comfortable saying they are bad at math even though they would be embarrassed to be thought illiterate. It's not entirely clear why this literacy/numeracy difference exists, but it may be because illiteracy is relatively uncommon whereas innumeracy is unexceptional. In one study, for example, 99% scored as having adequate literacy skills; only 17% had better than ninth-grade numeracy skills.[1] This difference in proportions of people with adequate literacy versus numeracy is common.

In a recent study of 382 individuals, we asked them if they agreed or disagreed with the following statement "I consider myself a math person." Thirty-eight percent of our participants said that they somewhat or strongly disagreed that they were a math person, 13% neither agreed nor disagreed, and 49% somewhat or strongly agreed that they were a math person.[2] Having lower subjective numeracy (operationalized in this book as having lower numeric confidence, aka self-efficacy, or higher math anxiety), however, may hold us back as individuals and as a society from realizing our numeric potential and its positive effects. In this chapter, I draw primarily from literatures in psychology and medical decision making to review emerging evidence concerning the psychological processes that underlie the effects of subjective numeracy on judgment and decision processes and life outcomes.

By the end of this chapter, you will understand that numbers exert motivational, and even emotional, impacts on our lives, separate from our actual abilities. You will learn that individuals who believe they are worse with numbers have more negative emotional reactions to numbers in judgments and choices, and they are more anxious about using numbers. These emotional reactions to math and numeric confidence (aka self-efficacy, how good or bad you believe you are at math) appear to drive whether people approach or avoid numeric information, how hard they try with numbers, and how much they persevere in ongoing tasks that involve numbers. You will also learn about some of our early studies concerning how numeric confidence and ability interact. Specifically, even when an individual with low numeric confidence has adequate objective ability with numbers, they may understand less and make

Innumeracy in the Wild. Ellen Peters, Oxford University Press (2020). © Oxford University Press 2020.
DOI: 10.1093/oso/9780190861094.003.0001

worse decisions nonetheless because they enjoy the process less, give up more easily, and ultimately perform less well. Conversely, people who do not score as objectively high in numeracy but believe they're quite good with numbers may tackle numeric tasks with zest but make significant errors. Their own numeric ignorance is invisible to them[3] but has negative consequences.

Numeric Competencies and Emotional Reactions to Math

Growing up, I sat on our old green couch with my three brothers and watched *Sesame Street*. The Count sang about loving to count, and we sang along with him. I'm not sure that the Count really made the difference, but all four of us graduated college with engineering degrees. For me, math was always fun. It was a series of interesting puzzles to solve. For some people, math is even beautiful.[4] But others report a very different experience. As one high school graduate wrote "I was having trouble figuring out how to maximize the amount I could pay off while minimizing interest payments across cards. It was stressful and made me feel inferior, because I should be better at this than I was at that particular time."[5] Embarrassment shows up frequently, too, when people talk about their everyday experiences with numbers. "When I first started couponing for groceries and other things, I had a hard time calculating how much things were going to cost. Several times I made errors and during one particular time with a cashier, I had to have her take everything off of my ticket and take back all the groceries to go buy more to do the deal. I was very embarrassed!"[6]

In recent research, we found that people who reported being less subjectively numerate also reported experiencing more negative emotions to math than those higher in subjective numeracy.[7] In fact, these emotional reactions to math were better predictors of subjective numeracy ratings than were objective numeracy scores[7] even though the subjective numeracy measure was developed to be a proxy for objective numeracy.[8]

These emotional reactions to math can feel debilitating. In fact, psychologist Sian Beilock and her colleague[9] have demonstrated that mere anticipation of doing math caused activation of the neural networks associated with visceral threat detection and the experience of pain among highly math-anxious individuals. The activation was specific to anticipating the pain of math; actually doing math problems did not increase activation in these same areas. For many people, math (and math in everyday decisions) provokes negative emotions. In one study, about 16% of participants reported experiencing "quite a bit" or "high anxiety" in dealing with numbers every day.[10]

Such anxiety may be particularly troublesome for decision making because anxiety takes up cognitive resources, such as working memory, that we need to do our best thinking.[11,12] Whereas those lower in *objective* numeracy do not understand numbers and are not inclined toward using number operations (comparing numbers, doing calculations) in judgments and decisions (see Chapters 2–8), those lower in *subjective* numeracy react negatively simply to the possibility of doing math.

With my colleague Pär Bjälkebring,[7] we explored relations among our three numeric competencies (objective numeracy, subjective numeracy, and approximate number system [ANS] acuity), gender, and math emotions (see Figure 14.1). We hypothesized and found that greater ANS acuity (assessed through symbolic number mapping) was associated with being more objectively numerate, consistent with ANS acuity underlying the development of math abilities (Chapter 11). Greater objective abilities then appeared to drive more positive math emotions and greater subjective numeracy; math emotions and subjective numeracy were also related. Gender differences emerged; females rated themselves lower than males in subjective numeracy and scored marginally lower in their objective abilities. The relations of objective numeracy to gender and ANS acuity held, even when controlling for intelligence proxies (working memory and vocabulary scores).

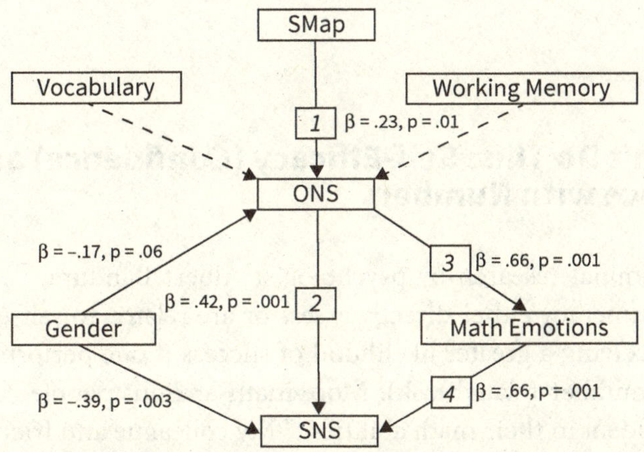

Figure 14.1 Structural equation model of symbolic number mapping (SMap), Objective Numeracy Scale (ONS), Subjective Numeracy Scale (SNS), Gender, Math Emotions, Vocabulary, and Working Memory. A dashed line indicates a path that was nonsignificant ($p > .10$).

We tested alternative models at the same time by reversing or eliminating various paths and concluded that (1) greater subjective numeracy did not lead to greater objective numeracy and more positive math emotions (the model in Figure 14.1 fit the data better than a model reversing paths 2 and 4, similar to prior research[13]); (2) despite the literature on stereotype threat,[14] gender did not lead to lower SNS, more negative math emotions, and worse objective numeracy scores in turn (a model that reversed Paths 2, 3, and 4 was not as good a fit to the data); and (3) more positive math emotions did not lead to greater objective numeracy. Instead, Figure 14.1's model was the best fit to the data (data fit was identical, however, if Path 4 was reversed).

We proposed that the link between emotional reactions to math and subjective numeracy might be explained by subjective numeracy tapping into a self-representation of "me as a math person" or "not a math person."[7] If so, then when a numeric self-representation is activated, that activation may spread among related (but not unrelated) self-representations to organize ongoing experiences and direct actions.[15] Thus, spreading activation of subjective numeracy as a self-representation should alter emotional reactions and related motivations and behaviors in numeric but not non-numeric tasks[15,16] and, thus, should have implications for judgment and choice. In the rest of this chapter, I present evidence consistent with those implications, including evidence concerning persistence with numeric information, wanting numbers, numeric comprehension, and choices. If the chapter piques your interest concerning subjective numeracy measures, I provide a brief review in Chapter 1's Appendix.

I Just Can't Do This: Self-Efficacy (Confidence) and Persistence with Numbers

Based on seminal research by psychologist Albert Bandura,[17] measures of subjective numeracy either directly assess or are related to self-efficacy (defined as perceiving a greater likelihood of success if one performs a task; in this case, a number-related task). More math-anxious people, for example, are less confident in their math abilities.[18] My colleague and friend, psychologist Nancy Betz, suggests that having this confidence is important because it determines "whether or not behavior will be initiated, how much effort will be expended, and how long behavior will be sustained in the face of obstacles and aversive experiences" (p. 328).[19] Thus, greater self-efficacy relates to approach (vs. avoidance) behaviors and persistence in the face of obstacles.[17,20]

According to self-efficacy theory, a person's belief in his or her ability to perform a task well is the major driver of behavior.

Thus, although greater objective numeracy has been associated with superior decision making and decision outcomes, being better at math may not guarantee optimal decision making. People also need to believe in their own numeric skills (they need self-efficacy) so that they will be active decision makers if the decisions require considerable engagement or re-engagement with numbers over time. Individuals who believe less in their numeric skills (they are lower in subjective numeracy) may be driven less to approach number-heavy decisions (e.g., selecting retirement funds) and may be more likely to avoid or fail to persist in boring or difficult tasks that must be completed time and time again. Such tasks are common and range from adhering to a doctor's instructions, making bill payments, counting carbohydrates in a meal, or following a budget.

Ultimately, the less subjectively numerate may be less likely to act in the face of numeric information. Consistent with this reasoning, we recently tested memory for numeric and non-numeric information simultaneously.[7] We asked participants to memorize a series of 18 numbers of objects in given locations (e.g., 20 skulls on a shelf) so that they could later recall the number (20) and object (skulls) when presented the location (shelf). Participants could respond correctly, incorrectly, or not respond (no penalty existed for wrong answers). We hypothesized and found that less subjectively numerate participants attempted to recall fewer numbers than those higher in subjective numeracy (controlling for intelligence and other numeric competencies). In other words, they persisted less either in encoding the numbers in the first place or in attempting to retrieve them. No such subjective numeracy differences existed in responses to a non-numeric vocabulary test.

One of my graduate students, Mary Kate Tompkins,[21] looked more directly at the relation of numeric self-efficacy and persistence with numbers. Undergraduate participants ($N = 292$) responded to the first four numeric confidence questions in a popular subjective numeracy scale.[8] They then attempted to answer two unsolvable math problems (e.g., "Imagine that you have 10 coins in your pocket [pennies, nickels, dimes, or quarters]. The value of the coins adds up to $1.53. What are the coins?"). She timed how long people were willing to try to solve them as an operationalization of persistence. As hypothesized, higher numeric confidence was associated with greater persistence (time spent) on these impossible problems.

Although persisting more on an impossible task is wasted effort, persistence often pays off. Recent survey research, for example, found that individuals with greater financial self-efficacy (defined as confidence in financial management capacities) reported better financial behaviors, owning more investment and savings products and fewer debt products than those with lower self-efficacy beliefs, controlling for objective financial knowledge.[22] Having greater subjective knowledge in specific content domains or more generally with numbers appears to have unique positive effects on related actions. To do well with numbers, one has to have ability and also the confidence to use them.

Decision Consequences of Emotional Reactions and Self-Efficacy

Wanting Versus Avoiding Numbers

Subjective numeracy also may drive wanting to receive versus avoid numbers in communications. As reviewed in Chapter 9, physicians with higher subjective numeracy were more likely to report communicating or intending to communicate numeric health information than those lower in subjective numeracy (controlling for objective numeracy).[23] These subjectively numerate physicians want to provide more numeric evidence, such as for prognosis at the end of life, to their patients.[24] Nonphysicians show a related effect: Greater subjective numeracy was associated with a greater preference to receive numeric risk information in hypothetical informed consent, controlling for objective numeracy.[25] Consistent with self-efficacy theory,[17] more subjectively numerate individuals initiate action with numbers more by wanting to provide and receive them in the first place as compared to those lower in subjective numeracy. When numeric information is computationally complex, these subjective numeracy effects may be stronger, and especially when assessed with the preference-for-numbers submeasure of one common measure.[8,26,27]

Consistent with the subjectively numerate wanting numeric information more, they also may seek it out more and enjoy the information-seeking process more. You read in Chapter 5, for example, about existing, albeit limited, research on numeracy and numeric information seeking (mostly conducted with objective numeracy and process-tracing methods). The link with information seeking, however, is particularly likely with subjective numeracy for three reasons. First, across domains, greater confidence in one's abilities is an important predictor of information-seeking behaviors.[28] Second, people tend to avoid information when it might lead to unpleasant emotions.[29] The less subjectively numerate, of course, experience more negative emotions in anticipation of doing math problems and dealing with numbers in everyday decisions[9,10] and, thus, may avoid numbers.[29,30] In fact, less subjectively numerate respondents from the 2007 Health Information National Trends Survey (HINTS) reported a more negative experience in seeking health information than those higher in subjective numeracy.[31] Information seeking is important though when choosing whether to find out about the likelihood of a disease such as the flu (and possibly be vaccinated for it) or the probability of benefits and adverse events from siting a nearby chemical plant (and possibly vote for it). No known studies exist on information seeking and subjective numeracy while controlling for objective numeracy.

Finally, people avoid information when they perceive it will present something difficult, demanding, or unpleasant.[27] Because doing numeric computations is perceived as more difficult by those lower in subjective numeracy (and interpreting numbers may be perceived in similar manner),[32,33] the less subjectively numerate likely will avoid numbers in decisions simply because they perceive numbers as hard. In addition, to be self-consistent, those higher and lower in subjective numeracy may choose environments strategically that allow them to select and avoid numeric information in line with their subjective numeracy.[34–38] Consistent with this research, the more subjectively numerate are more aware of numeric information. For example, individuals higher in subjective numeracy were more likely to be aware of (highly numeric) direct-to-consumer genetic tests, perhaps due to a greater desire to seek out numeric information.[39]

Thus, positive and negative motivations seem to drive part of the use and nonuse of numerical information in decisions. Numeric confidence (self-efficacy) and math anxiety, respectively, are sources of positive and negative motivation. Having less math self-efficacy and higher math anxiety can leave people (even if they are numerically able) potentially susceptible to a variety of problems in decision making where it matters if the decision maker engages with numerical information. These findings may help explain why individuals lower in subjective and objective numeracy prefer less active roles in medical decisions with their healthcare providers.[40] They do not seek out numeric health information, do not want it provided to them, and prefer not to reason with it because of its difficulty and/or emotional consequences for them. Let's continue with ways this avoidance likely matters to decisions independent of objective numeracy.

Understanding Numbers

Researchers have found that the less subjectively numerate (based on math anxiety and self-efficacy) avoid math courses and math content more and therefore learn less math than those who are higher in subjective numeracy.[41,42] As a result, any subjective numeracy effects on numeric comprehension in natural settings might be explained by differences in objective numeracy because the latter measure already takes into account this earlier avoidance of learning math. On the other hand, less subjectively numerate individuals also bring their negative emotional reactions, lack of confidence, and avoidance into current situations. By this logic, subjective numeracy may have additional effects on numeric comprehension separate from objective numeracy. In support of the first conjecture, individuals who rated themselves as more anxious to use numbers in everyday tasks misunderstood health statistics more and were less confident in their responses.[10] The confidence results held after controlling for objective numeracy, but the accuracy results did not; objective numeracy accounted for comprehension.

The second conjecture (that subjective and objective numeracy both have independent associations with comprehension) is more often supported. For example, middle-aged to older adults (50 years and older) were asked comprehension questions about colorectal cancer prevention information controlling for prose literacy and education;[43] both objective and subjective numeracy related to better comprehension. In a more stringent test of this hypothesis, researchers found independent subjective numeracy effects (using the first four questions of a popular subjective numeracy measure[8]). Specifically, those who rated their numeric ability lower also performed worse on medical data interpretation and tradeoffs, after controlling for objective numeracy, cognitive abilities (non-numeric fluid and crystallized intelligence measures), demographic variables (age, gender, marital status, education), and work experience.[44] In an applied genetics setting, both objective and subjective numeracy were positively related to more accurate understanding of an ambiguous genetic test result.[45] Thus, subjective numeracy, as measured with perceived ability (aka numeric self-efficacy or confidence), appears to exert independent effects on comprehension of numeric data, whereas math anxiety may not.

Separable roles for numeric self-efficacy and math anxiety have been little studied. Although related, they are different from one another. Numeric self-efficacy concerns confidence about the likelihood of math success (a more cognitive concept) whereas math anxiety is defined as feelings experienced in reaction to or anticipation of doing math (an emotional concept). Both concepts have been related to avoidance of math-related content and situations.[17,41] For example, in one study, participants read about statistical evidence of potential risks from genetically modified foods. Their math anxiety increased from before to after reading the information.[46] However, similar to other findings,[10] math anxiety did not predict comprehension of the information over and above math self-efficacy and objective numeracy, both of which did predict comprehension as expected.[46] Thus, math self-efficacy, as suggested by psychologist Albert Bandura,[17] as opposed to math anxiety, may be a more direct determinant of behaviors needed to understand numeric data. Math anxiety, however, may be a precursor to being less numerate in the first place.[47]

Given that the knowledge gained from information is a basic building block for making good decisions,[48] having greater subjective numeracy should be beneficial, independent of objective numeracy. However, for this statement to be true, people also have to use numeric information effectively, an assumption that is not always met—as you'll see later in this chapter's section "The Effects of Knowing More or Less Than What You Think You Know."

Forming Judgments and Making Decisions

The negative emotional reactions and lower self-efficacy of subjective numeracy seem to have consequences that include lower cognitive capacity, less persistence with and more avoidance of numbers, and inferior numeric comprehension. As a result, subjective numeracy likely also exerts an influence on judgments and choices independent of objective numeracy. In particular, individuals who *perceive* themselves higher versus lower in numeracy should find numeric tasks more attractive and be more willing to respond to them; the same should not be true for non-numeric tasks. Consistent with the numeric part of this reasoning, greater subjective (but not objective) numeracy has been associated with greater willingness to pay for (highly numeric) direct-to-consumer genetic testing results.[49,50] Worry that the test might find illness and risk perceptions related to developing breast cancer and having a genetic mutation did not explain the results. Thus, the test's value (how much people said they were willing to pay for it) related more to numeric self-efficacy and preferences for numeric information than it did to people's cognitive and emotional anticipations to getting emotionally aversive but potentially helpful information.

Evaluations of other numeric options relate similarly to subjective numeracy. Take the Loss versus No-Loss bets task reviewed in Chapter 6. You might recall that people judged the attractiveness of playing either a Loss bet (7/36 chances to win $9; otherwise lose 5¢) or a No-Loss bet (7/36 chances to win $9; otherwise win nothing). In responses to the bets, greater objective numeracy was associated with a number-comparison process that resulted in the objectively worse Loss bet being rated as more subjectively attractive than the No-Loss bet.[7] However, bets are highly numeric, and those higher versus lower in subjective numeracy rated both bets as more attractive (they were not affected by the presence of the small loss), independent of objective numeracy and intelligence proxies. Moreover, the result could not be explained by a positive-rating bias among those higher in subjective numeracy. In particular, they rated their subjective numeracy and the bet more positively, but did not rate (nonnumeric) self-reported health more positively. Thus, more subjectively numerate people valued highly numeric objects more than the less subjectively numerate.

Emotional learning about choice options also may relate to subjective numeracy. For example, more math-anxious people made worse decisions on a card task called the Iowa Gambling Task (IGT);[51] objective numeracy was unrelated to performance. In the task, participants initially know nothing about four card decks, but they learn as they win and lose money based on their choices. Participants who make better IGT choices develop stronger physiological reactions to the bad decks than the good decks and these reactions appear to guide their choices. The math anxious may have made worse choices for either of two reasons. First, because the math anxious experience greater physiological reactions to numeric processing,[9,52] their greater overall reactivity may have overwhelmed the physiological differentiation between good and bad decks so that the decks' difference went undetected by them, leading the math anxious to make worse decisions. Alternatively, individuals with greater math anxiety may have reacted more to the higher average loss amounts in the good decks than they did to the lower average loss amounts in the bad decks, with those reactions guiding them toward choosing the bad decks. Similar findings have emerged with related measures of negative reactivity.[53] However, neither math anxiety nor objective numeracy were associated with performance on the Balloon Analogue Risk Task.[51]

If lower subjective numeracy only affected decisions in lab tasks, they might be of little concern. However, it is also a roadblock to numeracy learning (see Chapter 12), and it appears to underlie taking fewer math-intensive courses[13] and being less likely to pursue math-related careers. In the next section, it also emerges as important to life outcomes in interaction with objective numeracy.[54,55]

The Effects of Knowing More or Less Than What You Think You Know

Former US President Calvin Coolidge is credited with saying "Nothing in this world can take the place of persistence. . . . Persistence and determination alone are omnipotent."[56] According to this quote, Coolidge believed that the persistence emerging from greater subjective numeracy should always be beneficial. This more-is-better prediction is borne out in some research. For example, more overconfidence appears to be an important driver of choosing math-related careers. In a recent study, male and female college students were asked to take a math test and estimate their score. Men overestimated how well they had done more than women did, and the overestimation accounted for men's greater intent to pursue math-related careers (they did not control for other math self-efficacy measures).[57] These data provide some support for the idea that being more confident could underlie people's tendency to pursue lofty goals. They may also help to explain males' overrepresentation in US science and engineering fields.[58]

However, a mismatch between one's actual and perceived number abilities could be problematic. In recent research on self-reported financial outcomes, we predicted an interactive effect of objective numeracy and numeric confidence. Specifically, among those individuals with higher objective numeracy, we reasoned that having more numeric confidence (greater numeric self-efficacy) would lead them to persist in numeric tasks and take action in financial decisions. Because they had the objective skills to support effective decisions, they would enjoy greater financial success based on our hypothesis.[59] However, if lower objective numeracy was paired with higher numeric confidence, these individuals may make the worst decisions because they persist in financial choices but lack the necessary numeric skills for success. Thus, they would be more prone to calculation errors (e.g., making debt repayment calculation errors, taking out payday loans without understanding the numeric terms, selecting a mortgage with higher interest rates) and bad financial decisions. You may recognize yourself or someone you know in this description and the paragraphs that follow.

Data on self-reported positive financial outcomes (e.g., having no credit card debt or payday loans) from 4,572 participants supported our hypotheses.[59] Individuals highest in objective numeracy reported 82% positive financial outcomes if they were also higher in numeric confidence but only 78% positive outcomes if they were lower in numeric confidence. This 4% difference was not small; it was equivalent to the effect of having an additional $93,905 in annual household income (controlling for other variables in the model, such as education). Furthermore, among those lowest in objective numeracy, the opposite pattern emerged with numerically confident individuals reporting only 78% positive outcomes compared to 80% positive outcomes for those lower in numeric confidence. Despite having worse outcomes, these individuals with lower objective numeracy and higher confidence nonetheless perceived themselves to be about as financially well-off as those with the same confidence but higher ability (see Appendix).[59] We think that their confidence combined with lack of ability may lead them to not see or not value opportunities to improve their finances.

If these individual differences (objective numeracy and numeric confidence) tap into basic psychological processes with respect to understanding and processing important numeric information, then we should see a similar interaction in other domains. Health decision making is a critical area in which numeric competencies could play a role and perhaps especially in chronic disease management that requires persistence over time. We recently studied a group of 91 patients with systemic lupus erythematosus.[59] They gave us permission to access their disease activity scores in their medical records (possible range = 0–24) and they completed measures of numeric confidence and objective numeracy. Lupus itself is an autoimmune disease in which the body attacks its own tissues, and it can cause widespread inflammation and tissue damage in affected organs. It has no cure, but medical interventions and lifestyle changes, if properly done, can help control symptoms and disease progression. Adhering to such a program, however, requires numeric skills to understand the risks and benefits of drugs, to adhere to medications such as prednisone, to perform healthy behaviors such as regular exercise, and to make good health insurance and health provider choices.

We reasoned that current disease activity may be affected by the same objective numeracy and numeric confidence factors that were related to financial outcomes. Consistent with this thinking, among patients highest in objective numeracy, if they were also higher in numeric confidence, their disease activity was lower (mean = 1.0) than if they were lower in numeric confidence (mean = 4.2), as if the latter group had the skills but not the necessary persistence. For patients lowest in objective numeracy, the opposite pattern emerged once again. Their average disease activity was higher if they were higher in numeric confidence (mean = 5.5, as if they persisted but did not have the necessary numeric skills to do their health tasks successfully) and lower if they were lower in numeric confidence (mean = 3.2). Those lower in both subjective and objective numeracy may compensate with a greater willingness to ask for and receive help and advice on their medical condition. Results were similar when examining which patients had sufficiently active disease (scores of ≥6) that they likely required additional treatment. Among patients higher in numeric confidence, for example, 7% and 44%, respectively, of those highest and lowest in objective numeracy likely required additional treatment.

Across financial outcomes and lupus disease activity, both numeric competencies mattered and in ways that were consistent with what we know about objective numeracy and its links with number operations *and* what we know about numeric confidence and the behavioral consequences of self-efficacy. Confidence supports success if you have skills consistent with the actions you take. Conversely, misplaced confidence can be an issue that puts people at financial and medical risk. Those higher in numeric confidence but lower in objective skills are perhaps the best exemplars of the *Dunning-Kruger effect.* "Not only does their incomplete and misguided knowledge lead them to make mistakes but those exact same deficits also prevent them from recognizing when they are making mistakes and other people [are] choosing more wisely" (p. 248).[3] Note, however, that those higher in objective skills and lower in numeric confidence had similarly problematic outcomes in health and finances.

Moving Forward with Subjective Numeracy

The truth is, you are a math person. You can tell at a glance about how many oranges are on your kitchen counter and you can even quickly approximate its combination with the fruit in your refrigerator. We come into this world with a sense of numeric magnitude and a rudimentary ability to do approximate arithmetic. Some differences exist in this evolutionarily older ability, but people differ considerably more in their objective numeracy abilities for a variety of reasons (see Chapters 11 and 12). One reason germane to this chapter is that you may not believe you are good at math. Theory and data point toward these preconceived notions of your ability driving how much you persevere to understand and use numbers effectively. It may also explain lower subjective numeracy's relation with avoiding healthcare.[60] Although more research is needed, believing less in your abilities leads to less persistence in numeric tasks even if you have adequate numeric skills. Believing more in your abilities, conversely, leads to greater persistence. If you also have the necessary objective numeracy skills to support the tasks you attempt, then you will achieve better success. However, despite former President Coolidge's beliefs about the omnipotence of persistence, persistence without requisite skills appears problematic.[59]

The importance of *calibration* (having a match between objective numeracy and numeric confidence) may depend on where you are in the decision process, however. Psychologist David Dunning suggests that the "road to a goal often contains two phases. The first is a planning and preparation phase, in which people must map out how they can reach their goal. The second is the actual execution of a plan. Overconfidence may be beneficial in the second phase, when people potentially must energize and persevere to press on to their goals, but it may be deadly in the first phase" (p. 289).[3] Thus, calibration may matter more in planning and preparation (and those higher in objective numeracy tend to be better calibrated on general knowledge and numeracy questions).[61] Overconfidence, and the persistence that comes from having more numeric confidence than warranted, may be beneficial, however, once a goal has been determined and action is needed. For example, men's greater overconfidence in math ability appears to explain their greater interest in pursuing math courses and careers relative to women.[57] It may be that having a positive illusion of one's math ability is particularly useful to learning in math and related courses that involve difficult concepts and negative feedback.[19,62] However, the activities critical to attainment of good overall financial outcomes and enjoy better health outcomes among lupus patients[59] may better match Dunning's planning and preparation phase.[3] We do not yet understand enough of what seems likely to be a complex interplay between greater math confidence and overconfidence in the quality of judgments we form and choices we make.

Furthermore, characteristics of the person (like subjective numeracy) are not the only motivational drivers, and motivations stemming from the decision situation itself also matter. Curiosity, a desire to increase positive emotions, and impulses to reduce worry or uncertainty can override personal traits.[28] For example, controlling for objective numeracy, women made higher quality hospital choices than men;[63] they may have worked harder to "run the numbers" to reduce concerns about their families' health. Experience with similar numeric processing also matters. In fact, in one study, Americans were less numerate than Germans but nonetheless made numerically superior choices.[64] The researchers speculated that Americans may have had more experience with trading off attributes in decisions (e.g., tradeoffs between monetary outcomes and probabilities). Thus, it is not inevitable that the less subjectively numerate will always avoid numeric information in decisions, but it is likely that they will do so in more situations than those higher in subjective numeracy.

You knew before reading this chapter that numbers can be difficult and that being more objectively numerate can help people choose better. Hopefully, you now also know that being more objectively numerate does not guarantee the best decisions and outcomes. Merely thinking you are not a math person likely limits your ability to learn math, and it also curbs how much you use numbers in the inevitable situations where math can help you avoid getting the wrong change, running out of a prescription drug, or investing in a bad venture. By believing you're not a math person when you really are at your core, you may avoid more math education and avoid important numbers in everyday life that you could otherwise handle. As a result, you may hamstring your own career, health, and wealth. The key is calibration and arriving at a better understanding of what you actually know.

References

1. Kumar, D., Sanders, L., Perrin, E. M., Lokker, N., Patterson, B., Gunn, V., . . . Rothman, R. L. (2010). Parental understanding of infant health information: Health literacy, numeracy, and the parental health literacy activities test (PHLAT). *Academic Pediatrics*, *10*(5), 309–316.
2. Shoots-Reinhard, B., Peters, E., & Petty, R. E. (in process). *Certainty, subjective numeracy, and objective numeracy in decision making*.
3. Dunning, D. (2011). The Dunning–Kruger effect: On being ignorant of one's own ignorance. In J. M. Olson & M. P. Zanna (Eds.), *Advances in experimental social psychology*, Vol. 44 (pp. 247–296). San Diego, CA: Academic Press.
4. Friedman, R. A. (2017, April 15). The world's most beautiful mathematical equation. *New York Times*. Retrieved from https://nyti.ms/2oepdry
5. Peters, E. (2018a). MTurk Cohort 2, ID A1PKCBFB4QY19G.
6. Peters, E. (2018b). MTurk Cohort 2, ID. AXJHKT9KSDEUF.
7. Peters, E., & Bjälkebring, P. (2015). Multiple numeric competencies: When a number is not just a number. *Journal of Personality and Social Psychology*, *108*(5), 802–822.
8. Fagerlin, A., Zikmund-Fisher, B. J., Ubel, P. A., Jankovic, A., Derry, H. A., & Smith, D. M. (2007). Measuring numeracy without a math test: Development of the Subjective Numeracy Scale. *Medical Decision Making*, *27*(5), 672–680.
9. Lyons, I. M., & Beilock, S. L. (2012). When math hurts: Math anxiety predicts pain network activation in anticipation of doing math. *PLoS ONE*, *7*(10), e48076.
10. Rolison, J. J., Morsanyi, K., & O'Connor, P. A. (2016). Can I count on getting better? Association between math anxiety and poorer understanding of medical risk reductions. *Medical Decision Making*, *36*(7), 876–886.
11. Ashcraft, M. H., & Kirk, E. P. (2001). The relationships among working memory, math anxiety, and performance. *Journal of Experimental Psychology: General*, *130*(2), 224–237.
12. Ashcraft, M. H., & Krause, J. A. (2007). Working memory, math performance, and math anxiety. *Psychonomic Bulletin & Review*, *14*(2), 243–248.
13. Peters, E., Shoots-Reinhard, B., Tompkins, M. K., Schley, D., Meilleur, L., Sinayev, A., . . . Crocker, J. (2017). Improving numeracy through values affirmation enhances decision and STEM outcomes. *PLoS ONE*, *12*(7): e0180674.
14. Martens, A., Johns, M., Greenberg, J., & Schimel, J. (2006). Combating stereotype threat: The effect of self-affirmation on women's intellectual performance. *Journal of Experimental Social Psychology*, *42*(2), 236–243.
15. McConnell, A. R. (2011). The multiple self-aspects framework: Self-concept representation and its implications. *Personality and Social Psychology Review*, *15*(1), 3–27.
16. Schwarzer, R., & Fuchs, R. (1996). Self-efficacy and health behaviours. In M. Conner & P. Norman (Eds.), *Predicting health behavior: Research and practice with social cognition models* (pp. 63–196). Maidenhead, UK: Open University Press.
17. Bandura, A. (1977). Self-efficacy: Toward a unifying theory of behavioral change. *Psychological Review*, *84*(2), 191–215.

18. Meece, J. L., Wigfield, A., & Eccles, J. S. (1990). Predictors of math anxiety and its influence on young adolescents' course enrollment intentions and performance in mathematics. *Journal of Educational Psychology, 82*(1), 60–70.

19. Hackett, G., & Betz, N. E. (1981). A self-efficacy approach to the career development of women. *Journal of Vocational Behavior, 18*(3), 326–339.

20. Betz, N. E. (2013). Assessment of self-efficacy. In K. F. Geisinger, B. A. Bracken, J. F. Carlson, J.-I. C. Hansen, N. R. Kuncel, S. P. Reise, & M. C. Rodriguez (Eds.), *APA handbooks in psychology. APA handbook of testing and assessment in psychology, Vol. 2. Testing and assessment in clinical and counseling psychology* (pp. 379–391). Washington, DC: American Psychological Association.

21. Tompkins, M. K. (2018). *The role of subjective numeracy in financial outcomes and interventions of numeric-ability beliefs* (Doctoral dissertation). The Ohio State University.

22. Farrell, L., Fry, T. R., & Risse, L. (2016). The significance of financial self-efficacy in explaining women's personal finance behaviour. *Journal of Economic Psychology, 54*, 85–99.

23. Anderson, B. L., Obrecht, N. A., Chapman, G. B., Driscoll, D. A., & Schulkin, J. (2011). Physicians' communication of Down syndrome screening test results: The influence of physician numeracy. *Genetics in Medicine, 13*(8), 744–749.

24. Han, P. K. J., Dieckmann, N. F., Holt, C., Gutheil, C., & Peters, E. (2016). Factors affecting physicians' intentions to communicate personalized prognostic information to cancer patients at the end of life: An experimental vignette study. *Medical Decision Making, 36*(6), 703–713.

25. Couper, M. P., & Singer, E. (2009). The role of numeracy in informed consent for surveys. *Journal of Empirical Research on Human Research Ethics, 4*(4), 17–26.

26. Suri, R., Monroe, K. B., & Koc, U. (2013). Math anxiety and its effects on consumers' preference for price promotion formats. *Journal of the Academy of Marketing Science, 41*(3), 271–282.

27. Sweeny, K., Melnyk, D., Miller, W., & Shepperd, J. A. (2010). Information avoidance: Who, what, when, and why. *Review of General Psychology, 14*(4), 340–353.

28. Hong, T. (2006). The Internet and tobacco cessation: The roles of Internet self-efficacy and search task on the information-seeking process. *Journal of Computer-Mediated Communication, 11*(2), 536–556.

29. Shepperd, J. A., & Howell, J. L. (2015). Responding to psychological threats with deliberate ignorance: Causes and remedies. In P. J. Carroll, R. M. Arkin, & A. L. Wichman (Eds.), *Handbook of personal security* (pp. 257–274). New York: Psychology Press.

30. Gigerenzer, G., & Garcia-Retamero, R. (2017). Cassandra's regret: The psychology of not wanting to know. *Psychological Review, 124*(2), 179–196.

31. Chen, Y. X., & Feeley, T. H. (2014). Numeracy, information seeking, and self-efficacy in managing health: An analysis using the 2007 Health Information Trends Survey (HINTS). *Health Communication, 29*(9), 843–853.

32. Afifi, W. A., & Weiner, J. L. (2004). Toward a theory of motivated information management. *Communication Theory, 14*(2), 167–190.

33. Peters, E., Dieckmann, N. F., Västfjäll, D., Mertz, C. K., Slovic, P., & Hibbard, J. H. (2009). Bringing meaning to numbers: The impact of evaluative categories on decisions. *Journal of Experimental Psychology: Applied, 15*(3), 213–227.

34. Moorman, C., Diehl, K., Brinberg, D., & Kidwell, B. (2004). Subjective knowledge, search locations, and consumer choice. *Journal of Consumer Research, 31*(3), 673–680.

35. Swann Jr, W. B., Rentfrow, P. J., & Guinn, J. S. (2002). Self-verification: The search for coherence. In M. R. Leary & J. P. Tangney. *Handbook of self and identity* (pp. 367–383). New York: Guilford.

36. Cialdini, R. (1993). *The psychology of influence*. New York: William Morrow.

37. Festinger, L. (1957). *A theory of cognitive dissonance*. Palo Alto, CA: Stanford University Press.

38. Heider, F. (1958). *The psychology of interpersonal relations*. New York: Wiley.

39. Langford, A. T., Resnicow, K., Roberts, J. S., & Zikmund-Fisher, B. J. (2012). Racial and ethnic differences in direct-to-consumer genetic tests awareness in HINTS 2007: Sociodemographic and numeracy correlates. *Journal of Genetic Counseling, 21*(3), 440–447.

40. Hanoch, Y., Miron-Shatz, T., Rolison, J. J., Omer, Z., & Ozanne, E. (2015). Shared decision making in patients at risk of cancer: The role of domain and numeracy. *Health Expectations, 18*(6), 2799–2810.

41. Ashcraft, M. H. (2002). Math anxiety: Personal, educational, and cognitive consequences. *Current Directions in Psychological Science, 11*(5), 181–185.

42. Betz, N. E. (1978). Prevalence, distribution, and correlates of math anxiety in college students. *Journal of Counseling Psychology, 25*(5), 441–448.

43. Donelle, L., Arocha, J. F., & Hoffman-Goetz, L. (2008). Health literacy and numeracy: Key factors in cancer risk comprehension. *Chronic Diseases in Canada, 29*(1), 1–8.

44. Låg, T., Bauger, L., Lindberg, M., & Friborg, O. (2014). The role of numeracy and intelligence in health-risk estimation and medical data interpretation. *Journal of Behavioral Decision Making, 27*(2), 95–108.

45. Hanoch, Y., Miron-Shatz, T., Rolison, J. J., & Ozanne, E. (2014). Understanding of BRCA1/2 genetic tests results: The importance of objective and subjective numeracy. *Psycho-Oncology, 23*(10), 1142–1148.

46. Silk, K. J., & Parrott, R. L. (2014). Math anxiety and exposure to statistics in messages about genetically modified foods: Effects of numeracy, math self-efficacy, and form of presentation. *Journal of Health Communication, 19*(7), 838–852.

47. Rolison, J.J., Morsanyi, K., & Peters, E. (2020). Understanding health risk comprehension: The role of math anxiety, subjective numeracy, and objective numeracy. *Medical Decision Making, 40*(2), 222–234.

48. Hibbard, J. H., & Peters, E. (2003). Supporting informed consumer health care choices: Data presentation approaches that facilitate the use of information in choice. *Annual Review of Public Health, 24*, 413–433.

49. Miron-Shatz, T., Hanoch, Y., Doniger, G. M., Omer, Z. B., & Ozanne, E. M. (2014). Subjective but not objective numeracy influences willingness to pay for BRCA1/2 genetic testing. *Judgment and Decision Making, 9*(2), 152–158.

50. Miron-Shatz, T., Hanoch, Y., Katz, B. A., Doniger, G. M., & Ozanne, E. M. (2015). Willingness to test for BRCA1/2 in high risk women: Influenced by risk perception and family experience, rather than by objective or subjective numeracy? *Judgment and Decision Making, 10*(4), 386–399.

51. Buelow, M. T., & Barnhart, W. R. (2017). The influence of math anxiety, math performance, worry, and test anxiety on the Iowa Gambling Task and Balloon Analogue Risk Task. *Assessment, 24*(1), 127–137.

52. Faust, M. W. (1992). *Analysis of physiological reactivity in mathematics anxiety*. Unpublished doctoral dissertation. Bowling Green State University, Bowling Green, Ohio.

53. Peters, E., & Slovic, P. (2000). The springs of action: Affective and analytical information processing in choice. *Personality and Social Psychology Bulletin, 26*(12), 1465–1475.

54. Betz, N. E., & Hackett, G. (1981). The relationship of career-related self-efficacy expectations to perceived career options in college women and men. *Journal of Counseling Psychology, 28*(5), 399–410.

55. Betz, N. E., & Hackett, G. (2006). Career self-efficacy theory: Back to the future. *Journal of Career Assessment, 14*(1), 3–11.

56. Calvin Coolidge Quotes. (n.d.). BrainyQuote.com. Retrieved from: https://www.brainyquote.com/quotes/calvin_coolidge_414555.

57. Bench, S. W., Lench, H. C., Liew, J., Miner, K., & Flores, S. A. (2015). Gender gaps in overestimation of math performance. *Sex Roles, 72*(11–12), 536–546.

58. National Science Board. (2015). *Revisiting the STEM workforce: A companion to science and engineering indicators 2014*. Arlington, VA: National Science Foundation.

59. Peters, E., Tompkins, M. K., Knoll, M., Ardoin, S. P., Shoots-Reinhard, B., & Meara, A. S. (2019). Despite high objective numeracy, lower numeric confidence relates to worse financial and medical outcomes. *Proceedings of the National Academy of Sciences (PNAS)*, doi.org/10.1073/pnas.1903126116.

60. Smith, K. T., Monti, D., Mir, N., Peters, E., Tipirneni, R., & Politi, M. C. (2018). Access is necessary but not sufficient: Factors influencing delay and avoidance of health care services. *MDM Policy & Practice, 3*(1), 1–11.

61. Ghazal, S., Cokely, E. T., & Garcia-Retamero, R (2014). Predicting biases in very highly educated samples: Numeracy and metacognition. *Judgment and Decision Making, 9*(1), 15–34.

62. Betz, N. E., & Hackett, G. (1983). The relationship of mathematics self-efficacy expectations to the selection of science-based college majors. *Journal of Vocational Behavior, 23*(3), 329–345.

63. Hibbard, J. H., Peters, E., Dixon, A., & Tusler, M. (2007). Consumer competencies and the use of comparative quality information: It isn't just about literacy. *Medical Care Research and Review, 64*(4), 379–394.

64. Pachur, T., & Galesic, M. (2013). Strategy selection in risky choice: The impact of numeracy, affect, and cross-cultural differences. *Journal of Behavioral Decision Making, 26*(3), 260–271.

NUMBERS ARE JUST NUMBERS

The Impotence of Data Versus the Power of Information

15

Evidence-Based Information Presentation Matters*

Poorly presented numbers represent a large part of the innumeracy problem. Communicators often provide information in forms that are familiar or easy for them or that serve their priorities and intentions, but that are not usable by those who need it. For example, a cable provider might inform its customers that this year's $100 monthly premium will increase by 2% next year. This math problem is easy for some people, but a sizable minority of participants in one study could not infer the new monthly premium of $102.[1]

This innumeracy extends to automobile sales, where consumers hold a systematic misunderstanding of fuel efficiency given how it is usually displayed. Imagine a couple, Bob and Lisa, who are in the process of deciding whose vehicle to replace. Bob has a truck that gets 10 miles per gallon (MPG) and would replace it with one that gets 20 MPG. Lisa currently drives a car that gets 25 MPG, but she has her eye on one that gets 50 MPG. Which vehicle should they replace? Based on studies of "The MPG illusion," business school professors Rick Larrick and Jack Soll[2] would predict the couple would buy a new car for Lisa. After all, her new car would get 25 MPG more compared to only 10 MPG more for Bob's new truck. However, switching out Bob's truck actually would save more gas if you work through the nonlinear thinking required (for every 10,000 miles driven, Bob's proposed 10 MPG savings would save 500 gallons of gas compared to a measly 200 gallons saved for Lisa's 25 MPG proposal). MPG is a poor, but common, representation of fuel efficiency that misleads people.

Communicators Add Barriers to Comprehension and Use of Information

The situation is not helped by some of the bad habits, inabilities, and biases of people, often experts, who communicate information. To communicate well,

*Modified with permission from the National Academy of Sciences, Courtesy of the National Academies Press, Washington, D.C.

Innumeracy in the Wild. Ellen Peters, Oxford University Press (2020). © Oxford University Press 2020. DOI: 10.1093/oso/9780190861094.003.0001

communicators have to properly identify what the communication should accomplish. They cannot simply provide all of the information and rely on consumers to pick out what is important and discard the superfluous to make wise choices. Instead, the communicator needs to decide first on the goal or goals of the communication. Psychologist Baruch Fischhoff[3] emphasizes that communicators first need to figure out what people know and don't know and what they should know. Such a decision about what people still need to know then alters communication goal(s) and the information that should be shown.

The communication process is also made more difficult by the fact that communicators (and especially experts) tend to overestimate what other people know[4,5] and how well they themselves communicate.[6,7] These overestimations are important because communicators adapt communications to intended recipients to improve effectiveness. But if they are unaware of these common problems, they may not recognize opportunities to adapt and improve their communications. Finally, even when they are aware and try to communicate better, communicators' intuitions about how best to provide information sometimes undermine, rather than support, comprehension.[8,9]

For example, information providers, including college professors, sometimes overlook the fact that numbers can be hard even for highly numerate people. I gave a talk recently in which I showed the results of two studies with conceptually similar results in two different domains. In one study on financial outcomes, bigger numbers on the y-axis of my bar chart meant better outcomes; in the other study on chronic disease activity, bigger numbers indicated worse outcomes.[10] Incredibly bright, quantitatively minded people told me afterward that the comparative results were confusing. The next time I spoke about these findings, I changed the y-axis in the disease-activity study so that bigger numbers meant better outcomes and the graphs "matched" better across the two studies. This seemingly minor change reduced cognitive effort for the audience and fostered greater comprehension, allowing me to communicate the meaning of my results better and more quickly.

Of course, I should have known better given the existing evidence base (reviewed in Chapter 16) that reducing cognitive effort helps people to understand and use numeric evidence better. In fact, in Chapters 15–17, you will learn that communications, and not just people, can be innumerate. Numeric information often does not have to be so difficult to use. It can be made easier through evidence-based information-presentation methods. The goal of these chapters is to teach you some of these techniques to use in your own communications and to request them when you are on the receiving end of communications (e.g., as a patient). After reading them, I hope that numbers don't get in the way as much for your audience and yourself.

Communication Is Not Easy but Evidence-Based Techniques Exist

Quantitative evidence is common whether in research or in finances (fees, expected returns, stock market prices and trends), health (laboratory test results, disease likelihood, uncertainty of treatment benefit), or other areas of science. Numeric-related evidence can be actual numbers (basic numbers, fractions, frequencies, money, percentages, proportions, or range information and trends in any of these numbers over time or between groups), mathematical operations (addition, division), or descriptive words (e.g., many, lower, annual, previously, associated, risk). Understanding and using such data gives us unparalleled ability to control and improve our world so long as the numbers can be understood and used by the people who need them. An analogy exists to running hurdles in track. Hurdling is also difficult, but it can be made easier in either of two ways: you can make the hurdles shorter or you can make the runner stronger. Either method will lead to greater success. See Figure 15.1. The same thing is true for the use of quantitative evidence in decisions: you can make it easier to comprehend and use by making

Figure 15.1 Jumping numeric hurdles is key to good decisions.

the hurdles shorter or you can improve the individual's numeric competencies. Chapter 18 will focus on methods to improve numeric competencies (to make the person stronger), whereas Chapters 15–17 focus on how information providers can shorten the numeric hurdles people face when making decisions. The challenge is not merely to communicate accurate numeric data to consumers, but also to understand how to present quantitative evidence so that it is used in decision making. When people access, understand, and use numeric data appropriately, they can increase control over their experiences, actions, and outcomes.

In particular, Chapters 15–17 link what we learned in earlier chapters about the psychology of how decision makers process information to formatting strategies that increase the likelihood that information will be used in judgments and decisions. I focus on methods to reduce the cognitive effort needed to understand numeric evidence and use results from math operations, to provide evaluative meaning concerning numeric evidence, and to increase attention to important numeric information. Research has demonstrated that using these methods increases comprehension; alters feelings about information; motivates behaviors; changes the relative valuing of information; reduces reliance on heuristics and concrete, easy-to-evaluate attributes; promotes sensitivity to and consistent use of numeric evidence; and increases comfort and satisfaction with a decision. Information providers need to take care, however, because they also can persuade.

According to risk communicator David Spiegelhalter,[11] "There are no absolute rules. It all depends on what you want to communicate." For example, the same information about average global temperatures from 1880 to 2018 can be presented to indicate little to no change (top panel of Figure 15.2) or significant change (bottom panel of Figure 15.2). The goal of the communication shaped how each communicator labeled the y-axis (0 to 110 degrees Fahrenheit in the top graph and 56.5 to 58.5 degrees Fahrenheit in the bottom graph).

By the end of Chapters 16–17, I want you to know how to change the formatting of numbers that you or others present to increase knowledge and promote informed decision making. We sometimes call this process *information architecture*. Table 15.1 summarizes the initial setup needed for good communication and then recommends strategies for communicating numeric evidence. Once designed, communications also need to be tested to ensure that the right message(s) are being heard.

Next, I introduce in more detail these evidence-based methods for presenting quantitative data that enable more informed decisions. As we'll

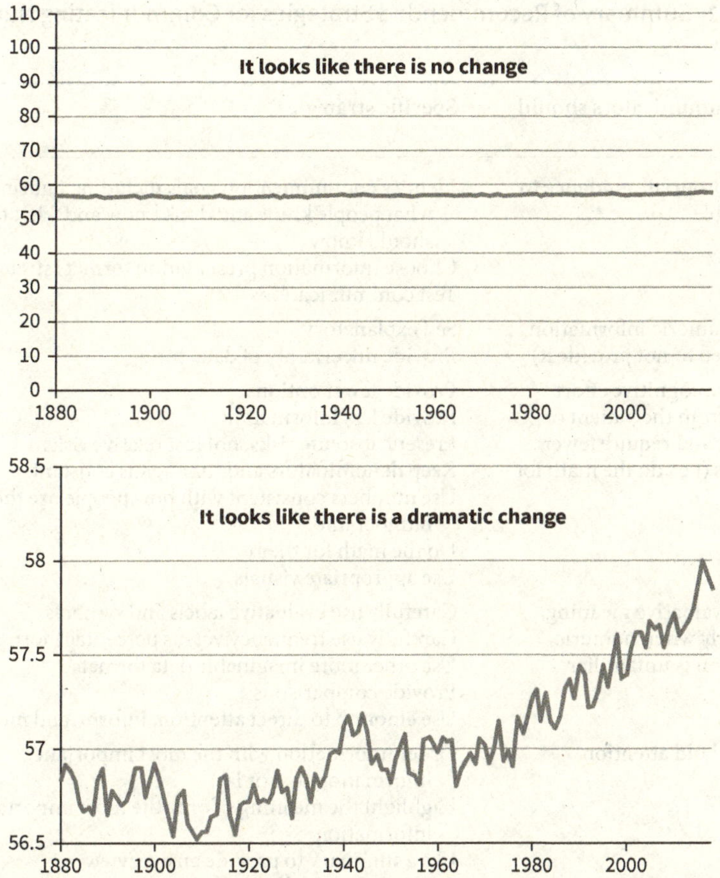

Figure 15.2 Two methods to present average global temperature trends from the year 1880 to 2018.

Data downloaded from: https://data.giss.nasa.gov/gistemp/graphs/graph_data/Global_Mean_Estimates_based_on_Land_and_Ocean_Data/graph.txt. The original data are in units of variation from the mean temperature for 1951 to 1980 (in centigrade). These data were converted by adding 57°F (the estimated global mean temperature for that period); https://earthobservatory.nasa.gov/world-of-change/DecadalTemp) to the Fahrenheit variation.

find out, the less numerate tend to be misled more often than the highly numerate by poorly presented numbers. These kinds of findings underscore the responsibility that communicators have to choose productive and defensible presentation methods. Although some communicators would argue that they simply want to present objective facts, their mindful or mindless choices of how they present information will have an impact on people. Whether that impact is defensible and known or ill thought out and unrecognized, it will be no more or less manipulative.

Table 15.1 Summary of Recommended Strategies for Communicating Numeric Evidence

What communicators should do:	Specific strategies
Set up appropriate guidance to assist people	Identify communication goals including figuring out what people know and don't know and what they should know Choose information presentation formats strategically Test communications
Provide numeric information (as opposed to not provide it)	Self explanatory Provide uncertainty of data, too
Reduce the cognitive effort required from the patient or consumer and require fewer inferences (i.e., do the math for them)	Provide fewer options Provide less information Present absolute risks, not just relative risks Keep denominators and time spans constant Use numbers consistent with how people use the number line Do the math for them Use appropriate visuals
Provide evaluative meaning, particularly when numeric information is unfamiliar	Carefully use evaluative labels and symbols Carefully use frequency versus percentage formats Use other more imaginable data formats Provide comparisons Use emotion to direct attention, inform, and motivate
Grab and hold attention	Order information with the most important information first or last Highlight the meaning of only the most important information Use a summary to provide an overview Increase visual salience to draw attention to important information

References

1. Finucane, M. L., Slovic, P., Hibbard, J. H., Peters, E., Mertz, C. K., & MacGregor, D. G. (2002). Aging and decision-making competence: An analysis of comprehension and consistency skills in older versus younger adults considering health-plan options. *Journal of Behavioral Decision Making, 15*(2), 141–164.
2. Larrick, R. P., & Soll, J. B. (2008). The MPG illusion. *Science 320*(5883), 1593–1594.
3. Fischhoff, B. (2013). Risk perception and communication. In B. Fischhoff (Ed.), *Risk analysis and human behavior* (pp. 17–46). New York: Earthscan.
4. Nickerson, R. S. (1999). How we know—and sometimes misjudge—what others know: Imputing one's own knowledge to others. *Psychological Bulletin, 125*(6), 737–759.
5. Nickerson, R. S. (2001). The projective way of knowing: A useful heuristic that sometimes misleads. *Current Directions in Psychological Science, 10*(5), 168–172.
6. Keysar, B., & Henly, A. S. (2002). Speakers' overestimation of their effectiveness. *Psychological Science, 13*(3), 207–212.

7. Chang, V. Y., Arora, V. M., Lev-Ari, S., D'Arcy, M., & Keysar, B. (2010). Interns overestimate the effectiveness of their hand-off communication. *Pediatrics 125*(3), 491–496.
8. Greene, J., Peters, E., Mertz, C. K., & Hibbard, J. H. (2008). Comprehension and choice of a consumer-directed health plan: An experimental study. *American Journal of Managed Care, 14*(6), 369–376.
9. Peters, E., Klein, W., Kaufman, A., Meilleur, L., & Dixon, A. (2013). More is not always better: Intuitions about effective public policy can lead to unintended consequences. *Social Issues and Policy Review, 7*(1), 114–148.
10. Peters, E., Tompkins, M. K., Knoll, M., Ardoin, S. P., Shoots-Reinhard, B., & Meara, A. S. (2019). Despite high objective numeracy, lower numeric confidence relates to worse financial and medical outcomes. *Proceedings of the National Academy of Sciences (PNAS)*, doi.org/10.1073/pnas.1903126116.
11. Rathi, A. (2016, March 26). A Cambridge professor on how to stop being so easily manipulated by misleading statistics. *Quartz*. Retrieved from https://qz.com/643234/cambridge-professor-on-how-to-stop-being-so-easily-manipulated-by-misleading-statistics/

16
Provide Numbers but Reduce Cognitive Effort[*]

Provide Numeric Information

Nobel Prize laureate Daniel Kahneman once said: "No one ever made a decision because of a number. They need a story."[1] However, receiving and comprehending needed information is a basic building block of making good choices. Providing numeric information, in particular, can inform decision makers in at least five ways.

1. *It can help correct people who have the wrong facts.* For example, the Pew Research Center recently pointed out that a majority of Americans reported each year from 1993–2015 that more crime had occurred in the United States compared to the year before; in reality, both violent and property crime rates declined sharply over this time period based on data from the FBI and the Bureau of Justice Statistics.[2]

2. *Providing numeric information can correct inappropriate interpretations.* A classic study found that many people incorrectly interpret an event such as a flood predicted "once in 100 years" to mean how often it will happen (i.e., if it happened last year, it won't again for 99 years), rather than correctly interpreting it as an annual probability of 1%.[3,4]

3. *Providing numeric information can help people avoid being surprised by an unexpected event and the possible decisional regret and even anger that can follow.*

4. *Emotion can divert attention from the unlikelihood of an event if numeric likelihoods are not emphasized.* We can get carried away by the emotion and hype that sometimes accompanies possible outcomes such as a multimillion-dollar Powerball lottery or a razor found in an apple at Halloween.

Innumeracy in the Wild. Ellen Peters, Oxford University Press (2020). © Oxford University Press 2020.
DOI: 10.1093/oso/9780190861094.003.0001

5. *Displaying quantitative information is perceived as more useful.* For example, we used quantitative information on a website to inform people about chemicals found in cigarettes.[5] Compared to a condition where we did not provide it, people given numeric information reported thinking more about the harms of smoking, and they wanted to use the website more.

Provide Quantitative Information

Thus, the first recommendation is to provide actual numbers, in part because people generally prefer to get them.[6] In one study, for example, nearly two-thirds of participants preferred to receive numerical risk information more than verbal risk information about breast cancer and mammography.[7] In fact, providing numbers (such as likelihoods of benefits and side effects when choosing a medical treatment) compared to not providing them improves patient understanding and willingness to take medications.[8,9]

Several reasons exist for the improvement. First, qualitative labels such as "low chance" or "common," that are often used as substitutes for numbers, are interpreted quite differently by different people. To one person, common might mean 50% whereas to others it means 25%.[8] Figure 16.1 shows what people think various verbal terms mean numerically. Vast disagreement exists. Most of the estimates for "Almost Certainly," for example, are in the 90–100% range, but some estimates are as low as 60–70%. The Intergovernmental Panel on Climate Change (IPCC) uses verbal descriptions, such as "likely" and "very likely," to convey uncertainty rather than providing numeric probabilities. In a recent study, respondents were asked to interpret the meaning of eight IPCC statements that included one of these verbal descriptions with help from an IPCC table that interpreted what these terms meant (e.g., "likely" and "very likely" were intended to convey >66% and >90%, respectively). For the statement "It is very likely that hot extremes, heat waves, and heavy precipitation events will continue to become more frequent," participants estimated that the statement meant an average of 72% (range = 57–83%), but they should have estimated greater than 90% to match the provided IPCC table.[10] Second, the average person overestimates the likelihood of risks and benefits in some domains (e.g., prescription medications) when provided only non-numeric information (e.g., risk labels such as "common," "rare"). These overestimates decline substantially when numeric information is provided.[11-13]

Some researchers believe, however, that less objectively numerate people may be unable to "handle" numeric information.[14] Recent studies contradict

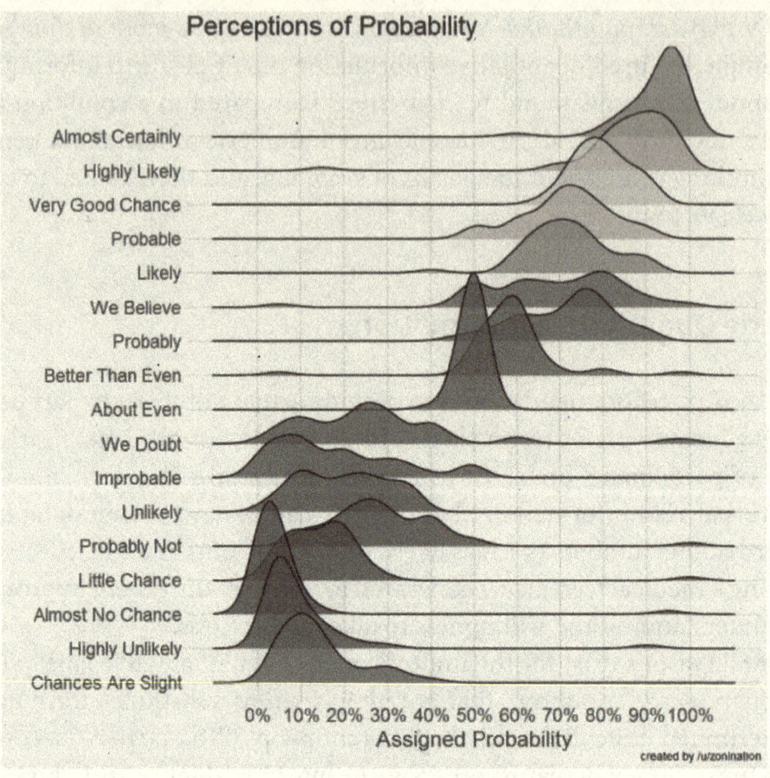

Figure 16.1 Perceptions of numeric probabilities given verbal terms (created by u/zonination).

this view. With physician Liana Fraenkel, for example, we found that both more and less objectively numerate respondents provided more accurate medication risk estimates and were more willing to take a hypothetical medication when provided numeric information about medication side effects as opposed to providing only non-numeric information.[15] For example, when provided numeric information, 18% and 6% of the less and more numerate, respectively, overestimated the risk of stomach upset. Such a result is consistent with previous findings that the less numerate tend to perceive more risk than the highly numerate.[16] However, this numeracy effect was swamped by the effect of giving only verbal descriptions of the likelihood of adverse events (e.g., stomach upset was "uncommon"). In this case, many more people overestimated risk (69% and 66%, respectively, of the less and more numerate). Furthermore, patients eligible for colorectal cancer screening ($N = 213$) were more likely to get screened when given quantitative information about the test's uncertainty and cancer incidence and mortality.[17] Similar benefits of numeric provision emerged in studies concerning scientific consensus about climate change,[18] numeric evidence of global warming effects on polar bears,[19] and numeric weather uncertainty.[20] Providing exact statistics has a bigger effect on judgments and choices than does providing imprecise verbal terms for both more and less numerate decision makers.

The positive effects of quantitative information extend to experts, too. With physician Paul Han and colleagues, we presented 93 physicians with quantitative prognostic information ("12-month mortality risk estimate of 78%") in a hypothetical vignette about an end-stage gastric cancer patient.[21] Such information is important to physician decisions about appropriate medical interventions and to patient decisions about medical, family, and other matters. As with other individuals, terminally ill patients tend to prefer getting such information.[22,23] Once they had access to good quality numeric estimates, physicians were more likely to intend to communicate prognosis to the patient and family and especially if the physician was higher in objective numeracy.

Providing numeric information, however, is not a guaranteed solution. In one study, for example, the simple presence versus absence of numbers was used as a heuristic shortcut. Pedersen[24] found that politicians were judged as more competent when they used arguments that included numeric information compared to when the same arguments did not include numbers. Furthermore, providing calorie counts for food and drinks appears insufficient to influence eating behavior.[25-29] Some exceptions exist, but positive effects of calorie count provision appear limited to individuals with higher education or numeracy or greater health consciousness.[30,31] At Starbucks (which tends to cater to more affluent consumers), for example, mandatory calorie counts were associated with a 6% decrease in average calories per transaction.[32] However, no influence of calorie labeling existed for adolescents in low-income communities even though more than half reported noticing the labels.[33] Behavioral economist George Loewenstein[34] speculated that low-income individuals may even view cheaper meals with more calories as a better "deal." Calorie counts may be one area where providing exact numeric information (about calories) may not be necessary on top of an interpretation of what the number of calories means (although providing the calorie counts does not hurt either[35]). This lack of numeric power for calorie counts may be due to the ongoing, incessant nature of the task (we eat throughout the day) and/or to memory failures and hedonic temptations that cause us to forget or neglect the information.[36,37] Future research may discover information presentation formats tailored to this unique issue that produce greater success.

Provide Uncertainty in Data

When I think about providing numeric information, it's often about likelihoods of future outcomes. For example, a new prescription drug may indicate that 27% of patients taking it will suffer headaches as a side effect. A patient will not know whether she will get headaches, but she will know how likely it is. Quantitative evidence can be uncertain in other ways, too. For example, even when an estimate is given (e.g., a Java chip Frappuccino has 600 calories), your actual calories depend on the heavy-handedness of your barista. This ambiguity, or uncertainty about the strength or validity of evidence[38,39] is a second type of uncertainty. Other forms of uncertainty include (3) uncertainty about the personal significance of outcomes (e.g., their severity or timing), (4) uncertainty arising from complexity (e.g., the variety of existing risks and benefits or their instability over time), and (5) uncertainty due to ignorance.[40]

We know little about best evidence–based approaches to presenting uncertainty other than the likelihoods of future outcomes (the first uncertainty form). We do know, however, that people have difficulty with uncertainty. In one study that gave participants 90% confidence intervals as a way of conveying uncertainty in the strength of the evidence, a participant commented "If you have an estimate of 10, but feel that it could be anywhere from 1–20, how can you be 90 percent certain of that?"[41]

Presenting each of these forms of uncertainty is important for several reasons. First, sometimes people prefer getting it.[42] Second, conveying a false sense of certainty can undermine trust if events do not turn out as expected or science changes.[42,43] In addition, presenting uncertainty promotes a sense of transparency that can foster trust[44] and it can be helpful to decision makers weighing risk.[45] However, communicating uncertainty can diminish perceived scientific authority.[46] It is also more difficult for people,[41] and it increases worry and decreases decision satisfaction.[47,48] People are also averse to ambiguity and prefer to receive less ambiguous information.[5,39] At the same time, stock market crashes and Nassim Taleb's[49] book on "black swan events" have taught us respect for extremely unlikely outcomes that may occur nonetheless. More research is needed with respect to how individuals who vary in numeracy respond to these various forms of uncertainty.

Although less numerate individuals find numeric information more difficult, providing numeric information is an ethically defensible decision from the perspective of informed choice and results such as those just described. The potential for misunderstandings, however, emphasizes the need to understand how to provide comprehensible and usable numeric information, the focus of the rest of this chapter and Chapter 17. By their end, you will know multiple ways that you can make yourself and others better understood.

Reduce Cognitive Effort and Required Inferences (i.e., Do the Math for Them)

Provide Fewer Options and Less Information

When presenting information, one of the first questions you should ask yourself (or the presenter) is whether all of the information is equally important. Often, less relevant information and options are presented beside relevant ones. This additional information can distract consumers.[50,51] Although having more choice options can have advantages, recent research has pointed toward the notion of a "paradox" or "tyranny" of choice. For example, research has demonstrated that having more options can lead to less comprehension, worse choices, and lower satisfaction.[52-54] In particular, researchers have suggested that an overabundance of choice can lead to information overload,[55-57] decreased motivation and an inability to choose,[58-60] decision-related anxiety,[61] and outcome dissatisfaction and regret.[62-64] The combination of large choice sets and a desire to choose the best can lead to more regret, reduced happiness, and less overall choice satisfaction.[65]

Providing fewer options may be particularly relevant to health choices. For example, in one study, when shown 20 health providers, only 69.5% successfully selected the top three healthcare providers, compared with 80.2% when given only five providers.[66] Those higher in objective numeracy made better decisions than the less numerate with small numbers of options but not with more options.[67,68] For example, when directed to choose the cheapest Medicare prescription drug plan, highly numerate physician trainees were able to do so 67% of the time when faced with three options but only 33% of the time when choosing among nine options.[69]

Instead of providing fewer options, you could present all options sequentially (one at a time). Public-health researcher Brian Zikmund-Fisher and colleagues[51] used information from a breast cancer communication tool called Adjuvant Online! (http://www.adjuvantonline.com) that was designed to help oncologists communicate the benefits of hormonal therapy and chemotherapy.[70] Typically, patients are presented simultaneously with the risks of four treatment options: no additional treatment, hormonal therapy, chemotherapy, and combined hormonal therapy and chemotherapy. With sequential presentation of the options instead, knowledge and sensitivity to risk reduction improved and especially among the less numerate.[51]

Although information is often provided for good reasons (respect for consumer and patient autonomy and to help them make better-informed decisions), cognitive drawbacks exist to providing more information. We tested whether providing consumers with less information, rather than more, could produce superior outcomes.[50] The results indicated that providing less information in hospital quality reports (i.e., removing non–quality-of-care information such as the number of general care beds) resulted in better decision making through improved comprehension and higher quality choices, particularly among participants with lower objective numeracy. Communicators should identify more and less critical elements of a decision (e.g., dominated options that are worse than other available options on every important dimension) so that information providers can delete them from the consideration set or strategically choose how to present them.

Present Absolute Risks, Not Just Relative Risks

People often say they prefer risk information in relative risk formats, but this format leads to misunderstandings.[71,72] For example, hormone replacement therapy can be used to relieve symptoms of menopause, but it more than doubles deaths from breast cancer (its relative risk). This seemingly large increase, however, can be put in an arguably more appropriate absolute context: it increases deaths from breast cancer by a relatively minor absolute change of .02%, from 12 out of 10,000 to 25 out of 10,000.[73] The relative-risk communication, not surprisingly, magnifies risk perceptions, and treatments are viewed less favorably than when the same information is presented using the absolute-risk format among lay people and medical experts.[74–76]

Providing absolute risk numbers, including baseline risks, disambiguates the situation and reduces cognitive effort and potential confusion by doing the math for people.[77] Providing benefit information works similarly[78] and it also should be presented in absolute terms because it, too, can mislead if presented only in relative terms. Although little studied, it is likely that these effects would be larger among the less objectively numerate.[79]

Keep Denominators and Time Spans Constant

People also experience greater difficulty comparing across options, such as medical treatments, when different denominators are used.[80] For example,

1-in-X ratios (e.g., 1 in 12 and 1 in 120) led to greater perceived probability and worry about health outcomes than when the same risks were conveyed using a fixed denominator (e.g., 10 in 120 and 1 in 120).[81–83] The 1-in-X ratios are problematic even among policy makers and other experts. Take, for example, Joe Scarborough, former US Representative from Florida and now co-host of MSNBC's "Morning Joe." In 2011, he discussed an anti-poverty program with a guest, commenting that "You want to help be a part of a process that cuts poverty in half in America. Right now one in six of Americans are in poverty. You want to make that one in three." Unfortunately, half of "one in six" is "one in twelve," and Scarborough had suggested doubling poverty instead.[84] A single denominator should be chosen when making comparisons (e.g., 1 in 10,000 and 400 in 10,000 rather than 1 in 10,000 and 4 in 100). Using the same logic, communicators should use the same time frame when presenting risks and benefits (e.g., provide annual costs for all health plans rather than monthly costs for some and annual costs for others).

Use Numbers in a Direction Consistent with People's Expectations

We found that less objectively numerate consumers, in particular, understood more and made better choices when the provided information required less cognitive effort.[50] In one study, we presented hospital quality-of-care information either in a format in which a higher number meant better (the number of registered nurses per 100 patients) or in the more usual format where a lower number meant better (the number of patients per registered nurse). Putting the numbers in a direction consistent with people's expectations (i.e., usually higher numbers mean something "better" than lower numbers) facilitated comprehension and choice. Do you recall my example of presenting disease activity and financial outcome results in the fourth paragraph of Chapter 15? Formatting the numbers so that higher numbers always meant better outcomes helped me communicate better.

This concept applies equally to other common information formats. For example, physicians often explain risks associated with treatment using the *number needed to treat* (NNT). With chemotherapy, for example, NNT is the number of women needed to take chemoprevention to prevent cancer in one of them; here, larger numbers mean a less effective treatment. NNT is a difficult format for people to understand, and it should not be used with laypeople (and arguably not with physicians, either, who can also be innumerate).[85,86]

Do the Math for Them

More generally, people understand and use numeric information more if information providers run the numbers for them, presenting the information in the form most applicable to their current decision. For example, when evaluating healthy behaviors such as taking medication, eating better, or exercising more, consumers and patients are often told about risks over one time period, and they are expected to extrapolate to other time periods. Nina might be told of the annual risk of taking birth control pills, but she intends to take them for many years, say 10. Understanding this 10-year risk requires a level of numeracy that few people have (e.g., 1% of college students answered a similar question correctly).[87] Similar cumulative-risk issues exist in understanding the long-term false-positive rates from annual cancer screenings,[88–91] the likelihood of HIV or other infection from repeated unprotected sex,[92] and the risks of driving distracted, among many others. Providing estimates for risks over longer time periods by doing the math for consumers would go a long way toward helping them understand the cumulative implications of their choices.

Many examples exist of doing the math for people. Psychologist Janet Kleber and colleagues[93] found that charity donations that operate through product prices should present absolute donation amounts ($2 will go toward this charity) rather than a percentage (20% of your purchase price will be donated), presumably because less numerate individuals have difficulty calculating the amount to be donated from a percentage and subsequently feel more uncertain and less confident, with resulting lower purchase intentions. Clarifying the math in a variety of ways helps, and especially for the less numerate (e.g., credit card debit,[94] per cent daily values [% DVs] on food labels[95,96]).

Even when choices require only simple quantitative reasoning steps, communicators may need to pay close attention to how numeric information is expressed, explained, and implemented. In particular, they should do the math for consumers whenever possible. This conclusion suggests that complicated choices, such as those found in health insurance plans or financial planning, should consider cost and other calculators as part of their implementation.[97–99]

Use Appropriate Visuals

"Graphs are an appealing alternative to numbers because they are visually interesting and exploit rapid, automatic visual perception skills" (p. 608).[100]

However, different types of visual displays exist, and communicators should choose a display best suited for their communication goal.

- *Line graphs are generally well understood, and they work well for communicating trends over time.*[101] However, they may increase the extent to which a local contrast versus a global trend over time affects judgments.[102] Line graphs can also be made more impactful through the use of trusted information sources, by showing data points one at a time, and by highlighting change over time through labeling (DECLINE!) and overlaid trend lines.[103]
- *Bar graphs, on the other hand, are effective at conveying magnitudes and comparisons across groups*[9,101,104] *whether presented in two or three dimensions.*[105] Risks presented in bar charts were also recalled better than when they were presented as numbers only (among more objectively numerate participants only).[106]
- *Tables were superior than bar charts, however, when estimating equality and sums.*[105]
- *Pie charts tend to be familiar and acceptable, and they have the advantage of being particularly useful for exhibiting single proportions*[107] *and providing part-to-whole comparisons (icon arrays also are useful for this purpose).* In addition, although pie charts did not improve comprehension over tables or bar charts, they also did not reduce comprehension significantly except when the pie charts were three-dimensional.[105]
- *Icon arrays (also called pictographs) have been shown to reduce several biases, including denominator neglect*[108,109] *and the use of anecdotes over more reliable statistical information.*[110] They also reduce framing effects[111] although pie charts and vertical and horizontal bars can be more effective than icon arrays in reducing framing effects.[112]

Recent research indicates that icon arrays effectively communicate to both more and less numerate individuals, whereas comprehension and risk perceptions with other visual aids such as line graphs and bar graphs depended more on numeracy levels.[113–116] Icon arrays' advantage may be due to them allowing more and less numerate individuals to process the information differently. Consistent with our earlier research,[117] the more numerate were more likely to perform a number operation (counting the icons) whereas the less numerate appeared to use large-area processing by comparing highlighted and nonhighlighted areas within the visual.[118,119]

Icon arrays have been tested extensively in health communication research, and some nuances to their use have arisen. For example, the icons are usually arranged in blocks (e.g., of those with vs. without the disease) rather than being scattered randomly. Scattering icons randomly can facilitate the perception of randomness (e.g., who gets a disease), but it also increases perceptions of risk magnitude.[120–122] However, when an individual needs to interpret the presented risk (e.g., is 5% a low, intermediate, or high chance?), icon arrays can result in lower comprehension and less satisfaction.[123] In such cases, communicators may need to provide an interpretation (see Chapter 17's section on evaluative meaning).

Most studies, however, have tested only single icon arrays, and little is known about the effects of icon arrays in situations that require integration across multiple arrays (e.g., displaying the 10 possible adverse effects of a prescribed medication). The complexity of multiple icon arrays may disadvantage the less numerate in particular.

Recent research has begun to examine dynamic displays. Interactive displays with images, avatars, or spinners are intended to encourage individuals to actively engage with the context. As a result, they may promote better understanding and retention and especially in less numerate individuals who ordinarily do not process numeric information as thoroughly.[120] For example, participants in one study "experienced" a hypothetical risk relevant to prenatal genetic testing by viewing a series of photographs of children with and without Down syndrome.[124] They demonstrated less probability neglect in this experiential format compared to the same risks presented in more abstract numeric formats, such as frequencies. We attempted to replicate their findings but did not find differences in lung cancer screening preferences among pulmonary patients randomized to a more complicated experiential task versus those receiving descriptive statistics.[125]

Spinners (with an arrow in the center of a donut-shaped ring containing a colored segment representing the risk of an adverse event) also might facilitate risk communication. In one study, knowledge scores were higher among patients (recruited from outpatient medicine clinics) randomized to the spinner format compared to those receiving numeric information only.[126] Patients also preferred the spinner format over the descriptive statistical information. More research is needed on interactive displays given their potential benefits but also their complexity and efficiency.

Some final notes on visual displays:

- Visual displays appear particularly helpful in less numerate populations but provide benefits even among physicians who tend to be higher in numeracy.[127,128]

- Just because consumers or patients prefer some graphs does not necessarily mean that they will understand them better than non-preferred graphs.[98]
- Some researchers claim that multiple representations of the same information work better.[129] However, in one study, a combined negative and positive frame elicited risk perceptions that were more similar to the negative than positive frame.[130] Additionally, it is possible that providing more information in the combined frame would reduce comprehension relative to either frame alone.[50] Multiple representations may not produce the desired "magical kind of convergence: by providing multiple presentations of information, participants will somehow be able to draw an element of truth from each perspective and combine them to arrive at a more true, or at least less biased, understanding" (p. 2081).[41] Groups will not necessarily converge on the best understanding but may, instead, rely on whatever was their favorite or easiest to process information source. This source, however, may not maximize comprehension or use of information.

Visual displays may help consumers reduce cognitive effort and/or reduce the perception that cognitive effort is needed. If the former, then objective numeracy differences should attenuate with their use. However, if they work through reducing perceived cognitive effort, then objective numeracy differences may be reduced primarily among those lower in subjective numeracy (who otherwise lacked the confidence to try).

Reducing the cognitive effort required to understand numbers means that less objectively numerate consumers will have more of a chance to use them in ways that are similar to the highly numerate. You should not stop there, however, because sometimes people don't pay attention to data in the first place, or they can tell you what the numbers are, but not what they mean for the decision at hand. Chapter 17 focuses on these two topics.

References

1. Leonhardt, D. (2017, December 24). What I was wrong about this year. *The New York Times*. Retrieved from https://www.nytimes.com/2017/12/24/opinion/2017-wrong-numbers.html

2. Gramlich, J. (2018, January 30). 5 facts about crime in the US. *Pew Research Center*. Retrieved from http://www.pewresearch.org/fact-tank/2017/02/21/5-facts-about-crime-in-the-u-s/.

3. Kates, R. W. (1962). *Hazard and choice perception in flood plain management*. Chicago, IL: Department of Geography, University of Chicago.

4. Lee, K. D., Torell, G. L. & Newman, S. (2021). A once-in-one-hundred-year event? A survey assessing deviation between perceived and actual understanding of flood risk terminology. *Journal of Environmental Management*, 275, 111209. https://doi.org/10.1016/j.jenvman.2020.111400.

5. Lazard, A. J., Byron, M. J., Vu, H., Peters, E., Schmidt, A., & Brewer, N. T. (2019). Website designs for communicating about chemicals in cigarette smoke. *Health Communication*, *34*(3), 333–342. doi:10.1080/10410236.2017.1407276

6. Wallsten, T. S., Budescu, D. V., Zwick, R., & Kemp, S. M. (1993). Preferences and reasons for communicating probabilistic information in verbal or numerical terms. *Bulletin of the Psychonomic Society*, *31*(2), 135–138.

7. Vahabi, M. (2010). Verbal versus numerical probabilities: Does format presentation of probabilistic information regarding breast cancer screening affect women's comprehension? *Health Education Journal*, *69*(2), 150–163.

8. Berry, D. C. (2006). Informing people about the risks and benefits of medicines: Implications for the safe and effective use of medicinal products. *Current Drug Safety*, *1*(1), 121–126.

9. Lipkus, I. M. (2007). Numeric, verbal, and visual formats of conveying health risks: Suggested best practices and future recommendations. *Medical Decision Making*, *27*(5), 696–713.

10. Budescu, D. V., Por, H. H., Broomell, S. B., & Smithson, M. (2014). The interpretation of IPCC probabilistic statements around the world. *Nature Climate Change*, *4*(6), 508–512.

11. Berry, D. C., Knapp, P. R., & Raynor, D. K. (2002). Provision of information about drug side effects to patients. *Lancet*, *359*(9309), 853–854.

12. Berry, D. C., Knapp, P., & Raynor, D. K. (2003). Communicating risk of medication side effects: An empirical evaluation of EU recommended terminology. *Psychology, Health & Medicine*, *8*(3), 251–263.

13. Berry, D., Raynor, T., Knapp, P., & Bersellini, E. (2004). Over the counter medicines and the need for immediate action: A further evaluation of European Commission recommended wordings for communicating risk. *Patient Education and Counseling*, *53*(2), 129–134.

14. Schwartz, P. H. (2011). Decision aids, prevention, and the ethics of disclosure. *Hastings Center Report*, *41*(2), 30–39.

15. Peters, E., Hart, P. S., Tusler, M., & Fraenkel, L. (2014). Numbers matter to informed patient choices: A randomized design across age and numeracy levels. *Medical Decision Making*, *34*(4), 430–442.

16. Peters, E. (2012). Beyond comprehension: The role of numeracy in judgments and decisions. *Current Directions in Psychological Science*, *21*(1), 31–35.

17. Schwartz, P. H., Perkins, S. M., Schmidt, K. K., Muriello, P. F., Althouse, S., & Rawl, S. M. (2017). Providing quantitative information and a nudge to undergo stool testing in a colorectal cancer screening decision aid: A randomized clinical trial. *Medical Decision Making*, *37*(6), 688–702.

18. Myers, T. A., Maibach, E., Peters, E., & Leiserowitz, A. (2015). Simple messages help set the record straight about scientific agreement on human-caused climate change: The results of two experiments. *PLoS ONE*, *10*(3), e0120985.

19. Hart, P. S. (2013). The role of numeracy in moderating the influence of statistics in climate change messages. *Public Understanding of Science*, *22*(7), 785–798.

20. Grounds, M. A., & Joslyn, S. L. (2018). Communicating weather forecast uncertainty: Do individual differences matter? *Journal of Experimental Psychology: Applied*, *24*(1), 18–33.

21. Han, P. K. J., Dieckmann, N. F., Holt, C., Gutheil, C., & Peters, E. (2016). Factors affecting physicians' intentions to communicate personalized prognostic information to cancer patients at the end of life: An experimental vignette study. *Medical Decision Making*, *36*(6), 703–713.

22. Clayton, J. M., Butow, P. N., & Tattersall, M. H. (2005). When and how to initiate discussion about prognosis and end-of-life issues with terminally ill patients. *Journal of Pain and Symptom Management, 30*(2), 132–144.

23. Hancock, K., Clayton, J. M., Parker, S. M., Wal der, S., Butow, P. N., Carrick, S., . . . Tattersall, M. H. (2007). Truth-telling in discussing prognosis in advanced life-limiting illnesses: A systematic review. *Palliative Medicine, 21*(6), 507–517.

24. Pedersen, R. T. (2017). Ratio bias and policy preferences: How equivalency framing of numbers can affect attitudes. *Political Psychology, 38*(6), 1103–1120.

25. Downs, J. S., Loewenstein, G., & Wisdom, J. (2009). Strategies for promoting healthier food choices. *American Economic Review, 99*(2), 159–64.

26. Elbel, B., Kersh, R., Brescoll, V. L., & Dixon, L. B. (2009). Calorie labeling and food choices: A first look at the effects on low-income people in New York City. *Health Affairs, 28*(6), w1110–w1121.

27. Finkelstein, E. A., Strombotne, K. L., Chan, N. L., & Krieger, J. (2011). Mandatory menu labeling in one fast-food chain in King County, Washington. *American Journal of Preventive Medicine, 40*(2), 122–127.

28. Girz, L., Polivy, J., Herman, C. P., & Lee, H. (2012). The effects of calorie information on food selection and intake. *International Journal of Obesity, 36*(10), 1340–1345.

29. Vadiveloo, M. K., Dixon, L. B., & Elbel, B. (2011). Consumer purchasing patterns in response to calorie labeling legislation in New York City. *International Journal of Behavioral Nutrition and Physical Activity, 8*(1), 51.

30. Bassett, M. T., Dumanovsky, T., Huang, C., Silver, L. D., Young, C., Nonas, C., . . . Frieden, T. R. (2008). Purchasing behavior and calorie information at fast-food chains in New York City, 2007. *American Journal of Public Health, 98*(8), 1457–1459.

31. Dumanovsky, T., Huang, C. Y., Nonas, C. A., Matte, T. D., Bassett, M. T., & Silver, L. D. (2011). Changes in energy content of lunchtime purchases from fast food restaurants after introduction of calorie labelling: Cross sectional customer surveys. *British Medical Journal, 343*, d4464.

32. Bollinger, B., Leslie, P., & Sorensen, A. (2011). Calorie posting in chain restaurants. *American Economic Journal: Economic Policy, 3*(1), 91–128.

33. Elbel, B., Gyamfi, J., & Kersh, R. (2011). Child and adolescent fast-food choice and the influence of calorie labeling: A natural experiment. *International Journal of Obesity, 35*(4), 493–500.

34. Loewenstein, G. (2011). Confronting reality: Pitfalls of calorie posting. *American Journal of Clinical Nutrition, 93*(4), 679–680.

35. VanEpps, E. M., Downs, J. S., & Loewenstein, G. (2016). Calorie label formats: Using numeric and traffic light calorie labels to reduce lunch calories. *Journal of Public Policy & Marketing, 35*(1), 26–36.

36. Peters, E., Shoots-Reinhard, B., Shoben, A., Evans, A. T., Klein, E., Tompkins, M. K., . . . Tusler, M. (2019). Pictorial warning labels and memory for cigarette health-risk information over time. *Annals of Behavioral Medicine, 53*, 358–371. https://doi.org/10.1093/abm/kay050

37. Hsee, C. K., & Rottenstreich, Y. (2004). Music, pandas, and muggers: On the affective psychology of value. *Journal of Experimental Psychology: General, 133*(1), 23–30.

38. Han, P. K., Klein, W. M., & Arora, N. K. (2011). Varieties of uncertainty in health care: A conceptual taxonomy. *Medical Decision Making, 31*(6), 828–838.

39. Ellsberg, D. (1961). Risk, ambiguity, and the savage axioms. *Quarterly Journal of Economics, 75*(4), 643–669.

40. Politi, M. C., Han, P. K., & Col, N. F. (2007). Communicating the uncertainty of harms and benefits of medical interventions. *Medical Decision Making, 27*(5), 681–695.

41. Gregory, R., Dieckmann, N., Peters, E., Failing, L., Long, G., & Tusler, M. (2012). Deliberative disjunction: Expert and public understanding of outcome uncertainty. *Risk Analysis*, *32*(12), 2071–2083.

42. Frewer, L. J., & Salter, B. (2007). Societal trust in risk analysis: Implications for the interface of risk assessment and risk management. In M. Siegrist, T. C. Earle, & H. Gutscher (Eds.), *Trust in cooperative risk management: Uncertainty and scepticism in the public mind* (pp. 143–158). London: Earthscan.

43. Binder, A. R., Hillback, E. D., & Brossard, D. (2016). Conflict or caveats? Effects of media portrayals of scientific uncertainty on audience perceptions of new technologies. *Risk Analysis*, *36*(4), 831–846.

44. Johnson, B. B., & Slovic, P. (1995). Presenting uncertainty in health risk assessment: Initial studies of its effects on risk perception and trust. *Risk Analysis*, *15*(4), 485–494.

45. Fischhoff, B., & Davis, A. L. (2014). Communicating scientific uncertainty. *Proceedings of the National Academy of Sciences*, *111*(suppl 4), 13664–13671.

46. Funtowicz, S. O., & Ravetz, J. R. (1992). Three types of risk assessment and the emergence of post-normal science. In S. Krimsky & D. Golding (Eds.), *Social theories of risk* (pp. 251–274). Westport, CT: Praeger.

47. Han, P. K. J., Klein, W. M. P., Lehman, T., Killam, B., Massett, H., & Freedman, A. N. (2011). Communication of uncertainty regarding individualized cancer risk estimates: Effects and influential factors. *Medical Decision Making*, *31*(2), 354–366.

48. Politi, M. C., Clark, M. A., Ombao, H., Dizon, D., & Elwyn, G. (2011). Communicating uncertainty can lead to less decision satisfaction: A necessary cost of involving patients in shared decision making? *Health Expectations*, *14*(1), 84–91.

49. Taleb, N. N. (2007). *The black swan: The impact of the highly improbable*. New York: Random House.

50. Peters, E., Dieckmann, N., Dixon, A., Hibbard, J. H., & Mertz, C. K. (2007). Less is more in presenting quality information to consumers. *Medical Care Research and Review*, *64*(2), 169–190.

51. Zikmund-Fisher, B. J., Angott, A. M., & Ubel, P. A. (2011). The benefits of discussing adjuvant therapies one at a time instead of all at once. *Breast Cancer Research and Treatment*, *129*(1), 79–87.

52. Hanoch, Y., Rice, T., Cummings, J., & Wood, S. (2009). How much choice is too much? The case of the Medicare prescription drug benefit. *Health Services Research*, *44*(4), 1157–1168.

53. Schwartz, B. (2005, January 5). Choose and lose. *The New York Times*. Retrieved from https://www.nytimes.com/2005/01/05/opinion/choose-and-lose.html.

54. Zikmund-Fisher, B. J., Fagerlin, A., & Ubel, P. A. (2008). Improving understanding of adjuvant therapy options via simpler risk graphics. *Cancer*, *113*(12), 3382–3390.

55. Huffman, C., & Kahn, B. E. (1998). Variety for sale: Mass customization or mass confusion? *Journal of Retailing*, *74*, 491–513.

56. Reutskaja, E., & Hogarth, R. M. (2009). Satisfaction in choice as a function of the number of alternatives: When "goods satiate." *Psychology & Marketing*, *26*(3), 197–203.

57. Scammon, D. L. (1977). Information load and consumers. *Journal of Consumer Research*, *4*(3), 148–155.

58. Dhar, R. (1997). Consumer preference for a no-choice option. *Journal of Consumer Research*, *24*(2), 215–231.

59. Iyengar, S. S., Huberman, G., & Jiang, W. (2004). How much choice is too much: Determinants of individual contributions in 401K retirement plans. In O. S. Mitchell & S. Utkus (Eds.), *Pension design and structure: New lessons from behavioral finance* (pp. 83–95). Oxford: Oxford University Press.

60. Iyengar, S. S., & Lepper, M. R. (2000). When choice is demotivating: Can one desire too much of a good thing? *Journal of Personality and Social Psychology, 79*(6), 995–1006.

61. Garbarino, E. C., & Edell J. A. (1997). Cognitive effort, affect, and choice. *Journal of Consumer Research, 24*(2), 147–158.

62. Botti, S., & McGill, A. L. (2006). When choosing is not deciding: The effect of perceived responsibility on satisfaction. *Journal of Consumer Research, 33*(2), 211–219.

63. Schwartz, B. (2000). Self-determination: The tyranny of freedom. *American Psychologist, 55*(1), 79–88.

64. Schwartz, B. (2004). *The paradox of choice.* New York: Harper Collins.

65. Schwartz, B., Ward, A., Monterosso, J., Lyubomirsky, S., White, K., & Lehman, D. R. (2002). Maximizing versus satisficing: Happiness is a matter of choice. *Journal of Personality and Social Psychology, 83*(5), 1178–1197.

66. Damman, O. C., De Jong, A., Hibbard, J. H., & Timmermans, D. R. M. (2016). Making comparative performance information more comprehensible: An experimental evaluation of the impact of formats on consumer understanding. *BMJ Quality & Safety, 25*(11), 860–869.

67. Szrek, H., & Bundorf, M. K. (2014). Enrollment in prescription drug insurance: The interaction of numeracy and choice set size. *Health Psychology, 33*(4), 340–348.

68. Hanoch, Y., Miron-Shatz, T., Cole, H., Himmelstein, M., & Federman, A. D. (2010). Choice, numeracy, and physicians-in-training performance: The case of Medicare Part D. *Health Psychology, 29*(4), 454–459.

69. Barnes, A. J., Hanoch, Y., Martynenko, M., Wood, S., Rice, T., & Federman, A. D. (2013). Physician trainees' decision making and information processing: Choice size and Medicare Part D. *PLoS ONE, 8*(10), e77096

70. Ravdin, P. M., Siminoff, L. A., Davis, G. J., Mercer, M. B., Hewlett, J., Gerson, N., & Parker, H. L. (2001). Computer program to assist in making decisions about adjuvant therapy for women with early breast cancer. *Journal of Clinical Oncology, 19*(4), 980–991.

71. Hux, J. E., & Naylor, C. D. (1995). Communicating the benefits of chronic preventive therapy: Does the format of efficacy data determine patients' acceptance of treatment? *Medical Decision Making, 15*(2), 152–157.

72. Sheridan, S. L., Pignone, M. P., & Lewis, C. L. (2003). A randomized comparison of patients' understanding of number needed to treat and other common risk reduction formats. *Journal of General Internal Medicine, 18*(11), 884–892.

73. Chlebowski, R. T., Anderson, G. L., Gass, M., Lane, D. S., Aragaki, A. K., Kuller, L. H., . . . Johnson, K. C. (2010). Estrogen plus progestin and breast cancer incidence and mortality in postmenopausal women. *JAMA, 304*(15), 1684–1692.

74. Forrow, L., Taylor, W. C., & Arnold, R. M. (1992). Absolutely relative: How research results are summarized can affect treatment decisions. *American Journal of Medicine, 92*(2), 121–124.

75. Baron, J. (1997). Confusion of relative and absolute risk in valuation. *Journal of Risk and Uncertainty, 14*, 301–309.

76. Chao, C., Studts, J. L., Abell, T., Hadley, T., Roetzer, L., Dineen, S., . . . McMasters, K. M. (2003). Adjuvant chemotherapy for breast cancer: How presentation of recurrence risk influences decision-making. *Journal of Clinical Oncology, 21*(23), 4299–4305.

77. Bodemer, N., Meder, B., & Gigerenzer, G. (2014). Communicating relative risk changes with baseline risk: Presentation format and numeracy matter. *Medical Decision Making, 34*(5), 615–626.

78. Malenka, D. J., Baron, J. A., Johansen, S., Wahrenberger, J. W., & Ross, J. M. (1993). The framing effect of relative and absolute risk. *Journal of General Internal Medicine, 8*(10), 543–548.

79. Rolison, J. J., Hanoch, Y., & Miron-Shatz, T. (2012). What do men understand about lifetime risk following genetic testing? The effect of context and numeracy. *Health Psychology*, *31*(4), 530–533.

80. Fagerlin, A., & Peters, E. (2011). Quantitative information. In B. Fischhoff, N. Brewer, & J. Downs (Eds.), *Evidence-based communication of risk and benefits: A user's guide* (pp. 53–64). Silver Spring, MD: Food and Drug Administration.

81. Pighin, S., Savadori, L., Barilli, E., Cremonesi, L., Ferrari, M., & Bonnefon, J. F. (2011). The 1-in-X effect on the subjective assessment of medical probabilities. *Medical Decision Making*, *31*(5), 721–729.

82. Oudhoff, J. P., & Timmermans, D. R. M. (2015). The effect of different graphical and numerical likelihood formats on perception of likelihood and choice. *Medical Decision Making*, *35*(4), 487–500.

83. Sirota, M., Juanchich, M., Kostopoulou, O., & Hanak, R. (2014). Decisive evidence on a smaller-than-you think phenomenon: Revisiting the 1-in-x" effect on subjective medical probabilities. *Medical Decision Making*, *34*(4), 419–429.

84. Sheppard, N. (2011, October 26). Scarborough's impeccable math: Half of one sixth is one third. Retrieved from https://www.newsbusters.org/blogs/nb/noel-sheppard/2011/10/26/scarboroughs-impeccable-math-half-one-sixth-one-third.

85. Anderson, B. L., Obrecht, N. A., Chapman, G. B., Driscoll, D. A., & Schulkin, J. (2011). Physicians' communication of Down syndrome screening test results: The influence of physician numeracy. *Genetics in Medicine*, *13*(8), 744–749.

86. Sheridan, S. L., & Pignone, M. (2002). Numeracy and the medical student's ability to interpret data. *Effective Clinical Practice*, *5*(1), 35–40.

87. Peters, E., Kunreuther, H., Sagara, N., Slovic, P., & Schley, D. R. (2012). Protective measures, personal experience, and the affective psychology of time. *Risk Analysis*, *32*(12), 2084–2097.

88. Gigerenzer, G. (2002). *Calculated risks: How to know when numbers deceive you.* New York: Simon & Schuster.

89. Sakr, W. A., Gringon, D. J., Hass, G. P., Heilbrun, L. K., Pontes, J. E., & Crissman, J. D. (1996). Age and racial distribution of prostatic intraepithelial neoplasia. *European Urology*, *30*(2), 138–144.

90. USPSTF. (2011, October). Screening for prostate cancer: A review of the evidence for the US Preventive Services Task Force. Retrieved from http://www.uspreventiveservicestaskforce.org/uspstf/uspsprca.htm

91. Welch, G., Schwartz, L., & Woloshin, S. (2011). *Overdiagnosed: Making people sick in the pursuit of health.* Boston, MA: Beacon Press.

92. Linville, P. W., Fischer, G. W., & Fischhoff, B. (1993). AIDS risk perceptions and decision biases. In J. B. Pryor & G. D. Reeder (Eds.), *The social psychology of HIV infection* (pp. 5–38). Hillsdale, NJ: Lawrence Erlbaum.

93. Kleber, J., Florack, A., & Chladek, A. (2016). How to present donations: The moderating role of numeracy in cause-related marketing. *Journal of Consumer Marketing*, *33*(3), 153–161.

94. Soll, J. B., Keeney, R. L., & Larrick, R. P. (2013). Consumer misunderstanding of credit card use, payments, and debt: Causes and solutions. *Journal of Public Policy & Marketing*, *32*(1), 66–81.

95. Miller, L. M. S. (2014). Quantitative information processing of nutrition facts panels. *British Food Journal*, *116*(7), 1205–1219.

96. Tangari, A. H., Burton, S., & Davis, C. (2014). Do they have your number? Understanding the moderating role of format effects and consumer numeracy for quantitative front-of-package nutrition claims. *Journal of Consumer Affairs*, *48*(3), 620–633.

97. Goldstein, D. G., Hershfield, H. E., & Benartzi, S. (2016). The illusion of wealth and its reversal. *Journal of Marketing Research, 53*(5), 804–813.

98. Greene, J., Peters, E., Mertz, C. K., & Hibbard, J. H. (2008). Comprehension and choice of a consumer-directed health plan: An experimental study. *American Journal of Managed Care, 14*(6), 369–376.

99. Politi, M. C., Kuzemchak, M. D., Liu, J., Barker, A. R., Peters, E., Ubel, P. A., . . . Philpott, S. E. (2016). Show me my health plans: Using a decision aid to improve decisions in the federal health insurance marketplace. *MDM Policy & Practice, 51*(supl1), S1503.

100. Ancker, J. S., Senathirajah, Y., Kukafka, R., & Starren, J. B. (2006). Design features of graphs in health risk communication: A systematic review. *Journal of the American Medical Informatics Association, 13*(6), 608–618.

101. Lipkus, I. M., & Hollands, J. G. (1999). The visual communication of risk. *Journal of the National Cancer Institute Monographs, 9*(25), 149–63.

102. Hutchinson, J. W., Alba, J. W., & Eisenstein, E. M. (2010). Heuristics and biases in data-based decision making: Effects of experience, training, and graphical data displays. *Journal of Marketing Research, 47*(4), 627–642.

103. Jamieson, K. H., & Hardy, B. W. (2014). Leveraging scientific credibility about Arctic sea ice trends in a polarized political environment. *Proceedings of the National Academy of Sciences, 111*(suppl 4), 13598–13605.

104. Hilton, N. Z., Ham, E., Nunes, K. L., Rodrigues, N. C., Frank, C., & Seto, M. C. (2017). Using graphs to improve violence risk communication. *Criminal Justice and Behavior, 44*(5), 678–694.

105. Schonlau, M., & Peters, E. (2012). Comprehension of graphs and tables depend on the task: Empirical evidence from two web-based studies. *Statistics, Politics, and Policy, 3*(2). https://www.degruyter.com/view/j/spp.2012.3.issue-2/2151-7509.1054/2151-7509.1054.xml

106. Mason, D., Boase, S., Marteau, T., Kinmonth, A. L., Dahm, T., Minorikawa, N., & Sutton, S. (2014). One-week recall of health risk information and individual differences in attention to bar charts. *Health Risk & Society, 16*(2), 136–153.

107. Nelson, D. E., Hesse, B. W., & Croyle, R. T. (2009). *Making data talk: Communicating public health data to the public, policy makers, and the press.* New York: Oxford University Press.

108. Garcia-Retamero, R., Galesic, M., & Gigerenzer, G. (2010). Do icon arrays help reduce denominator neglect? *Medical Decision Making, 30*(6), 672–684.

109. Garcia-Retamero, R., & Galesic, M. (2009). Communicating treatment risk reduction to people with low numeracy skills: A cross-cultural comparison. *American Journal of Public Health, 99*(12), 2196–2202.

110. Fagerlin, A., Wang, C., & Ubel, P. A. (2005). Reducing the influence of anecdotal reasoning on people's health care decisions: Is a picture worth a thousand statistics? *Medical Decision Making, 25*(4), 398–405.

111. Garcia-Retamero, R., & Cokely, E. T. (2011). Effective communication of risks to young adults: Using message framing and visual aids to increase condom use and STD screening. *Journal of Experimental Psychology: Applied, 17*(3), 270–287.

112. Garcia-Retamero, R., & Galesic, M. (2010). Who profits from visual aids: Overcoming challenges in people's understanding of risks. *Social Science & Medicine, 70*(7), 1019–1025.

113. Hamstra, D. A., Johnson, S. B., Daignault, S., Zikmund-Fisher, B. J., Taylor, J. M. G., Larkin, K., . . . Fagerlin, A. (2015). The impact of numeracy on verbatim knowledge of the longitudinal risk for prostate cancer recurrence following radiation therapy. *Medical Decision Making, 35*(1), 27–36.

114. Hawley, S. T., Zikmund-Fisher, B., Ubel, P., Jancovic, A., Lucas, T., & Fagerlin, A. (2008). The impact of the format of graphical presentation on health-related knowledge and treatment choices. *Patient Education and Counseling, 73*(3), 448–455.

115. Tait, A. R., Voepel-Lewis, T., Zikmund-Fisher, B. J., & Fagerlin, A. (2010a). The effect of format on parents' understanding of the risks and benefits of clinical research: A comparison between text, tables, and graphics. *Journal of Health Communication*, *15*(5), 487–501.

116. Tait, A. R., Voepel-Lewis, T., Zikmund-Fisher, B. J., & Fagerlin, A. (2010b). Presenting research risks and benefits to parents: Does format matter? *Anesthesia and Analgesia*, *111*(3), 718–723.

117. Peters, E., & Bjälkebring, P. (2015). Multiple numeric competencies: When a number is not just a number. *Journal of Personality and Social Psychology*, *108*(5), 802–822.

118. Kreuzmair, C., Siegrist, M., & Keller, C. (2016). High numerates count icons and low numerates process large areas in pictographs: Results of an eye-tracking study. *Risk Analysis*, *36*(8), 1599–1614.

119. Kreuzmair, C., Siegrist, M., & Keller, C. (2017). Does iconicity in pictographs matter? The influence of iconicity and numeracy on information processing, decision making, and liking in an eye-tracking study. *Risk Analysis*, *37*(3), 546–556.

120. Ancker, J. S., Weber, E. U., & Kukafka, R. (2011). Effects of game-like interactive graphics on risk perceptions and decisions. *Medical Decision Making*, *31*(1), 130–142.

121. Schapira, M. M., Nattinger, A. B., & McAuliffe, T. L. (2006). The influence of graphic format on breast cancer risk communication. *Journal of Health Communication*, *11*(6), 569–582.

122. Wright, A. J., Whitwell, S. C., Takeichi, C., Hankins, M., & Marteau, T. M. (2009). The impact of numeracy on reactions to different graphic risk presentation formats: An experimental analogue study. *British Journal of Health Psychology*, *14*(1), 107–125.

123. Brewer, N. T., Richman, A. R., DeFrank, J. T., Reyna, V. F., & Carey, L. A. (2012). Improving communication of breast cancer recurrence risk. *Breast Cancer Research and Treatment*, *133*(2), 553–561.

124. Tyszka, T., & Sawicki, P. (2011). Affective and cognitive factors influencing sensitivity to probabilistic information. *Risk Analysis*, *31*(11), 1832–1845.

125. Fraenkel, L., Peters, E., Tyra, S., & Oelberg, D. (2016). Shared medical decision making in lung cancer screening: Experienced versus descriptive risk formats. *Medical Decision Making*, *36*(4), 518–525.

126. Eyler, R. F., Cordes, S., Szymanski, B. R., & Fraenkel, L. (2017). Utilization of continuous "spinners" to communicate risk. *Medical Decision Making*, *37*(6), 725–729.

127. Garcia-Retamero, R., & Hoffrage, U. (2013). Visual representation of statistical information improves diagnostic inferences in doctors and their patients. *Social Science & Medicine*, *83*, 27–33.

128. Garcia-Retamero, R., Cokely, E. T., Wicki, B., & Joeris, A. (2016). Improving risk literacy in surgeons. *Patient Education and Counseling*, *99*(7), 1156–1161.

129. Spiegelhalter, D., Pearson, M., & Short, I. (2011). Visualizing uncertainty about the future. *Science*, *333*(6048), 1393–1400.

130. Peters, E., Hart, P. S., & Fraenkel, L. (2011). Informing patients: The influence of numeracy, framing, and format of side effect information on risk perceptions. *Medical Decision Making*, *31*(3), 432–436.

17

Provide Evaluative Meaning and Direct Attention[*]

You might recall from Chapters 5–8 that people higher in objective numeracy have different inclinations with numbers compared to the less numerate. These inclinations of the highly numerate mean that they are more likely to understand numeric information even when it is difficult. In Chapter 16, you also learned that, when information providers reduce the cognitive effort required to understand numbers, people understand the numbers better and especially if they are less numerate. The habits of the highly numerate also give them two other decision-making advantages over the less numerate. First, they understand the feeling of numbers better and thus know their good/bad meaning so they can be used in decisions. Second, they pay more attention to numeric evidence, for example by thinking longer in decisions that involve them. Information architecture based on these processes, the focus of the present Chapter 17, can help the less numerate.

Provide Evaluative Meaning or Highlight Meaning

Having data and comprehending them are necessary but insufficient steps to making good choices. Decision makers also need to be able to evaluate the good or bad meaning of the information (see Chapter 6). Information, however, varies in how easy it is to evaluate. Consider, for example, a choice between hospitals that vary in post-treatment survival rates. Survival is clearly an important attribute, and people know bigger numbers are better. Nonetheless, they may not understand the meaning of small differences that exist (e.g., 93% vs. 96% survival) and especially when juxtaposed against familiar, salient, and easy-to-evaluate cost differences.[1] Particularly in unfamiliar domains, we may be able to identify correctly what a number is without having a clue as to what it means for the decision at hand.

[*] Modified with permission from the National Academy of Sciences, Courtesy of the National Academies Press, Washington, D.C.

Innumeracy in the Wild. Ellen Peters, Oxford University Press (2020). © Oxford University Press 2020.
DOI: 10.1093/oso/9780190861094.003.0001

This difference between comprehension and comprehension of meaning is highlighted in research on evaluability.[2] When a decision maker cannot map a numeric value onto an affective good/bad scale (the meaning of an attribute's value), then she also cannot weigh it properly in decisions.[3] Not only that, but information that is easier to evaluate (e.g., a narrative's compelling power) will affect decision making more (and especially for the less numerate) when numeric information is difficult to evaluate.[4,5]

By the end of this chapter, you will know a variety of ways to help people determine the meaning of numeric information. By improving evaluability, consumers transform data into meaningful information and are able to use it in choice.[6] In particular, evaluability changes appear to make the goodness or badness of choice information more accessible.[1] This simpler information then seems to alter understanding of choice attributes, which subsequently affects how they are weighted and used in choice.

Provide Comparisons

One way to improve information evaluability is to provide other relevant comparisons. For example, we found that providing numeric likelihoods of possible side effects associated with a medication reduced the number of people who overestimated them, and it increased their willingness to take the medication in a hypothetical scenario.[7] We concluded that providing numeric risk-likelihood information allowed "for comparisons between various [side effects] and other risks that put into perspective the risks posed by the medication" (p. 439).[7] This speculation was consistent with the reasons people gave for their reported willingness to take the medication. In particular, when we gave respondents numeric likelihoods, 50% of them said that most side effects were not serious or not likely; only 30% said so when not given the numeric likelihoods. Conveying numeric information appropriately may cause decision makers to process information more deeply, draw their own conclusions, and, ultimately, allow the numeric information to have greater impact due to elaborative processes.[8,9]

Furthermore, numbers can be provided for comparison in different ways. You can furnish comparison numbers to other risks, as we did with medication side effects, or you can ask the individual to estimate a number (e.g., the likelihood of a disease or other outcome) and then show the actual numbers. In an example of the latter, psychologist Angie Fagerlin[10] asked half of her female respondents to estimate the lifetime chance that the average woman would develop breast cancer; the other half did not make an estimate.

The estimators tended to overestimate (their mean estimate was 46%). The experimenters then told both groups that women have an average 13% lifetime risk of breast cancer and asked how they felt about it. The estimators felt relieved and perceived less risk, presumably because they compared the surprisingly low 13% risk to their own estimates. The nonestimators were much more anxious about the risk. Results were similar across objective-numeracy levels. We extended these findings when we examined beliefs in the rate of scientific consensus on human-caused climate change (the current consensus estimate is about 97%[11]). In this case, people tend to underestimate the consensus, with one study finding an average perceived consensus rating of 67%.[12] We asked participants to estimate the consensus before and after reporting the actual 97% consensus to them. Reported consensus was 65% pre-message and a significantly higher 89% post-message; increases were similar among liberals and conservatives.[13] Thus, active comparisons change how people process information.

Thus, with unfamiliar numbers, we often know what a number is but not what it means. With a numerical comparison, however, the number can come alive with affective meaning and become evaluable.[2,14–17]

In some cases, comparisons are made possible because you evaluate two options together instead of evaluating a single option by itself. In one study, subjects assessed either one or two infertility clinics that differed in in vitro fertilization success rates and distance from the patient.[18] When evaluating a single clinic, participants tended to weigh the easy-to-evaluate distance factor more than the difficult-to-evaluate—but important—success-rate factor, and they favored the nearby clinic over the more distant one. However, when the clinics were compared side by side (Hsee[14], calls this "joint evaluation" in his work on the evaluability hypothesis), participants instead preferred the clinic that was farther away but had a higher success rate, demonstrating that the difficult-to-evaluate attribute (success rates) received little weight in preference without a provided comparison. Provision of similar numeric comparisons has been shown to alter people's perceptions of food products based on information in a nutrition facts label.[19] Similarly, adding a 2,000-calories-a-day recommendation to restaurant menus increased the immediate effect of numeric calorie information on menus.[20] Presumably, a 1,600-calorie breakfast evokes a different feeling when you know that experts recommend eating only 2,000 calories all day.

Research has also demonstrated that social comparisons can alter cancer risk estimates, decrease ambivalence about cancer screening, and increase adoption of healthy behaviors.[21–23] For example, telling people that their personal risk was above or below average changed attitudes toward the risks and benefits of treatments.[24] Furthermore, women told that the proportion of women who chose chemotherapy was 15% (a low social norm) were less interested in chemotherapy than those told that 60% chose it (a high social norm).[25] It is unclear whether the effects of social comparison information will differ by numeracy. It may be that numeracy differences will not appear given that people make social comparisons automatically,[26,27] in the presence of objective standards,[28] and with inappropriate comparison targets.[26]

Experts instead can provide contextual meaning using comparisons such as with size. The press, for example, compared the size of the July 2017 iceberg that broke away from the Antarctic Peninsula[29] to the size of Delaware (in the United States), London (in the United Kingdom), and Lake Erie (by the original researchers). Such comparisons are intended to convey an intuitive sense of the numeric magnitude of the iceberg. They may be particularly useful with the very large numbers our minds have difficulty representing (think about icebergs, federal budgets, and evolutionary time, for example).

Providing numeric comparisons, including magnitude comparisons, can help people discover the meaning of numerical data on their own. Such a process respects their intelligence more in some ways (compared to providing evaluative labels in the next section, for example) and it may lead to greater elaboration, personal meaning, and use of the data. However, choosing the best comparison can be difficult given its effects on perceptions of risk magnitude (e.g., a 12% risk may seem low relative to a 30% risk but high when compared to a 1% risk).

You might recall from Chapter 6 though that the highly numerate compare numbers more, suggesting that providing comparisons may not help the less numerate much. Existing data, however, are equivocal. From prior research, we know that more and less objectively numerate people respond similarly sometimes (e.g., when motivated to understand disease risk[10,30,31]), whereas other times the highly numerate use comparative information more.[5,32–35] For example, participants read about a woman learning that her baby's risk of having a chromosomal anomaly was either 1 in 110, 1 in 770, or 1 in 5,390.[33] Experimenters then randomly assigned participants to read or not read a comparison scenario (e.g., "For comparison purposes consider that in Europe, the risk of contracting an infection that can damage the fetus during pregnancy is 1 in 1,428, but if the woman does not observe personal hygiene the risk is 1 in 500"). Participants discriminated more between risk levels when provided the comparison and especially if they were higher in objective numeracy. Notice though that the risks were always presented as 1-in-X so that participants had to compare numbers with different denominators. The less numerate may have discriminated less simply because the changing denominator was too difficult for them. Similarly, a graphical risk ladder depicting comparison risks at varying levels of probability made it easier for the highly numerate to discriminate between different levels of probability but had little effect on the less numerate, who were generally insensitive to risk levels.[34,35] Using a simpler risk ladder with a familiar cigarette-smoking comparison, however, did improve the less numerate's evaluation of risk levels.[30,36]

Generally, numeric comparisons have less effect on those lower in objective numeracy, perhaps because the data are perceived as less relevant. However, providing greater description of what the numbers represent can increase perceptions of their relevance and ultimately increase their use. In a collaboration between psychologists and a lawyer, participants made hypothetical decisions about committing a mental-health patient based on an actuarial estimate of the person's likelihood of violence and a description of violence risk factors.[37] The experimenters varied the numeric likelihood (8/100, 26/100, vs. 76/100) and the number of violence risk factors described (either six, three, or no risk factors such as alcohol abuse diagnosis, high in anger reaction, prior hospitalization). Providing more risk factors increased the perceived relevance of and sensitivity to the provided numeric risk level. This "unpacking" of risk factors (without provision of any comparative numbers) affected only the less numerate and may be an alternative for increasing perceived relevance and elaboration of numeric risk information among the less numerate, similar to the use of narratives.[38]

However, most studies with comparative information have not included objective numeracy measures, making such effects less known. Numeracy effects seem less likely to emerge when motivation is high (e.g., breast cancer risk)[10] and when concrete, easy-to-evaluate comparisons are provided.[30] Numeracy differences, on the other hand, seem more likely when numbers are perceived as less relevant or trusted,[37,38] they are complex,[33] or they require a number operation which the highly numerate are more likely to do[32]. Thus far, I've suggested that providing numeric comparisons is helpful because it often allows people to discriminate better between numeric levels. However, is more discrimination always better? Is it possible that providing comparisons might cause numeric information to be overused and especially by the highly numerate? More research is needed including to identify boundary conditions for when more and less numerate individuals are sensitive to numbers critical to their decisions.

Carefully Use Evaluative Labels and Symbols

Because people (and especially the less numerate) can be quite poor at using unfamiliar numeric information even when provided comparisons, communicators should consider directly furnishing the meaning of numeric information (e.g., by telling patients how good or bad a 9% risk is). In one set of studies, we provided half of our participants with labels (poor, fair, good, and excellent) that evaluated numeric quality-of-care information about hospitals and health insurance plans.[1] Compared to those given numbers only, evaluative-label participants formed judgments more sensitive to numeric differences in the quality-of-care offered and less sensitive to how they felt in the moment (their current mood state), especially if they were less numerate. Follow-up studies in this paper revealed that participants given evaluative labels processed numeric information similarly to those given only numbers (e.g., they had similar numeric memory). However, they accessed their feelings about choice options faster than their thoughts about the same options with evaluative labels; thoughts and feelings came to mind equally quickly when only numbers were provided. Because information that comes to mind first tends to have a disproportionate influence on choices,[39] we interpreted these results to mean that the labels influenced choice through an affective mechanism. Supplying evaluative labels (e.g., "high," "low") also improves risk comprehension[40,41] and user experience of provided information.[42] Marketers have even started to tout its benefits (in combination with other psychological techniques) for weight loss.[43]

Evaluative labels are used at some cost, however. In one study, providing evaluative labels changed what information was understood. We asked participants to evaluate different environmental management actions with or without evaluative labels that described the uncertainty inherent in each possible option.[44] Participants given evaluative labels (e.g., uncertainty is High or Low) understood the general concept of uncertainty better (they understood in which option scientists had the greatest confidence). However, the presence of the labels reduced understanding about specific possible outcomes (e.g., "For which option is a final saved population of 8,500 most likely?") and caused participants to choose value-inconsistent options more often. For example, in our Study 2, participants with strong economic values unexpectedly chose the environmentally friendly, economically unfriendly option more often in the presence of evaluative labels. Evaluative labels for medical test results (the test came back "positive" or "abnormal") also induced larger changes to risk perceptions and behavioral intentions than did numeric results alone.[45] The authors argued that these changes could be inappropriate so that evaluative labels should be applied with great care. Thus, evaluative labels provide both advantages (they help people integrate information and improve understanding of certain global aspects of uncertainty information) and disadvantages (decreased understanding of specific information; questionable effects on value-inconsistent choices and risk perceptions).

Evaluative symbols can be used in place of labels. In health insurance plan studies, consumers chose high-value plans more often when stars were understood to indicate the quality of the health plan, when the stars were displayed adjacent to cost information, and when high-value plans were highlighted with a check mark or blue ribbon. These approaches, unlike some of the earlier evaluative label studies, were equally effective for participants with higher and lower numeracy.[46] In a study focused on comparative performance information concerning 20 healthcare providers, the use of colored dots resulted in more selections of the top three providers (84.3%), compared with word icons (76.6% correct), star ratings (70.6% correct), numbers (62.0%), and bars (54.2%).[47] Less numerate parents similarly understood more when provided color-coded charts about their child's body mass index chart.[48]

Results across these studies imply that, even when decision makers understand what the numbers are, they sometimes need help understanding what they mean. Using evaluative labels and symbols has the potential to influence behaviors and choices but also requires information providers to take responsibility for and make decisions about the meaning of the numbers they provide. This process is likely to be difficult and rife with ethical and political concerns (e.g., what scores are fair vs. good, what costs come with their use) and it requires the use of expert judgment or consensus. However, making numerical information easier to evaluate may increase use of information and assist decision makers in making better quality choices in health, financial, and other domains.[49]

Carefully Use Frequency Versus Percentage Formats

You might recall from Chapter 4 that choosing to present risk information in frequentistic versus percentage formats can increase people's affective reactions to and perceptions of provided risk information.[50] For instance, we asked participants to imagine they could take a medication to decrease the frequency of their severe headaches.[51] Participants read about a possible side effect of the drug in a percentage format (10% of patients get a blistering rash) or in a frequency format (10 patients out of 100 get a blistering rash). Less numerate participants (but not the highly numerate) perceived the medicine as less risky when side-effect information was presented using percentages. We interpreted these results as being due to the frequency formats eliciting greater emotional imagery compared to percentage formats, which were thought to be perceived as relatively abstract. Because information providers have to choose some format to provide likelihood information about side effects and no format is neutral, they should think carefully about whether they would definitely recommend taking the medication (in which case they should use the abstract percentage format to convey possible risks) or they want the patient to take the side effect seriously (they might use a frequency format instead). The choice of format will make little difference to risk perceptions of the highly numerate but may matter to the less numerate (see similar results for terrorism risk perceptions,[52] possible violence from a mental patient,[5] and for effects on donations[53]). One set of researchers did not replicate these results, however, for reasons that are unclear.[54]

Use Other More Imaginable Data Formats

Just as data presented in a frequentistic format may be easier (and more emotional) to imagine than the same data presented in a probabilistic format, changes in life expectancy appear easier to imagine than changes in disease risk. Psychologists Mirta Galesic and Rocio Garcia-Retamero[55] found that, when information about consequences of risky behaviors was presented as months of life lost or gained, recall was better than when it was presented in terms of disease likelihood. The effect held for both short-term and longer term memory among individuals higher and lower in objective numeracy. The improved recall seemed to be due to better imaginability of changes in life expectancy. Similarly, displaying the minutes of brisk walking needed to burn calories for menu items had a bigger effect than calorie counts alone on calories ordered and consumed.[56] Another potentially easy to imagine format for communicating risk is the use of a person's calculated heart age. However, communicating heart age as compared to 5-year absolute risk did not improve lifestyle intentions and behaviors. It also inflated risk perceptions and was perceived as less credible across levels of numeracy.[57]

The use of analogies, such as a visual analog scale (a thermometer where the lowest "temperature" was death and the highest "temperature" was perfect health[58]), may improve imaginability of unfamiliar concepts, too. For example, imagine a friend considering an emotionally appealing investment that had a low likelihood of success. You might tell them "That's as useful as rearranging deck chairs on the *Titanic*." Such an analogy could help overcome the overweighting of small probabilities (often called *probability neglect*) common to events that elicit emotional responses in us.[59] In health studies, the use of analogies (e.g., comparing the effect of a new drug for stroke to the effect of broccoli for cancer) improved understanding of medical problems, such as risk reduction from preventive medical treatments.[60] The analogies were more helpful for difficult problems among participants higher in objective numeracy and for easy problems among those lower in objective numeracy.[60]

Use Emotion to Direct Attention, Inform, and Motivate

Affective reactions also appear to be powerful sources of information and motivation, including with respect to numeric information.[15,61] A recent example comes from tobacco, the leading cause of preventable death worldwide, killing 1 person every 6 seconds and more than 6 million each year.[62–64] To combat this epidemic, a series of strategies have been implemented (e.g., taxes, clean air laws, advertising bans). In addition, at least 100 countries have implemented pictorial health warnings on the front and back of cigarette packages that include basic statements of health risks (e.g., "smoking kills") and large images illustrating the risks.[65] Pictorial warnings elicit negative emotion that spills over onto risk perceptions, quit intentions, and cessation.[66–71] These and other findings have led the Court (and others) to misperceive that these warnings work by merely "browbeat[ing] consumers into quitting" (p. 1216)[72] as if emotions are irrational impulses, without value.

This view of emotions as irrational, however, conflicts with behavioral research on the multiple roles that emotion plays in knowledge, risk perceptions, and decisions.[69,73–75] In particular, emotions act as information, informing our perceptions of risk quickly and efficiently as they have throughout humans' evolutionary history. They also motivate behaviors that benefit our well-being because emotions signal what is important to us. And, finally, emotions act as a spotlight in a two-stage process in which the emotion first highlights information that is critical and then that information affects later decisions. In the domain of pictorial cigarette risk warnings, warnings that elicit greater emotional reactions caused smokers to retain more risk knowledge over time, including knowledge about the numeric risks of smoking.[76,77] These pictorial warning labels appear to have greater effects among less numerate smokers who otherwise may have more superficial understanding of smoking's risks,[78] although current data are limited.

Communicators should consider the use of emotion to inform, motivate, and direct attention to important information, thus supporting knowledge and the motivation to use it. For example, smokers exposed to cigarette advertisements looked at the warnings for longer when embedded health warnings also included emotional images. In particular, they spent 24% of their time looking at the warning labels embedded in the ads when they included images compared to only 10% of their time when the ads included only text warnings.[79] The attention effects mediated effects of the pictorial warning labels on recall of health effects.[80]

Thus, emotion causes cognitive elaboration, which can lead to long-lasting positive behavioral and knowledge changes. Of course, these benefits of emotion need to be balanced with potential manipulative concerns that emotion can be used more superficially to persuade in the short term.[9] In addition, negative emotion, in particular, has been found to increase message reactance, which can decrease emotion's informational and motivational effects on risk perceptions and quit intentions, respectively.[81] Testing of messages can help the communicator determine the effects of particular messages.

What Did We Learn About Evaluative Meaning in Communications?

Let's pause for a moment and consider what we have learned. First, if you want to use numbers in decisions, you may have to understand their good/bad meaning: They have to be evaluable. Second, you might already know their meaning from past experience (100% correct on a test feels fantastic!), but without experience, it's harder. That difficulty does not mean that using them is impossible. Instead, it means that you have to make the numbers evaluable or ask someone to do so for you. In this chapter thus far, we found that information can be made easier to evaluate in ways that require more cognitive effort from the decision maker (using numeric comparisons) or less effort (using evaluative labels, frequencies, and other more imaginable formats). The use of emotion is an interesting example because its effects may require less effort in some ways (affect motivates behaviors directly) but potentially more cognitive effort when it acts as a spotlight on relevant information[73] and supports memory for information over time.[76]

Grab and Hold Attention to Important Information

Just as emotion can function as a spotlight, directing attention to particular information similarly can alter the relative salience of decision information.[69,73] Altering attention also can change preference directly because looking longer at a liked object drives choices of it.[82,83] As you'll see, a number of techniques exist for grabbing and holding people's attention besides the use of emotion.

Order Information So That the Most Important Information Is First or Last

Ordering information can help consumers by drawing attention to important information and reducing the cognitive effort required to locate and understand the goodness or badness of information. Marketing professor Jay Russo,[84] for example, found that providing unit prices on separate shelf tags in a supermarket saved consumers 1% at grocery checkout; also providing an ordered list of unit cost information from lowest to highest on a grocery store shelf saved them 3% compared to not providing unit prices. We found that ordering health plans by performance within premium cost strata resulted in more choices of higher performing plans compared with presenting the information unordered.[6] Although unstudied, it seems likely that the effect would be larger among the less objectively numerate, who have more difficulty understanding the meaning of numeric information. However, simplifying very complex Medicaid information, including ordering the plans based on their generosity in terms of costs and extra benefits, improved comprehension only among those higher in subjective numeracy.[85]

Highlight the Meaning of Only the Most Important Information

Making only a more important quality measure easier to evaluate through the use of evaluative symbols (rather than making all indicators easier to evaluate) led to more choices of higher quality hospitals,[86] presumably because it directed attention to this quality measure (which was then easy to evaluate). These results were particularly strong among the less objectively numerate. Making the meaning of all information easier to evaluate (the more and less important information) worsened health choices among those with lower numeracy in this same paper.

Use a Summary to Provide an Overview

When choices are unfamiliar, communicators could consider providing an overview, but should be aware of the costs of doing so. We examined consumer understanding and use of information when choosing between more and less familiar types of health plans.[87] Less objectively numerate consumers understood less of the information provided about the new type of health plan at the same time as they were substantially more likely to choose it. Providing an overarching framework to explain and highlight the differences between the two types of health plans boosted comprehension on items related to the framework message. However, it reduced comprehension on items that were not related to the framework and particularly among the less objectively numerate. The study highlighted the difficulty many less numerate consumers have in understanding comparative information and in making informed healthcare choices.

Summary evaluations can be used instead.[88] In one study, participants examined hospital options one at a time to form an overall evaluation of each one, and they either received or did not receive a summary evaluation of each option. Getting the summary helped older and less numerate individuals, in particular, to overcome the effects of choice and information overload. Thus, providing a framework or summary can help, but information providers need to ensure that critical information is appropriately mentioned and weighted.

Increase Visual Salience to Draw Attention to Important Information

Sometimes consumers don't use numeric information because they never looked at it in the first place. This neglect may be particularly prevalent among less numerate consumers (see review of numeracy-related attention effects in Chapter 5). Methods can be used, however, to explicitly draw attention to numeric information in these cases. Stimuli that are perceptually salient draw attention[89] and tend to have greater influence on choice.[90] For example, in a men's clothing store, a red tie placed in a display of neutrally colored ties may capture attention and be chosen more often than the same red tie in a display of vibrant colors.

The visual salience of numeric information can be manipulated similarly, including through larger, bolder, and more salient fonts. In an unpublished dissertation, for example, numeric product information that was italicized and printed in gray (in contrast with the regular black font of the surrounding information) had a greater impact on product judgments.[91] Similar results were demonstrated in hypothetical vaccine studies when font size was varied.[92] Increasing the font size of the numeric risk information drew participant attention toward it, increased sensitivity to numeric risk levels, and altered vaccination decisions. Increased salience of information (management fees and costs) also affected the ability to locate important information in retirement savings funds and to evaluate fund performance. In this case, effects were limited to those people with moderate numeracy.[93]

Moving Forward

I hope this chapter has sharpened your sense that how information is presented matters to how you and others judge and decide. It is simply not enough to provide or receive the best information when how information is presented influences comprehension and use of it. These effects are stronger for the less objectively numerate who have fewer skills to navigate unfamiliar numeric decisions in finances, employment, health, and science. This population varies considerably in what we called "education-based numeracy skills" (from basic arithmetic to understanding cumulative risk) and also in emergent decision-based numeracy skills (from seeking out numeric information to deriving affective meaning from it).[94] For you and others to get the most from numeric information, information providers need to better understand to whom they are talking (in terms of their numeric abilities) and they need to know how to apply the science of communication to maximize informed decisions and, in turn, well-being.

Communicating effectively is more difficult than it initially appears. Nonetheless, "those who disseminate information have a responsibility to be aware of how they use that influence and to direct it in productive and defensible ways. The alternative is to manipulate people in ways that are unknown, are not thought out, or are not defensible, but are no less manipulative" (p. 291).[6] The evidence-based strategies reviewed in this chapter will help you communicate numbers better and assist you in asking others to make meaningless numbers come alive for you.

Many challenges exist. For example, in a specific situation where you want to present information well, we may not know yet exactly what to do. Furthermore, as mentioned earlier, our intuitions about how to present information do not always help and sometimes hurt comprehension of the people we want to help. In those situations, ideally, you would test communications with the appropriate populations. This possibility highlights the need to consider communication early on in order to plan for the necessary resources.

Other logistical constraints exist, too. The US Food and Drug Administration (FDA), for example, makes judgments about prescription medicines and other products with respect to whether their benefits outweigh their risks, in which case that product can go to market. When I was a member of their Risk Communication Advisory Committee, we recommended that the FDA provide quantitative information to the public about the likelihoods of drug risks and benefits. The FDA, however, considered their numeric data inadequate for communication purposes.

Political pushback provides further constraints (see Figure 15.2). But effective communication matters even more in politically divisive contexts where misinformation and knowledge resistance are persistent and, in some cases, more so among highly numerate audiences.[95,96] A recent meta-analysis revealed that generating reasons in support of initial misinformation makes persistence stronger whereas providing a detailed debunking message had more beneficial effects.[97] Solving misinformation and knowledge resistance may require supporting numeric understanding using the evidence-based techniques reviewed in this chapter combined with reducing motivated reasoning. Multiple reasons exist for such motivated reasoning and multiple solutions likely are need to solve it. We need to know more though about how to select best strategies based on individual and situational factors.[98]

If no communication is "neutral," then communicators need to choose to exercise influence consciously or mindlessly. If consciously, they also need to consider what types of influence are justifiable. I argue for five areas of defensible influence. First, it seems defensible to use presentation approaches that help consumers weight attributes more that they want to weight more (e.g., performance quality in choices among health insurance plans).[6] A second defensible approach is using graded performance standards (e.g., unacceptable, poor, excellent performance). Data are more evaluable with them, and they allow people to understand numeric information and use it. However, determining fair and accurate categories and labels requires expert judgment or consensus. This process inherently concerns both ethics and politics. For example, when hospitals were graded on performance and these reports were made public, the hospitals thought the report less valid especially if they had low performance scores.[99] Third, summarizing data simply to reduce the information-processing burden on consumers is harder to justify and smacks of "dumbing it down." However, combining expert consensus about high-importance information with consumer values and preferences for data could determine the critical information to include. Less important information (but that is perhaps desired by a subset of consumers) could be accessed by drilling down further in the provided information.

Fourth, communicators commonly provide information for the general public side by side with information specific to subgroups of the population. The research reviewed here suggests that this practice is problematic (remember, less can be more). Instead, consumers with special information needs should be directed to a separate source that includes information tailored to their circumstances, leaving the more general report targeted at a more general population and its information needs.

Finally, given the potential to manipulate, consumers need protection from both unscrupulous and naïve purveyors of information. For example, an employer could unknowingly "simplify" information and skew choice in one direction or another. A company could manipulate shoppers by displaying comparative data in a format that advantages a more profitable product relative to other products. Standardization in how comparative performance is presented (e.g., Medicare health insurance plans) would provide an element of protection. Experts, in consultation with consumers, could determine what data displays and inherent biases are acceptable, and any inherent bias in the data display approach would at least be known. By recognizing the limitations of human judgment and decision making as well as communicators' own potential influence, communicators can make better choices about how to provide information in ways that promote individual and social goals.

References

1. Peters, E., Dieckmann, N. F., Västfjäll, D., Mertz, C. K., Slovic, P., & Hibbard, J. H. (2009). Bringing meaning to numbers: The impact of evaluative categories on decisions. *Journal of Experimental Psychology: Applied*, *15*(3), 213–227.
2. Hsee, C. K., Loewenstein, G. F., Blount, S., & Bazerman, M. H. (1999). Preference reversals between joint and separate evaluations of options: A review and theoretical analysis. *Psychological Bulletin*, *125*(5), 576–590.
3. Slovic, P., Finucane, M., Peters, E., & MacGregor, D. G. (2002). Rational actors or rational fools: Implications of the affect heuristic for behavioral economics. *Journal of Socio-Economics*, *31*(4), 329–342.
4. Betsch, C., Haase, N., Renkewitz, F., & Schmid, P. (2015). The narrative bias revisited: What drives the biasing influence of narrative information on risk perceptions? *Judgment and Decision Making*, *10*(3), 241–264.
5. Peters, E., Västfjäll, D., Slovic, P., Mertz, C. K., Mazzocco, K., & Dickert, S. (2006). Numeracy and decision making. *Psychological Science*, *17*(5), 407–413.
6. Hibbard, J. H., Slovic, P., Peters, E., & Finucane, M. L. (2002). Strategies for reporting health plan performance information to consumers: Evidence from controlled studies. *Health Services Research*, *37*(2), 291–313.
7. Peters, E., Hart, P. S., Tusler, M., & Fraenkel, L. (2014). Numbers matter to informed patient choices: A randomized design across age and numeracy levels. *Medical Decision Making*, *34*(4), 430–442.

8. Jamieson, K. H., & Hardy, B. W. (2014). Leveraging scientific credibility about Arctic sea ice trends in a polarized political environment. *Proceedings of the National Academy of Sciences, 111*(suppl 4), 13598–13605.

9. Petty, R. E., & Cacioppo, J. T. (1979). Issue involvement can increase or decrease persuasion by enhancing message-relevant cognitive responses. *Journal of Personality and Social Psychology, 37*(10), 1915–1926.

10. Fagerlin, A., Zikmund-Fisher, B. J., & Ubel, P. A. (2005). How making a risk estimate can change the feel of that risk: Shifting attitudes toward breast cancer risk in a general public survey. *Patient Education and Counseling, 57*(3), 294–299.

11. Cook, J., Nuccitelli, D., Green, S. A., Richardson, M., Winkler, B., Painting, R., . . . Skuce, A. (2013). Quantifying the consensus on anthropogenic global warming in the scientific literature. *Environmental Research Letters, 8*(2), 024024.

12. van der Linden, S. L., Leiserowitz, A. A., Feinberg, G. D., & Maibach, E. W. (2015). The scientific consensus on climate change as a gateway belief: Experimental evidence. *PloS ONE, 10*(2), e0118489.

13. Myers, T. A., Maibach, E., Peters, E., & Leiserowitz, A. (2015). Simple messages help set the record straight about scientific agreement on human-caused climate change: The results of two experiments. *PLoS ONE, 10*(3): e0120985.

14. Hsee, C. K. (1996). The evaluability hypothesis: An explanation for preference reversals between joint and separate evaluations of alternatives. *Organizational Behavior and Human Decision Processes, 67*(3), 242–257.

15. Slovic, P., Finucane, M. L., Peters, E., & MacGregor, D. G. (2004). Risk as analysis and risk as feelings: Some thoughts about affect, reason, risk, and rationality. *Risk Analysis, 24*(2), 311–322.

16. Teigen, K. H., & Brun, W. (2000). Ambiguous probabilities: When does p = 0.3 reflect a possibility, and when does it express a doubt? *Journal of Behavioral Decision Making, 13*(3), 345–362.

17. Windschitl, P. D., Martin, R., & Flugstad, A. R. (2002). Context and the interpretation of likelihood information: The role of intergroup comparisons on perceived vulnerability. *Journal of Personality and Social Psychology, 82*(5), 742–755.

18. Zikmund-Fisher, B. J., Fagerlin, A., & Ubel, P. A. (2004). "Is 28% good or bad?" Evaluability and preference reversals in health care decisions. *Medical Decision Making, 24*(2), 142–148.

19. Visschers, V. H., & Siegrist, M. (2009). Applying the evaluability principle to nutrition table information. How reference information changes people's perception of food products. *Appetite, 52*(2), 505–512.

20. Roberto, C. A., Larsen, P. D., Agnew, H., Baik, J., & Brownell, K. D. (2010). Evaluating the impact of menu labeling on food choices and intake. *American Journal of Public Health, 100*(2), 312–318.

21. Dillard, A. J., McCaul, K. D., Kelso, P. D., & Klein, W. M. (2006). Resisting good news: Reactions to breast cancer risk communication. *Health Communication, 19*(2), 115–123.

22. Lipkus, I. M., & Klein, W. M. (2006). Effects of communicating social comparison information on risk perceptions for colorectal cancer. *Journal of Health Communication, 11*(4), 391–407.

23. Schmiege, S. J., Klein, W. M., & Bryan, A. D. (2010). The effect of peer comparison information in the context of expert recommendations on risk perceptions and subsequent behavior. *European Journal of Social Psychology, 40*(5), 746–759.

24. Fagerlin, A., Zikmund-Fisher, B. J., & Ubel, P. A. (2007). "If I'm better than average, then I'm ok?": Comparative information influences beliefs about risk and benefits. *Patient Education and Counseling, 69*(1), 140–144.

25. Zikmund-Fisher, B. J., Windschitl, P. D., Exe, N., & Ubel, P. A. (2011). "I'll do what they did": Social norm information and cancer treatment decisions. *Patient Education and Counseling, 85*(2), 225–229.

26. Gilbert, D. T., Giesler, R. B., & Morris, K. A. (1995). When comparisons arise. *Journal of Personality and Social Psychology, 69*(2), 227–236.

27. Mussweiler, T., & Bodenhausen, G. V. (2002). I know you are, but what am I? Self-evaluative consequences of judging in-group and out-group members. *Journal of Personality and Social Psychology, 82*(1), 19–32.

28. Klein, W. M. (1997). Objective standards are not enough: Affective, self-evaluative, and behavioral responses to social comparison information. *Journal of Personality and Social Psychology, 72*(4), 763–774.

29. Victor, D. (2017, July 12) How big Is the iceberg? That depends on where you live. *The New York Times.* Retrieved from https://www.nytimes.com/2017/07/12/climate/iceberg-antarctica-size.html

30. Keller, C. (2011). Using a familiar risk comparison within a risk ladder to improve risk understanding by low numerates: A study of visual attention. *Risk Analysis, 31*(7), 1043–1054.

31. Mata, A., Sherman, S. J., Ferreira, M. B., & Mendonça, C. (2015). Strategic numeracy: Self-serving reasoning about health statistics. *Basic and Applied Social Psychology, 37*(3), 165–173.

32. Peters, E., Fennema, M. G., & Tiede, K. E. (2019). The loss-bet paradox: Actuaries, accountants, and other numerate people rate numerically inferior gambles as superior. *Journal of Behavioral Decision Making, 32*, 15–29. https://doi.org/10.1002/bdm.2085.

33. Pighin, S., Savadori, L., Barilli, E., Rumiati, R., Bonalumi, S., Ferrari, M., & Cremonesi, L. (2013). Using comparison scenarios to improve prenatal risk communication. *Medical Decision Making, 33*(1), 48–58.

34. Keller, C., & Siegrist, M. (2009). Effect of risk communication formats on risk perception depending on numeracy. *Medical Decision Making, 29*(4), 483–490.

35. Siegrist, M., Orlow, P., & Keller, C. (2008). The effect of graphical and numerical presentation of hypothetical prenatal diagnosis results on risk perception. *Medical Decision Making, 28*(4), 567–574.

36. Keller, C., Siegrist, M., & Visschers, V. (2009). Effect of risk ladder format on risk perception in high- and low-numerate individuals. *Risk Analysis, 29*(9), 1255–1264.

37. Scurich, N., Monahan, J., & John, R. S. (2012). Innumeracy and unpacking: Bridging the nomothetic/idiographic divide in violence risk assessment. *Law and Human Behavior, 36*(6), 548–554.

38. Shaffer, V. A., Tomek, S., & Hulsey, L. (2014). The effect of narrative information in a publicly available patient decision aid for early-stage breast cancer. *Health Communication, 29*(1), 64–73.

39. Weber, E. U., Johnson, E. J., Milch, K. F., Chang, H., Brodscholl, J. C., & Goldstein, D. G. (2007). Asymmetric discounting in intertemporal choice: A query-theory account. *Psychological Science, 18*(6), 516–523.

40. Brewer, N. T., Richman, A. R., DeFrank, J. T., Reyna, V. F., & Carey, L. A. (2012). Improving communication of breast cancer recurrence risk. *Breast Cancer Research and Treatment, 133*(2), 553–561.

41. Khandpur, N., Graham, D. J., & Roberto, C. A. (2017). Simplifying mental math: Changing how added sugars are displayed on the nutrition facts label can improve consumer understanding. *Appetite, 114*, 38–46.

42. Lazard, A. J., Byron, M. J., Vu, H., Peters, E., Schmidt, A., & Brewer, N. T. (2019). Website designs for communicating about chemicals in cigarette smoke. *Health Communication, 34*(3), 333–342. doi: 10.1080/10410236.2017.1407276

43. Shapa. (2017). How it works. Retrieved from: https://www.shapa.me/how-it-works

44. Dieckmann, N. F., Peters, E., Gregory, R., & Tusler, M. (2012). Making sense of uncertainty: Advantages and disadvantages of providing an evaluative structure. *Journal of Risk Research, 15*(7), 717–735.

45. Zikmund-Fisher, B. J., Fagerlin, A., Keeton, K., & Ubel, P. A. (2007). Does labeling prenatal screening test results as negative or positive affect a woman's responses? *American Journal of Obstetrics & Gynecology, 197*(5), 528.e1–528.e6.

46. Greene, J., Hibbard, J. H., & Sacks, R. M. (2016). Summarized costs, placement of quality stars, and other online displays can help consumers select high-value health plans. *Health Affairs, 35*(4), 671–679.

47. Damman, O. C., De Jong, A., Hibbard, J. H., & Timmermans, D. R. M. (2016). Making comparative performance information more comprehensible: An experimental evaluation of the impact of formats on consumer understanding. *BMJ Quality & Safety, 25*(11), 860–869.

48. Oettinger, M. D., Finkle, J. P., Esserman, D., Whitehead, L., Spain, T. K., Pattishall, S. R., . . . Perrin, E. M. (2009). Color-coding improves parental understanding of body mass index charting. *Academic Pediatrics, 9*(5), 330–338.

49. Hibbard, J. H., & Peters, E. (2003). Supporting informed consumer health care choices: Data presentation approaches that facilitate the use of information in choice. *Annual Review of Public Health, 24*(1), 413–433.

50. Slovic, P., Monahan, J., & MacGregor, D. G. (2000). Violence risk assessment and risk communication: The effects of using actual cases, providing instructions, and employing probability versus frequency formats. *Law and Human Behavior, 24*(3), 271–296.

51. Peters, E., Hart, P. S., & Fraenkel, L. (2011). Informing patients: The influence of numeracy, framing, and format of side effect information on risk perceptions. *Medical Decision Making, 31*(3), 432–436.

52. Dieckmann, N. F., Slovic, P., & Peters, E. M. (2009). The use of narrative evidence and explicit likelihood by decisionmakers varying in numeracy. *Risk Analysis, 29*(10), 1473–1488.

53. Dickert, S., Kleber, J., Peters, E., & Slovic, P. (2011). Numeracy as a precursor to pro-social behavior: The impact of numeracy and presentation format on the cognitive mechanisms underlying donations. *Judgment and Decision Making. 6*(7), 638–650.

54. Brase, G. L., & Hill, W. T. (2017). Adding up to good Bayesian reasoning: Problem format manipulations and individual skill differences. *Journal of Experimental Psychology: General, 146*(4), 577–591.

55. Galesic, M., & Garcia-Retamero, R. (2011). Graph literacy: A cross-cultural comparison. *Medical Decision Making, 31*(3), 444–457.

56. James, A., Adams-Huet, B., Crisp, K., Mitchell, J., Dart, L., Turner, M., . . . Shah, M. (2013). The effect of menu labels, displaying minutes of brisk walking needed to burn food calories, on calories ordered and consumed in young adults. *Journal of the Federation of American Societies for Experimental Biology, 27*(1supl), 367.2.

57. Bonner, C., Jansen, J., Newell, B. R., Irwig, L., Teixeira-Pinto, A., Glasziou, P., . . . McCaffery, K. (2015). Is the heart age concept helpful or harmful compared to absolute cardiovascular disease risk? An experimental study. *Medical Decision Making, 35*(8), 967–978.

58. Woloshin, S., Schwartz, L. M., Moncur, M., Gabriel, S., & Tosteson, A. N. A. (2001). Assessing values for health: Numeracy matters. *Medical Decision Making, 21*(5), 382–390.

59. Rottenstreich, Y., & Hsee, C. K. (2001). Money, kisses, and electric shocks: On the affective psychology of risk. *Psychological Science, 12*(3), 185–190.

60. Galesic, M., & Garcia-Retamero, R. (2013). Using analogies to communicate information about health risks. *Applied Cognitive Psychology, 27*(1), 33–42.

61. Loewenstein, G. F., Weber, E. U., Hsee, C. K., & Welch, E. S. (2001). Risk as feelings. *Psychological Bulletin, 127*(2), 267–286.

62. Centers for Disease Control and Prevention. (2012). Smoking & tobacco use: Fast facts. Retrieved from http://www.cdc.gov/tobacco/data_statistics/fact_sheets/fast_facts/

63. World Health Organization. (2012). Tobacco. Retrieved from http://www.who.int/mediacentre/factsheets/fs339/en/index.html

64. World Health Organization. (2013). *WHO report on the global tobacco epidemic, 2013: Enforcing bans on tobacco advertising, promotion and sponsorship*. Geneva: World Health Organization.

65. Canadian Cancer Society. (2016). Cigarette package health warnings: International status report (5th ed.). Retrieved from www.tobaccolabels.ca/wp/wp-content/uploads/2016/11/Cigarette-Package-Health-Warnings-International-Status-Report-English-CCS-Oct-2016.pdf.

66. Peters, E., Hibbard, J., Slovic, P., & Dieckmann, N. (2007). Numeracy skill and the communication, comprehension, and use of risk-benefit information. *Health Affairs, 26*(3), 741–748.

67. Hammond, D. (2011). Health warnings on tobacco packages: A review. *Tobacco Control, 20*(5), 327–337.

68. White, V., Webster, B., & Wakefield, M. (2008). Do graphic health warning labels have an impact on adolescents' smoking-related beliefs and behaviours? *Addiction, 103*(9), 1562–1571.

69. Evans, A. T., Peters, E., Strasser, A. A., Emery, L. F., Sheerin, K. M., & Romer, D. (2015). Graphic warning labels elicit affective and thoughtful responses from smokers: Results of a randomized clinical trial. *PloS ONE, 10*(12), e0142879.

70. Brewer, N. T., Hall, M. G., Noar, S. M., Parada, H., Stein-Seroussi, A., Bach, L. E., . . . Ribisl, K. M. (2016). Effect of pictorial cigarette pack warnings on changes in smoking behavior: A randomized clinical trial. *JAMA Internal Medicine, 176*(7), 905–912.

71. Romer, D., Ferguson, S. G., Strasser, A. A., Evans, A. T., Tompkins, M. K., Macisco, J., . . . Peters, E. (2017). Effects of pictorial warning labels for cigarettes and quit-efficacy on emotional responses, smoking satisfaction, and cigarette consumption. *Annals of Behavioral Medicine, 52*(1), 53–64.

72. *R. J. Reynolds Tobacco Co. v Food and Drug Administration*, 696 F.3d 1205 (D.C. Cir. 2012).

73. Peters, E. (2006). The functions of affect in the construction of preferences. In S. Lichtenstein & P. Slovic (Eds.), *The construction of preference* (pp. 454–463). New York: Cambridge University Press.

74. Peters, E., Lipkus, I., & Diefenbach, M. A. (2006). The functions of affect in health communications and in the construction of health preferences. *Journal of Communication, 56*(suppl 1), S140–S162.

75. Peters, E., Evans, A. T., Hemmerich, N., & Berman, M. (2016). Emotion in the law and the lab: The case of graphic cigarette warnings. *Tobacco Regulatory Science, 2*(4), 404–413.

76. Peters, E., Shoots-Reinhard, B., Shoben, A., Evans, A. T., Klein, E., Tompkins, M. K., . . . Tusler, M. (2019). Pictorial warning labels and memory for cigarette health-risk information over time. *Annals of Behavioral Medicine, 53*, 358–371. https://doi.org/10.1093/abm/kay050.

77. Shoots-Reinhard, B., Erford, B., Romer, D., Evans, A. T., Shoben, A., Klein, E. G., & Peters, E. (2020). Numeracy and memory for risk probabilities and risk outcomes depicted on cigarette warning labels. *Health Psychology, 39*(8), 721–730. https://doi.org/10.1037/hea0000879

78. Klein, E. G., Quisenberry, A. J., Shoben, A. B., Romer, D., & Peters, E. (2018). The influence of health numeracy and health warning label type on smoking myths and quit-related reactions. *Nicotine & Tobacco Research, 21*(7), 974–978. https://doi.org/10.1093/ntr/nty207

79. Klein, E. G., Shoben, A. B., Krygowski, S., Ferketich, A., Berman, M., Peters, E., . . . Wewers, M. E. (2015). Does size impact attention and recall of graphic health warnings? *Tobacco Regulatory Science, 1*(2), 175–185.

80. Klein, E. G., Quisenberry, A. J., Shoben, A. B., Cooper, S., Ferketich, A. K., Berman, M., . . . Wewers, M. E. (2017). Health warning labels for smokeless tobacco: The impact of graphic images on attention, recall, and craving. *Nicotine & Tobacco Research, 19*(10), 1172–1177.

81. Hall, M. G., Sheeran, P., Noar, S. M., Boynton, M. H., Ribisl, K. M., Parada, H., . . . Brewer, N. T. (2017). Negative affect, message reactance and perceived risk: How do pictorial cigarette pack warnings change quit intentions? *Tobacco Control.* doi: 10.1136/tobaccocontrol-2017-053972

82. Krajbich, I., Armel, C., & Rangel, A. (2010). Visual fixations and the computation and comparison of value in simple choice. *Nature Neuroscience, 13*(10), 1292–1298.

83. Armel, K. C., Beaumel, A., & Rangel, A. (2008). Biasing simple choices by manipulating relative visual attention. *Judgment and Decision Making, 3*(5), 396–403.

84. Russo, J. E. (1977). The value of unit price information. *Journal of Marketing Research, 14*(2), 193–201.

85. Greene, J., & Peters, E. (2009). Medicaid consumers and informed decisionmaking. *Health Care Financing Review, 30*(3), 25–40.

86. Peters, E., Dieckmann, N., Dixon, A., Hibbard, J. H., & Mertz, C. K. (2007). Less is more in presenting quality information to consumers. *Medical Care Research and Review, 64*(2), 169–190.

87. Greene, J., Peters, E., Mertz, C. K., & Hibbard, J. H. (2008). Comprehension and choice of a consumer-directed health plan: An experimental study. *American Journal of Managed Care, 14*(6), 369–376.

88. Fasolo, B., Reutskaja, E., Dixon, A., & Boyce, T. (2010). Helping patients choose: How to improve the design of comparative scorecards of hospital quality. *Patient Education and Counseling, 78*(3), 344–349.

89. Parkhurst, D., Law, K., & Niebur, E. (2002). Modeling the role of salience in the allocation of overt visual attention. *Vision Research, 42*(1), 107–123.

90. Bettman, J. R., Luce, M. F., & Payne, J. W. (1998). Constructive consumer choice processes. *Journal of Consumer Research, 25*(3), 187–217.

91. Sagara, N. (2009). *Consumer understanding and use of numeric information in product claims.* (Doctoral dissertation). University of Oregon. Retrieved from ProQuest. Publication No. AAT 3395194.

92. Meilleur, L. R. (2012). *Manipulating attention to improve health behaviors.* Master's thesis. The Ohio State University. Retrieved from OhioLink ETD. Publication No. OSU1354291552.

93. Foster, F. D., Ng, J., & Wee, M. (2015). Presentation format and financial literacy: Accessibility and assessability of retirement savings statements. *Journal of Consumer Affairs, 49*(3), 519–549.

94. Peters, E., Meilleur, L., & Tompkins, M. K. (2014). Numeracy and the Affordable Care Act: Opportunities and challenges. Appendix A. IOM (Institute of Medicine). In *Health Literacy and Numeracy: Workshop Summary* (pp. 91–132). Washington, DC: The National Academies Press.

95. Kahan, D. M., Peters, E., Wittlin, M., Slovic, P., Ouellette, LL., Braman, D., & Mandel, G. (2012). The polarizing impact of science literacy and numeracy on perceived climate change risks. *Nature Climate Change, 2*(10), 732–735.

96. Kahan, D. M., Peters, E., Dawson, E. C., & Slovic, P. (2017). Motivated numeracy and enlightened self-government. *Behavioural Public Policy, 1*(1), 54–86.

97. Chan, M. P. S., Jones, C. R., Jamieson, K. H., & Albarracín, D. (2017). Debunking: A meta-analysis of the psychological efficacy of messages countering misinformation. *Psychological Science, 28*(11), 1531–1546.

98. National Academies of Sciences, Engineering, and Medicine. (2017). *Communicating science effectively: A research agenda.* Washington, DC: National Academies Press.

99. Hibbard, J. H., Stockard, J., & Tusler, M. (2003). Does publicizing hospital performance stimulate quality improvement efforts? *Health Affairs, 22*(2), 84–94.

SECTION VIII

BECOMING MORE NUMERATE

18

Training Numeracy

In this chapter, I want you to learn how people can become more numerate beyond the specific "tricks" taught in the boxes of Chapters 2–8. Those tricks are intended to teach you about intuitive biases that many people hold and how to avoid them. By themselves, though, this informational approach has limited effectiveness.[1] Its inefficacy may be due to the compelling power of intuitive biases. However, I believe it is better ascribed to innumeracy. This chapter focuses on methods to improve objective numeracy, numeric self-efficacy, and symbolic number mapping and their subsequent effects on decision processes and outcomes.

In particular, I focus on the case for formal schooling (years of education) and specific numeracy trainings as long-term foundations for good decision making through these three numeric competencies. Some of the research simultaneously tests causal influences of numerical competencies on decision-making processes and outcomes, a critical direction for future numeracy research. Improving numeric competencies means that you and others won't neglect numbers as much or get distracted by other information in your decisions. It is simply not the case that you cannot change your numeric ability. Instead, interventions can build adult numeric capacity—foster additional human capital—and propel decision makers not just to have more knowledge, but also to bring it to bear on decisions, think probabilistically, use heuristic processing less, consider alternative scenarios, and reason better numerically.

However, when it comes to improving adult numeracy and its subsequent effects on decision making, research is in its early stage. Where research exists, effect sizes also have been relatively small, with the exception of formal schooling in childhood. More targeted studies are needed to improve these effect sizes among adults and to understand whether small improvements may nonetheless have powerful cumulative effects. We'll talk more about these points.

Innumeracy in the Wild. Ellen Peters, Oxford University Press (2020). © Oxford University Press 2020.
DOI: 10.1093/oso/9780190861094.003.0001

Getting More Formal Education Increases General Intelligence

It is well known at this point that people who complete more years of formal education lead healthier and wealthier lives.[2-4] However, the causal impacts of education on decision processes and outcomes are not entirely clear because children cannot be randomly assigned to particular years of education (random assignment, of course, is the gold standard to determine causation but is unethical in this case). However, state-initiated changes to compulsory schooling laws in the United States from 1914 to 1978 offered a natural experiment because adults who were children at specific ages in those states received different numbers of years of schooling. Using these state-initiated changes, researchers found that more education increased later wages and savings rates, and it improved investment decisions.[5] These effects then mediated other superior financial outcomes in adulthood. In particular, each additional year of education increased the likelihood of having investment income by 7.5 percentage points and decreased the chances of going bankrupt by 3.3 percentage points. Each additional year of education also led to higher credit scores and fewer delinquent credit card payments.

Education appears to produce these and other positive outcomes through increases to general intelligence. For example, people with more years of formal education score higher on tests of domain-general cognitive processes (e.g., working memory, inhibitory control, attention-shifting processes).[6,7] In fact, some studies have concluded that schooling-related intelligence (IQ) increases are three to four times more than maturation-related increases.[8] Greater cognitive abilities, including objective numeracy, then appear to support better decision making and improved health and financial behaviors and outcomes.[5,9-13] "Education improves cognitive ability and cognitive ability appears to improve . . . outcomes (controlling for family background and other potentially confounding effects), likely by helping individuals reason through complex . . . decisions" (p. 2047).[5]

These studies of education-related intelligence and life outcomes have been conducted primarily in Western countries, leaving it unclear whether other variables endemic to Western societies (e.g., greater disparities in healthcare access) could explain what look like education differences. To examine this phenomenon with fewer such alternative explanations, we traveled to Ghana in sub-Saharan Africa and to the highlands of Peru.[9,14] These locations allowed us to study populations that were quite different from Western societies. In particular, individuals differed more in education and less in other variables proven critical to health and cognitive-functioning differences in Western countries (healthcare access, income, parental education, post-schooling employment).

We tested a schooling decision-making hypothesis that more years of schooling would enhance cognitive capacities and, in turn, risk-assessment and decision-making abilities. In collaboration with sociologist David Baker at Pennsylvania State University, we thought that these superior decision skills, and not simply health knowledge or income, then would lead individuals to undertake healthier behaviors and avoid unhealthy risks. Thus, we hypothesized that mass schooling would spread cognitive and decision skills, and these skills subsequently would lead to better health behaviors and outcomes (see Figure 18.1).

In Ghana, we collected data from schooled and unschooled rural villagers ($N = 181$) and focused on HIV/AIDS risk, a major health hazard in sub-Saharan Africa.[9] Consistent with prior research concerning education's link with better health, more educated villagers indeed practiced more protective health behaviors, such as being tested for HIV/AIDS and using condoms, than did less educated villagers. They also were wealthier and had greater cognitive abilities and HIV/AIDS knowledge. Wealth, abilities, and knowledge all were correlated with practicing more protective behaviors. Thus, simple correlations were consistent with greater education leading to all of the following: (1) more wealth and therefore affordability of health behaviors, (2) greater HIV/AIDS knowledge (and, thereby, the necessary tools to take charge and protect oneself against a potentially life-threatening disease), and (3) greater cognitive abilities that allowed people to understand *and* reason appropriately about health behaviors. However, and consistent with our model, cognitive abilities (and not HIV/AIDS knowledge or wealth) explained the effects of education on taking health-protective behaviors.

Endogenous variables did not offer good explanations of the data. First, although it is possible that more intelligent individuals completed more schooling, participants' reasons for continuing or discontinuing schooling were unrelated to intelligence. Instead, they reported having to quit school due

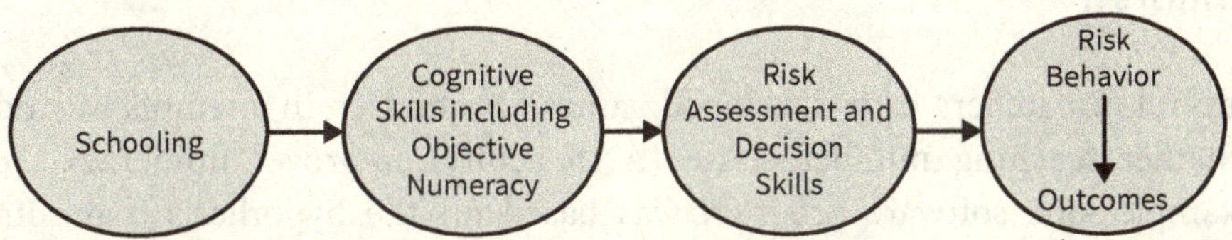

Figure 18.1 A model of the schooling decision-making hypothesis.

to noncognitive factors (e.g., access to schooling) or financial circumstances (e.g., death of a parent.) Second, post-schooling employment was largely similar; 86% of our Ghanaian participants reported farming as their primary or secondary occupation. Third, preschool impacts were likely similar as parent education usually produces these differences, and schooling was rare in Ghana when participants' parents were children. Thus, potential employment and pre-school impacts on cognitive abilities were relatively constant across our participants. The best explanation of our data is that schooling has many effects, but one of its most important is to build cognitive and decision skills to augment reasoning and decision-making competence.[15]

Education further has "silver bullet" properties in health and financial outcomes that appear due to these education-produced increases; people with more education do better than those with less, and educational inequalities produce further inequalities. An obvious solution is to increase education for all. This proposition is short-term expensive, with long-term payoffs, especially for early-childhood schooling when education dollars produce a "bigger bang for the buck."[13] More formal schooling for adults also may produce more benefits than costs if we consider its effects on better health, financial, and employment outcomes.

Training Approximate Number System Acuity

Given the expense and opportunity costs of more years of formal schooling, especially among adults, I turn in the remainder of this chapter to training methods that target our three numeric competencies. In Chapter 11, we discovered that the emergence of early math ability relates to the development of the approximate number system (ANS), our so-called intuitive number sense. This number sense or ANS acuity appears to lay the foundation for learning complex numeric skills in children. Could improving ANS acuity among children or adults improve objective numeracy and decision making, in turn?

Children

Several researchers have developed games for children in attempts to study whether teaching number sense (ANS acuity) improves numeracy. For example, one software program was based on the hypothesis that some children may have a core ANS deficit or a deficit in the mapping of magnitude representations to symbolic numbers.[16] In a proof-of-concept study, researchers examined nine children with persistent and/or severe difficulties in mathematics (called "acalculia") and found that playing their Number Race game speeded numerical-comparison ability and marginally improved ANS acuity. However, with more data, they concluded that their training did not improve ANS acuity per se, but it may allow children better access to their number sense or may improve mental mappings between symbolic and non-symbolic number representations.[17]

Psychologist Robert Siegler designed another intervention, a linear math board game called The Great Race, that has had stronger effects on numeric abilities.[18] It was designed to enhance preschoolers' numerical knowledge compared to a circular version of the same game or doing other mathematical activities. They hypothesized that the linear game more closely resembled our linear representation of numbers (e.g., a line running from 1 to 9) and thus should improve math skills more. Consistent with hypothesis, low-income preschoolers who played the linear board game for an hour made more accurate numerical magnitude comparisons (Which is more: one cookie or six cookies?) and number-line estimations (placing a "3" on a visual line ranging from "0" to "10"). They also scored higher on an arithmetic test compared to other participants. For example, children who played the linear game later scored 45% correct on a difficult addition test compared to children who played a circular board game or did other numerical activities and scored, respectively, 30% and 28% correct.

Other visual training programs that rely on ANS representations to improve children's arithmetic skills also have had some success. For example, children, who were trained with visual representations (colored bars) of the magnitudes of addends and sums in addition problems, scored higher on subsequent novel addition problems.[19] Similar training generalized beyond math. For example, children given corrective feedback about their estimates of number location on number lines had greater recall for numbers presented in vignettes than those given no feedback.[20] Child-centered math interventions have received much focus. You can learn more in some of the many existing reviews.[21,22]

Adults

Adults' ANS acuity could plausibly be improved through experimental practice, but mixed results exist. First, several days (and 1,600 trials) of training with college students did not alter one measure of ANS ability, the size of the distance effect[23] (see Chapter 13 and its Appendix to remind yourself of what that is). Other similar experimental studies also have revealed nonsignificant improvements in ANS acuity after controlling for testing effects.[24] However, significant effects have emerged of approximate arithmetic training on adults' symbolic arithmetic scores.[25-27] ANS acuity itself did not improve in these studies, but training may have improved mental mappings between symbolic and nonsymbolic representations of number.

Potentially consistent with this latter result, training on another measure of ANS acuity, symbolic number mapping (SMap), has yielded some positive results. In one study, less educated (but not more educated) patients who placed numbers on a line with subsequent feedback performed better on a posttest SMap task compared to pretest.[28] Participants did not respond to any decision tasks or health outcomes, however, to examine spillover effects. In a modified intervention, participants responded to an arithmetic problem by indicating its answer either on a number line (intervention) or a free response (control condition).[29] Feedback was provided after each trial and block. Intervention participants again improved SMap scores more than controls. However, this improvement did not generalize to objective numeracy scores (nor did it alter subjective numeracy). It also did not change performance on any decision task except one price-estimation task that used a similar sliding scale (it did not generalize, however, to typed responses in that same task), suggesting that results could have been due to the shared sliding scale rather than to any SMap improvement.

Thus, SMap responses are trainable among adults. However, improvements have generalized little to objective numeracy or decision performance. Current results could be explained by feedback increasing participant effort (a less interesting explanation) or feedback improving linkages between symbolic and nonsymbolic representations of number (but then we might expect to see better objective numeracy and decision performance). Researchers could examine long-term effects[30] by including decision tasks most likely to reflect theoretical effects of ANS-acuity improvements.[31] Overall, however, attempts to improve adult ANS acuity have shown little generalizability to other tasks.

Altering Subjective Numeracy

You might recall from Chapter 14 that decision makers also can be high or low in their numeric self-efficacy, and this numeric confidence may or may not match their objective numeracy performance. You yourself might be one of these people who are underconfident or overconfident about your numeric abilities. By the end of this section, you will learn what we know about how to alter subjective numeracy. Thus far, studies have focused primarily on altering numeric self-efficacy or math anxiety to establish their causal links with objective numeracy and numeric persistence.

In one study intended to test whether increasing subjective numeracy causally improves objective numeracy, we turned to a theoretically motivated psychological intervention called *values affirmation*. In it, people reflect on the importance and meaningfulness of core values.[30] By doing so, they remind themselves about positive self-aspects that then act as psychological resources to buffer against potential stress.[32,33] Our study's source of stress was a required statistics course thought to enhance statistical and methodological reasoning. The course, however, involves difficult numeric concepts and negative feedback, which can stress students, reduce their numeric self-efficacy, and interfere with learning.[34] We hypothesized that affirming one's own values (compared to a control condition) would reduce the course's perceived threat, improve subjective numeracy, and, through these beliefs, improve objective numeracy learning in the course. Values affirmation thus should lead to a cycle of greater confidence, more positive appraisals about failures, and good performance; its effects should be self-reinforcing and recursive.[35]

To test these ideas, we randomly assigned participants ($N = 194$) to a self-affirmation condition in which they wrote about a value important to them or we assigned them to an other-affirmation condition in which they wrote about a value important to someone else.[30] Nine weeks later, we found that the intervention had protected subjective numeracy (particularly numeric self-efficacy) and improved objective numeracy. It also had causal effects on two decision-related outcomes (financial literacy and healthy behaviors such as not having unsafe sex). We further detected indirect-only effects on financial outcomes, grades, and taking additional math courses. Changes in objective and/or subjective numeracy mediated all effects and with similar and robust enhancements for all outcomes. Thus, we were able to alter both subjective and objective numeracy and demonstrate causal effects on some decision outcomes. Effect sizes over 9 weeks were significant but small (e.g., a 4 percentile point difference in healthy-behavior change between conditions). Our current research focuses on methods to increase these effect sizes.

Theoretically, greater self-efficacy should propel more action and persistence in the face of difficult and tedious numeric tasks,[36,37] but little causal evidence exists with respect to numeric self-efficacy. According to self-efficacy theory, self-efficacy beliefs are the major determinant of how much effort one will expend on an activity and how long effort will be sustained in the face of obstacles and aversive experiences over and above objective abilities.[38,39]

Numeric self-efficacy beliefs can be increased, for example, by suggesting students set proximal subgoals to finish a certain number of pages of math problems each session compared to having them set a distal goal of finishing all pages by the end of the last session.[40] Children in the proximal-goals condition reported greater numeric self-efficacy and arithmetic attainment by the study's end than the distal-goal group and two other control conditions. They also persisted longer on difficult problems from the beginning to end of the study although not more than the other groups (other than the no-treatment control). Thus, the intervention improved numeric self-efficacy and performance but did not provide clear evidence of persistence as a causal mechanism.

We were interested in whether a brief, more targeted intervention among college students could alter numeric self-efficacy and persistence in turn. With psychologist Mary Kate Tompkins,[41] a former graduate student, we randomized participants ($N = 292$) into one of three conditions: a control condition (they did no a priori math problems), an easy condition (they completed eight second-grade-level math problems, e.g., $2/3 - 1/3 =$), or a hard condition (they completed eight middle-school-level math problems, e.g., $\sqrt{0.0025} =$). Participants then responded to two unsolvable math problems ("Imagine that you have 10 coins in your pocket [pennies, nickels, dimes, or quarters]. The value of the coins adds up to \$1.53. What are the coins?"). We timed how long participants were willing to try to solve them as an operationalization of persistence.

Our manipulation was partially successful. Individuals in the hard condition were less subjectively numerate than control participants and they spent less time attempting to solve the unsolvable math problems. As hypothesized, their decreased subjective numeracy mediated persistence effects. Results held after removing those few participants who recognized that the problems were impossible. In the easy condition, however, participants did not become more subjectively numerate compared to control (nor did they persist longer). Thus, we successfully altered subjective numeracy and established causal effects on numeric persistence, but only in one direction.

Having greater confidence in a specific domain exerted unique causal effects on related actions. Untested in these studies was (1) whether the effects were specific to related actions or whether unrelated actions might be affected as well and (2) whether long-term effects might exist.

Understanding that numeric self-efficacy produces motivation and action with respect to numeric tasks also points toward other motivational interventions that might improve number use in decisions. Possibilities include interventions such as positive mood, social support, and monetary incentives.[42] In a somewhat tongue-in-cheek example, when the media reported a link between eating processed meat and developing cancer, Underwood[43] tweeted that "A stubborn love of bacon just taught more Americans the difference between p values and effect size than 100 stats courses could." In other words, the motivation and persistence required to understand difficult numbers can come from sources other than numeric confidence!

In addition, some people believe that they are not math people and never will be; they have fixed mindsets about math and their unchangeable abilities.[44] However, math skills (with unusual exceptions of individuals with dyscalculia[45]) are malleable, and a *growth mindset* (having the belief that you can cultivate and improve upon your abilities through practice and effort) can lead to greater numeracy skills. For example, children and adults who believe that math intelligence can develop over time were more likely to learn and develop those abilities even when faced with setbacks.[44,46] Growth mindset training, in particular, improved math grades among students.[46] Effects were small, but training helped low socioeconomic status and at-risk students the most.[47] With this kind of training, students are taught about the malleability of intelligence and, for example, that working on new kinds of problems helps their math brain grow and helps them become smarter; trained versus control students improved in how well they performed on subsequent math problems.[48] Untested is whether these math improvements will generalize to increased numeric self-efficacy as well as better decision skills and outcomes, but the research is promising.

Some research has focused instead on reducing math anxiety because it has been linked to poor math scores and avoidant behavior toward math and math education.[49,50] Math anxiety is thought to influence cognitive processes by producing performance-related worries (distracting thoughts) and disrupting central executive processes and especially working memory, thus making math calculations more difficult.[51] Expressive writing, shown to reduce intrusive thoughts and improve working memory availability, enhanced the math performance of math-anxious participants in one study.[52] Relaxation before engaging in math may reduce math anxiety.[53] In fact, it and similar treatments have improved math scores in some studies.[54,55] In my lab, however, relaxation and mindfulness manipulations were ineffective at increasing subjective numeracy or objective numeracy.[56] And none of these studies examined subsequent effects on decision-related tasks.

In each of the studies in this section (except values affirmation in a statistics course[30]), interventions were conducted in the absence of additional math training. As a result, they likely did not enhance objective numeracy per se.

Instead, they probably relieved math anxiety and/or improved numeric self-efficacy to allow a clearer picture of participants' true math competence to emerge because they tried harder. As Malcolm Gladwell once said "Success is a function of persistence and doggedness and the willingness to work hard for twenty-two minutes to make sense of something that most people would give up on after thirty seconds" (p. 246).[57] Pairing a subjective numeracy-related intervention with math training, however, likely would allow greater learning to occur.

Finally, simply increasing or decreasing subjective numeracy (by whatever means) could do more harm than good if we created or increased a mismatch between objective and subjective numeracy. For example, as we learned in Chapter 14, superior health and financial outcomes emerged among patients and consumers whose objective numeracy and numeric confidence were more calibrated.[58] I am unaware of any attempts to increase numeric calibration but it is an important focus for future research. In a different domain (biology), improving this metacognitive awareness among undergraduates in an introductory course improved course performance.[59] Only more empirical research can reveal whether we can improve numeric calibration and whether this improvement will enhance decision making and life outcomes, in turn.

Training Objective Numeracy

Last, but not least, is the potential of improving objective numeracy so that decision makers comprehend and deliberate more about numbers, forecast better into the future, balance risks and benefits appropriately, and, ultimately, make better health, financial, and other choices. Studies of objective numeracy and decision making have been primarily correlational in nature, and we know less about objective numeracy's causal effects. Here, we focus on objective numeracy training with adults and its effects on decision processes and outcomes. This approach has much promise given what we know from earlier chapters.

To begin, long-term formal objective numeracy education likely will be the most impactful method for improving objective numeracy because deep learning requires practice with concentrated effort and feedback.[60] As you will see, other shorter term interventions nonetheless support theoretical predictions but may not yet be practically useful. I say "may not" because they create small improvements in objective numeracy (suggesting limited practical import), but objective numeracy effects may accumulate over many situations and time so that small effects could be practically significant. We need to understand the ecology of numeracy.

To foreshadow the rest of this section, you can become more numerate, although it is not easy. Thus far, outside of taking formal courses, objective numeracy training results are encouraging and demonstrate causal effects on decision competence and outcomes. More research is needed to identify methods that are as brief as possible and produce sustained and large enough effects for practical purposes. Studies fall into two categories: (1) training on specific statistical rules and its proximal effects on using that trained rule and (2) training in objective numeracy and its more distal effects on decision tasks or outcomes.

Training Specific Statistical Rules

Training specific statistical rules has proceeded in a few ways. Such training is a more extended version of the "tricks" taught in the boxes of Chapters 2–8. First, researchers have tested whether exposure to a health statistics priming manual improved medical data interpretation skills.[61] They provided participants with copies of the primer or a general health booklet and asked them to read it and complete a survey within 2 weeks. The 80-page primer was designed to increase comprehension of disease risk (using colon cancer as an example) and of medical treatment risks and benefits (using a drug advertisement as an example). It used cartoons, figures, and examples in an attempt to make the material more appealing and less threatening. The control group received a 70-page general health booklet. The researchers then tested the same medical data interpretation skills taught in the primer (but with different data). Compared to the control condition, participants who received the primer were more interested in and better interpreted medical statistics. The groups, however, reported similar confidence in their ability to interpret medical statistics (a measure of subjective numeracy). It may be that the health statistics primer increased interest, which motivated people to work harder and score higher on the medical data interpretation test, but they still perceived it as difficult. Ultimately, their greater interest, if stable over time, might lead to a cascade of greater interest leading to greater abilities and, in turn, more confidence with health statistics.[62]

Extended specific rule training also leads to improvements in numeracy skills, for example, such as using the "law of large numbers."[63–66] As you might recall from Chapter 3, in the law of large numbers, all else equal, larger samples better represent the population from which they were drawn than do smaller samples. However, people, and particularly the less numerate, often make judgments as if large and small samples are equally representative (see Box 3.1).[67,68] In research by psychologist Richard Nisbett and his colleagues, participants were taught rudimentary, intuitive versions of the law of large numbers.[63] This training improved their statistical responses (related to the law of large numbers) in hypothetical scenarios. They replicated these results across cohort and longitudinal studies with undergraduate and graduate student populations.[63,64,69] Similar results emerge with brief training on best strategies in conjunction problems like "Linda the feminist bank teller"[70] (see Box 3.4).

These training studies on the "law of large numbers" and conjunction problems, however, tested rule use immediately post-training. As a result, any effects could have been due to priming appropriate rules rather than statistical training per se: "It is no doubt crucial to the difference that the testing took place in the same setting as the training: subjects were prepared to look for [and] use the appropriate logical rules" (p. 528).[70] Although unstudied, training may also have had larger effects on more objectively numerate participants given recent studies indicating that explicitly asking participants to consider correct responses reduces conjunction fallacies only among numerically more able participants.[71] Sometimes, the highly numerate must be reminded of statistical rules to use them.

Broader Objective Numeracy Training

Broader objective numeracy training also has demonstrated causal effects, supporting correlational findings. For example, a longitudinal study of undergraduate education on use of the law of large numbers produced expected changes in reasoning from the first to fourth year.[65] Specifically, undergraduates in probabilistic sciences such as psychology and other social sciences improved their statistical reasoning based on the law of large numbers, whereas undergraduates in nonprobabilistic majors (natural science and humanities) improved instead in deductive logic. Neither group of undergraduates differed in changes to non-numeric verbal reasoning.

Broader training also influences financial outcomes. Recent research has demonstrated that state-mandated high school mathematics courses, but not personal finance courses, led to greater investment income, better credit management, and fewer foreclosures in adulthood.[5,72] Interestingly, economics training was associated with worse financial outcomes, such as holding outstanding debt and having difficulty with repayments; economics, financial, and numeracy training all delayed home ownership.[72]

We attempted a brief intervention to test objective numeracy's possible causal impacts on decision skills,[25] using a technique modified from earlier studies.[26,27] In it, we asked participants over the Internet (using Amazon Mechanical Turk) to estimate answers to arithmetic problems (without time to calculate the correct responses and with feedback). We then tested the consistency of their risk perceptions. Specifically, participants were randomly assigned to six sessions of practice over 2 weeks with either arithmetic estimation (the intervention) or working memory (the control condition). Intervention participants made fast estimates of either the sum of or difference between presented numeric stimuli, using symbolic numbers (Arabic integers such as 11 and 27) or nonsymbolic dot arrays. We told them each time whether their answer was correct or incorrect. Training difficulty in all conditions was adjusted, becoming more difficult when participants answered correctly and easier when participants answered incorrectly.

Compared to working-memory training, estimating arithmetic problems improved post-intervention numeracy performance (48% vs. 44% correct, respectively, in the intervention and memory-training conditions). Improvements, however, depended both on participants' subjective numeracy and whether he or she completed symbolic or nonsymbolic arithmetic estimations. Specifically, we hypothesized that less subjectively numerate participants who have more negative emotions to math might be less reactive when working with dots (nonsymbolic quantities) than with Arabic integers (symbolic quantities) because dots estimation would feel less like doing math. Consistent with this reasoning, objective numeracy improved more among the less subjectively numerate when their training focused on estimates with (presumably less threatening) non-symbolic dots than symbolic numbers.[25] Conversely, individuals higher in subjective numeracy improved more when trained on symbolic numbers than non-symbolic dots.

These numeracy improvements also caused positive changes in risk perceptions.[25] Intervention participants demonstrated greater consistency in risk perceptions compared to control participants. For example, intervention participants were more likely than controls to perceive correctly that their 5-year mortality risk was greater than or equal to their 1-year risk, rather than the reverse. They also were more likely to assign a smaller chance to someone breaking into their house and stealing something than to someone stealing something from them. Based on mediation analysis, objective numeracy improvements explained the intervention's effects on risk-perception consistency. However, because we tested risk-perception consistency immediately after the last training session, the intervention could have primed the use of appropriate mathematical rules instead.

Nonetheless, so far, it looks like even adults can improve objective numeracy and decision-making skills, in turn. Research and effect sizes are limited, but objective numeracy training generalizes, both short-term and (somewhat) long-term, in ways that other cognitive trainings do not.[30,73]

The ultimate goal should be truly long-lasting effects. Because innumeracy appears to produce cumulative risks for the quality of decisions and life outcomes over time, research needs to turn to those potential lasting and cumulative effects of enhanced numeracy. Researchers could combine numeracy interventions in a multipronged approach. For example, a school system might want to combine interventions aimed at children to improve both subjective and objective numeracy with interventions aimed at their parents to reduce parental math anxiety. Such combined approaches offer the potential for stronger and longer lasting effects.[74] Even longer term, intergenerational effects could emerge as less math-anxious and more math-competent parents may be more likely and more able to teach their own children better numeracy skills.

Numeracy-training research, however, is in an early stage with only a small amount of research focused on whether and how it might improve decision skills and outcomes. Based on what we know so far, boosting numeric competence while promoting numeric self-efficacy should elevate decision skills, improving comprehension and reducing heuristic use. These individuals then should make strides over time in financial, employment, and health outcomes. For domains that require numeric persistence (e.g., chronic disease management), improving numeric calibration (the match between objective numeracy and numeric confidence) in tandem with overall improvements in these competencies may be key to improving health and wealth outcomes.

References

1. Arkes, H. R. (1991). Costs and benefits of judgment errors: Implications for debiasing. *Psychological Bulletin, 110*(3), 486.
2. Goesling, B., & Baker, D. P. (2008). Three faces of international inequality. *Research in Social Stratification and Mobility, 26*(2), 183–198.
3. Goldman, D. P., & Smith, J. P. (2002). Can patient self-management help explain the SES health gradient? *Proceedings of the National Academy of Sciences, 99*(16), 10929–10934.
4. Deary, I. (2008). Why do intelligent people live longer? *Nature, 456*(7219), 175–176.
5. Cole, S., Paulson, A., & Shastry, G. K. (2014). Smart money? The effect of education on financial outcomes. *Review of Financial Studies, 27*(7), 2022–2051.

6. Ceci, S. J. (1991). How much does schooling influence general intelligence and its cognitive components? A reassessment of the evidence. *Developmental Psychology, 27*(5), 703–722.

7. Nisbett, R. E. (2009). *Intelligence and how to get it: Why schools and cultures count.* New York: WW Norton.

8. Cliffordson, C., & Gustafsson, J. E. (2008). Effects of age and schooling on intellectual performance: Estimates obtained from analysis of continuous variation in age and length of schooling. *Intelligence, 36*(2), 143–152.

9. Peters, E., Baker, D. P., Dieckmann, N. F., Leon, J., & Collins, J. (2010). Explaining the effect of education on health: A field study in Ghana. *Psychological Science, 21*(10), 1369–1376.

10. Baker, D. P., Leon, J., & Collins, J. M. (2011). Facts, attitudes, and health reasoning about HIV and AIDS: Explaining the education effect on condom use among adults in sub-Saharan Africa. *AIDS and Behavior, 15*(7), 1319–1327.

11. Baker, D. P., Salinas, D., & Eslinger, P. J. (2012). An envisioned bridge: Schooling as a neurocognitive developmental institution. *Developmental Cognitive Neuroscience, 2*(suppl 1), S6–S17.

12. Nisbett, R. E., Aronson, J., Blair, C., Dickens, W., Flynn, J., Halpern, D. F., & Turkheimer, E. (2012). Intelligence: New findings and theoretical developments. *American Psychologist, 67*(2), 130–159.

13. Heckman, J. J. (2007). The economics, technology, and neuroscience of human capability formation. *Proceedings of the National Academy of Sciences, 104*(33), 13250–13255.

14. Dieckmann, N. F., Peters, E., Leon, J., Benavides, M., Baker, D. P., & Norris, A. (2015). The role of objective numeracy and fluid intelligence in sex-related protective behaviors. *Current HIV Research, 13*(5), 337–346.

15. Baker, D. P., Eslinger, P. J., Benavides, M., Peters, E., Dieckmann, N. F., & Leon, J. (2015). The cognitive impact of the education revolution: A possible cause of the Flynn Effect on population IQ. *Intelligence, 49*, 144–158.

16. Wilson, A. J., Revkin, S. K., Cohen, D., Cohen, L., & Dehaene, S. (2006). An open trial assessment of "The Number Race," an adaptive computer game for remediation of dyscalculia. *Behavioral and Brain Functions, 2*(1), 20.

17. Wilson, A. J., Dehaene, S., Dubois, O., & Fayol, M. (2009). Effects of an adaptive game intervention on accessing number sense in low-socioeconomic-status kindergarten children. *Mind, Brain, and Education, 3*(4), 224–234.

18. Siegler, R. S., & Ramani, G. B. (2009). Playing linear number board games—but not circular ones—improves low-income preschoolers' numerical understanding. *Journal of Educational Psychology, 101*(3), 545–560.

19. Booth, J. L., & Siegler, R. S. (2008). Numerical magnitude representations influence arithmetic learning. *Child Development, 79*(4), 1016–1031.

20. Thompson, C. A., & Opfer, J. E. (2016). Learning linear spatial-numeric associations improves accuracy of memory for numbers. *Frontiers in Psychology, 7*, 24–32.

21. Siegler, R. S., & Lortie-Forgues, H. (2017). Hard lessons: Why rational number arithmetic is so difficult for so many people. *Current Directions in Psychological Science, 26*(4), 346–351.

22. McLean, J. F., & Rusconi, E. (2014). Mathematical difficulties as decoupling of expectation and developmental trajectories. *Frontiers in Human Neuroscience, 8*, 44.

23. Dehaene, S. (1997). *The number sense: How the mind creates mathematics.* New York: Oxford University Press.

24. Knoll, L. J., Fuhrmann, D., Sakhardande, A. L., Stamp, F., Speekenbrink, M., & Blakemore, S. J. (2016). A window of opportunity for cognitive training in adolescence. *Psychological Science, 27*(12), 1620–1631.

25. Chesney, D., Shoots-Reinhard, B., & Peters, E. (2021). The causal impact of numeracy on normative judgments: Improving numeracy via symbolic and non-symbolic arithmetic practice improves risky judgments. *Journal of Numerical Cognition (JNC), 7*(3), 351–367.

26. Park, J., & Brannon, E. M. (2013). Training the approximate number system improves math proficiency. *Psychological Science, 24*(10), 2013–2019.

27. Park, J., & Brannon, E. M. (2014). Improving arithmetic performance with number sense training: An investigation of underlying mechanism. *Cognition, 133*(1), 188–200.

28. Eyler, R. F., Cordes, S., Szymanski, B. R., & Fraenkel, L. (2018). Use of feedback to improve mental number line representations in primary care clinics. *BMC Medical Informatics and Decision Making, 18*(1), 40.

29. Sobkow, A., Fulawka, K., Tomczak, P., Zjawiony, P., & Traczyk, J. (2019). Does mental number line training work? The effects of cognitive training on real-life mathematics, numeracy, and decision making. *Journal of Experimental Psychology. Applied.* doi: 10.1037/xap0000207

30. Peters, E., Shoots-Reinhard, B., Tompkins, M. K., Schley, D., Meilleur, L., Sinayev, A., . . . Crocker, J. (2017). Improving numeracy through values affirmation enhances decision and STEM outcomes. *PLoS ONE, 12*(7), e0180674.

31. Peters, E., Slovic, P., Västfjäll, D., & Mertz, C. K. (2008). Intuitive numbers guide decisions. *Judgment and Decision Making, 3,* 619–635.

32. Cohen, G. L., Garcia, J., Apfel, N., & Master, A. (2006). Reducing the racial achievement gap: A social-psychological intervention. *Science, 313*(5791), 1307–1310.

33. Miyake, A., Kost-Smith, L. E., Finkelstein, N. D., Pollock, S. J., Cohen, G. L., & Ito, T. A. (2010). Reducing the gender achievement gap in college science: A classroom study of values affirmation. *Science, 330*(6008), 1234–1237.

34. Betz, N. E., & Hackett, G. (1983). The relationship of mathematics self-efficacy expectations to the selection of science-based college majors. *Journal of Vocational Behavior, 23*(3), 329–345.

35. Cohen, G. L., & Sherman, D. K. (2014). The psychology of change: Self-affirmation and social psychological intervention. *Annual Review of Psychology, 65,* 333–371.

36. Hadar, L., Sood, S., & Fox, C. R. (2013). Subjective knowledge in consumer financial decisions. *Journal of Marketing Research, 50*(3), 303–316.

37. Farrell, L., Fry, T. R., & Risse, L. (2016). The significance of financial self-efficacy in explaining women's personal finance behaviour. *Journal of Economic Psychology, 54,* 85–99.

38. Bandura, A. (1977). Self-efficacy: Toward a unifying theory of behavioral change. *Psychological Review, 84*(2), 191–215.

39. Betz, N. E. (2013). Assessment of self-efficacy. In K. F. Geisinger, B. A. Bracken, J. F. Carlson, J.-I. C. Hansen, N. R. Kuncel, S. P. Reise, & M. C. Rodriguez (Eds.), *APA handbooks in psychology. APA handbook of testing and assessment in psychology, Vol. 2. Testing and assessment in clinical and counseling psychology* (pp. 379–391). Washington, DC: American Psychological Association.

40. Bandura, A., & Schunk, D. H. (1981). Cultivating competence, self-efficacy, and intrinsic interest through proximal self-motivation. *Journal of Personality and Social Psychology, 41*(3), 586.

41. Tompkins, M. K. (2018). *The role of subjective numeracy in financial outcomes and interventions of numeric-ability beliefs.* Doctoral dissertation. The Ohio State University.

42. Strough, J., Bruine de Bruin, W., & Peters, E. (2015). New perspectives for motivating better decisions in older adults. *Frontiers in Psychology, 6,* 783. doi:10.3389/fpsyg.2015.00783.

43. Underwood. (2015, October 27). A stubborn love of bacon just taught more Americans the difference between p values and effect size than 100 stats courses could. (Twitter Post). Retrieved from https://twitter.com/Ted_Underwood/status/658983555008040960

44. Dweck, C. S. (2006). *Mindset: The new psychology of success.* New York: Random House.

45. Butterworth, B. (2010). Foundational numerical capacities and the origins of dyscalculia. *Trends in Cognitive Sciences, 14*(12), 534–541.

46. Rattan, A., Savani, K., Chugh, D., & Dweck, C. S. (2015). Leveraging mindsets to promote academic achievement: Policy recommendations. *Perspectives on Psychological Science, 10*(6), 721–726.

47. Sisk, V. F., Burgoyne, A. P., Sun, J., Butler, J. L., & Macnamara, B. N. (2018). To what extent and under which circumstances are growth mind-sets important to academic achievement? Two meta-analyses. *Psychological Science, 29*(4), 549–571.

48. Yeager, D. S., Paunesku, D., Walton, G. M., & Dweck, C. S. (2013, May). How can we instill productive mindsets at scale? A review of the evidence and an initial R&D agenda. White paper prepared for the White House meeting on "Excellence in Education: The Importance of Academic Mindsets." Retrieved from http://homepage.psy.utexas.edu/HomePage/Group/YeagerLAB/ADRG/Pdfs/Yeager et al R&D agenda-6-10-13.pdf.

49. Betz, N. E. (1978). Prevalence, distribution, and correlates of math anxiety in college students. *Journal of Counseling Psychology, 25*(5), 441–448.

50. Meece, J. L., Wigfield, A., & Eccles, J. S. (1990). Predictors of math anxiety and its influence on young adolescents' course enrollment intentions and performance in mathematics. *Journal of Educational Psychology, 82*(1), 60–70.

51. Ashcraft, M. H., & Kirk, E. P. (2001). The relationships among working memory, math anxiety, and performance. *Journal of Experimental Psychology: General, 130*(2), 224–237.

52. Park, D., Ramirez, G., & Beilock, S. L. (2014). The role of expressive writing in math anxiety. *Journal of Experimental Psychology: Applied, 20*(2), 103–111.

53. Furner, J. M., & Duffy, M. L. (2002). Equity for all students in the new millennium: Disabling math anxiety. *Intervention in School and Clinic, 38*(2), 67–74.

54. Hembree, R. (1990). The nature, effects, and relief of mathematics anxiety. *Journal for Research in Mathematics Education, 21*(1), 33–46.

55. Martens, A., Johns, M., Greenberg, J., & Schimel, J. (2006). Combating stereotype threat: The effect of self-affirmation on women's intellectual performance. *Journal of Experimental Social Psychology, 42*(2), 236–243.

56. Bjälkebring, P., Tompkins, M. K., Shoots-Reinhard, B., & Peters, E. (2017, November). Altering number motivations through subjective numeracy influences objective numeracy speed but not accuracy. Poster session presented at the annual meeting of the Society for Judgment and Decision Making, Vancouver, BC.

57. Gladwell, M. (2008). *Outliers: The story of success.* New York: Little, Brown and Company.

58. Peters, E., Tompkins, M. K., Knoll, M., Ardoin, S. P., Shoots-Reinhard, B., & Meara, A. S. (2019). Despite high objective numeracy, lower numeric confidence relates to worse financial and medical outcomes. *Proceedings of the National Academy of Sciences (PNAS),* doi.org/10.1073/pnas.1903126116.

59. Osterhage, J. L., Usher, E. L., Douin, T. A., & Bailey, W. M. (2019). Opportunities for self-evaluation increase student calibration in an introductory biology course. *CBE—Life Sciences Education, 18*(2), ar16.

60. Ericsson, K. A. (2006). The influence of experience and deliberate practice on the development of superior expert performance. In K. A. Ericsson, N. Charness, P. J. Feltovich, & R. R. Hoffman (Eds.), *The Cambridge Handbook of Expertise and Expert Performance* (pp. 685–705). Cambridge University Press.

61. Woloshin, S., Schwartz, L. M., & Welch, H. G. (2007). The effectiveness of a primer to help people understand risk: Two randomized trials in distinct populations. *Annals of Internal Medicine, 146*(4), 256–265.

62. Ganley, C. M., & Lubienski, S. T. (2016). Mathematics confidence, interest, and performance: Examining gender patterns and reciprocal relations. *Learning and Individual Differences, 47,* 182–193.

63. Fong, G. T., Krantz, D. H., & Nisbett, R. E. (1986). The effects of statistical training on thinking about everyday problems. *Cognitive Psychology, 16*(3), 253–292.

64. Lehman, D. R., Lempert, R. O., & Nisbett, R. E. (1988). The effects of graduate training on reasoning: Formal discipline and thinking about everyday-life events. *American Psychologist, 43*(6), 431–442.

65. Lehman, D. R., & Nisbett, R. E. (1990). A longitudinal study of the effects of undergraduate training on reasoning. *Developmental Psychology, 26*(6), 952–960.

66. Nisbett, R. E., Fong, G. T., Lehman, D. R., & Cheng, P. W. (1987). Teaching reasoning. *Science, 238*(4827), 625–631.

67. Kahneman, D., & Tversky, A. (1972). Subjective probability: A judgment of representativeness. *Cognitive Psychology, 3*(3), 430–454.

68. Chesney, D. L., & Obrecht, N. A. (2012). Statistical judgments are influenced by the implied likelihood that samples represent the same population. *Memory & Cognition, 40*(3), 420–433.

69. Fong, G. T., & Nisbett, R. E. (1991). Immediate and delayed transfer of training effects in statistical reasoning. *Journal of Experimental Psychology: General, 120*(1), 34–45.

70. Agnoli, F., & Krantz, D. H. (1989). Suppressing natural heuristics by formal instruction: The case of the conjunction fallacy. *Cognitive Psychology, 21*(4), 515–550.

71. Scherer, L. D., Yates, J. F., Baker, S. G., & Valentine, K. D. (2017). The influence of effortful thought and cognitive proficiencies on the conjunction fallacy: Implications for dual-process theories of reasoning and judgment. *Personality and Social Psychology Bulletin, 43*(6), 874–887.

72. Brown, M., Grigsby, J., van der Klaauw, W., Wen, J., & Zafar, B. (2016). Financial education and the debt behavior of the young. *Review of Financial Studies, 29*(9), 2490–2522.

73. Melby-Lervåg, M., Redick, T. S., & Hulme, C. (2016). Working memory training does not improve performance on measures of intelligence or other measures of "far transfer" evidence from a meta-analytic review. *Perspectives on Psychological Science, 11*(4), 512–534.

74. Hawkins, J. D., Kosterman, R., Catalano, R. F., Hill, K. G., & Abbott, R. D. (2008). Effects of social development intervention in childhood 15 years later. *Archives of Pediatrics & Adolescent Medicine, 162*(12), 1133–1141.

19

Reflections on Numeracy and the Power of Reasoning Numerically

By now, I hope you realize that disconnects can exist between people's comprehension and perceptions of numbers versus their reality. For example, my good friend and colleague, psychologist Hal Arkes (Personal communication, June 21, 2018) once agreed that his neighbor could have an easement over his property to build an out-sized garage. A lawyer from an expensive law firm drew up the document. However, the lawyer thought that 12 feet and 2 inches was 12.2 feet, and 12 feet and 11 inches was 12.11 feet. Therefore, the latter was shorter than the former! Apparently, the mysteries of our number system perplexed him. Hal ultimately drafted and filed the easement himself. Policy makers and others generally assume that, provided appropriate numbers, people will understand and use them, but, clearly, this is not always true even for well-educated experts. Instead, people are often tricked by numbers, whether they concern measurements, relative versus absolute risk, or sales prices where you take an additional 25% off the 40% off sales price (hint: it's not 65% off; it's 55% off).

In fact, innumeracy is rampant in the United States and around the world.[1] About 68 million US adults (29% of the population) can do only simple numeric operations; they can count, sort, and do basic arithmetic operations with whole numbers or money. Only 9% of US adults (about 21 million adults) are thought to be at the highest numeracy levels so that they can understand and use the complex numeric information needed for some decisions, as in diabetes management. Estimates in other countries follow a similar pattern although the US scored 21st out of 23 member countries of the Organisation for Economic Cooperation and Development (OECD) surveyed.

This innumeracy presents major challenges because math is part of our daily decisions, both big and small (recipes, shopping for bargains, paying bills, budgets, taxes, medical treatments, retirement savings, support for policy options). People often make jokes about being innumerate ("Did you know that 5 out of 4 people have trouble with fractions and other numbers?"), but innumeracy's consequences can be enormous. Take George as an example "As a person with diabetes, you're required to constantly be 'on.' Diabetes

Innumeracy in the Wild. Ellen Peters, Oxford University Press (2020). © Oxford University Press 2020.
DOI: 10.1093/oso/9780190861094.003.0001

management takes a ton of mental effort. From remembering appointments, to counting carbs and taking medication, you rarely get a day to truly relax."[2]

Objective Numeracy

As we learned in Chapters 2–8, individuals lower and higher in objective numeracy process the same information differently in decisions. More objectively numerate people are equipped with durable tools that seem to allow them to take charge of the numeric aspects of their lives. They think harder about numbers than the less numerate and do more explicit number operations (e.g., number comparisons and expected-value calculations,[3] likely because they have more chronically activated numeric knowledge structures.[4] The objectively numerate also derive more feeling from numbers, with those feelings guiding their judgments and choices.[5,6] Overall, individuals higher in objective numeracy access a richer gist from numbers.[7]

Having a numeric "hammer" (it's probably more of a toolbox, but let's keep with the hammer metaphor) then is associated with better decision-making competence, allowing the highly numerate to avoid the compelling power of narratives and other easier-to-use information. The less objectively numerate potentially can learn their habits and inclinations with numbers. However, as we saw in Chapter 18, teaching people about these habits of mind may have limited effectiveness if they do not also improve their objective numeracy.

Objective numeracy differences, however, do not always emerge in decision making, and we need to know more about how to identify certain situations such as the following:

- When the more objectively numerate understand and decide better than the less numerate (most of Chapters 2–7),
- When the more and less numerate similarly understand and make sensible decisions,[8] and
- When nobody understands or uses numeric information appropriately (see Chapter 8)

From what we know so far, the highly numerate understand and use numbers more than the less objective numerate 259 when (1) situational motivation is lower (e.g., the decision is abstract and less important; e.g., not like bacon![9]); (2) the domain is unfamiliar (e.g., few people are familiar with hospital quality ratings); (3) the numeric information is difficult to evaluate (e.g., cadmium in cigarette smoke occurs in units of nanograms); and (4) the decision maker makes a single response as opposed to a repeated series of them, as are often required in experiments (see Chapters 7 and 10).

Chapters 2–4 focused on the less objectively numerate understanding less and relying more on mental shortcuts in evaluating evidence and making choices across situations. In Chapters 4 and 9, I suggested that their persistent incomprehension and heuristic reliance poses a risk factor for them that accumulates over time, leading them to experience worse outcomes. This speculation has not been tested, although it is consistent with other correlational and experimental results.[10,11] For example, the average annual income difference between participants scoring the lowest versus highest on an eight-item numeracy test was about $30,000 controlling for education, verbal intelligence, and personality.[12] Furthermore, this and other numeracy differences were stronger at older than younger ages, as if we accumulate more of numeracy's benefits and of innumeracy's costs across the adult lifespan.[13] If true, we should be able to identify the magnitude of negative and positive cumulative effects over time at different numeracy levels. We should also be able to pinpoint the objective numeracy improvements needed for an individual to experience identifiable positive effects over a specific time period.

This cumulative risk argument depends, in part, on persistent heuristic use (and their resulting biases) by the less objective numerate. However, let's pause for a moment and consider the types of heuristics that have been tested with objective numeracy because more than one heuristic type exists. The mental shortcuts tested thus far with objective numeracy include the availability, representativeness, and affect heuristics, as well as framing effects. When using these traditional heuristics, decision makers generally ignore statistics that are more relevant. For example, they might rely on their fears about cancer rather than its objective chance of recurrence. Nonetheless, researchers consider heuristic use generally effective because using heuristics is faster and less effortful. Their use also produces decisions that tend to be "good enough." However, they lead to less accurate decisions, presumably due to the compelling power of our non-numeric intuitions. In this book, I have emphasized a different interpretation: namely, that heuristic use is due more to innumeracy and cognitive inaccessibility of appropriate known statistical rules. In other words, sometimes we are too innumerate to know the rule, and, even when numerate enough, the rule does not always pop to mind when deciding.

A second type of heuristics, however, may not depend on poor statistical use. Researchers believe these fast-and-frugal heuristics exploit structures of information that exist naturally in the environment so that they can be more accurate than more complex ways of making decisions.[14] As a result, formal statistical inferences may be less necessary for good decisions, and people at all levels of numeracy may use these heuristics. However, these fast-and-frugal heuristics have not been a focus of numeracy research.

The question then becomes whether researchers can identify which heuristics, traditional or fast-and-frugal, matter for life outcomes and how and why they matter. Traditional-heuristic and fast-and-frugal-heuristic perspectives are different. Theoretically, traditional heuristic use might worsen life outcomes whereas fast-and-frugal heuristic use might improve outcomes. From the literature so far, you now know that less objectively numerate people are more susceptible to using traditional heuristics. In addition, those who are more prone to traditional heuristic use also experience worse life outcomes (see Chapter 9).[10,15] These combined results support my conjecture that low numeracy is a risk factor that accumulates over time and causes worse outcomes. However, might fast-and-frugal heuristics act as useful tools that compensate for these negative effects on the less numerate, at least in "kind" environments (as opposed to "wicked" ones)? I think the answer is likely yes. But, as researchers, we need to understand the ecology of numeracy, heuristic use, and their interaction much better before being able to provide definitive answers.

Multiple Numeric Competencies

At this point, you also know that objective numeracy is one part of a larger puzzle. Until recently, numeracy research had largely ignored distinctions between the three numeric competencies introduced in this book. As you learned in Chapter 13, approximate number system (ANS) acuity, which allows for greater discriminability of numeric magnitudes, relates to valuation and numeric memory. Subjective numeracy relates to emotional reactions to and motivation/confidence in numeric tasks, as described in Chapter 14.

Let's start with subjective numeracy. You know by now that subjective numeracy measures are not always good diagnostic indicators of objective numeracy.[16,17] This fact does not make the measure less important. Subjective numeracy, while correlated with objective numeracy, instead appears critical to regulating emotional responses, motivation, and action in numeric tasks.[18–20] Although researchers have linked objective numeracy to numeric information seeking and attention (see Chapter 5), I suspect that subjective numeracy may underlie these action-oriented processes also or instead of objective numeracy.

Furthermore, you know that people higher in objective numeracy possess a numeric hammer that the less objectively numerate do not. However, owning a hammer is inadequate if it sits in your toolbox. You hopefully discovered in Chapter 14 that decision makers also need to persist with numbers to understand and use them appropriately. Studies thus far support the idea that this persistence comes from subjective numeracy and especially numeric self-efficacy (confidence).

Although extensive correlational research has demonstrated objective numeracy's potential to increase the quality of health and financial outcomes (Chapter 9), emerging evidence points toward subjective numeracy as another possible underlying cause of better outcomes. In particular, as you learned in Chapter 14, interactions of objective numeracy and numeric confidence may be critical to health and financial outcomes that require knowing how to run the numbers and persisting with numeric tasks over time. It appears that being numerically indolent can harm you, but so can being numerically zealous if you do not have the objective skills to back up your actions.[18] However, we need more data explicitly testing whether numeric self-efficacy leads to greater numeric persistence in concrete tasks such as health management, which then leads to better decisions and outcomes over time if the patient has adequate objective numeracy.

Finally, we have approximate number abilities (a so-called intuitive number sense) that can compensate for objective skills in decision making (see Chapter 13). Using it is like using a brick instead of your trusty hammer to drive a nail. It gets the job done, but the results aren't as pretty or precise. This third numeric competency emerges in development. Specifically, an ANS is shared by human and non-human animals and has been associated with the development of human symbolic math ability. In decisions, it helps us to discriminate, approximately and imprecisely, how far apart are two numeric magnitudes (which hand holds more M&Ms?) or two symbolic numbers (how much smaller is this mortgage rate?). An outstanding research question is which of two sources of imprecision relate to complex decisions involving symbolic numbers: Is it inexactness in the ANS's internal magnitude representations, or is it the related inexactness in the mapping of symbolic numbers to those mental magnitudes?[21,22] The first inexactness in internal magnitude representations has an evolutionary basis. Decision making, however, often involves symbolic numbers, and people must learn how symbolic numbers map onto mental magnitudes. I suspect that it is the second inexactness that will emerge as key to decision making. The answer to this question has theoretical and practical implications, for example, to whether research should include measures with symbolic or nonsymbolic quantities (see the Appendix).

Overcoming Innumeracy

Innumeracy, of course, is not inevitable.[23] As a short-term fix, communicators can make materials (as opposed to people) more numerate (Chapters 15–17). The less numerate, in particular, comprehend numeric information better when it is presented in more digestible forms.

Knowledge alone, however, is often insufficient to produce choices consistent with a decision maker's values and best interests.[24] People know, for example, that smoking is bad and exercise is good, but deep knowledge of risks can be uncommon[25] and behavior change is difficult. Also, you can know that purchasing $40 a day in lottery tickets is unlikely to yield the big winner but still hope that it might (and continue to buy tickets). Such motivated beliefs contrast with facts but are not uncommon in personal, business, and policy decisions. For example, marketing managers persist with new products despite obvious indicators of failure from sales and profit figures, budgets and forecasts, and market research results.[26]

Knowing basic facts is necessary but insufficient for making good decisions in a wide variety of domains.[27,28] In a surprising example from our own studies, we assessed HIV/AIDS knowledge among 181 individuals from four small, agrarian villages in eastern Ghana that had a high prevalence of HIV infection.[29] With yes/no questions (e.g., "Can AIDS be transmitted by a blood transfusion?") posed in their local language, Twi, we followed up responses by asking participants how to reduce the targeted health risk. Responses were coded as correct only if the risk reduction question was also answered correctly. Thus, we could identify presumably correct responses that actually exemplified poor reasoning. One participant, a middle-aged villager, responded correctly that blood transfusions could infect him with HIV. However, he further stated "but not if I wear a condom." His incorrect response indicated fundamental misunderstandings about disease transmission and prevention even while he had some correct knowledge. Clearly, Chapter 15–17's insights and tools concerning evidence-based communication techniques cannot solve all of our numeracy problems.

You also can improve your numeracy and that of others in order to enhance the quality of decision processes and life outcomes, in turn. As mathematicians Marilyn Carlson and Michael Pearson wrote: "As students begin to experience the power of reasoning mathematically, they are more likely to persist and continue in STEM fields. Perhaps just as important, students who develop mathematical competency are likely to make better decisions across a variety of domains."[30]

We know a little about the causal influences of the numeric competencies (see Chapter 18). Adult numeracy can be improved, but it is not easy.[11,31] We need to know more about how to create new human capital when it comes to numeric abilities (objective numeracy, subjective numeracy, and our intuitive number sense). We also need to avoid unintended consequences, such as increasing numeric confidence for someone who has inadequate objective numeracy to accomplish necessary numeric tasks or recognize ensuing mistakes. Doing so requires understanding the numeric competencies of the individual and the numeric requirements of the situation. By appropriately building your (and others') numeric understanding, I hope that numbers will no longer get in your way and that you can take charge of your decisions and improve your well-being. Overall, building numeracy should allow us to open doors to better opportunities and a healthier and wealthier nation of individuals.

I hope, by now, however, that I have convinced you that numeracy issues deserve attention whether you are a researcher, a communicator (and who among us is not?), someone who is highly numerate, or someone who wants to be. As responsible citizens, we need numeric abilities to understand and react appropriately to the inevitable uncertainty and complications in current events, science, and even our health and finances. Some jobs also obviously require numeric faculties (actuaries); other jobs do not seem mathematical (nurses) but require numeric ability nonetheless. As a result, you are not a geek if you are numerate. Instead, you are someone who can make more insightful choices in health and finances and be a more productive citizen of our world.

References

1. Desjardins, R., Thorn, W., Schleicher, A., Quintini, G., Pellizzari, M., Kis, V., & Chung, J. E. (2013). *OECD Skills Outlook 2013: First Results from the Survey of Adult Skills*. Paris, France: OECD.
2. L. D. (2018, January 9). *Diabetes and Exhaustion: You're Not Alone*. [Blog post]. Retrieved from http://blog.thediabetessite.com/diabetes-is-tiring/
3. Peters, E., & Bjälkebring, P. (2015). Multiple numeric competencies: When a number is not just a number. *Journal of Personality and Social Psychology, 108*(5), 802–822.
4. Srull, T. K., & Wyer, R. S. (1979). The role of category accessibility in the interpretation of information about persons: Some determinants and implications. *Journal of Personality and Social Psychology, 37*(10), 1660–1672.

5. Peters, E., Västfjäll, D., Slovic, P., Mertz, C. K., Mazzocco, K., & Dickert, S. (2006). Numeracy and decision making. *Psychological Science, 17*(5), 407–413.

6. Petrova, D. G., van der Pligt, J., & Garcia-Retamero, R. (2014). Feeling the numbers: On the interplay between risk, affect, and numeracy. *Journal of Behavioral Decision Making, 27*(3), 191–199.

7. Reyna, V. F., Nelson, W. L., Han, P. K., & Dieckmann, N. F. (2009). How numeracy influences risk comprehension and medical decision making. *Psychological Bulletin, 135*(6), 943.

8. Fagerlin, A., Zikmund-Fisher, B. J., & Ubel, P. A. (2005). How making a risk estimate can change the feel of that risk: Shifting attitudes toward breast cancer risk in a general public survey. *Patient Education and Counseling, 57*(3), 294–299.

9. Underwood. (2015, October 27). A stubborn love of bacon just taught more Americans the difference between p values and effect size than 100 stats courses could. (Twitter Post). Retrieved from https://twitter.com/Ted_Underwood/status/658983555008040960

10. Bruine de Bruin, W., Parker, A. M., & Fischhoff, B. (2007). Individual differences in adult decision-making competence. *Journal of Personality and Social Psychology, 92*(5), 938–956.

11. Peters, E., Shoots-Reinhard, B., Tompkins, M. K., Schley, D., Meilleur, L., Sinayev, A., . . . Crocker, J. (2017). Improving numeracy through values affirmation enhances decision and STEM outcomes. *PLoS ONE, 12*(7), e0180674.

12. Bjälkebring, P. & Peters, E. (2021). Money matters (especially if you are good at math): Numeracy, verbal intelligence, education, and income in satisfaction judgments. *PLOS ONE, 16*(11), e0259331.

13. Bjälkebring, P., & Peters, E. (in preparation). Numeracy's effects accumulate across the lifespan.

14. Gigerenzer, G., Todd, P. M., & The ABC Research Group. (1999). *Simple heuristics that make us smart.* New York: Oxford University Press.

15. Stanovich, K. E., West, R. F., & Toplak, M. E. (2016). *The rationality quotient: Toward a test of rational thinking.* Cambridge, MA: MIT Press.

16. Dunning, D., Heath, C., & Suls, J. M. (2004). Flawed self-assessment: Implications for health, education, and the workplace. *Psychological Science in the Public Interest, 5*(3), 69–106.

17. Liberali, J. M., Reyna, V. F., Furlan, S., Stein, L. M., & Pardo, S. T. (2012). Individual differences in numeracy and cognitive reflection, with implications for biases and fallacies in probability judgment. *Journal of Behavioral Decision Making, 25*(4), 361–381.

18. Peters, E., Tompkins, M. K., Knoll, M., Ardoin, S. P., Shoots-Reinhard, B., & Meara, A. S. (2019). Despite high objective numeracy, lower numeric confidence relates to worse financial and medical outcomes. *Proceedings of the National Academy of Sciences (PNAS)*, doi. org/10.1073/pnas.1903126116.

19. McConnell, A. R. (2011). The multiple self-aspects framework: Self-concept representation and its implications. *Personality and Social Psychology Review, 15*(1), 3–27.

20. Schwarzer, R., & Fuchs, R. (1996). Self-efficacy and health behaviours. In M. Conner & P. Norman (Eds.), *Predicting health behavior: Research and practice with social cognition models.* (pp. 63–196). Maidenhead, UK: Open University Press.

21. Izard, V., & Dehaene, S. (2008). Calibrating the mental number line. *Cognition, 106*(3), 1221–1247.

22. Siegler, R. S., & Opfer, J. E. (2003). The development of numerical estimation: Evidence for multiple representations of numerical quantity. *Psychological Science, 14*(3), 237–250.

23. Kersey, A. J., Braham, E. J., Csumitta, K. D., Libertus, M. E., & Cantlon, J. F. (2018). No intrinsic gender differences in children's earliest numerical abilities. *NPJ Science of Learning, 3*(1), 12.

24. National Academies of Sciences, Engineering, and Medicine. (2016). *Communicating science effectively: A research agenda.* Washington, DC: National Academies Press.

25. Peters, E., Shoots-Reinhard, B., Shoben, A., Evans, A. T., Klein, E., Tompkins, M. K., . . . Tusler, M. (2019). Pictorial warning labels and memory for cigarette health-risk information over time. *Annals of Behavioral Medicine, 53*, 358–371, https://doi.org/10.1093/abm/kay050.

26. Hutchinson, J. W., Alba, J. W., & Eisenstein, E. M. (2010). Heuristics and biases in data-based decision making: Effects of experience, training, and graphical data displays. *Journal of Marketing Research, 47*(4), 627–642.

27. Baker, D. P., Leon, J., & Collins, J. M. (2011). Facts, attitudes, and health reasoning about HIV and AIDS: Explaining the education effect on condom use among adults in sub-Saharan Africa. *AIDS and Behavior, 15*(7), 1319–1327.

28. Hibbard, J. H., & Peters, E. (2003). Supporting informed consumer health care choices: Data presentation approaches that facilitate the use of information in choice. *Annual Review of Public Health, 24*(1), 413–433.

29. Peters, E., Baker, D. P., Dieckmann, N. F., Leon, J., & Collins, J. (2010). Explaining the effect of education on health: A field study in Ghana. *Psychological Science, 21*(10), 1369–1376.

30. Carlson, M., & Pearson, J. M. (2019, March 25) Co-requisite math doesn't result in weak foundational knowledge. *The Chronicle of Higher Education.* Retrieved from https://www.chronicle.com/blogs/letters/co-requisite-math-doesnt-result-in-weak-foundational-knowledge/

31. Peters, E., Meilleur, L., & Tompkins, M. K. (2014). Numeracy and the Affordable Care Act: Opportunities and challenges. Appendix A. IOM (Institute of Medicine). In *Health literacy and numeracy: Workshop summary* (pp. 91–132). Washington, DC: National Academies Press.

APPENDIX

Chapter 1

Measuring Objective Numeracy and Subjective Numeracy

In this part of the Appendix, I briefly review measures of objective numeracy and subjective numeracy. We'll discuss measures of the approximate number system (ANS) later in the Appendix for Chapter 13 after I introduce this complex and interesting topic in more depth. The present section is relatively technical, and you can certainly skip it until a time when you're curious about how to measure objective or subjective numeracy or how to identify someone (including yourself!) as high or low in numeracy.

Measuring Objective Numeracy

Objective numeracy is measured using a math test (usually the total number of correct responses, with missing responses coded as incorrect). A variety of measures have been proposed and used. Measures most often involve probabilistic concepts, but they have also focused on arithmetic and algebra. No one best measure exists so far, and which measure to choose depends on your sample's likely numeric ability and potential prior exposure to particular measures. We also generally do not have nationally representative data for the measures. One exception exists, however. See Table A.1 for the proportion of respondents who answered each question correctly in representative samples (US and Germany)[1] and in convenience samples of low and high education individuals[2] and of accountants.[3]

Researchers have not yet proposed standardized norms (e.g., categorizing people as having adequate or inadequate numeracy) for any of the objective numeracy measures reviewed here. Instead, research has focused on developing brief, reliable measures with enough variability in scores to predict comprehension, judgments, and choices. In this section, I review these measures, including each measure's number and type of questions (e.g., arithmetic, statistical, algebra), reliability, predictive validity, and limitations (e.g., answers that can be found easily online). See Table A.2. I also include my subjective assessment of each measure's difficulty level based on my experiences with these measures across studies that included diverse participants. Many measures are too easy or too difficult if used alone.[4,5] That evaluation depends, however, on the sample being studied. The same measure can be too easy for some groups (e.g., college students) and too hard for others (older patients). As a result, choosing a "best" measure for your study will involve your prior judgment about their likely numeracy.

The *Numeracy Scale* developed by psychologist Isaac Lipkus and his colleagues[6] is one of the most widely used. Completing its 11 questions requires understanding risk magnitudes, percentages, and proportions, including converting percentages and proportions. It is comprised of three questions from physician Lisa Schwartz and colleagues' *Numeracy Assessment*[7] plus eight additional questions. Among college students, the *Lipkus Numeracy Scale* is often too easy and highly skewed. Nonetheless, it is a reasonable predictor of simple judgment and decision tasks, such as attribute framing and ratio biases[8] that are described in Chapters 2–7. We developed an *Expanded Numeracy Scale*[2] to increase the difficulty range by adding four questions concerning probabilities and base rates.

Later, we developed the *Rasch-Based Numeracy Scale*,[5] a briefer, psychometrically improved eight-question measure based on Rasch analysis of two large, diverse Internet samples whose participants had responded to 18 objective numeracy questions. The final version of the measure included questions with a wider range of difficulty and discriminated more finely between different levels of numeracy. The measure includes five questions from the original

Table A.1 Comparison of Percent Correct on Numeracy Items in a Nationally Representative Sample, Among Low/High Education Adults and Among Accountants

Numeracy Questions	Nationally representative samples[1]		High- and-low education adults[2]		Accountants[3]
	United States	Germany	More education (> high school)	Less education (< ≤ high school degree)	
Which of the following represents the biggest risk of getting a disease? 1%, 10%, 5%	83%	79%	96%	88%	95%
If the chance of getting a disease is 10%, how many people would be expected to get the disease out of 1,000?	83%	89%	86%	69%	91%
Which of the following numbers represents the biggest risk of getting a disease? 1 in 100, 1 in 1,000, 1 in 10	75%	72%	94%	83%	95%
Imagine that we flip a fair coin 1,000 times. What is your best guess about how many times the coin will come up heads in 1,000 flips?	73%	73%			88%
If the chance of getting a disease is 20 out of 100, this would be the same as having a ____% chance of getting the disease.	70%	73%	90%	70%	91%
In the Bingo Lottery, the chance of winning a $10 prize is 1%. What is your best guess about how many people would win a $10 prize if 1,000 people each buy a single ticket for Bingo Lottery? ___persons out of 1,000	58%	68%	60%	36%	86%
If person A's chance of getting a disease is 1 in 100 in 10 years, and person B's risk is double that of A, what is B's risk?	57%	55%	76%	49%	86%
Imagine that we roll a fair, six-sided die 1,000 times. Of 1,000 rolls, how many times do you think the die would come up even (2, 4, or 6)?	57%	64%	65%	50%	85%
In the Daily Times Sweepstakes, the chance of winning a car is 1 in 1,000. What percent of tickets of Daily Times Sweepstakes win a car?	23%	46%	33%	13%	57%
The chance of getting a viral infection is .0005. Out of 10,000 people, about how many of them are expected to get infected?			44%	29%	79%
Imagine that you are taking a class and your chances of being asked a question in class are 1% during the first week of class and double each week thereafter (i.e., you would have a 2% chance in Week 2, a 4% chance in Week 3, and an 8% chance in Week 4). What is the probability that you will be asked a question during Week 7?			73%	38%	85%

Suppose that 1 out of every 10,000 doctors in a certain region is infected with the SARS virus; in the same region 20 out of every 100 people in a particular at-risk population also are infected with the virus. A test for the virus gives a positive result in 99% of those who are infected and in 1% of those who are not infected. A randomly selected doctor and a randomly selected person in the at-risk population in the region both test positive for the disease. Who is more likely to actually have the disease?   54%   38%   67%

Suppose you have a close friend who has a lump in her breast and must have a mammogram. Of 100 women like her, 10 of them actually have a malignant tumor and 90 of them do not. Of the 10 women who actually have a tumor, the mammogram indicates correctly that 9 of them have a tumor and indicates incorrectly that 1 of them does not have a tumor. Of the 90 women who do not have a tumor, the mammogram indicates correctly that 81 of them do not have a tumor and indicates incorrectly that 9 of them do have a tumor. The table below summarizes all of this information. Imagine that your friend tests positive (as if she had a tumor), what is the likelihood that she actually has a tumor? [Note that a later version of this question modified the 81 who do not have a tumor to 80 and the 9 who do have a tumor to 10 in order to reduce guessing.]   14%   7%   12%

	Tested positive	Tested negative	Totals
Actually has cancer	9	1	10
Does not have cancer	9	81	90
Totals	18	82	100

Note: The correct answer to the objective numeracy question in the "Moving Forward" section of Chapter 1 is 25%.

Missing responses indicate items that were not asked.

Table A.2 Objective Numeracy Measures Summary

Scale name and authors	Difficulty level	Administration time	# of items	Types of items	Internal reliability	Test-retest reliability[a]	Response format
Numeracy Assessment[7]	Moderate	Very brief	3	Probability and converting metrics (percentages and proportions)	α = .52 to .80	r = .72	Open-ended
Numeracy Scale[6]	Easy	Brief	11	Magnitude, probability, converting metrics, arithmetic	α = .54 to .76	[b]	Open-ended and multiple choice
Expanded Numeracy Scale[2]	Moderate	Moderate	15	Magnitude, probability, converting metrics, arithmetic	α = .53 to .83	[b]	Open-ended and multiple choice
Rasch-Based Numeracy Scale[5]	Moderate	Brief-Moderate	8	Probability, converting metrics, arithmetic, algebra	α = .53 to .71	[b]	Open-ended (multiple choice version)[9]
Berlin Numeracy Test[10]	Difficult	Brief	4	Probability, statistical	α = .59	NA	Open-ended
Berlin Numeracy Test (adaptive)[10]	Difficult	Very brief	2–3	Probability, statistical	NA	NA	Open-ended
Cognitive Reflection Test[11]	Difficult	Very brief	3	Algebra, arithmetic	α = .60	[b]	Open-ended

Note: Administration time in relatively educated populations (at least some college; MTurk): Very brief (1–3 minutes); brief (3–6 minutes); moderate (6–10 minutes)

[a] Where acceptable test–retest correlations are r > .5, Spearman–Brown > .66, an 18-question objective numeracy measure comprised of items from scales marked with the letter b showed r = .88 and Spearman-Brown = .94.[12]

Lipkus Numeracy Scale,[6] two questions from the cognitive reflection test (CRT[11]), and one from the Expanded Numeracy Scale.[2] Note that this latter question was modified slightly at a later date to retain its difficulty but reduce guessing the correct response. The Rasch-Based Numeracy Scale successfully predicted responses on a variety of tasks related to numeracy in prior research (ratio bias, attribute framing, bets task, risk perceptions of terrorist attacks and salmon extinction). A multiple-choice version of this eight-question measure has been used to predict comprehension of debt repayments.[9]

The more recent *Berlin Numeracy Test* assesses "statistical numeracy," an understanding of the operations of probabilistic and statistical computation.[10] The measure was designed for use in highly educated participants and professionals so it should be used with great care if you study less educated individuals or populations who would likely find it too difficult. The standard version of the test, however, is quite short (four questions) and has very good reliability and predictive validity.[13,14] They simultaneously designed an adaptive version of the test that requires answering only 2–3 questions.

General health objective numeracy measures also exist, including the *Numeracy Understanding in Medicine Instrument* (NUMi)[15] and domain-specific measures in asthma, anticoagulation control, and diabetes.[16–18]

Potential Issues in Objective Numeracy Measures

Inclusion of CRT Questions   Our choice to include two CRT questions in our Rasch-based measure has been controversial.[5,9,19] To us, CRT questions obviously concern objective numeracy (and algebra in particular). One item reads "A bat and a ball cost $1.10 in total. The bat costs $1.00 more than the ball. How much does the ball cost?" Correct responses depend critically on the ability to set up and solve a math equation. Some researchers have ignored its mathematical basis and focused instead on cognitive reflection being needed to override the intuitive response (10¢ is the intuitive response in the preceding example above).[11,20] In developing our Rasch-Based Numeracy Scale, however, confirmatory factor analysis revealed that CRT questions were appropriate to use with standard numeracy questions. In fact, four of five published studies that employed exploratory or confirmatory factor analyses concluded that CRT and other objective numeracy questions load onto the same factor.[5,21–23] Only one study (out of two studies in the paper) concluded otherwise.[23] Psychologist Jon Baron[22] further surmised that CRT questions were less similar to non-numeric CRT-like verbal problems (that also included an intuitively compelling incorrect response) and were more similar to math questions without intuitive answers. These studies support the idea that CRT questions are most like objective numeracy questions.

In addition, we can divide CRT scores into components of calculation (identifying the correct response) and cognitive reflection (avoidance of the intuitive response) and examine the predictive validity of the individual components (how well each one predicts decisions, for example).[24] If cognitive reflection is indeed the critical driver of good decisions, then its subcomponent should be a better predictor than the calculation subcomponent. Contrary to original thinking on the measure, the calculation subcomponent (and not the cognitive reflection subcomponent) was associated with performance on decision tasks traditionally associated with CRT scores (i.e., incentivized measures of impatient and risk-averse choices, the consistency of risk perceptions, and self-reported financial outcomes). The latter cognitive reflection subcomponent lacked the same predictive validity. Instead, it related to having stronger religious beliefs, traditional moral values, and disgust-based moral judgments independent of calculation.[20] Thus, at least in traditional decision tasks, CRT questions acted as objective numeracy questions, supporting how we constructed our Rasch-based measure.

General Versus Specific Math Intelligences   Several researchers have discussed the potential importance of general math intelligence versus specific facets of mathematical skills (e.g., probabilistic vs. arithmetic),[5,25,26] but little published data exist. Analyses in one paper uncovered some specific components of objective numeracy in exploratory factor analysis.[23] Although plausible as objective numeracy components, the researchers appeared to use the Kaiser-Guttman criterion to choose how many factors to retain (retaining all factors with eigenvalue >1.00 without considering other solutions). This criterion, however, is an unreliable method to estimate the number of retained factors.[27–29] In fact, their factor structure was not fully stable across two studies. In addition, some resulting factors included only two questions, and statisticians recommend that three questions per factor are needed to identify common stable factors.[27] Finally, although these researchers concluded that "the CRT is not just another numeracy scale" (p. 361),[23] the CRT loaded on the same factor with other numeracy questions in one of their two studies (and in all of the remaining four published studies).[24] These points question the stability of their subcomponents and therefore relations between them and decision tasks.

We do know that general math intelligence matters because different objective numeracy measures have similar predictive power in the identical decision task. For example, in a study conducted with rural villagers in Ghana, our participants did not understand symbols for probability and we switched to measuring arithmetic performance.[30,31] The number of correct arithmetic answers among Ghanaians had similar value in predicting choices in a ratio-bias task[32] as a traditional objective numeracy measure had in an earlier college student sample.[33]

This question about general versus specific numeracy skills is complicated by the fact that current research has not distinguished well between the difficulty of numeracy questions (where higher scores may indicate higher general math intelligence) and specific numeracy skills. For example, CRT[11] and Berlin Numeracy Test[10] questions are more difficult than Lipkus Numeracy Scale[6] questions. As a result, they may add additional power to predicting decision performance because they tap into a critical specific objective numeracy skill or because they allow for finer discrimination of individuals with greater ability (easier measures would lump all of these people into the same top score). I am unaware of published research that distinguishes difficulty from specific skills in predicting decisions. At this point, I believe researchers can use arithmetic, algebra, or probabilistic questions interchangeably in predicting judgments and decisions so long as they choose a measure with an appropriate difficulty level for their target sample (I suspect geometry, calculus, and trigonometry questions will be different but have not tested them). Future research may prove otherwise, however. Overall, the jury is out on whether measures of specific numeracy skills might be better predictors of specific types of decisions than a general numeracy intelligence measure.

Recommended Objective Numeracy Measures

To summarize, no one best objective numeracy measure exists at this time. To choose a best measure, interested researchers should consider the likely range of numerical ability in the group they plan to study and the difficulty ranges of various objective numeracy measures. If you are studying older adults or patients, you should consider one of the easier measures in Table A.2. If MBA students are your participants, consider the Berlin Numeracy Test.

One final pragmatic issue exists. Study participants can easily find correct answers on the Internet to most, if not all, popular objective numeracy questions. As a result, in my lab, we are developing a large pool of objective numeracy questions that can be used interchangeably. In addition, when conducting studies online, we present images of numeracy questions so that participants cannot copy and paste them into a web browser. This technique should cut down on cheating. Researchers also should ask participants at a study's end if they used any assistance, such as available answers or calculators, and exclude their data in final analyses.

Measuring Subjective Numeracy

Subjective numeracy measures are self-reported measures rather than math tests. As a result, they are easier to administer and briefer; they are also preferred by many participants.[34]

However, subjective measures are not good diagnostic indicators of their objective proxies, and subjective numeracy is no exception.[23,35,36] As in other domains, impressions people have of their numeracy skills are only modestly correlated with their objective numeracy performance.[37] More importantly, subjective numeracy measures simply assess a different numeric competence (see Chapter 14).

Two categories of subjective numeracy measures exist and are used regularly in published studies. One category of measures assesses numeric self-efficacy (i.e., numeric confidence) and (sometimes) preferences for numbers over words. The second category measures the related concept of math emotion or anxiety. In addition, one could measure self-identity by asking people's level of agreement with the statement "I consider myself a math person" (-2 = strongly disagree, -1 = somewhat disagree, 0 = neither disagree nor agree, $+1$ = somewhat agree, $+2$ = strongly agree). However, researchers have rarely tested this latter measure.

Numeric Confidence or Self-Efficacy

Subjective numeracy measures were developed and have been used as proxies (replacements) for objective numeracy measures. The most popular eight-question subjective numeracy measure from psychologist Angie Fagerlin and her colleagues has two four-question sub measures: perceptions of one's numeric confidence and preferences for numbers over words (e.g., in weather forecasts).[34] The numeric confidence sub measure assesses an individual's beliefs about her objective numeracy skills (e.g., "How good are you at figuring out how much a shirt will cost if it's 25% off?" on a 6-point scale from 1 = not at all good to 6 = extremely good). The number-preference sub measure assesses an individual's preference for numeric versus non-numeric information (e.g., "When people tell you the chance of something happening, do you prefer that they use words ['it rarely happens'] or numbers ['there's a 1% chance']?" on a 6-point scale from 1 = always prefer words to 6 = always prefer numbers). The full eight-question measure shows good test-retest reliability after a 1-week delay (Spearman-Brown = .95 with no significant mean change over this time period).[12] Originally intended as a proxy for objective numeracy, its correlation with objective numeracy tends to r = .45, but this correlation varies across studies (r = .46,[38] r = .36 to .50,[39] r = .19 to .44,[40] r = 0.45 to .47[23]). It has been used widely in the medical decision-making literature[36,40–42] and (less so) in the judgment and decision-making literature.[9,23,38] A short three-question version was validated in patient populations.[43,44]

Physicians Steven Woloshin, Lisa Schwartz, and Gilbert Welch[45] developed another popular measure to assess level of interest and confidence in using medical statistics. The STAT-interest sub measure consists of five questions (e.g., "To make wise decisions about my health it is important to know how to interpret statistics") assessed on a 5-point scale from strongly disagree, disagree, neither, agree, strongly agree. The STAT-confidence sub measure consists of three questions (e.g., "I am confident that I can make sense of medical statistics") assessed on a 5-point scale from strongly disagree, disagree, neither, agree, strongly agree. Physicians have used the measures widely.[36,46]

Education researchers have related other numeric confidence (self-efficacy) measures to math performance. One three-question measure assesses students' sense of their math ability and performance.[47] A more recent 12-question measure asks participants to respond to everyday questions (e.g., "I am confident in my ability to understand a graph accompanying an article on business profits" and "I am confident in my ability to understand how much interest I will earn on my savings account in 6 months, and how that interest is computed") on 5-point scales ranging from 1 (strongly disagree) to 5 (strongly agree).[48]

Each of the preceding measures has somewhat limited variance, especially in educated populations, because people tend to report high numeric confidence. Greater variance is available when participants do a numeracy test and then rate confidence in their performance.[49] For example, confidence in multiplication estimations can be assessed on an 11-point scale ranging from no confidence at all (0%) to total confidence (100%).[50,51] Alternatively, researchers can ask participants to indicate how many questions they believe they answered correctly (so that researchers can compare the number of questions estimated vs. answered correctly). Overall, people who are lower in objective numeracy tend to overestimate their skills more whereas those higher in objective numeracy underestimate their skills or are calibrated more often (they are more likely to know what they know).[3,52] Understanding the relations of numeric confidence (the estimated number correct) versus overconfidence (the estimated number correct minus the actual number correct) to decision making is an interesting future research direction.

Math Anxiety

The most used measures of math anxiety are the 98-question *Mathematics Anxiety Rating* measure[53] or its briefer 25-question version, the *Short Mathematics Anxiety Rating* Scale[54]). They assess how anxious one feels during everyday math-related experiences (e.g., "reading a cash register receipt after you buy something," "studying for a math test") on a 5-point scale (1 = not at all, 2 = a little, 3 = a fair amount, 4 = much, 5 = very much). The sMARS correlates highly with overall MARS scores ($r > .90$) and has acceptable test-retest reliability ($r = .75$ at a 2-week retest interval).[55] The sMARS has been used widely in studies of math anxiety.[56–58] A single question "On a scale from 1 to 10, how math anxious are you?" also correlated anywhere from .49 to .85 with sMARS scores.[59]

Psychologist Nancy Betz's *Mathematics Anxiety Scale* (MAS)[60] was designed to measure the extent of mathematics anxiety in college students. Since then, it has been used extensively at the college, high school, and middle school levels and has excellent split-half reliability of .92.[39,50,61] The 10-question measure is equally divided between positive and negative statements concerning attitudes and experiences encountered in mathematics and mathematics-related tasks (e.g., "I get nervous before mathematics tests," "My mind goes blank and I am unable to think clearly when doing mathematics") answered on 5-point scales (1 = extremely uncharacteristic; 5 = extremely characteristic). A *Child Math Anxiety Questionnaire* (C-MAQ) also exists[62,63] and has good reliability.[56]

Other related measures also have good reliability. For example, on a modified MAS for non-students, participants respond on 5-point scales (1 = strongly disagree to 5 = strongly agree) to 10 modified questions including "Mathematics makes me feel uneasy and confused" and "I am unable to think clearly when working mathematics".[48] We instead assessed six bipolar math emotions ("Please describe your attitude toward math on the following scales": bad/good, sad/happy, disgusting/delightful, ugly/beautiful, avoid/approach, afraid/unafraid) on 7-point scales (from −3 to +3) (Cronbach's alpha = .92).[38]

More recently, a 13-question everyday math anxiety measure was designed to assess how much anxiety one feels in everyday situations (e.g., "having to present numerical information at a work meeting") on 5-point scales (1 = low anxiety, 2 = some anxiety, 3 = moderate anxiety, 4 = quite a bit of anxiety, 5 = high anxiety).[64] The measure included some modified questions from the most popular subjective numeracy measure[34] (e.g., how anxious are you "when having to work out a 15% tip"). The measure had good internal reliability (Cronbach's alpha = 0.93).

Recommended Subjective Numeracy Measures

To measure subjective numeracy, I recommend the *Subjective Numeracy Scale* and especially its numeric confidence sub measure.[34] However, if you are doing a medical study, you could select the STAT-interest sub measure[45] instead. At this point, it is unclear whether math-anxiety measures will add appreciably on top of other subjective numeracy measures in predictions of comprehension and information processing in judgments and choices. As indicated in Chapter 14 and consistent with theorizing by psychologist Albert Bandura,[65] numeric confidence may be a more proximal determinant of behaviors needed to understand numeric data than is math anxiety.[64] However, if I wanted to measure math anxiety with students, I would recommend the sMARS[54] or MAS.[60] With non-students (who might not respond reliably to questions about anxiety studying for math tests), the everyday math anxiety measure is a good choice.[64] Overall, if I had to choose a single subjective numeracy measure for a study, I would choose the numeric confidence sub measure of the Subjective Numeracy Scale to assess subjective numeracy.[34]

Moving Forward

In this section, we discussed measures of both objective and subjective numeracy so that you can make sense of their evidence in the remainder of the book. I also recommended measures at the end of both sections. As a reminder, we'll discuss measures of the ANS later in the Appendix under Chapter 13 after I introduce this complex and interesting topic in more depth.

If you have read the rest of the book by now (and especially Chapter 14), you hopefully know that you sometimes might want to measure both objective numeracy and subjective numeracy. For example, in predicting numeric comprehension in a relatively brief task, objective numeracy should certainly predict greater comprehension. However, across levels of objective numeracy, people who are more subjectively numerate may enjoy the tasks more than those lower in subjective numeracy, work harder, and answer more questions correctly.[21] In addition, those higher versus lower in objective numeracy may deploy their skills strategically in tasks (using them to make numerically appropriately choices when it is to their advantage and not bothering otherwise); those higher versus lower in subjective numeracy again may enjoy the task more than those lower in subjective numeracy and make numerically appropriate choices more often even when it benefits them very little.[66]

Finally, some tasks require running the numbers well, as well as long-term persistence in the face of tedium, difficulty, and obstacles. Environments that require self-management come to mind, for example in chronic disease and personal finances. In such cases, people higher in subjective numeracy may enjoy daily tasks more and be more likely to persist at them. If they also have adequate objective numeracy skills, then they should succeed more often than those lower in subjective numeracy; however, absent appropriate skills, they may suffer worse outcomes.[67] Thus, objective and subjective numeracy may interact to predict outcomes. In fact, although unexamined, this interaction hypothesis also may apply to the comprehension and strategic deployment studies described earlier if those tasks are difficult enough for high persistence and low skills to be problematic.

This latter point highlights some important unanswered questions.

- What level of objective numeracy do we need to be successful? It must depend on the ease or difficulty of the task at hand. What level of difficulty does the world tend to present to us?
- Do we adjust to our environments differently based on our numeric ability, placing ourselves in more numerically difficult situations when we are numerically adept (think about actuaries) and in easier environments otherwise? If so, do these choices depend more on subjective numeracy or objective numeracy? And what problems occur depending upon which numeracy we use? I could imagine that choosing based on subjective numeracy scores could be problematic if one's numeric ability fails to match this confidence. The reverse may be equally problematic.

Overall, objective numeracy measures are most likely to be useful when task performance requires running the numbers well, whereas subjective measures may be as important when numeric persistence is key. Pragmatically, subjective measures may also be more useful if research participants will be asked to return (they are less likely to return if they respond to an objective numeracy measure[34]) and you expect a large correlation with your outcome variable (such as with numeric comprehension). In these cases, the correlation with comprehension will be lower for subjective numeracy than objective numeracy, but at least more of your participants will return.

Chapter 9

Numeracy and Other Disease-Management Issues

As reviewed in Chapter 9, the less numerate suffer from more diseases, take more prescription medications, and may make worse choices about cancer treatments (and certainly make less informed choices). They also control active disease, like diabetes, less well. Here, I detail a number of other numeracy-related disease-management issues for the interested reader.

Kidney Disease

Kidney disease requires numerical skills to manage it effectively. Patients must adhere to daily medications and dietary restrictions, as well as undergo dialysis multiple times a week.[68,69] Lower numeracy in these and other transplant patients has been associated with a lower likelihood of being listed for or receiving a transplant as well as a greater likelihood to be readmitted post-transplant, even after controlling for reading ability and cognitive functioning.[70,71] Although the reasons are not completely clear, researchers have speculated that lower numeracy may result in lower understanding or appreciation of the health benefits of transplantation.

Asthma

Higher numeracy appears beneficial to supporting asthma patient health as well. Patients with higher numeracy reported higher asthma-related quality of life after controlling for potential demographic confounders.[72,73] They also reported being more able than the less numerate to access and use healthcare effectively for diagnosis and treatment.[74] In particular, less numerate adult asthma patients were less able to navigate their healthcare (e.g., recall medication instructions, such as their recommended number of puffs of inhaled steroid; understand copay requirements). Perhaps because of this navigation difficulty, less numerate asthma patients were hospitalized more often than the more numerate whereas health literacy did not predict hospitalization.[16]

Hospital Admissions

Less numerate individuals are generally more likely to end up in the hospital or emergency room based on data from 28 emergency departments in 17 US states.[75] In another study of 709 patients hospitalized for acute heart failure, the less numerate were more likely than the highly numerate to have an unplanned return to the hospital or emergency room within 30 days; health literacy was not a significant predictor.[43] Finally, getting hospital care quickly can be critical to decreasing risks of death and disability. A recent study revealed that patients with higher (vs. lower) numeracy were about four times more likely to seek medical attention within the critical first hour after coronary symptom onset (e.g., chest pain or tightness).[76]

Following Complex Medication Regimens

Numeracy-related disparities in health outcomes may sometimes be due to the less numerate having difficulty with their medications. As mentioned earlier, the less numerate take more prescription medications but have more difficulty recalling correct dosages.[74,77] In addition, less numerate HIV patients were less able than highly numerate patients to manage a simulated complex HIV medication regimen.[78] Less numerate patients at risk for stroke demonstrated less adequate anti-coagulation control, as if they were less able to follow their complex medication regimen (controlling for age).[17] Finally, medication errors occurred more often among previously hospitalized patients who were lower versus higher in subjective numeracy.[79]

More generally, numeracy may play a role in widespread nonadherence to prescription medications. Studies "have consistently shown that 20% to 30% of medication prescriptions are never filled and that approximately 50% of medications for chronic disease are not taken as prescribed . . . [with] dramatic effects on health" (p. 785).[80] Lower numeracy has been associated with less adherence. This numeracy-adherence association may be greater for preventive medications given that one study indicated that the less numerate perceived less value from them than the highly numerate.[81] For example, less numerate cardiovascular patients were less adherent than highly numerate ones in the period just before they were hospitalized for their disease.[82] However, no numeracy effect emerged in a study on diabetes medication adherence.[83]

Health Self-Management

Some numeracy associations may be explained by better health self-management skills.[74] For example, people who successfully monitor their blood pressure at home have lower cardiovascular and other risks independent of measures taken at a healthcare provider. However, less numerate patients monitored less well than the highly numerate.[84] Among older adults, higher numeracy and higher literacy independently predicted a variety of skills including organizing and dosing medication, comprehension of print and multimedia information, and use of patient portals.[85,86]

Numeracy May Relate Broadly to Healthy Behaviors

Although less research is available, other medical concerns are also thought to rely heavily on patient numeracy skills because of the complex nature of the tasks required. For example, numeracy's wide-ranging associations with better health outcomes could be due to more numerate patients practicing more protective behaviors.[30]

- *Condom usage.* In a study conducted in the Peruvian Highlands, we found a unique protective effect of numeracy on sex-related protective behavior (condom use), controlling for measures of fluid intelligence and potential confounding factors.[31]
- *Exercise.* An Australian study found that more numerate 9- to 11-year-old children exercised more than the less numerate, after controlling for child body mass index (BMI), ethnicity, and gender, as well as household demographics (highest education, income, marital status, mother's employment hours, and number of siblings).[87]
- *Informed consent and benefit expectations.* Patients sometimes expect more benefit from treatments than is warranted. This expectation can be particularly problematic in the face of unknown treatment risks. For example, researchers found that lower numeracy was associated with greater expectations of benefit from Phase I clinical cancer trials.[88] Their study included 328 advanced cancer patients who had agreed to participate in a Phase I trial for an experimental cancer therapy. Although the historic benefit rate of Phase I trials has been 5% or less, all participants overestimated benefits, with the less numerate overestimating more (the less and more numerate expected, respectively, a 70% and 62% chance of benefit).

Chapter 12

Scope and Sequence of Mathematics Education in the United States

In the United States, 42 states have agreed on a consensus standard for math achievement from kindergarten through grade 8 (e.g., Common Core State Standards Initiative). The curriculum provides clear standards for children at each grade to develop mathematical understanding. A strong focus exists on counting and understanding place values at early grades. Later grades then take advantage of early mastery to progress into more difficult mathematical operations with single-digit and then multidigit numbers. Geometric understanding and reasoning are also a focus, with links made to arithmetic operations. Very basic statistics are first introduced in Grade 6, and greater conceptual statistical understanding is enhanced in later grades. Developed by a consortium of state governors and chief state education officers, its adoption is expected to bring "a new level of uniformity and coherence to US mathematics education" (p. v)[89] A brief review of ideal standards at each grade level is listed here; they can be seen in more detail at http://www.corestandards.org/Math/.

- In kindergarten, children should learn number names, counting from 1–20, and how to identify comparative magnitudes of numbers ("Which one is bigger, 18 or 13?").
- First-graders are focused on number operations (addition and subtraction) with quantities 1–20 including some early algebraic thinking with word problems. They extend their counting sequence up to 120 and begin to understand place values (e.g., "10 can be thought of as a bundle of ten ones") and how to use place values in addition and subtraction (the base-10 notation system). First-graders also work on measurement, telling and writing time, and begin to study algebra and how to reason with shapes and their attributes. Through geometry, first-graders are introduced to concepts such as halves and quarters of shapes such as rectangles.
- In Grade 2 of the common core standards, children increase understanding of base-10 notation and improve their fluency with addition and subtraction with numbers up to 20 and with measuring and estimating lengths, including linking such processes with addition and subtraction. They continue to work with time and money. Finally, they extend their understanding of geometry and reasoning with more shapes and their attributes (e.g., identifying triangles, quadrilaterals, pentagons, hexagons, and cubes).
- Grade 3 extends many of these same concepts and moves into multiplication and division with numbers up to 100 and using place values to perform multidigit arithmetic (including addition and subtraction up to 1000 and more advanced multiplication). Fractions are introduced, and third-graders are expected to learn, for example, the equivalence of different fractions (e.g., $2/3 = 4/6 = 8/12$). Concepts in measurement and estimation, geometry, and data representation and interpretation become more advanced and are related back to multiplication and division.
- In Grade 4, children learn place values up to 1,000,000 and become more fluent with multidigit multiplication and division. With fractions, they generalize their understanding of fraction equivalence, addition and subtraction of fractions when the denominator is the same, and multiplication of fractions by whole numbers. They continue to extend geometric understanding of two-dimensional figures.
- Fifth-graders continue to learn more about and to develop fluency with addition and subtraction of fractions with multiplication and limited division of fractions introduced to them in this grade. Division of whole numbers is extended to multiple digits, and decimals are introduced as part of the place value system. They also develop an understanding of three-dimensional volumes.
- Math in Grade 6 is focused on more advanced reasoning about multiplication and division, including understanding ratios and rates. They extend their understanding of division with fractions and use this understanding to solve problems. Negative numbers are introduced. They also start to write equations that correspond to given situations ($y = 2x + 4$), and they begin to develop abilities to think statistically about concepts such as means, medians, and measures of variability.

- In Grade 7, students learn more about ratios and proportions in math problems, and they develop a more complete understanding of numbers from integers to fractions, decimals, and percentages and how to perform operations with them using equations. They also extend their problem-solving abilities within geometric shapes. Finally, they improve their understanding of statistics, including beginning to understand random sampling and representative samples and to examine population differences from two data distributions.
- Eighth-graders then are expected to understand concepts of rational and irrational numbers and to use exponents, proportional relations, and more advanced linear equations including implementing procedures efficiently to solve them. They are expected to understand and use functions to describe quantitative relationships. They extend their understanding of geometry and learn the Pythagorean Theorem. Finally, in statistics and probability, they learn to investigate patterns of association in bivariate data such as in two-way tables.

Chapter 13

Measuring the ANS at the Group or Individual Level

Researchers believe that the ANS produces our ability to discriminate quantities. Individuals with a more precise ANS can discriminate better (i.e., they can discriminate between quantities that are numerically closer) than those with a less precise ANS. They also perceive those numbers as more numerically different (as further apart from each other). *ANS acuity* (also called *ANS precision*) can be assessed using tasks that involve symbolic numbers (e.g., "9" and "127") or with tasks that use nonsymbolic quantities shown with the equivalent numbers of dots (e.g., 9 dots and 127 dots). In this section, I review the three most popular tasks in the decision literature: distance-effect, symbolic number mapping, and dot discrimination.

Distance-Effect Task

The original distance-effect task[90] has occasionally been used as an individual-difference measure of ANS acuity.[91] In it, participants are asked to make rapid judgments of the numerical order of Arabic numerals ("Is 2 greater than or less than 4?") or dot sets ("Is : greater than or less than ::?"). The distance effect is measured as the slope or difference of reaction times when comparing quantities that are close together (5 and 6) versus far apart (5 and 9). People respond more quickly when quantities are numerically farther apart. The size of the distance effect for each individual can be modeled using hierarchical linear modeling[91] or diffusion modeling.[92] Once modeled as an individual difference, it represents each person's ability to discriminate magnitudes. A smaller slope indicates superior ability to discriminate quantities that are closer together (i.e., more precise ANS).

For example, we used nonsymbolic quantities (dots) and symbolic numbers (Arabic integers, frequencies, percentages, and decimals), with the first three notations as magnitudes between 1 and 9 and the latter three notations as quantities between 0 and 1.[91] Younger and older adult participants responded to 160 experimental trials of each notation type and, ultimately, demonstrated the usual effect of distance. Specifically, they took longer to respond and made more errors to close magnitudes (5 and 6) than those farther apart (5 and 9). The distance effect, measured in this manner, was a reliable individual-difference construct across notations (Cronbach's alpha = .76). Unclear was whether a performance bias existed based on speed-accuracy tradeoffs.

Diffusion models can be used instead to improve the measure by disaggregating ANS acuity from speed–accuracy tradeoffs and other components of cognitive processing.[92,93] However, the task is time-consuming and boring for participants, and these tasks have been criticized recently with respect to their reliability and ability to distinguish individual differences in ANS acuity.[94–100]

Symbolic Number Mapping Task

Another task that generally involves symbolic numbers is the *symbolic number mapping* (SMap) task originally developed by psychologists Robert Siegler and John Opfer[101,102] (it is also called the *number-to-position line task*). In the task, participants generally are given a set of 6–14 symbolic numbers one-at-a-time. They are then asked to place a tick mark where a provided number (e.g., 4, 71, and 780) falls on a line usually marked from 0 to 1,000. Participants typically complete this task quickly, in 2–5 minutes. Researchers then either model responses in linear and/or logarithmic fashion,[12,102] or they calculate the mean absolute error of responses by summing the absolute deviations between each response on the 0–1,000 line and the objective number presented. Researchers who use this latter method often then log-transform scores to correct for positive skew and then multiply by −1 so that higher scores indicate more exact mapping and better SMap ability.[12,38,103] Split-half reliability on this task was better in one study based on mean absolute response errors ($r = .58$, Spearman–Brown = .73) than linear modeling ($r = .31$, Spearman–Brown = .47).[12] Mean absolute errors also have been used more often in the decision-making studies described in Chapter 13.[38,103] Experimenters generally use symbolic numbers in this line task but sometimes use nonsymbolic dots. However, using dots in the task may not yield consistently reliable performance.[12]

SMap and distance-effect tasks that use symbolic numbers have been criticized as measures of ANS acuity per se, however, because the ANS directly responds to nonsymbolic magnitudes (e.g., dots), but not to values of symbolic numbers. Instead, we learn to map symbolic numbers to the numerical magnitudes that we have in memory.[104] Thus, accuracy in these tasks using symbolic numbers is likely influenced by ANS acuity as well as the exactness of the mapping between symbolic numbers and their analog magnitudes.[12,98,101,105-108] The SMap task may also be influenced by higher order math skills since values can be placed relatively accurately by bisecting the line (e.g., "On a 1–1,000 line, locate 500, then 250").[109] As a result, the relation of SMap performance with ANS acuity may be attenuated further. Nonetheless, SMap scores correlate modestly with performance on the dot-discrimination task described next.[12]

Dot-Discrimination Task

Measures such as the dot-discrimination task use nonsymbolic magnitudes (i.e., dots) and assess ANS acuity more directly (without the additional noise of mapping symbolic numbers onto underlying representations). Psychologists Justin Halberda, Michèle Mazzocco, and Lisa Feigenson[110] developed the most well-known dot-discrimination task to assess ANS acuity. In it, participants responded to 80 trials of blue and yellow dot sets presented on a computer screen too rapidly (200 ms) to count the dots. On each trial, participants indicated whether there were more blue or yellow dots. Each set included 5–16 dots, and the ratio between the two sets varied randomly between ratios of 1:2, 3:4, 5:6, and 7:8. ANS acuity is then assessed by psychophysical modeling of performance (see panamath.org for an online test, including for researcher use). The Weber fraction that emerges is calculated based on the ratios an individual successfully discriminates. The measure demonstrated acceptable split-half reliability but low test-retest reliability.[110] It has been criticized for this limited reliability, and some researchers have found that the relation between ANS acuity (the Weber fraction) and mathematical achievement depends on the two dot sets being spatially intermixed versus spatially segregated,[95,111] perceptual factors such as area and density,[112] and inhibitory control processes endemic to the dots task.[113]

To improve reliability, we modified Halberda et al.'s original task by increasing the number of trials from 80 to 312, increasing controls on the size of the dots, and introducing "catch" trials to estimate inattention to the task.[12] Our modified 5- to 10-minute version of the task showed good split-half reliability (Spearman-Brown > .73) and good test-retest reliability after a 1-week delay (Spearman–Brown > .87).

The dot-discrimination task, is conceptually the closest measure of the ANS given its use of nonsymbolic magnitudes and no need to transform symbolic numbers into underlying magnitude representations. It is further, however, from the numbers used in everyday decisions for the same reasons.

Recommended ANS Measure

At this point, I recommend using the SMap task in decision-making studies because of its use of symbolic numbers, ease of use, and relatively high reliability and predictive validity. More research is needed, however, to understand the psychological mechanisms that underlie its predictive validity versus, for example, dot-discrimination tasks.

References

1. Galesic, M., & Garcia-Retamero, R. (2010). Statistical numeracy for health a cross-cultural comparison with probabilistic national samples. *Archives of Internal Medicine, 170*(5), 462–468.

2. Peters, E., Dieckmann, N., Dixon, A., Hibbard, J. H., & Mertz, C. K. (2007). Less is more in presenting quality information to consumers. *Medical Care Research and Review, 64*(2), 169–190.

3. Peters, E., Fennema, M. G., & Tiede, K. E. (2019). The loss-bet paradox: Actuaries, accountants, and other numerate people rate numerically inferior gambles as superior. *Journal of Behavioral Decision Making, 32*, 15–29. https://doi.org/10.1002/bdm.2085.

4. Schapira, M. M., Walker, C. M., & Sedivy, S. K. (2009). Evaluating existing measures of health numeracy using item response theory. *Patient Education and Counseling, 75*(3), 308–314.

5. Weller, J. A., Dieckmann, N. F., Tusler, M., Mertz, C. K., Burns, W. J., & Peters, E. (2013). Development and testing of an abbreviated numeracy scale: A Rasch analysis approach. *Journal of Behavioral Decision Making, 26*(2), 198–212.

6. Lipkus, I. M., Samsa, G., & Rimer, B. K. (2001). General performance on a numeracy scale among highly educated samples. *Medical Decision Making, 21*, 37–44.

7. Schwartz, L. M., Woloshin, S., Black, W. C., & Welch, H. G. (1997). The role of numeracy in understanding the benefit of screening mammography. *Annals of Internal Medicine, 127*(11), 966–972.

8. Peters, E., Västfjäll, D., Slovic, P., Mertz, C. K., Mazzocco, K., & Dickert, S. (2006). Numeracy and decision making. *Psychological Science, 17*(5), 407–413.

9. Soll, J. B., Keeney, R. L., & Larrick, R. P. (2013). Consumer misunderstanding of credit card use, payments, and debt: Causes and solutions. *Journal of Public Policy & Marketing, 32*(1), 66–81.

10. Cokely, E. T., Galesic, M., Schulz, E., Ghazal, S., & Garcia-Retamero, R. (2012). Measuring risk literacy: The Berlin Numeracy Test. *Judgment and Decision Making, 7*(1), 25–47.

11. Frederick, S. (2005). Cognitive reflection and decision making. *Journal of Economic Perspectives, 19*(4), 25–42.

12. Chesney, D., Bjälkebring, P., & Peters, E. (2015). How to estimate how well people estimate: Evaluating measures of individual differences in the approximate number system. *Attention, Perception, & Psychophysics, 77* (8), 2781–2802.

13. Ghazal, S., Cokely, E. T., & Garcia-Retamero, R. (2014). Predicting biases in very highly educated samples: Numeracy and metacognition. *Judgment and Decision Making, 9*(1), 15–34.

14. Lindskog, M., Kerimi, N., Winman, A., & Juslin, P. (2015). A Swedish validation of the Berlin numeracy test. *Scandinavian Journal of Psychology, 56*(2), 132–139.

15. Shapira, M. M., Walker C. M., Cappaert, K. J., Ganschow, P. S., Fletcher, K. E., McGinley, E. L., . . . Jacobs, E. A. (2012). The Numeracy Understand in Medicine Instrument (NUMi): A measure of health numeracy developed using Item Response Theory. *Medical Decision Making, 32*, 851–865.

16. Apter, A. J., Cheng, J., Small, D., Bennett, I. M., Albert, C., Fein, D. G., . . . Van Horne, S. (2006). Asthma numeracy skill and health literacy. *Journal of Asthma, 43*(9), 705–710.

17. Estrada, C. A., Martin-Hryniewicz, M., Peek, B. T., Collins, C., & Byrd, J. C. (2004). Literacy and numeracy skills and anticoagulation control. *American Journal of the Medical Sciences, 328*(2), 88–93.

18. Huizinga, M. M., Elasy, T. A., Wallston, K. A., Cavanaugh, K., Davis, D., Gregory, R. P., . . . Rothman, R. L. (2008). Development and validation of the Diabetes Numeracy Test (DNT). *BMC Health Services Research, 8* (96).

19. Hoover, J. D., & Healy, A. F. (2017). Algebraic reasoning and bat-and-ball problem variants: Solving isomorphic algebra first facilitates problem solving later. *Psychonomic Bulletin & Review, 24*(6), 1–7.

20. Pennycook, G., & Ross, R. M. (2016). Commentary: Cognitive reflection vs. calculation in decision making. *Frontiers in Psychology, 7*, 9.

21. Låg, T., Bauger, L., Lindberg, M., & Friborg, O. (2014). The role of numeracy and intelligence in health-risk estimation and medical data interpretation. *Journal of Behavioral Decision Making, 27*(2), 95–108.

22. Baron, J., Scott, S., Fincher, K., & Metz, S. E. (2015). Why does the Cognitive Reflection Test (sometimes) predict utilitarian moral judgment (and other things)? *Journal of Applied Research in Memory and Cognition, 4*(3), 265–284.

23. Liberali, J. M., Reyna, V. F., Furlan, S., Stein, L. M., & Pardo, S. T. (2012). Individual differences in numeracy and cognitive reflection, with implications for biases and fallacies in probability judgment. *Journal of Behavioral Decision Making, 25*(4), 361–381.

24. Sinayev, A., & Peters, E. (2015). Cognitive reflection vs. calculation in decision making. *Frontiers in Psychology, 6*, 532.

25. Brand, M., Schiebener, J., Pertl, M. T., & Delazer, M. (2014). Know the risk, take the win: How executive functions and probability processing influence advantageous decision making under risk conditions. *Journal of Clinical and Experimental Neuropsychology, 36*(9), 914–929.

26. Cokely, E. T., Feltz, A., Ghazal, S., Allan, J. N., Petrova, D., & Garcia-Retamero, R. (2018). Skilled decision theory: From intelligence to numeracy and expertise. In K. A. Ericsson, R. R. Hoffman, A. Kozbelt, & A. M. Williams (Eds.), *Cambridge handbook of expertise and expert performance* (pp. 476–505). New York: Cambridge University Press.

27. Floyd, F. J., & Widaman, K. F. (1995). Factor analysis in the development and refinement of clinical assessment instruments. *Psychological Assessment, 7*(3), 286–299.

28. Henson, R. K., & Roberts, J. K. (2006). Use of exploratory factor analysis in published research: Common errors and some comment on improved practice. *Educational and Psychological Measurement, 66*(3), 393–416.

29. Costello, A. B., & Osborne, J. W. (2005). Best practices in exploratory factor analysis: Four recommendations for getting the most from your analysis. *Practical Assessment, Research & Evaluation, 10*(7), 1–9.

30. Peters, E., Baker, D. P., Dieckmann, N. F., Leon, J., & Collins, J. (2010). Explaining the effect of education on health: A field study in Ghana. *Psychological Science, 21*(10), 1369–1376.

31. Dieckmann, N. F., Peters, E., Leon, J., Benavides, M., Baker, D. P., & Norris, A. (2015). The role of objective numeracy and fluid intelligence in sex-related protective behaviors. *Current HIV Research, 13*(5), 337–346.

32. Peters, E. (2008, November 5). Numeracy and decision making. Talk given at the Social Science Research Institute, Duke University, Durham, NC.

33. Peters, E., Västfjäll, D., Slovic, P., Mertz, C. K., Mazzocco, K., & Dickert, S. (2006). Numeracy and decision making. *Psychological Science, 17*(5), 407–413.

34. Fagerlin, A., Zikmund-Fisher, B. J., Ubel, P. A., Jankovic, A., Derry, H. A., & Smith, D. M. (2007). Measuring numeracy without a math test: Development of the Subjective Numeracy Scale. *Medical Decision Making, 27*(5), 672–680.

35. Dunning, D., Heath, C., & Suls, J. M. (2004). Flawed self-assessment: Implications for health, education, and the workplace. *Psychological Science in the Public Interest, 5*(3), 69–106.

36. Nelson, W. L., Moser, R. P., & Han, P. K. J. (2013). Exploring objective and subjective numeracy at a population level: Findings from the 2007 health information national trends survey (hints). *Journal of Health Communication, 18*(2), 192–205.

37. Dunning, D. (2011). The Dunning–Kruger effect: On being ignorant of one's own ignorance. In M. P. Zanna & J. Olson (Eds.), *Advances in experimental social psychology, Vol. 44* (pp. 247–296). New York: Academic Press.

38. Peters, E., & Bjälkebring, P. (2015). Multiple numeric competencies: When a number is not just a number. *Journal of Personality and Social Psychology, 108*(5), 802–822.

39. Peters, E., Shoots-Reinhard, B., Tompkins, M. K., Schley, D., Meilleur, L., Sinayev, A., . . . Crocker, J. (2017). Improving numeracy through values affirmation enhances decision and STEM outcomes. *PLoS ONE, 12*(7), e0180674.

40. Dolan, J. G., Cherkasky, O. A., Li, Q. H., Chin, N., & Veazie, P. J. (2016). Should health numeracy be assessed objectively or subjectively? *Medical Decision Making, 36*(7), 868–875.

41. Hanoch, Y., Miron-Shatz, T., Rolison, J. J., & Ozanne, E. (2014). Understanding of brca1/2 genetic tests results: The importance of objective and subjective numeracy. *Psycho-Oncology, 23*(10), 1142–1148.

42. Zikmund-Fisher, B. J., Smith, D. M., Ubel, P. A., & Fagerlin, A. (2007). Validation of the Subjective Numeracy Scale: Effects of low numeracy on comprehension of risk communications and utility elicitations. *Medical Decision Making, 27*(5), 663–671.

43. McNaughton, C. D., Collins, S. P., Kripalani, S., Rothman, R., Self, W. H., Jenkins, C., . . . Storrow, A. B. (2013). Low numeracy is associated with increased odds of 30-day emergency department or hospital recidivism for patients with acute heart failure. *Circulation-Heart Failure, 6*(1), 40–46.

44. Greene, J., Hibbard, J. H., & Sacks, R. M. (2017). Testing a personal narrative for persuading people to value and use comparative physician quality of care information: An

experimental study. *Medical Care Research and Review*. Online publication September 9, 2017. doi: 10.1177/1077558717730156

45. Woloshin, S., Schwartz, L. M., & Welch, H. G. (2005). Patients and medical statistics. *Journal of General Internal Medicine, 20*(11), 996–1000.

46. Han, P. K. J., Dieckmann, N. F., Holt, C., Gutheil, C., & Peters, E. (2016). Factors affecting physicians' intentions to communicate personalized prognostic information to cancer patients at the end of life: An experimental vignette study. *Medical Decision Making, 36*(6), 703–713.

47. Meece, J. L., Wigfield, A., & Eccles, J. S. (1990). Predictors of math anxiety and its influence on young adolescents' course enrollment intentions and performance in mathematics. *Journal of Educational Psychology, 82*(1), 60–70.

48. Silk, K. J., & Parrott, R. L. (2014). Math anxiety and exposure to statistics in messages about genetically modified foods: Effects of numeracy, math self-efficacy, and form of presentation. *Journal of Health Communication, 19*(7), 838–852.

49. Shoots-Reinhard, B., Peters, E., & Petty, R. E. (in process). Certainty, subjective numeracy, and objective numeracy in decision making.

50. Hoffman, B. (2010). I think I can, but I'm afraid to try: The role of self-efficacy beliefs and mathematics anxiety in mathematics problem-solving efficiency. *Learning and Individual Differences, 20*(3), 276–283.

51. Lopez, F. G., Lent, R. W., Brown, S. D., & Gore, P. A. (1997). Role of social–cognitive expectations in high school students' mathematics-related interest and performance. *Journal of Counseling Psychology, 44*(1), 44–52.

52. Tompkins, M. K. (2018). *The role of subjective numeracy in financial outcomes and interventions of numeric-ability beliefs*. Doctoral dissertation. The Ohio State University.

53. Richardson, F. C., & Suinn, R. M. (1972). The mathematics anxiety rating scale: Psychometric data. *Journal of Counseling Psychology, 19*(6), 551–554.

54. Alexander, L., & Martray, C. (1989). The development of an abbreviated version of the Mathematics Anxiety Rating Scale. *Measurement and Evaluation in Counseling and Development, 22*(3), 143–150.

55. Ashcraft, M. H., & Kirk, E. P. (2001). The relationships among working memory, math anxiety, and performance. *Journal of Experimental Psychology: General 2001,130*(2), 224–237.

56. Maloney, E. A., Ramirez, G., Gunderson, E. A., Levine, S. C., & Beilock, S. L. (2015). Intergenerational effects of parents' math anxiety on children's math achievement and anxiety. *Psychological Science, 26*(9), 1480–1488.

57. Berkowitz, T., Schaeffer, M. W., Maloney, E. A., Peterson, L., Gregor, C., Levine, S. C., & Beilock, S. L. (2015). Math at home adds up to achievement in school. *Science, 350*(6257), 196–198.

58. Lyons, I. M., & Beilock, S. L. (2012). When math hurts: Math anxiety predicts pain network activation in anticipation of doing math. *PloS One, 7*(10), e48076.

59. Ashcraft, M. H. (2002). Math anxiety: Personal, educational, and cognitive consequences. *Current Directions in Psychological Science, 11*(5), 181–185.

60. Betz, N. E. (1978). Prevalence, distribution, and correlates of math anxiety in college students. *Journal of Counseling Psychology, 25*(5), 441–448.

61. Pajares, F., & Urdan, T. (1996). Exploratory factor analysis of the Mathematics Anxiety Scale. *Measurement and Evaluation in Counseling and Development, 29*, 35–47.

62. Ramirez, G., Chang, H., Maloney, E. A., Levine, S. C., & Beilock, S. L. (2016). On the relationship between math anxiety and math achievement in early elementary school: The role of problem solving strategies. *Journal of Experimental Child Psychology, 141*, 83–100.

63. Suinn, R. M., Taylor, S., & Edwards, R. W. (1988). Suinn mathematics anxiety rating scale for elementary school students (MARS-E): Psychometric and normative data. *Educational and Psychological Measurement, 48*(4), 979–986.

64. Rolison, J. J., Morsanyi, K., & O'Connor, P. A. (2016). Can I count on getting better? Association between math anxiety and poorer understanding of medical risk reductions. *Medical Decision Making, 36*(7), 876–886.

65. Bandura, A. (1977). Self-efficacy: Toward a unifying theory of behavioral change. *Psychological Review, 84*(2), 191–215.

66. Traczyk, J., Sobkow, A., Fulawka, K., Kus, J., Petrova, D., & Garcia-Retamero, R. (2018). Numerate decision makers don't use more effortful strategies unless it pays: A process tracing investigation of skilled and adaptive strategy selection in risky decision making. *Judgment and Decision Making, 13*(4), 372–381.

67. Peters, E., Tompkins, M. K., Knoll, M., Ardoin, S. P., Shoots-Reinhard, B., & Meara, A. S. (2019). Despite high objective numeracy, lower numeric confidence relates to worse financial and medical outcomes. *Proceedings of the National Academy of Sciences (PNAS)*, doi.org/10.1073/pnas.1903126116.

68. Narva, A. S., Norton, J. M., & Boulware, L. E. (2016). Educating patients about CKD: The path to self-management and patient-centered care. *Clinical Journal of the American Society of Nephrology, 11*(4), 694–703.

69. Wright Nunes, J. A., Osborn, C. Y., Ikizler, T. A., & Cavanaugh, K. L. (2015). Health numeracy: Perspectives about using numbers in health management from African American patients receiving dialysis. *Hemodialysis International, 19*(2), 287–295.

70. Abdel-Kader, K., Dew, M. A., Bhatnagar, M., Argyropoulos, C., Karpov, I., Switzer, G., & Unruh, M. L. (2010). Numeracy skills in CKD: Correlates and outcomes. *Clinical Journal of American Society of Nephrology, 5*(9), 1566–1573.

71. Miller-Matero, L. R., Bryce, K., Hyde-Nolan, M. E., Dykhuis, K. E., Eshelman, A., & Abouljoud, M. (2016). Health literacy status affects outcomes for patients referred for transplant. *Psychosomatics, 57*(5), 522–528.

72. Apter, A. J., Wan, F., Reisine, S., Bender, B., Rand, C., Bogen, D. K., . . . Morales, K. H. (2013). The association of health literacy with adherence and outcomes in moderate-severe asthma. *Journal of Allergy and Clinical Immunology, 132*(2), 321–327.

73. Apter, A. J., Wang, X. M., Bogen, D., Bennett, I. M., Jennings, R. M., Garcia, L., . . . Ten Have, T. (2009). Linking numeracy and asthma-related quality of life. *Patient Education and Counseling, 75*(3), 386–391.

74. Perez, L., Morales, K. H., Klusaritz, H., Han, X. Y., Huang, J. R., Rogers, M., . . . Apter, A. J. (2016). A health care navigation tool assesses asthma self-management and health literacy. *Journal of Allergy and Clinical Immunology, 138*(6), 1593–1599.

75. Ginde, A. A., Clark, S., Goldstein, J. N., & Camargo, C. A. (2008). Demographic disparities in numeracy among emergency department patients: Evidence from two multicenter studies. *Patient Education and Counseling, 72*(2), 350–356.

76. Petrova, D., Garcia-Retamero, R., Catena, A., Cokely, E., Heredia Carrasco, A., Arrebola Moreno, A., & Ramírez Hernández, J. A. (2017). Numeracy predicts risk of pre-hospital decision delay: A retrospective study of acute coronary syndrome survival. *Annals of Behavioral Medicine, 51*(2), 292–306.

77. Garcia-Retamero, R., Andrade, A., Sharit, J., & Ruiz, J. G. (2015). Is patients' numeracy related to physical and mental health? *Medical Decision Making, 35*(4), 501–511.

78. Waldrop-Valverde, D., Osborn, C. Y., Rodriguez, A., Rothman, R. L., Kumar, M., & Jones, D. L. (2010). Numeracy skills explain racial differences in HIV medication management. *AIDS and Behavior, 14*(4), 799–806.

79. Mixon, A. S., Myers, A. P., Leak, C. L., Jacobsen, J. M. L., Cawthon, C., Goggins, K. M., . . . Kripalani, S. (2014). Characteristics associated with postdischarge medication errors. *Mayo Clinic Proceedings, 89*(8), 1042–1051.

80. Viswanathan, M., Golin, C. E., Jones, C. D., Ashok, M., Blalock, S. J., Wines, R. C., . . . Lohr, K. N. (2012). Interventions to improve adherence to self-administered medications for chronic diseases in the United States: A systematic review. *Annals of Internal Medicine, 157*(11), 785–795.

81. Hutchins, R., Viera, A. J., Sheridan, S. L., & Pignone, M. P. (2015). Quantifying the utility of taking pills for cardiovascular prevention. *Circulation-Cardiovascular Quality and Outcomes, 8*(2), 155–163.

82. Kripalani, S., Goggins, K., Nwosu, S., Schildcrout, J., Mixon, A. S., McNaughton, C., . . . Wallston, K. A. (2015). Medication nonadherence before hospitalization for acute cardiac events. *Journal of Health Communication, 20*(supl2), 34–42.

83. Osborn, C. Y., Cavanaugh, K., Wallston, K. A., Kripalani, S., Elasy, T. A., Rothman, R. L., & White, R. O. (2011). Health literacy explains racial disparities in diabetes medication adherence. *Journal of Health Communication, 16*(supl3), 268–278.

84. Rao, V. N., Sheridan, S. L., Tuttle, L. A., Lin, F. C., Shimbo, D., Diaz, K. M., . . . Viera, A. J. (2015). The effect of numeracy level on completeness of home blood pressure monitoring. *Journal of Clinical Hypertension, 17*(1), 39–45.

85. Smith, S. G., Curtis, L. M., O'Conor, R., Federman, A. D., & Wolf, M. S. (2015). ABCs or 123s? The independent contributions of literacy and numeracy skills on health task performance among older adults. *Patient Education and Counseling, 98*(8), 991–997.

86. Taha, J., Sharit, J., & Czaja, S. J. (2014). The impact of numeracy ability and technology skills on older adults' performance of health management tasks using a patient portal. *Journal of Applied Gerontology, 33*(4), 416–436.

87. Maher, C., Lewis, L., Katzmarzyk, P. T., Dumuid, D., Cassidy, L., & Olds, T. (2016). The associations between physical activity, sedentary behaviour and academic performance. *Journal of Science and Medicine in Sport, 19*(12), 1004–1009.

88. Weinfurt, K. P., Castel, L. D., Li, Y., Sulmasy, D. P., Balshem, AM., Benson, A. B., . . . Meropol, N. J. (2003). The correlation between patient characteristics and expectations of benefit from phase I clinical trials. *Cancer, 98*(1), 166–175.

89. Dosey, J. A., McCrone, S. S., & Halvorsen, K. T. (2016). Mathematics education in the United States 2016. National Council of Teachers of Mathematics. Retrieved from https://www.nctm.org/uploadedFiles/About/MathEdInUS2016.pdf.

90. Moyer, R. S., & Landauer, T. K. (1967). Time required for judgements of numerical inequality. *Nature, 215*(5109), 1519–1520.

91. Peters, E., Slovic, P., Västfjäll, D., & Mertz, C. K. (2008). Intuitive numbers guide decisions. *Judgment and Decision Making, 3*(8), 619–635.

92. Ratcliff, R. (1978). A theory of memory retrieval. *Psychological Review, 85*(2), 59–108.

93. Ratcliff, R., & McKoon, G. (2008). The diffusion decision model: Theory and data for two-choice decision tasks. *Neural Computation, 20*(4), 873–922.

94. Inglis, M., & Gilmore, C. (2014). Indexing the approximate number system. *Acta Psychologica, 145*, 147–155.

95. Lindskog, M., Winman, A., Juslin, P., & Poom, L. (2013). Measuring acuity of the approximate number system reliably and validly: The evaluation of an adaptive test procedure. *Frontiers in Psychology, 4*, 510.

96. Price, G. R., Palmer, D., Battista, C., & Ansari, D. (2012). Nonsymbolic numerical magnitude comparison: Reliability and validity of different task variants and outcome measures, and their relationship to arithmetic achievement in adults. *Acta Psychologica, 140*(1), 50–57.

97. Gilmore, C., Attridge, N., & Inglis, M. (2011). Measuring the approximate number system. *Quarterly Journal of Experimental Psychology, 64*(11), 2099–2109.

98. Holloway, I. D., & Ansari, D. (2009). Mapping numerical magnitudes onto symbols: The numerical distance effect and individual differences in children's mathematics achievement. *Journal of Experimental Child Psychology, 103*(1), 17–29.

99. Maloney, E. A., Risko, E. F., Preston, F., Ansari, D., & Fugelsang, J. (2010). Challenging the reliability and validity of cognitive measures: The case of the numerical distance effect. *Acta Psychologica, 134*(2), 154–161.

100. Sasanguie, D., Defever, E., Van den Bussche, E., & Reynvoet, B. (2011). The reliability of and the relation between non-symbolic numerical distance effects in comparison, same-different judgments and priming. *Acta Psychologica, 136*(1), 73–80.

101. Siegler, R. S., & Opfer, J. E. (2003). The development of numerical estimation: Evidence for multiple representations of numerical quantity. *Psychological Science, 14*(3), 237–250.

102. Opfer, J. E., Thompson, C. A., & Kim, D. (2016). Free versus anchored numerical estimation: A unified approach. *Cognition, 149*, 11–17.

103. Schley, D. R., & Peters, E. (2014). Assessing economic value symbolic-number mappings predict risky and riskless valuations. *Psychological Science, 25*(3), 753–761.

104. Dehaene, S., & Cohen, L. (1997). Cerebral pathways for calculation: Double dissociation between rote verbal and quantitative knowledge of arithmetic. *Cortex, 33*(2), 219–250.

105. Chesney, D. L., & Matthews, P. G. (2013). Knowledge on the line: Manipulating beliefs about the magnitudes of symbolic numbers affects the linearity of line estimation tasks. *Psychonomic Bulletin & Review, 20*(6), 1146–1153.

106. Izard, V., & Dehaene, S. (2008). Calibrating the mental number line. *Cognition, 106*(3), 1221–1247.

107. Rips, L. J. (2013). How many is a zillion? Sources of number distortion. *Journal of Experimental Psychology: Learning, Memory, and Cognition, 39*(4), 1257–1264.

108. Sekuler, R., & Mierkiewicz, D. (1977). Children's judgments of numerical inequality. *Child Development*, 630–633.

109. Barth, H. C., & Paladino, A. M. (2011). The development of numerical estimation: Evidence against a representational shift. *Developmental Science, 14*(1), 125–135.

110. Halberda, J., Mazzocco, M. M., & Feigenson, L. (2008). Individual differences in non-verbal number acuity correlate with maths achievement. *Nature, 455*(7213), 665–668.

111. Norris, J. E., & Castronovo, J. (2016). Dot display affects approximate number system acuity and relationships with mathematical achievement and inhibitory control. *PLoS ONE 11*(5): e0155543

112. Anobile, G., Cicchini, G. M., & Burr, D. C. (2014). Separate mechanisms for perception of numerosity and density. *Psychological Science, 25*(1), 265–270.

113. Gilmore, C., Attridge, N., Clayton, S., Cragg, L., Johnson, S., Marlow, N., . . . Inglis, M. (2013). Individual differences in inhibitory control, not non-verbal number acuity, correlate with mathematics achievement. *PLoS ONE, 8*(6), e67374.

Name Index

For the benefit of digital users, indexed terms that span two pages (e.g., 52–53) may, on occasion, appear on only one of those pages.